2 Vols
10/

A HISTORY OF MODERN LIBERTY

By the same Author.

THE GROWTH AND DECLINE OF THE FRENCH MONARCHY.

8vo, pp. xx. and 840.   21s. net.

Longmans, Green, & Co., London, New York, and Bombay.

"'The Growth and Decline of the French Monarchy' cannot fail to be recognised by any impartial historian as the production of a fellow-worker which can hardly be too highly appreciated."—R. FLINT, D.D., LL.D., *Correspondent of the Institute of France; Emeritus-Professor of Edinburgh University.*

"L'historien qui a traité de main de maître le règne d'Edouard III. et l'Union d'Angleterre et de l'Ecosse a rendu un service considérable à l'Histoire de France, en recherchant, dans un volume récent, les causes de la grandeur et de la décadence de la monarchie française. Cette large synthèse, puisée aux sources originales et pleine d'aperçus élevés et lumineux, a popularisé chez nous le nom du savant professeur de St Andrews. Par sa connaissance approfondie de notre langue, de nos documents, et de nos livres, il est devenu un des facteurs intellectuels de l'union, si nécessaire aujourd'hui, entre la Grande Brétagne et la France."—ACHILLE LUCHAIRE, *Member of the Institute; Professor of Mediæval History in the University of Paris.*

"Il me semble que les livres de M. le Professeur James MacKinnon sur Edouard III. et sur la monarchie française, principalment dans les derniers siècles, se recommandent à la fois par la solidité du fond et par la netteté et l'élégance sévère de la forme. Ce sont les livres d'un érudit qui sait se mettre à la portée du grand public."—PAUL MEYER, *Member of the Institute; Professor at the Collège de France; Directeur de l'Ecole Nationale des Chatres; D.C.L., Oxon.*

"Après votre Histoire d'Edouard III., cet ouvrage apporte un nouveau et solide témoignage de votre connaissance de l'Histoire de France. Votre érudition est très étendue, et vous avez su présenter l'évolution de notre ancienne monarchie avec assez de vigueur et d'originalité pour rendre la lecture de votre œuvre utile à tous les lecteurs français."—A. COVILLE, *Rector of the University of Clermont-Ferrand; Hon. Professor of the University of Lyons.*

"Ich habe mit Freuden beobachtet, dass mir, bei jeder Stichprobe, sprechende Belege desselben umfassenden Wissens, desselben eisernen Fleisses, derselben geistvollen Auffassung und Durchdringung des Stoffes, derselben kraft- und lebensprühenden Darstellung entgegen getreten sind, an denen ich in Ihren früheren Werken stets meine Freude gehabt habe."—*The late* Dr W. ONCKEN, *Professor of History in the University of Giessen; formerly Member of the Reichstag.*

"Gia il nome suo, come di Storico valente, m'era noto per cio che nostre Reviste Storiche era stato scritto d'un altro lodato lavoro suo, La Storia di Edoardo Terzo; onde col maggiore interesse mi sono posto subito ad esaminare la nuova pubblicazione. Le sono grato di avermi procurato una tanto piacevole ed interessante lettura. Ella a riusuto con forma concettada e brillante a raccogliare in un solo quadro efficacissime e sempre vivo tutte le svolgersi attraverso i seccoli della monarchia francese."—*The Commendatore,* VITTORIO FIORINI, *Director-General of Public Instruction; Professor in the University of Rome.*

A HISTORY

OF

MODERN LIBERTY.

BY

JAMES MACKINNON, Ph.D.

VOL. I.—INTRODUCTION.
(ORIGINS—THE MIDDLE AGES.)

LONGMANS, GREEN, AND CO.,
39 PATERNOSTER ROW, LONDON;
NEW YORK AND BOMBAY.
1906.
All Rights Reserved.

323.44
M216h
v.1

AUG 8 1933
339735
May. Hist.

Printed at THE DARIEN PRESS, *Edinburgh.*

TO

MY WIFE.

"Liberty is the Life,
Despotism the Death of Nations."

PREFACE TO VOLUMES I. AND II.

I PURPOSE in this work to trace the history of liberty throughout what is called the modern age.

Liberty in the general sense I take to be the free development of man, subject of course to the limits of such development inseparable from human life. Absolute liberty is the prerogative of no mortal. Man is subject to the conditions of his being. He derives his existence from another. He is dependent on others as well as himself for its maintenance. Its span is short and uncertain at the best. Looking at human life merely from the material standpoint, man's insufficiency, dependence are patent enough. They are equally patent from the spiritual point of view. The human spirit is instinctively conscious of subjection to an intelligence infinitely superior to it, and this feeling of subjection is expressed in one form or another in its religious beliefs and usages. Again, as a political and social unit, the individual is conscious of restraints as well as rights. In whatever relation we regard him—material, moral, political, social—limitation, subjection is the law of his life.

So much granted as a matter of course, it is nevertheless true that liberty, within certain limits, is also a law of human life. The human will is free, to a certain extent at least, as is evidenced by our consciousness of the fact, and exemplified in countless acts of volition. A great part of my experience is a matter of my own volition, for which I must hold myself, as well as circumstances, responsible. Man is not a mere machine driven by the motor force of necessity. He has, to a certain extent, his destiny in his own hands. If it were not so, to speak of liberty, far less to attempt to write a history of it, would be an utter delusion. If there is any meaning at all in the word, if history is to be regarded as something higher than a mere tissue of necessity, we are bound to believe in the freedom of the will, though we may dispute about its extent, its operation. Both nature and history must, in fact, be accepted as a vast manifestation of will, natural and human activity as the reflection of intelligence and volition. To offer any other explanation is to ignore the human as well as the divine mind and substitute for it a meaningless philosophic, or rather pseudo-philosophic jargon. History can only be explained as a revelation of cause and effect; and without the operation of the free human will we should look in vain, in human affairs, for either the one or the other. Minus this factor, history would simply be an enigma. Nay, there would be no history at all.

The fact of free will involves the right to exercise it. I am, for instance, free to choose the good, and no one ought to prevent me from choosing it. Or, I am entitled to resist evil, and no one ought to compel me not to resist. Or, I have a right to live, and no one ought to hinder me from enjoying this right. There is a certain liberty of action, as well as a certain subjection, which we owe to nature, and this liberty is as indisputable as the subjection inherited from nature. Hence the old doctrine of natural rights, which, though in some respects erroneous, expressed some patent truths. Among these is the right to be free, within certain limits at least.

Assuming, then, the fact of human liberty as well as human dependence, and leaving the philosophy of the subject in abeyance, my object in the following volumes is to trace the development of liberty as exemplified in modern history. The work being a history, and not a philosophic disquisition, it is with man as a member of the community, the State, that I am specially concerned. Individual liberty has indeed its province, and it would, in my opinion, be a calamity if individuality were so absorbed by the State as to leave the liberty of the individual the minimum sphere of activity. We shall have occasion enough to note the evil effects of the encroachment of an absolute monarch, or a universal Church, or a dominant system like that of feudalism, on individual rights. But while taking into account the abuses of corporate power, we shall assume the fact that individual liberty must be more or less limited by the community, the State. It is with man as a citizen that the historian has to do. The individual man may be largely left to the philosopher.

It is, then, liberty, as exemplified in history, that will chiefly engage our attention. Moreover, as the subject of investigation is the history of modern liberty, our attention will be further restricted to the period denominated modern. I have, however, devoted a preliminary volume to the origins of liberty so restricted, and these origins I have sought in what have come to be known as the Middle Ages, from which the modern world directly emanated.

In pursuing this investigation we must bear in mind the fact that the history of liberty is the history of an evolution. The meaning, the compass of the word varies from one age to another. It had, for instance, a much more restricted compass in mediæval, compared with that which it came to acquire in modern times. In the Middle Ages we are at the beginning of an evolution ; in the twentieth century the evolution has run a large part of its course.

Not only would it be vain to seek in the Middle Ages for that larger conception which the word possesses for us in these modern days. It would be equally vain to read into it the same significance in one modern century as compared with another. Liberty in the century of the Reformation, for example, meant something much more restricted than what it means to us in the beginning of the twentieth century, and modern historians have grievously erred in thus reading into such terms as "liberty," "people," "democracy" the significance of their own time, because they happen to find them in some chronicle or State document of a former age. The language of the General Privilege of Aragon, or of the Groote Privilegie of the Netherlands, or of some of the demands of the English Commons in the fourteenth century, may, for example, sound very democratic. We might fancy ourselves at times, on reading the debates of a mediæval assembly of Estates, listening to the orators of the Long Parliament, or even of the Constituent Assembly. No words recur oftener in mediæval parliamentary documents than the words "liberties," "rights," "privileges." But the liberties, rights, privileges were reserved for certain classes, not for the people in the larger sense of the term. The people, politically, did not exist outside these classes. All that we can say of such documents is that the language of them is an anticipation of larger modern political ideas. The anticipation is very partial indeed. It only serves to show to what a height of political power certain classes had attained. Serfdom was the lot of the masses. In the age of the Reformation social emancipation had made considerable progress, in some countries at least. After the French Revolution serfdom disappeared among enlightened European nations. In writing or speaking of popular rights, from the historical point of view, we must, therefore, be careful to discriminate century and circumstance. Popular rights in the modern sense did not exist in, say, the year 1100 A.D. "The liberty of the subject" did not apply to the servile class. Popular liberty, as we understand it, was non-existent, despite specious phrases which can only deceive the uninitiated.

Religious liberty, to take another example, cannot be said to have existed at all in the Middle Ages. It existed in only a very imperfect degree in the days of Luther and Calvin. It is, happily, a concrete conception among all truly civilised peoples in this year 1906. There is no danger now that a freethinker will be sent to the stake by an intolerant Church, as in the days of a St Dominic, or even of a Calvin. Nevertheless, we occasionally meet in the works of writers who ought to know better, especially Protestant writers on the Reformation, glowing descriptions of Protestantism, as if it had then been identical with religious liberty in the modern sense.

We must, then, beware, in our quest of the origins of modern liberty, of trying to discover in the Middle Ages what is not there. Religious and intellectual liberty, even personal liberty in the case of the masses, were practically unknown. But we should greatly err if we were to conclude that, because some components of modern liberty were incomprehensible to the age of a Hildebrand, that age was utterly barren of any germs of liberty. That age might be the age of the universal intolerant Church, of an intellectual system, dominated by that Church, which held the minds of all but a few daring doubters in thraldom, of a social system which doomed the toiling mass to a degrading servitude. It might be, in many essential respects, the age of unquestioned authority on the one hand, absolute subjection on the other. Religious and intellectual liberty might be stifled by ecclesiastical dogma, papal supremacy. The feudal system might cramp the existence of the masses in its tyrannic vice. Nevertheless, the aspiration of liberty—religious, intellectual, political, social—was not dormant. There were always a few bold champions of freedom of thought and conscience to challenge traditional authority and dare persecution and death for the sake of their convictions. They were doomed to tragic failure, of course; hardly, as we shall see, made any impression on the dominant system in Church and school. Far otherwise was it in the case of the struggle for political rights, social emancipation. The mediæval equally with the modern age had its revolutions, though these revolutions were, as a rule, more gradual, less dramatic than those which swept over the Netherlands in the sixteenth, Great Britain in the seventeenth, France in the eighteenth, and Europe in the nineteenth centuries. The feudal system might be for long supreme, but the reaction against it produced, even within the Middle Ages, a most fruitful movement in favour of social and political emancipation.

The initial factor of this movement was economic. The Crusades gave an impulse to the revival of commerce and industry, and led to the growth of towns. The effect of this revival and this growth is apparent in the demand for emancipation from feudal subjection and the assertion of the right of municipal self-government in Italy, France, Spain, Germany, England, and Scotland. In the twelfth and thirteenth centuries this movement became general in all these countries, and its result was the establishment of the City Republics of Italy, the Communes of France, the Communeros of Spain, the Freistädte of the Empire, the Municipalities of England and Scotland. Along with it, and consequent on it, may be discerned the aspiration, on the part of the masses, for the amelioration of their lot which led to the recognition of the rights of the craft gilds or artisans, and the relative elevation of the peasantry in the social scale. The movement was at the same time a training for the political *rôle* which the representatives of the towns, or the Third Estate at least, played in the mediæval Parliament, or States-General. The municipality was the foster-father of the Parliament. By the admission of the Third Estate, or, as we should say, the Commons (though in a restricted sense), the council of lay and clerical magnates became the assembly of the three orders of clergy, nobles, and commons, and the organisation of the modern Parliament was thus, in form at all events, complete in the twelfth or the thirteenth century in most of the countries of Western and Central Europe. In Castile and Aragon this assembly of the three orders appears as the Cortes, in France and the Low Countries as the States-General, in Germany as the Reichstag, in England and Scotland as the Parliament. The political power to which the Third Estate attained was, however, greater in some countries than in others. In Spain, in the fourteenth century in particular, the Commons exercised political functions which were substantially those of the modern Parliament. In England, too, the Commons succeeded during the same century in making good their claim to control legislation and administration. In the Low Countries the democracy of the gilds, championed by the Arteveldes, bade fair to gain the supremacy. In France the claims of the Third Estate were equally high, though the struggle, during the Hundred Years War, to substantiate them failed. Unfortunately, this development of parliamentary institutions in their mediæval form was blasted in some countries, checked in others, by the rising force of absolutism, which the bane of mediæval anarchy induced, and which was, from this point of view, a needful antidote in the interest both of nationality and order.

The Middle Ages witnessed, too, the rise of independent nations, which finally vindicated the idea of nationality in opposition to that of a universal empire, as embodied in the emperors of the Holy Roman Empire. In the case of the Swiss confederation, they furnished to the world the example of a small people of mountaineers revolting against the oppression of their overlord, and maintaining their national liberty against the aggressor on many a bloody battlefield. And, thanks to the long and bitter strife between pope and kaiser, these centuries were fruitful of political theories which forestalled the modern conception of popular sovereignty, and reminded both would-be universal potentates that there was a power greater even than theirs—the power of the people, as the word people was then understood, at all events.

Thus it comes to pass that in order to understand the beginnings of some aspects at least of modern liberty, we must turn to those ages which are conventionally regarded as the ægis of universal chaos and darkness. The first volume or introduction will, I trust, make this fact abundantly clear in detail.

I had better say, in reference to this introduction, that much contention exists in connection with some of the subjects with which it deals. Hot dispute has long raged among specialists over such questions as the origin of feudalism and the mediæval municipalities, the institutions of the barbarian peoples that conquered the Roman empire, the relation of the village community to the manor in Anglo-Saxon Britain, &c. Where no final conclusion seems to me to have been reached, I have contented myself merely with stating the fact, or have qualified my statements with the indispensable "probably" or "seemingly." The object of the introduction is not controversial. I have not entered the lists for or against rival theories of this sort, but have tried to expound from the best sources—original and secondary—the development of those germs of modern liberty which struck root in these mediæval centuries.

The second volume deals with the age of the Reformation in Central and Western Europe. It may seem partial to devote so large a part of this volume to England and Scotland. My justification may be found in the fact that it was in England and Scotland in the seventeenth century that the great battle of constitutional liberty was fought out, and that the struggles of the Reformation age in these countries formed the preliminary of that great constitutional drama.

The Renascence and the Reformation mark a superlatively important stage in the evolution of modern liberty. It was, for instance, by means of these movements that the aspiration after intellectual and religious liberty became a mighty factor in modern history. The revolt of the intellect against the dominant system of thought and culture, the revolt of the conscience against the dominant Church and theology, ushered in that tremendous conflict of the individual mind with corporate authority, of Biblical Protestantism with traditional orthodoxy, which convulsed the greater part of Europe and was finally fought out on the battlefield in France, Holland, Germany, Scotland. With this conflict was combined the forcible attempts, on the part of the masses, more particularly in Germany, to sweep away the social abuses which pressed hard on "the common man." The Reformation was, in fact, as we shall see, a social as well as a religious movement. On every hand arose the cry for justice for the poor man, based on the Bible and natural right—justice as against an oppressive caste in Church and State—and in Southern Germany in particular the cry roused tens of thousands of sturdy peasants to do battle for Christian brotherhood and natural justice.

The influence of this conflict on political liberty was, too, of superlative importance. As the struggle progressed, the champions of the pope, the persecutors in high places, were met by the appeal, not only to the Bible and the conscience, but to the right of the subject to resist oppression on political as well as religious grounds. The intellectual and religious movement thus became a political as well as a social movement. It not only made war on the pope. It deposed monarchs, as in Holland and Scotland. It forced them to compromise and recognise the right of the Protestant equally with the Catholic subject to profess his creed in peace. It forced the emperor to agree to even the exclusive predominance of the Protestant creed in the Protestant States of the empire.

From both the conflicts and the theories of the sixteenth century liberty thus received an impulse which came to full maturity in the French Revolution, and is still potently felt in the world of to-day. The remaining volumes of this work will, in fact, be largely the history of this impulse as displayed in the constitutional struggle in England and Scotland in the seventeenth century, the American and the French Revolutions in the eighteenth, and in those revolutionary and progressive movements in the nineteenth which have inaugurated the era of full intellectual, religious, political, and social liberty as the distinctive feature of the life of all enlightened nations.

I had already completed the second volume before I learned from "The Letters of Lord Acton to Mary Gladstone," published in 1904 under the editorship of Mr Herbert Paul, that the late lamented Professor of History at Cambridge had cherished for many years the plan of writing a History of Liberty. It is deeply to be regretted that Lord Acton could never summon up the resolution to write what was evidently intended to be his *opus magnum*. He, unfortunately, gave to the world only the merest snatches of his vast erudition. But the specimens he has left of his literary power and his historical learning suffice to show that, had he carried out his plan, he would probably have enriched English historical literature with one more masterpiece. In it would have been distilled, full, and clear, and flowing, the nectar of forty years of reading and reflection on one of the greatest of themes. I cannot hope to equal his unrivalled erudition in this special field, but I may say that, while I have for a number of years independently worked at the realisation of an idea similar to, though more restricted than his, I have done my best to master the authorities, both primary and secondary, bearing on the subject. Unfortunately, I am precluded from indulging in the luxury of footnotes, as I have done so freely in the case of previous works, and have had to content myself with a list of the special works studied, appended to each chapter.

THE UNIVERSITY,
ST ANDREWS, *January* 1906.

CONTENTS—VOL. I.

CHAPTER I.

BEGINNINGS OF THE MIDDLE AGES—TRANSFORMATION OF WESTERN EUROPE UNDER ROMANO-GERMANIC AUSPICES.

PAGES

The Origins of Modern Liberty—The Barbarians and the Empire—Influence of Imperial Institutions—Lombards and Anglo-Saxons—The Early Barbarian Kingship—Growth of the Royal Power—The Merovingian Kings—Insubordination of Magnates—Mayors of the Palace—Cæsar Redivivus—Charlemagne as Emperor—Reaction towards Feudalism—Election of Hugh Capet—The Fittest Person to Rule—The Feudal Monarch—The Holy Roman Empire—Emperor and Pope—Sources of Chapter I. 1-18

CHAPTER II.

GROWTH OF THE FEUDAL SYSTEM—ITS EFFECTS ON THE LOWER CLASSES.

Roots of Feudalism—Wholesale Dependence—Force and Usurpation—Policy of Charlemagne—The Feudal System—The Feudal Hierarchy—Burdens and Privileges—The Unfree—Villeins and Franc-Villeins—Charges and Burdens—The Feudal *Régime* Odious—Society an Active Volcano—Feudalism and Liberty—Defects and Characteristics—Critical Estimate—Sources of Chapter II. . . 19-35

CHAPTER III.

THE EMANCIPATION OF THE ITALIAN COMMUNES AND THE ITALIAN CITY REPUBLICS.

Decline of Roman Civic Life—Effects of Barbarian Conquests—Revival of Commerce and Industry—The Emancipation Movement in Italy—The Emperor and the Lombard Cities—Treaty of Constance—Guelfs and Ghibelines—Frederick II.—" Italy full of Tyrants "—Venice—Florence and Genoa—Rome—Arnold de Brescia—Negative Lessons in Liberty—Lack of Moderation—Italy against Germany—Sources of Chapter III. 36-53

VOL. I. *b*

CHAPTER IV.

REPUBLICAN FLORENCE AND THE MEDICI.

Class Feuds—Revolt of the Ciompi—Greater and Lesser Arts—A Democratic Orator—An Abortive Revolution—The Early Medici—Liberty Equivalent to Anarchy—Cosimo de Medici—A Republic in Leading Strings—Corruption—Lorenzo—Mæcenas and Politician—Villari's Estimate—Florence and Savonarola—His Incipient Failure—Savonarola as Preacher—Savonarola and Lorenzo—Savonarola and Piero—Prophecies and Denunciations—Invasion of Charles VIII.—Expulsion of Piero—Reform of the Government—"The Will of the People"—The Reformed Constitution—Savonarola Denounces the Parliament—Puritan Florence—Reaction and Doom—The Castigation of Italy—Savonarola's Mission—Sources of Chapter IV.   54-84

CHAPTER V.

THE EMANCIPATION OF THE COMMUNES IN FRANCE.

Growth of Cities in France—Subjection to a Superior—The Conjuration—Circumstances Favour Emancipation—A Practical Movement—Death the Great Philanthropist—Tyranny of Feudal Superiors—Hostility of Bishops and Abbots—The Clergy and their Serfs—Heroic Side of the Movement—Fighting and Ferocity—Variety of the Communes—The Municipality a Collective Superior—Powers of the Municipality—Attitude of French Kings—Mixed Motives—Encroachment of the Royal Power—Sources of Chapter V. .   . 85-103

CHAPTER VI.

THE THIRD ESTATE AND THE STATES-GENERAL IN FRANCE.

Early French Political Assemblies—Philip IV. and the States-General—Function of the Estates—Growing Strength of the Crown—Position in the Fourteenth Century—States-General of 1356—Etienne Marcel—Constitutional Demands—Navarre and Normandy—Attack on the Royal Palace—Dissension and Civil War—Rising of the Peasants—Its Excesses—A Terrible Vengeance—A Desperate Situation—Murder of Marcel—His Vindication—Failure Inevitable—Sources of Chapter VI.   104-123

CHAPTER VII.

THE THIRD ESTATE AND THE STATES-GENERAL IN FRANCE—CONTINUED TILL THE END OF THE FIFTEENTH CENTURY.

Popular Outbreaks under Charles VI.—Repression—Party Feuds and Civil War—The Cabochiens as Reformers—Charles VII. Rehabili-

Contents. xix

tates the Monarchy—Standing Army and Arbitrary Taxation—Louis
XI. and the Magnates—The States-General of 1484—Democratic
Theories—People Unfit for Political Power—Sources of Chapter VII. 124-134

CHAPTER VIII.

THE EMANCIPATION MOVEMENT IN GERMANY AND THE GERMAN FREE CITIES.

The Mediæval Empire—Weakness of the Emperors—Power of the Magnates—The Growth of Local Liberty—The Barbarians and the Roman Cities—Growth of Cities in Germany—Origin of German Municipalities—Rival Theories—Where the Theorists Err—Slow Development of Civic Life—Influence of Commerce and Industry—The Conjuration in Germany—Early Domination of Merchant Gild —Craft Gilds *versus* Oligarchy—Results of the Struggle—Contribution of the Gilds to Liberty—Powers of Imperial Municipalities—Leagues of the Cities—Their Ultimate Failure—The Hansa League —Brilliance and Decline—Sources of Chapter VIII. . 135-157

CHAPTER IX.

RELIGIOUS AND SOCIAL REVOLT IN BOHEMIA AND GERMANY IN THE FIFTEENTH CENTURY.

Wicklif and Hus—Hus at Constance—His Attitude as Reformer—The Appeal to Conscience—Calixtines and Taborites—Revolutionary Doctrines—The Revolutionary Movement—A Christian Theocracy —The Appeal to the Sword—Hussite Influence in Germany— Risings of the Peasants—" The Noble Peasant "—Peasant Conjurations—Hans Böheim as Democratic Preacher—The Bundschuh— Something goes Wrong—Condition of the Peasants—Luxury and Oppression—Reform of Society and Church—The Democratic Movement in the Towns—German Cities in the Fifteenth Century— Splendour and Prosperity—The Discontented Masses—The Tyranny of the Rich—Revolutionary Factors—Sources of Chapter IX. . 158-184

CHAPTER X.

THE SWISS AND THE FRISIANS.

Independent Spirit of the Swiss—The Freemen of Schwyz and Uri— Germ of a Free Confederation—The Bund of 1291—Its Historical Significance—The Earlier Versions of the Story—Justinger's Account —Later Versions—The Story according to Tschudi—William Tell— Criticism and Controversy—Decisive Victories—Ancient Frisian Democracy—Criticism of Von Richthofen—Subjection and Vassalage—The Assembly at Upstalboom—The Germ of a Free State—A Mettlesome Race—Frisians and Swiss—Spirit of the Frisian Laws—"Hail, Free Frisian!"—Sources of Chapter X. . . . 185-207

CHAPTER XI.

EMANCIPATION AND REVOLUTION IN THE NETHERLANDS.

The Netherlands in the Middle Ages—The Counts of Flanders—The Flemish Cities—The Rule of the Oligarchy—Count Guy and Philip IV.—Worsted by Philip—Victory of Courtrai—Revolt of Flanders—Battle of Cassel—Flanders and the Anglo-French Quarrel—An Embarrassing Situation—Jacques van Artevelde—Anglo-Flemish Alliance—Artevelde Triumphant—Reaction and Hostility—The Martyr of Mob Rage—Vindication of Artevelde—Anti-democratic Reaction—Renewed Revolt—Roosebeke—The Work of the Arteveldes—*Joyeuse Entrée* of Brabant—Liège, Holland, Hainault—Results of Struggle for Liberty—Philip the Good—Revolt Again and its Suppression—Charles the Bold—The "Groote Privilegie"—Relapse under Autocratic *Régime*—Sources of Chapter XI. . 208-238

CHAPTER XII.

COMMUNEROS AND CORTES IN MEDIÆVAL SPAIN.

Spanish Mediæval Kingdoms—Bellicose Spirit—Early Spanish Municipalities—The Estates or Cortes—The Hermandad—The Castilian Monarchy—The Castilian Grandees—Castilian Cortes Control Taxation—Legislation and Control of Executive—Constitutional Government—Dissension of the Orders—Aragon and its Nobility—The "General Privilege" of Aragon—Rights of Class *versus* Mass—The "Privilege of Union"—The Cortes of Aragon—The Justiza—Valencia and Catalonia—Barcelona—Sources of Chapter XII. . 239-259

CHAPTER XIII.

CONSTITUTIONAL AND SOCIAL PROGRESS IN MEDIÆVAL ENGLAND.

The Anglo-Saxon Settlements—Invaders not all Freemen—King and Witan—Powers of Witan and King—System of Local Government—Increase of the Royal Power—William I. and the Feudal Hierarchy—Actual, not Titular Sovereign—William II. and Henry I.—Government of Henry II.—Henry and the Clergy—John and the Barons—The Great Charter—Significance of the Charter—The Provisions of Oxford—De Montfort's Policy—Bracton and the Supremacy of the Law—The Apparition of the Jurist—The Model Parliament—Parliament and Taxation—Who were the Commons?—Parliament and People—The Servile Classes—Servile Burdens—

Contents.

Gradual Amelioration—Customary Tenants—The Church and the Villeins—The English Towns—The Communal Movement in England—Diversity of Municipalities—Merchant Gild and Craft Gild—Rule of the Oligarchy—Sources of Chapter XIII. . . . 260-293

CHAPTER XIV.

POLITICAL AND SOCIAL REVOLUTION IN ENGLAND IN THE FOURTEENTH CENTURY.

Misgovernment of Edward II.—His Deposition—The Opposition to Edward III.—Friction with Parliament—The Good Parliament—Its Reforms and Failure—The Merciless Parliament—English Tradition in Favour of Liberty—Richard's Despotism—His Deposition—Parliament the Source of Law—English Constitutional History an Evolution towards Liberty—The Black Death—Economic Effects—Landlord and Peasant—The Determination to be Free—John Ball—Langley—The Revolt against Convention—Political Side of the Revolt—Rising of the Peasants—" Kill All without Mercy"—Attack on the Capital—Vengeance and Failure—Reign of Terror—Where the Blame Lies—Wicklif and the Social Movement—His Doctrine of Lordship—Wicklif and the Right of Resistance—The Wicklifite Movement—The Revolt against Ecclesiastical Domination—Significance of the Fourteenth Century—Restriction of Representative Rights—Power of the House of Commons—Sources of Chapter XIV. 294-329

CHAPTER XV.

THE ENGLISH PARLIAMENT FROM HENRY IV. TO HENRY VIII.

Activity of Parliament in the Fifteenth Century—Principles Exemplified—Sir John Fortescue—The " De Laudibus "—The " Governance of England "—Democratic Tone—Significance of the Fifteenth Century—The Rule of the Tudors—Parliament under the Tudors—Inconsistency and Subservience—Danger to Liberties and Rights—Forces Unfavourable to Despotism—Sources of Chapter XV. . . 330-343

CHAPTER XVI.

CONSTITUTIONAL AND SOCIAL PROGRESS IN MEDIÆVAL SCOTLAND.

Monarchy in Early Scottish History—The Scoto-Pictish Kingdom—Malcolm II.—Serfage in Saxon Lothian—Identity of Saxon and Celtic Social Institutions—And of their Political Institutions—Develop on Parallel Lines—Where is the Essential Difference?—The Feudal Tendency—Effects on the Lower Classes—The Mediæval Scottish Burghs—Their Government—The Gild and the

xxii Contents.

PAGES

Craftsman—Public Spirit and Institutions—Origins of the Scottish Parliament—The Parliament of Cambuskenneth—Activity of Parliament in the Fourteenth Century—Comparison with the English Parliament—Faction and Anarchy—Misery of the People—Sources of Chapter XVI. 344-364

CHAPTER XVII.

Mediæval Political Thought in Relation to Liberty.

Discussion in the Schools—Mediæval Idea of Unity—This Idea Hostile to Liberty—The Papal Claim to Supremacy—Superiority of the Spiritual to the Temporal Power—Victory and Defeat of the Theory—The Conciliar Opposition—Champions of the Imperial Power—Contentions of the Rival Champions—Exaltation of the Emperor—The Divine Right of Kings—Service of the Doctrine to Liberty—The "Antique-Modern" Spirit—Resistance to Tyranny—The Sovereignty of the People—Manegold, Marsilius, and Cusanus—Natural and Positive Law—The Doctrine of the Contract—Representative Government—Slavery an Accepted Institution—Views of Aquinas—Sources of Chapter XVII. 365-387

A HISTORY
OF
MODERN LIBERTY.

CHAPTER I.

BEGINNINGS OF THE MIDDLE AGES—TRANSFORMATION

ERRATA.

Page 115, line 33, *for* "southern" *read* "northern."
Page 260, line 2, *for* "Briton" *read* "Britain."
Page 262, line 33, *for* "Briton" *read* "Britain."

by Charlemagne. Though the imperial name survived in the Holy Roman Empire, the Holy Roman Emperor was in reality only King of Germany. A number of independent monarchies gradually displaced the old empire, as the result of the break-up of that vast dominion which, in the fourth century, stretched from the Tiber to the Forth. Over this vast stretch of territory, too, the feudal system ultimately supplanted the barbarian and the Roman institutions. The establishment of the monarchy in place of the empire, the growth of the feudal system in place of the imperial institutions, are the cardinal political and social facts of the history of Western and partly of Central Europe during the earlier Middle Ages. King and aristocracy shared the domination of the State between them, and in some of these kingdoms the aristocracy wielded sovereign jurisdiction within their own domains. The people, the "freemen" of the barbarian nations, by whose authority, according to Tacitus, all important affairs were formerly decided, gradually lost political power and sank in the social scale. There is, in fact, some reason for believing that the process of degradation had begun among the Teutonic invaders before—perhaps long before—they crossed the Rhine or the Danube. This degradation helped to swell the servile class, and the servile class came to be synonymous with the mass. It was the reaction of the mass from subjection to the feudal class which produced the emancipation of the communes or towns, improved the social condition of the serfs or peasantry, and paved the way for the rise of the Third Estate to political rights. It is this emancipation movement which I purpose to trace in the following chapters.

I need hardly emphasise the interest of the subject, for in this emancipation movement lie the origins of modern liberty. We are apt to look on the Middle Ages as dreary wastes of war and anarchy, as ages of barbarism from which the modern world escaped by way of the Renascence and the Reformation. We accordingly date the beginning of modern history from the middle of the fifteenth century—usually from the fall of Constantinople—and with certain meagre generalisations of what we conclude to be the distinctive features of the mediæval world, we usher ourselves into a new period, in which everything is supposed to be different from the period of a Barbarossa, a Gregory VII., an Aquinas. Beyond 1452 we imagine that all is as dead to us as the dusty tomes of the mediæval schoolmen. The fall of Constantinople is the beginning of life in the midst of death, of light in the midst of darkness. We forget that the Middle Ages are the threshold of the modern ages, and that politically and socially what is arbitrarily called modern grew out of what is as arbitrarily called mediæval. We forget, more especially, that our parliaments and our municipalities sprang from these same ages of barbarism, and this not in Great Britain only, but all over Western and Southern Europe. Barbarous they doubtless were in some respects, as we shall see; shockingly anarchic and bellicose; but their barbarism, their anarchy, their pugnacity did not succeed in stifling the seeds of progress which struggled in that rough environment into a life full of promise. To inquire how these mediæval parliaments and municipalities came into being is thus no merely antiquarian investigation. It is to trace to their source, amid wild and rugged scenes, it may be, the rights and liberties which have fed the broad and mighty stream of modern political and social progress.

We speak of the fall of the Roman empire, but the empire did not really fall in the fifth century. At most it was only disrupted. In the eastern half the imperial power remained intact, in spite of seasons of anarchy, and even in the west it suffered transformation rather than destruction. It was indeed impossible that so mighty a fabric could disappear. The barbarians did not succeed in sweeping it away, and an Ataulf, who purposed its destruction and the establishment of a barbarian empire in its stead, was fain to confess the impossibility of the task. The barbarians for the most part had no wish to sweep it away. They were driven by an irresistible impulse westwards and southwards, by the pressure of new hordes on their rear, by the increase of population which induced emigration, by the love of plunder, the allurement of a luxurious civilisation. They were not actuated by hatred of Rome in their inroads into the empire. Barbarian corps are found serving in the imperial armies. Barbarian tribes undertook the defence of the frontier in return for the benefices of land allotted to them. The hordes of the great migration itself offered their services to the emperor for the time being in return for lands and offices, if they did not scruple to take what was denied them. They even created emperors to confer on their leaders the coveted dignity of consul or patrician. Odoacer, Theodoric, were barbarian kings, but it was not as barbarian kings, it was as imperial consuls or patricians, that they ruled Italy, as Alaric vainly demanded to rule it before them, and as Clovis after them ruled Gaul. They were masters of Italy in virtue of force, but they exercised their mastery as imperial functionaries, and thus paid tribute to the enchantment of a mighty name, an irresistible, if fading, prestige. They did not supplant the imperial institutions by barbarian customs, Roman law by barbarian codes; they preserved the Roman law for the conquered Roman alongside their own customary law, and even, in some cases, commingled them. Theodoric made use of the administrative machinery of Rome, retained the fiscal system, incorporated the Roman law in his legislation (Edict of Theodoric), assimilated Roman civilisation. "All the new barbarian royalties," says Mr Hodgkin, "even that of the Vandals in Africa, preserved much of the laws and machinery of the Roman empire; but Theodoric's Italian kingdom preserved the most of all."

Though this "preservation" becomes less marked the further we recede from the centre of the western empire, it is more or less apparent among the Burgundians in the south-east of Gaul, among the Visigoths in the south-west and in Spain, among the Franks in the north, and, to some extent, even among the Anglo-Saxons in Roman Britain. Burgundians and Visigoths not only dispensed justice to the conquered Roman provincials in accordance with the principles of the Roman law,—witness the Lex Romana Burgundiorum and the Lex Romana Wisigothorum,—their native codes show, according to M. Rambaud, considerable traces of borrowing from the legal system of Rome. The Burgundian Gondebaud and the Visigothic Alaric II. were enlightened enough to pay in this respect the tribute of Teutonic barbarism to Roman civilisation.

The influence of a mighty tradition, of institutions that stood for all that was highest in the decaying splendours of a dying past, acted like a magnet on the inrushing hordes of wild men from beyond the Rhine or the Danube. Even a pagan barbarian of the fierce stamp of a Clovis respected the laws and coveted the honours of the power whose weakness might excite his contempt or his ambition. While he ruled his Franks in virtue of his hereditary right, he was as eager as his barbaric predecessors to plume himself with the title of Roman Consul with which the Emperor Anastasius invested him, and in virtue of which he exercised jurisdiction over his Gaulish subjects. These early Frankish kings were undoubtedly the leaders of the strongest subdivision of the Teutonic invaders, but even these founders of an undying dominion paid tribute to immortal Rome. They respected the majesty not only of imperial offices that had lost their former efficacy, but of the system of law that has continued to mould a large part of Europe to our own day. Thus we read in a decree of Clotaire II., "We have ordained that the conduct of cases between Romans shall be decided by the Roman law."

From Clovis to Charlemagne is a long interval, yet although the fiction of the imperial delegation of authority to the barbarian chiefs disappeared during this interval, it was in the future great Frankish king that the empire of the west was to be revived, that Rome once more, for a short period, ruled the west. Charlemagne, as we shall see, was the Roman imperator come to life again. It was Charlemagne that extinguished the Lombardic kingdom of North Italy, and in substituting his own imperial dominion for that of the Lombardic kings, he restored the empire of Rome. These Lombards, who came in the wake of the Ostrogoths, did not show themselves so susceptible to imperial institutions. Their irruption was purely destructive, for their civilisation was ruder, their organisation looser than those of their predecessors. They represent the fierce barbarian horde over which the king wielded but little authority (in the age of Tacitus they had no king), and for long North Italy was the prey of their lawless insubordination. They ravaged, plundered, slew without stint, imposed their laws on the vanquished, and established the purely barbarian domination which Charlemagne swept away. In the Roman diocese of Britain, too, where the fierce Anglo-Saxons settled, the imperial institutions were largely, if not wholly, swept away. They founded a State, or rather a series of petty States, which were subsequently unified into one powerful kingdom, and which, though subsequently coming, directly or indirectly, under Roman influences, seem at first to have felt but little the plastic touch of Rome. The positive assertions of most modern English historians as to the absolute immunity of the Anglo-Saxon settlers from Roman influence are, however, as we shall see later, not above question. Even among English historians there appears an occasional champion of the continuity of Roman institutions in Britain. "The conquering hordes of Gothic and Wendic origin," says Sir Travers Twiss, for example, in his introduction to his edition of Bracton, "which overran the southern portions of the western empire, equally with the Alemannic tribes which subsequently overran the northern portions, accepted the civil laws of the people whom they conquered, and the Saxon invaders of England were no exception to this rule."

The tendency to assimilate Roman institutions on the part of the invaders of Italy and Gaul is patent in the enhanced power of the barbarian king. Imperialism, Cæsarism, perpetuated itself in these nations of Teutonic freemen, who yielded to the spell of Roman autocracy. The king described by Tacitus was elected, and though distinguished ancestry was a qualification for election, and the election seems to have been confined to those of reputed royal descent, his power was very limited. He was not necessarily the leader of the nation in war. For this office the most capable man was selected. The king was merely the representative head of the nation. For the discussion and decision of questions of general interest the people met at stated times on the Marzfeld or the Maifeld. In these assemblies every important measure, such as the election of the king and the magistrates appointed to dispense justice in the various sub-divisions (*pagi*) of the kingdom, and the trial of State criminals, was decided by the free vote expressed by a murmur of dissent, or by the brandishing of spears to indicate assent, of all freemen present. The decision of matters of lesser importance was left to the smaller assembly of these chiefs or magistrates, who likewise prepared the measures to be submitted to the general council of the people. The kingship was not even universal, for some of these States were republics. They were governed by elective chiefs; but, whether republican or monarchic, the sovereignty belonged in all essential respects to the people. This sovereignty, however, was only exercised by the freemen. Slaves and serfs, even freedmen, had no political rights, and in this respect the Germanic democracy was different from what we in modern times understand by the sovereignty of the people. Even among the freemen the noble class seems to have enjoyed a distinction and a power that are hardly compatible with the traditional conception of equal rights for all. The renowned warrior, whose prowess attracted a number of "companions" who lived under his patronage and fought under his leadership; the wealthy landowner, whose herds and serfs were numerous, would inevitably exert a dominant influence on the government both of the district and the nation.

During the three centuries that intervened between the

age of Tacitus and the irruption of the barbarians, the Teutonic kingship underwent, among some of the Germanic peoples at least, a marked change. The tendency during this interval had been towards the formation of larger national unions. The small nation swelled into the combination of small nations for offence or defence, and the larger combination needed a larger authority to weld and keep it together for aggressive purposes. This larger authority was further enhanced, after the irruption, by the titles of consul, patrician, master of militia, which, as we have seen, the barbarian kings solicited and obtained from the emperors. Procopius denotes this larger authority, as invested in Theodoric, as well as emphasises the admirable manner in which he used it, when he says that the great Goth was a tyrant in name, but a true imperator in deed. Among the Frankish kings, in particular, these dignities led up to the imperial attributes themselves. Clovis is a sort of barbarian Cæsar. His successors are as absolute as Diocletian himself. They assume the imperial insignia—the crown of gold, the sceptre, the purple. They have their court, their courtiers, their grand dignitaries of the palace. They affect pompous titles, and usurp at last that of majesty itself. They are the masters (*domini*) of the State, and the people have become their subjects (*subjecti*). Even the magnates own subjection, and subscribe themselves as their slaves (*vestri servi*). They preface their ordinances with the high-flown phraseology of the imperial edicts. Their authority is derived from heaven, not from the people. They reign by the grace of God and in virtue of hereditary right. Election has lapsed, and the magnates meet at the death of the king, not to elect another, but to acclaim his son or nearest heir in his place, and swear fidelity to his person. "It is the King of the heavens that has confided the royal authority to us," asserted Gontram. "No one is ignorant," said Dagobert, "that the people have been placed in subjection to us by the goodness of God." The government — whether local or national—passes out of the hands of the people into that of the king and his officials—mayor of the palace, dukes, counts, &c. The sovereignty of the people has receded into the mists of time, or survives merely in certain usages which have only a retrospective significance. The assembly of the people on the Marzfeld or the Maifeld has become merely an armed review, and the occasion of offering gifts and paying tributes to the king. The king indeed takes council with the magnates as in the days of Tacitus, but the magnates are composed of the great officers of State, the bishops, and the *antrustions* or personal dependants of the monarch, and do not represent the people. They are an aristocratic class, dependent on the king, who seeks their advice, but is not subject to their control. In spite of an occasional phrase which seems to show the consent of the people to legislative or administrative acts, there is no evidence of the convocation of a single national deliberative assembly during the Merovingian period. The political assemblies of the later Merovingian kings were aristocratic, not popular assemblies.

The king is the head of the army, the head of the Church, the lawgiver and judge, and his will is supreme in all these capacities. "Liberty," says M. de Coulanges, "gained nothing from the fall of the Roman empire. The royalty which succeeded it was a despotism without legal limits." Insurrection, assassination, revolution are the only remedies against this despotism, but such expedients, while sometimes successfully applied, only show how completely all political control through the traditional public assemblies had slipped from the hands of the people. The Roman idea of the State, with its absolute head, its centralised administration, reappears in the Frankish kingdom of the Merovingian monarchs.

The Merovingian kings proved, however, too weak to sustain this usurpation of absolute power. Within less than a century after the death of Clovis a strong current of aristocratic opposition to centralised authority is traceable, especially in Austrasia, the eastern half of the Frankish kingdom. The *antrustions*, who had obtained grants of land from the king, appear as powerful territorial magnates, and with the privilege of "immunity" from the jurisdiction of the royal officials,—the dukes and counts in whom the provincial and local administration resided,—acquire large rights within their own domains. Their insubordination towards the king tends to increase in the ratio of their power over the people, and their freedom from official control. The partition of the kingdom among the sons, first of Clovis, and then of Clotaire, contributed still more materially to the undoing of the royal power. Clotaire's sons fought with one another like wild beasts, and their ferocity was fanned by the fury of these two terrible women, Fredegonde and Brunechilde. These Frankish kings were most horrible Christians—orthodox Christians, too. It would have been better for the honour of Christianity had they remained pagans, or rather savages. Savages they were, in spite of their veneer of Christian civilisation. They were the greatest adepts in patricide and fratricide on record. " An age of crimes," is the melancholy reflection of Gregory of Tours, whose sombre recital, as well as those of his fellow-annalists, Fredegaire and the author of the " Life of St Leger," forms a sickening tale of incessant war and savage outrage. It is a century of murder, whose dark and foul deeds are lighted up only by the gleam of the assassin's dagger. In this truculent strife the virility of the race of Clovis exhausted itself and invited its ultimate nullity. The power of the magnates—dukes, counts, bishops, territorial aristocracy— grew as that of the monarch declined, and against these magnates Brunechilde vainly struggled in Austrasia to her terrible fate. The reactionary character of their opposition to the crown is evident from the fact that they profess, like the English barons in the reign of King John, to vindicate the law, particularly their own proprietary rights, against the royal despotism. They claim, too, a voice in legislation and administration, and in their political assemblies we may see at least a partial revival of the old Germanic constitution as the result of the reaction against the usurped authority of a Clovis or a Clotaire.

Their leaders were the Austrasian mayors of the palace of the doughty race of Pippin, and with their support these mayors ultimately became the hereditary masters of the king and the kingdom.

The later Merovingian kings were in truth poor specimens of both royalty and human nature. In the hands of these forcible hereditary mayors they seem to lack all power of volition, let alone the ability to wield the sword in an age in which the sword was the only effective instrument of government. Their kingship consisted mainly in being paraded once a year on an ox-waggon in the presence of the assembled magnates, and in performing certain ceremonies for which they were primed like any child in a pantomime. "For many years," says Eginhard, in the introduction to his "Life of Charlemagne," "the house of the Merovings was destitute of vigour, and had nothing illustrious about it save the empty name of king, for the rulers of their palace possessed both the wealth and power of the kingdom, bearing the name of mayor, and had charge of all high matters of State."

A Chilperic, a Theuderic, a Childeric—the last of these pitiable remnants of the race of Clovis—still ruled in the first half of the eighth century by hereditary right, and by the lingering reverence for the memory of their mighty ancestor. The *de facto* king was the mayor of the palace, and by the sanction of Pope Zacharias and the assembled magnates and people, the mayor, in the person of Pippin the Short, became, in 752, *de jure* king as well. Three years later his kingly dignity was hallowed by his coronation by Zacharias' successor, the fugitive Stephen II.

This appeal to the pope is important. Zacharias might have no right to decide *ex cathedra* a question which it was for the people, according to ancient Germanic precedent, to solve; but his arbitration was pat to the purpose of the usurper, and the appeal was certainly advantageous to the pope. He was serving his own interests in conferring the sanction of Heaven on the new kingship. He was gaining a mighty ally to champion his cause in Italy, where he was impotent enough against the Lombard king; he was paving the way, too, for the assertion of a pretension which was to play a tremendous *rôle* in mediæval history. Pippin becomes king by the will of Heaven, but it is the pope that interprets that will and consecrates him to his office. In the future sequence of things his kingship is the gift of the pope, and the pope is consequently superior to the king. And when the kingly dignity is enhanced by the imperial sceptre of the great Charles, Pippin's masterful son, it is again the pope (this time Leo III.) that confers it. Leo had no more right to make Charles an emperor than his predecessors had to make Pippin a king, but he was all the same forging a precedent whereon future popes might found some startling conclusions. In the meantime the ecclesiastical ancestor of Gregory and Innocent comported himself with meet humility before his patron, the newly fabricated Cæsar of the west. For, apart from a questionable title, this Cæsar Redivivus was a truly imperial man, and fairly earned, as far as the merit of vast ability and force of character went, his exalted honours. He was in very deed the embodiment of the imperial dream which, throughout these shadowy centuries of brutal despots and *rois fainéants*, had not ceased to appeal to the imagination, and which the torpid empire of the east, under the unspeakable *régime* of a feminine head, had ceased to represent. He assumed the imperial power as well as the imperial name. He owed his imperial crown directly to the pope, not to the Frankish *leudes*, far less to the people. He was the absolute ruler of a vast State, and he strove to arrest the growth of feudal institutions which had begun to strike root with the rise of the Merovingian aristocracy, and re-establish the imperial State. He reorganised the administrative hierarchy by his *missi*, or deputies on mission, who exercised a strict supervision over all officials, from the duke or count downwards. He made use of the bishops as political agents for the same purpose. No detail of the administration but was guided directly or indirectly by his supreme will. The larger assembly of the old Germanic Volk still gathered on the Maifeld, but it was convened mainly for military and fiscal purposes. There was still the smaller assembly of officials and magnates of Church and State, but it too had no legislative power. It might give advice, express an opinion on the laws, or capitularies, submitted to it, but this opinion the emperor might accept or reject as he pleased. The decision lay in the imperial will, not in the independent votes of those present, though there is still a trace of ancient usage in the profession that the law is made by the imperial will and the consent of the people. It was the ostentatious policy of the emperor to cultivate the people, the freemen, who also formed the army, by phrases of this sort, which had really only an antiquarian meaning. The freemen, the people, equally with the magnates, swear fidelity to his person, but it is fidelity to a master. They renew their oaths on special occasions, such as the proclamation or the partition of the empire, but the emperor is limited by no earthly power in his actions as their sovereign lord. In the person of the mighty emperor the State again emerges into the foreground out of the mists of Merovingian chaos. The pope even becomes his subject, owning allegiance in return for patronage and protection, and submitting his election for the imperial confirmation and sanction. It is the emperor that nominates to vacant benefices, presides over the ecclesiastical assemblies as lord of Church and State, exacts the services and subjection of bishops and abbots as well as of the lay nobles. In his person the State is supreme over Church, aristocracy, and people.

The figure of the mighty emperor was, however, but an apparition between the age of contention and anarchy that preceded, and the age of contention and anarchy that followed his reign. "The Frank empire, in both its stages," remarks Mr Jenks, "was, in a very important sense, a sham empire. . . . (It) was from first to last a great anachronism. . . . The Germans of Continental Europe found themselves called upon to live up to the elaborate civilisation of the Roman empire. They broke down under the strain." The work and the system of Charles may almost be said to have died with him. The principle of partition, maladroitly applied by Louis the Pious in favour of a son by a second wife, in addition to his three sons by the first, resulted in the dismemberment of the empire and the establishment of several independent kingdoms. The imperial dignity, indeed, survived in the emperors Lothaire, Louis, Charles the Bald, Charles the Fat, Arnulf of Germany, Louis of Arles, and the Italians, Wido and Berengar, but it was little more than a dignity, and the dignity certainly did not rise in general estimation from its association with the Italian adventurers who contested its possession, or from the character of the sorry popes who claimed the right to confer it.

In the scramble for aggrandisement at its expense, these popes took care not only to enhance their temporal possessions, but to secure independence of imperial control. Nor did the royal authority gain with the disruption of the empire. The relapse of the successors of the great Charles is the repetition of the relapse of the later successors of the great Clovis. They steadily lost many of their prerogatives to the magnates, for the continuation of Charlemagne's policy of protecting the smaller freemen from subjection to the great lords was impossible in an age of civil strife and individual violence, which favoured this second reaction against absolute power, and gave scope to the selfish pretensions of dukes, counts, prelates, barons. The legislation of the reign of Charles the Bald shows clearly this advance towards feudalism, testifies alike to the impotence of the king and the increasing enslavement of the people. The king does nothing without the consent and advice of the magnates, is, in truth, more subject to them than they are to him, while the magnates are absolute lords of the people within their domains. The tone of some of these later capitularies is in fact that of the suppliant rather than of the master, in spite of the official "We will and command," and the equally impotent pains and penalties against omnipresent lawlessness. That of Mersen (847) enjoins all freemen to place themselves under a lord, under whose jurisdiction they are bound to remain and whom they must serve in war. That of 856, on the other hand, legitimates the right of resistance to the king in case he infringes the rights of these lords, and virtually puts a premium on rebellion against the royal authority. That of 857 fulminates severe pains and penalties against the prevailing brigandage, and reveals the fact that the only law that is respected is the law of force, and that the right of private warfare has become the universal right. That of Kiersey (877) recognises the hereditary transmission of offices and dignities, of dukedoms, countships, and benefices of the royal vassals, and thus creates a multitude of petty rivals of the hereditary sovereign. That of Pistes (864) commands the demolition of the castles and strongholds erected without the royal permission, and threatens the refractory lord with the royal vengeance. But these pugnative lords paid no heed to either command or threat, and continued to war with one another and with the king in the spirit of feudal insubordination. The Bald Charles' successors in the western Frankish kingdom, Charles the Fat and Charles the Simple, Louis d'Outremer, Lothaire, and Louis V., were not the men to cope with the growing anarchy. During the next century every strong man was a law unto himself, and it was ultimately as easy for one of these strong men to appropriate, with the consent of his fellows, the royal dignity of the last of the western Carolingian kings, as it had been for the mayor of the palace to brush aside the last of the Merovingians.

With the advent, in 987, of this strong man, Hugh Capet, Duke of France, the feudal monarchy emerges into full view. King Hugh was no hereditary monarch. He owed his dignity to the election of his fellow-magnates who had already made and unmade kings during the previous hundred years of anarchy. The kingship, which the strong men of Merovingian and Carolingian race had made hereditary and absolute, became a mere institution of expediency. The stress of the time, the dangers of the kingdom, exposed to perpetual broils within, Norman and Germanic inroads from without, suggested the choice of the fittest man for the post, and this fittest man Duke Hugh, as the master of broad domains, the skilful leader in war and diplomacy, was adjudged to be. "The office of king," proclaimed Archbishop Adalbéron of Reims in the assembly at Senlis, "does not belong by hereditary right to any family. It belongs to him whose military prowess, wisdom, faith mark as the fittest to fill it. It is Hugh of France that possesses all these qualities. He alone can maintain the prosperity of the republic and guarantee the interests of all." Thus the principle of hereditary succession was flatly discarded as irrational and dangerous, and though reverence for the memory of the Great Karl and his family survived in a small legitimist party, expediency carried it as the only possible alternative in the circumstances. These legitimists could hardly adduce experience in support of their fidelity to the old line. With the exception of a few strong men, who owed their ability to rule to nature, not to their ancestors, the hereditary rulers, whether of Carolingian or Merovingian race, had amply proved their incompetence to wear a crown, let alone their inability to govern as absolute sovereigns. The very epithets which distinguish many of these kings by descent do not reveal any inborn qualifications for a crown. If the most striking feature of a king consists in his baldness, or his fatness, or his simplicity, it is pretty evident that the "greatness" of Charles was not hereditary, and there was certainly some excuse for the determination of these magnates to apply a more rational test of fitness to rule than royal fatness, baldness, or simplicity. The principle of rationality in government, exemplified in the old Celtic as well as Germanic right of electing the fittest person to rule, and in the self-government of the Athenian democracy and the Roman republic, thus returned for a brief space to the world.

Its return was by no means final, however. The feudal king did not remain for long elective; the election of Hugh Capet proved to be the establishment of a new dynasty, which erelong vindicated the principle of hereditary succession and the monarchic power against the feudal magnates. Nor was it the sovereignty of the people that found expression in the rational discourse of Adalbéron at Senlis. It was rather the sovereignty of a caste, of the feudal magnate, who alone possessed political rights, and whose action is open to the suspicion of self-seeking. The last of the Carolingians had no lands to gift away, and as Hugh Capet was the greatest landowner of his day, there was a good prospect for the greedy lords of further aggrandisement in his elevation. It was the expediency of self-interest, of class privilege, that really triumphed at Senlis. These magnates did not give the State a master; they merely selected a patron of their own order. In reality, the patron was to prove the master in the persons of some of Hugh Capet's redoubtable successors; but, in the meantime, the royal power was practically null. Hugh Capet might imagine himself the successor of Charlemagne and Clovis in virtue of the consecration of the Church, and surround himself with the grand functionaries and the pomp of the old royalty. In reality, he was only the first among equals with a more dignified title. He had no jurisdiction over the vassals of the magnates. He could tax only his own vassals, and if the magnates rendered him homage as king, he rendered them homage, paid them dues for lands held within their domains, of which they, not he, were the superiors. There were practically as many kings in France as there were feudal grandees. While one of their number represented the State in matters of general policy and could demand the assistance of the others in its defence, each was virtual king over his own broad lands.

The striving of the Capetian kings was, however, to extend their rights as magnates over the whole kingdom, to substitute subordination for feudal equality, and make the monarchy supreme. They sought to revive the imperial tradition of the centralisation of power, and the pretension of absolute right derived from God was not long in reappearing. Their consecration to their office invested them and it with a sacredness, an indefeasibility on which churchmen like Suger and Abbon laid stress, and which the lawyers, trained by the revived study of Roman jurisprudence, by-and-by raised into a principle of law.

What meanwhile had become of the emperor? Not the Basileus of Constantinople, who still affected the headship of old Rome, but the successors of the great Charles, the Cæsar Redivivus of the west? The empire of Charles went to pieces, as we have noted, on the rock of partition which reft its unity. The Carolingian unity rested on the genius of Charles, and Louis le Debonnaire did not inherit the genius of his father in inheriting his imperial sceptre. With his death the empire became more and more a fiction as far as the west was concerned, split into the three kingdoms of France, Lotharingia, and Germany. Even imperial Lotharingia suffered subdivision on the death of Lothaire, and the imperial dignity was further restricted to the kingdom of Italy in the person of Louis II. For a short time it distended once more to its old proportions (with the exception of Provence or Arles) under the sceptre of Charles the Fat, Emperor and King of Germany, France (or Neustria), and Italy. With his abdication in 887 the imperial phantom lingered only in the title of some petty adventurer, like Wido and Berengar, to whom the pope solemnly gave the insignia of an imaginary universal sovereignty, until Otto of Saxony, King of Germany, appeared at Rome to claim and receive it from Pope John XII. in 962. The tenacity of the imperial idea must have been great indeed when such a travesty of universal sovereignty could pass in the imagination of the time for the embodiment of the ancient mastery of the western world. The Eternal City was still regarded as the seat of empire. "As long as the Colosseum shall stand, Rome will live; when the Colosseum shall fall, Rome will fall; and when Rome falls, the world will succumb." So dreamed the devotees of a hoary tradition, and the great Otto, whom the pope called to his aid against his oppressors, as his predecessor had appealed to the great Charles, should substantiate their sanguine dream. "The Holy Roman Empire of the German nation" was the embodiment of this dream. The German emperor meant subjection, not supremacy, for Rome, however, and induced recurring contention and revolt in Italy against an alien domination. It was a factor of disunion, not of unity; disunion in Germany, where, after the death of the great Otto, the ambition of rival princes and the growth of feudalism rent the land; disunion in Italy, where the Roman and German factions, Guelfs and Ghibelines, fought for predominance. The struggle lasted throughout the period of the imperial dynasties of Saxony, Franconia, and Hohenstaufen, and culminated in the grand duel for supremacy between pope and emperor, the spiritual and the temporal power, Gregory VII. and Henry IV., Adrian IV. and Barbarossa, Innocent III. and Henry VI., Gregory IX., Innocent IV. and Frederick II. The pontiff—theocracy—confronted the emperor—autocracy. Of old, the emperor was Pontifex Maximus, head of the Church as well as the State; the mediæval pontiff claimed the function, and not only disputed the imperial headship of the Church, as wielded by Charlemagne, but proclaimed himself virtual head of the State, king of kings, universal superior on earth. The pontiff, the theocrat, eventually triumphed over the emperor, the autocrat, but the pretension to universal superiority did not triumph in the emperor's defeat. Nationality grew and hardened during the struggle, and the kingly power, which likewise grew and hardened outside the arena of the struggle, in France and England, repelled the papal pretension to universal supremacy. Unity, whether based on the autocratic or the theocratic idea, became a fiction and remained a mere pretension in spite of a great Charles and a great Otto, a Gregory and an Innocent.

SOURCES OF THIS CHAPTER.—Cæsar, De Bello Gallico; Tacitus, Germania; Procopius, De Bello Gotthico (Corpus Scriptorum Historiæ Byzantinæ); Gregory of Tours, Historia Francorum (Monumenta Germaniæ Historica, and Guizot, Collection des Mémoires relatifs à l'Histoire de France);

Sources of Chapter I.

Chronicle ascribed to Fredegaire (in *ibid.*); The Vitæ of St Leger and Dagobert I. (Guizot); Einhard or Eginhard, Vita Caroli, and Annales (Guizot); The Gesta, by a monk of St Gall, translated by Guizot under the title of "Faits et Gestes"; Thegan, Vita Sancti Ludovici, and The Astronomer, Sancti Ludovici Imperatoris Vita (Guizot); Nithard, Historiæ (Guizot); Annales de Saint Bertin et de Metz; Frodoard, Histoire de l'Église de Rheims, and Chronique; Abbon, Siege de Paris par les Normands;—all in Guizot's Collection. Richter, Annalen des Fränkischen Reiches (1872), and Annalen des Fränkischen Reiches unter den Karolingen (1877); Gibbon, Decline and Fall of the Roman Empire; Fustel de Coulanges, Histoire des Institutions Politiques de l'Ancienne France (1875); Dahn, Urgeschichte der Germanischen und Romanischen Völker, in Oncken's Welt-Geschichte (1881-89); Guizot, Histoire de la Civilisation en France, t. i. (1884); Littré, Etudes sur les Barbares et le Moyen Age (1867-74); Rambaud, Histoire de la Civilisation Française, t. i. (1886); Gasquet, Précis des Institutions Politiques et Sociales de l'Ancienne France, t. i. (1885); Berthelot, Le Monde Barbare, &c., in t. i. of Histoire Générale, edited by Lavisse et Rambaud (1893); Langlois et Luchaire, Le Royaume de France, in *ibid.*; Hodgkin, Theodoric the Goth (1891), and Charles the Great (1897); Oman, European History (476-918), (1893); Jenks, Law and Politics in the Middle Ages (1898); Emerton, Introduction to the Study of the Middle Ages (1891) (written too exclusively from the Germanic standpoint); Twiss, Introduction to Vol. II. of edition of Bracton, De Legibus Angliæ.

CHAPTER II.

GROWTH OF THE FEUDAL SYSTEM—ITS EFFECTS ON THE LOWER CLASSES.

IT was from this long period of revolution that the feudal system sprang. The western empire was first broken into barbarian kingdoms. These kingdoms were in turn effaced by anarchy or conquest, and gave place to the empire of Charlemagne. Charlemagne's empire was in turn broken in pieces by the disintegrating forces within it, and the universal sovereignty gave place once more to the sovereignties of a number of kings, whose jurisdiction was gradually limited by that of the feudal magnates in France, Germany, Italy, and part of Spain. The State in the Roman sense disappeared, and was only to reappear later with the assertion of the royal authority at the expense of the feudal magnate. This process of disintegration lasted from the fifth to the tenth century, and for the next three hundred years its results were crystallised in what is termed the feudal system in the greater part of Western Europe.

To trace this process would be a lengthy undertaking, and would carry us outside the scope of this work into a multitude of contentious questions, for the origin and development of the feudal system are obscure enough, however simple its maturity. We may at least assert that the roots of feudalism lie in the social institutions of the Romans as well as of the barbarians—in dependence on a superior, involving restriction of liberty and of rights of property, common to Romans, Celts, and Teutons alike. In the Roman empire property in land was of two kinds. It was either the absolute, hereditary possession (*potestas*, *proprietas*) of the proprietor, and could be disposed by will, or it was a benefice (*beneficium*), held by a tenant, or beneficiary, under obligation to pay certain dues, render certain services, and revocable by the proprietor. In the third and fourth centuries, when the empire entered on its decline, a large part of the land, held by small free proprietors, became beneficiary, and the class of *coloni*, who held land on a servile or semi-servile tenure, consequently swelled enormously. In these anarchic centuries the small proprietor alienated his proprietary rights to the large proprietor in return for protection from the oppression of rapacious officials; or the large proprietor seized the opportunity of anarchy and misgovernment to deprive the small. Whether the alienation were voluntary or constrained, the smaller proprietor thus became the dependant of the larger in virtue of the change in the tenure of his estate from that of an absolute to a beneficiary possession. Many of these miserable freemen were, moreover, driven by destitution or despair to resort to another expedient, as fatal to liberty as to property—that of commendation. Commendation seems to have grown out of the old relation of client and patron, common to Romans, Celts, and Teutons. In return for maintenance and protection, the freeman, in this case, bound himself not merely to alienate his property to a superior, but to serve him as his lord (*dominus*).

The later period of the empire displays this twofold alienation of property and liberty in common operation, as the result of the weakening of the central power, and the consequent misgovernment and lawlessness. While the imperial officials victimised the weak by their extortions, the strong took advantage of their opportunity to increase their possessions and power. There was no philanthropy in these contracts. Official rapacity, rampant lawlessness on the one hand, the greed, the violence of the rich on the other, placed the small proprietor between a veritable Scylla and Charybdis. It was only a question of choosing the lesser evil, and, as we learn from Salvian, the lesser evil meant the exploitation of the poor, the weak by the rich, the strong. "The defence of the weak is not dictated by humanity, but by cupidity. While professing to protect the poor, the rich despoil them, and by defending the unfortunate, they render them more unfortunate. For those who seem to be defended are forced to make over almost all their property to their defenders, even before protection is accorded." The inevitable result of this policy was, he further tells us, to rob them of their liberty as well as of their property—"to make the *protégés* the serfs of the rich."

This wholesale dependence, by alienation, of property and liberty is a sure sign of the subversion both of the State and of society. A sin nature, so in history. Force unrestrained by law bursts forth in some terrible upheaval, some eruption, some shock which rends a world, or turns a fair region into a desert. The shock, the upheaval, came to that anarchic Roman world, when lawless force within, lawless force from without, brought doom to those whose only alternative was surrender to the inevitable. Imperial rule had, latterly at least, only taught the masses how to submit, and submission, in such an age, meant slavery. Certainly a terrible commentary on any political system when a nation is reduced to the necessity of helplessly bending before the social shock of aggression within, invasion from without. And when that nation is an empire, embracing a vast totality of human beings, the effects of such a shock, such an outburst of lawless force, are far-reaching indeed. It meant social desolation, the slavery of the small freeman in a large part of Europe for centuries to come.

For this twofold alienation continued not only throughout the period of the barbarian irruptions and settlements, but far into the Middle Ages, until it became the dominant system in Western and Central Europe. The small free proprietor disappeared over vast regions under the operation of the law so fatal to personal and political liberty, that the weak must submit to the strong. Throughout these rough centuries the cry of the small proprietor is raised against the rapacity, the violence of the large proprietor, who forces him to forfeit both his property and his freedom to a master. The desire to escape military service by alienating his property to the Church was doubtless responsible to some extent for the loss of rights; but force, not volition, is in general the basis of this all-devouring system of usurpation. Force, usurpation are everywhere —force acting with irresistible effect on those who have lost all active consciousness of the higher qualities of human worth, and are actuated chiefly by the instinct of self-preservation— usurpation which in such an age comes to be the natural course of things. There are times when human nature becomes false to itself, and only its lower instincts come into play in the arena of human life. Such a time was that succession of cast-iron centuries which gave birth to the feudal system. There are insurrections in these degenerate centuries; eternal broils, in which the magnates of the time are concerned chiefly; dynastic quarrels which draw blood like water; anarchic combinations, in which the strong man asserts himself, and carries away the profit or loss accruing therefrom, as the case may be. There is no rising of human nature against its own declension: no insurrection on behalf of its highest rights. The freeman, while uttering his complaint against usurpation and oppression, submits to the prevailing doctrine that rights are for the few, servility for the many. So universal is this tendency towards dependence, that there must have been a sort of law of social gravitation towards it. It is a period of collapse, following a tremendous political and social upheaval; and it is this fact of social comatose, induced by the misgovernment of the later empire, that alone explains the ultimate relapse of almost the whole body of small freemen, within and partially without the limits of the western empire, under the domination of a caste, based on landed possession.

The disappearance of the small free proprietor was contemporaneous with the rise of this landed aristocracy, lay and cleric, which throve at its expense. Its territorial aggrandisement was, of course, not due solely to the spoliation of the weak, though it owed much to this invidious source. Many of its members had profited from the generosity of the kings of Merovingian or Carolingian race, who conferred benefices on their *leudes*, their *antrustions*, in reward of their services. Some had inherited their domains from their Gallo-Roman ancestors, whose estates were by no means generally confiscated in favour of the barbarian invaders. The lands in the hands of the ecclesiastical dignitaries had been swelled by the gifts of the faithful, and portions of these lands had furnished the unscrupulous Charles Martel, or his immediate successors, with benefices for his greedy lay supporters. However they came by their broad acres, whether by spoliation of the weak, inheritance, or royal generosity, the significant fact is patent in the ninth century that a powerful landed aristocracy overshadows emperor, king, and people. Its members are the superiors of a greater or lesser number of dependants in virtue of the beneficiary tenure of the land which they hold. They enjoy, moreover, as superiors, certain immunities from the royal jurisdiction, and are consequently invested with certain rights of "justice," as they were called, over their dependants. Further, in virtue of the increasing usage of commendation, which binds the dependant to the superior in the close relation of personal service, including military service, the beneficiary tends more and more to become the vassal, the superior the lord.

Charlemagne, as we have seen, strove to depress this powerful aristocracy as dangerous to the unity of the State. He subjected their jurisdiction over their dependants, as well as that of the counts and lesser royal officials, to the supervision of his *missi dominici*, with the object of checking the tendency towards feudalism, and bringing the central authority to bear on all the members of the State. He continued, however, the practice of granting benefices out of the royal domains or the Church lands, and while he inveighed against the spoliation of the weak by the strong, he permitted the magnates similarly to grant benefices out of their own vast domains, and thus to increase the number of their dependants. He unwittingly, too, gave an impulse to the very tendency he strove to repress by encouraging, for military purposes, the practice of commendation, which bound the dependant, *inter alia*, to serve his superior in arms. If the dependant were bound to follow his superior in war, the emperor could, by merely summoning the superior, bring the whole army of the nation into the field. In the hands of a strong ruler the device might thus consolidate the force of the State. Relax the central authority, as happened under Charlemagne's weak successors, and the effect must be exactly the opposite. The magnate must, perforce, virtually become a petty sovereign, a great feudal lord, within his own domains. In the first place, the beneficiary form of tenure makes him the superior of a large number of dependants. In the second place, the beneficiary form of tenure, in virtue of its union with commendation, now obliges his dependant to serve him in war. The benefice becomes a fief, the dependant a vassal. In the third place, he possesses jurisdiction, the rights of "justice" over his dependants, or rather his vassals, in virtue of the immunities which he enjoys at the expense of the royal authority. This union of the benefice, of commendation, of immunity, it was that, under the *régime* of Charles' weak successors, went to the constitution of the feudal system. Society became a hierarchy cemented by land tenure, the personal relation of lord and vassal, and in this society the State became disintegrated, for that which cemented society disrupted the State. This disruption, this revolution, which, at other times, might have led to the emancipation of society, of the individual, led to the subordination of both to a feudal caste.

Examine now the constitution of this social and political hierarchy as consummated in the tenth and eleventh centuries in Western and Central Europe, and more particularly in France. At its head stands the king, who, in Germany, is invested with the imperial dignity. Both king and emperor are elected, though in France the hereditary principle erelong prevails once more in the successors of Hugh Capet. In Germany after the days of the Ottos, the Henrys, the Fredericks, the emperor is little more than a figure-head, the impotent representative of the fiction of a unity that has long passed away. The imperial power is still more shadowy in Italy, where predominance is divided between the great territorial magnates and the factions of the cities. The same feature of a fictive supremacy over a ruling aristocracy presents itself in France as in Germany, at least under the earlier Capetian kings. The great magnates—the dukes and counts, the peers of the realm—are sovereign within their vast domains and owe the king but a formal allegiance, expressed in the ceremonies of homage and fealty, which binds them to aid him in the defence of the kingdom. Only within his own domains is the feudal king a real sovereign, and this in virtue of his rights as a feudal magnate, not as a king. The other great magnates are practically his equals in everything but the title. They exercise sovereign rights within their domains, coin their own money, wage their own wars, make laws and dispense justice for their vassals, impose taxes on them, and are exempt from nearly all public burdens except military service. These represent the highest class of the feudal hierarchy, and to it belong the great dignitaries of the Church. Next come the barons, or magnates of lesser territorial power, who, in France, while possessed of sovereign jurisdiction within their domains, profess for the most part homage and fealty to the duke or count—the provincial magnates *par excellence*. In France they are termed seigneurs, in Germany herren, in England lords, in Spain ricos hombres. On a lower plane stand the noble vassals of these greater or lesser magnates—the chevalier, ritter, knight, caballero—who do homage and swear fealty to them for their fiefs. Last of all comes the grade of simple squire, ecuyer, edelknecht, infanzon, who possess a small fief in return for certain services to their superiors, and may be, in turn, the superiors of the peasants who cultivate it for them. Thus the members of each grade may be both superior and vassal according to their relation to the grade above or the grade beneath them. The duke or count is the vassal of the king, but the superior of most of the barons of his dukedom or countship. The baron, or seigneur, again, is the vassal of the duke or count, or of the king, but the superior of the chevalier, the knight, as the chevalier, the knight, may be the superior of the squire.

This vassalage involves military service and certain mutual obligations on the part of all, whatever their rank. It involves, too, certain burdens in the form of aids and reliefs to the lord. The vassal must pay an aid or tax on being invested with his fief, a relief or indemnity on the accession of his lord to his domain, or his own accession to his fief. He may further be called on to pay an aid on the marriage of his lord's eldest son or daughter, or for an expedition to the Holy Land. He is subject, in England and Normandy, and in some parts of Germany, to his lord's wardship during his minority, and the lord may appropriate the revenue of his estate to his own use till he come of age. He must obtain his lord's consent to the marriage of his daughters, and in the case of female wards a fine may be levied for refusing to marry the lord's nominee. Nay, in the case of the mighty kingdom of Jerusalem the lord may present three candidates from whom the lady must choose, unless she takes a desperate refuge in the confession that she is over sixty years of age.

He is bound to resort to the lord's court and assist in the dispensation of justice.

The feudal castle is the monument of this system of petty sovereignty, of subordination to a lord on which this sovereignty rests. Each castle is a citadel built for defence, and intended as a basis of attack. Hither the lord summons his vassals to rally in resistance to the aggression of a neighbour, or to sally forth for a foray into a hostile neighbour's domain. The massive donjon reminds us that society is in a state of war, and has hardened into its feudal form in the mould of a long period of lawlessness, usurpation, violence.

Whatever the gradation of power and rank, all the members of this hierarchy are noble, all outside it are ignoble. They alone, in the strict period of feudalism, can hold a fief and inscribe armorial bearings, which now came into vogue, as the badge of their nobility. They constitute, especially in France and Germany, a veritable caste, which regards intermarriage between noble and non-noble as degradation, dishonour. It is equally degrading for a "gentleman" to engage in trade or follow any profession but that of arms. None but nobles can be members of any order of chivalry, or appear at the court of the territorial magnate. It is only in the Church that the lack of nobility is not a barrier to social progress, and even in the Church the higher dignities are usually reserved for scions of noble families. The people is the victim of a social tyranny which, in France and Germany, lasted into the eighteenth century.

It is, in fact, impossible to speak of the people, in any real sense, in feudal times. The people, the populace, have shrunk into far narrower limits than at Rome or Athens; that is to say, the inferior, the unfree element, which was large enough at Rome or Athens, and among the ancient Germans and Celts as well, has swelled enormously in size during the period that produced the feudal system. The people, the mass of freemen possessed of civil and political rights in the Greek democracy, the later Roman republic, have almost disappeared, for not only has the ancient institution of slavery and serfage continued into the Dark Ages, but the small freeman has lapsed into a state of virtual bondage. We have seen the freeman agreeing or being forced to become the dependant of a superior, the small landowner becoming the beneficiary owner. A still worse fate overtook many of these victims of anarchy. They gradually sank into the position of serfs, of the *colonus* of the later empire, who, though free in principle, was bound to the soil which he cultivated for the proprietor, and was subject to a variety of restrictions, burdens, services. War, famine, pestilence, misfortune have swelled the crowd of miserables who have been despoiled of their birthright of freemen. The lack of money to pay a fine, the failure to join the king's levy, the credulity that alienated liberty as well as property to a religious house in return for the efficacy of the monks' prayers, the need of protection from pillage, the want of bread in times of famine—all these factors have contributed to increase the number of the unfree.

There were, indeed, degrees of servitude, which is almost equivalent to saying that there were degrees of misery. All the small cultivators on a domain or a fief have become the tenants of a lord or a lord's vassal, and whether technically free or unfree, whether villeins or franc villeins, are practically in a condition of serfage. They all bear a variety of burdens more or less onerous, are subject to a variety of vexatious restrictions. All are the victims of disabilities more or less galling, of usurpation often selfish and heartless, of the abuse of power often harsh and arbitrary.

There were, however, shades of difference in burdens, restrictions, disabilities, according as the cultivator was a serf or a so-called free tenant, a villein merely, or a franc villein. Many of the serfs—the lowest of their class—had absolutely no rights, were wholly at the mercy of their masters, who might seize their property, imprison and ill-treat them without possibility of remedy. Others were at least protected by custom, and custom came to acquire, if not the force of law—there was no law for the serf—at least the force of usage. If the serf fulfilled the conditions of serfage, he could count on a tolerable immunity from arbitrary encroachment on usage, and might ultimately buy the privilege of emancipation. The conditions of serfage were, nevertheless, hard enough, though they were not the same for all. Needless to say, his bondage was hereditary, transmissible from parents to children. He was bound to the soil, and was sold along with it. He could not marry any one above his condition, or outside the domain or the fief on which he lived, without obtaining his master's consent and paying a certain sum for the privilege (*droit de formariage*). If he died without legitimate children, his master took possession of his holding, and his next-of-kin must pay a heavy due before he could take possession (*mainmorte*). If he ran away, his master might pursue and seize him (*droit de suite*). He was subject to an annual poll-tax (*capitation*), and was bound to render certain services; was, in fact, in theory and often in practice, chargeable both in kind and services at his lord's discretion (*taillable et corvéable à merci*).

In contrast to the serf, the franc villeins, the free tenants, enjoyed certain rights, if, like the serfs, subjected to certain burdens. The relation between franc villein and lord was not that of master and serf, but of tenant and proprietor, and as long as the tenant acquitted the charges inherent in his tenure, the proprietor could not displace him. The free tenant, unlike the serf, could bequeath, even alienate, divide his holding at will, and the charges to which he was subject inhered in the land, not in the person. They were, nevertheless, both numerous and onerous, and in reality the difference between serf and non-serf, the free and non-free peasant, was not, in the matter of burdens, an appreciable one. The franc villein was subject to payments in money, in kind, in labour. Besides his rent, he was liable in an ordinary tax (*taille*) at the discretion of the proprietor, and might be called on to pay an extraordinary tax on special occasions, such as the marriage of the proprietor's daughter; was bound to pay dues in kind, so many sheaves of corn, so much wine, so many chickens or pigs; was liable to succession dues, market dues, dues on the sale of his produce, dues or tolls on roads, rivers, bridges, harbours. He was hampered by a number of monopolies (*banalités*) from which the proprietor drew a large revenue. He had to pay for the right of felling trees or pasturing his cattle in the proprietor's woods, and was compelled to grind his corn at the proprietor's mill, bake his bread in his oven, press his grapes at his press, and pay for the privilege with a part of the produce. He could not sell his corn or wine until the proprietor had disposed of his, and might not kill the game that destroyed his crops. He was forced to labour for the proprietor during a certain number of days in the year, till his fields, reap and transport his crops, keep his roads and buildings in repair, mount guard in his castle, and follow him in arms, lodge him and his escort when hunting or travelling.

These charges and burdens represent a widely ramified domination over the peasant cultivators, and afforded ample scope for applying the screw of oppression. There was no eternal superior, in the form of the State, to limit the power of the lord and his intendant or steward, or to see that justice was done to the poor man. For the lord had supreme jurisdiction over his tenants, the right of trying them and levying fines, and of condemning to death, banishment, confiscation in the case of the more serious crimes. In matters of civil jurisdiction he was equally absolute. He might be both judge and accuser, but his judgment was final. He was accountable to God only. "Between thy villein and thee there is no judge but God." His villeins might not assemble together to protest against his jurisdiction, or discuss their common interests, without his permission on pain of a fine, whose amount depended on his discretion. They might appeal to usage, and usage might become a safeguard of justice, but it was no effective substitute for rights, if the proprietor or his agents were not disposed by integrity or self-interest to respect it.

In general it *was* the interest, if not the legal duty, of the proprietor to refrain from oppression and injustice, for the prosperity of his fief or domain depended on the well-being of his serfs and tenants. Ordinarily the proprietor was prudent enough to observe tolerably the operation of this economic law to his own advantage. Its observation led, too, to the amelioration of the condition of the serf, the moderation of arbitrary seigneurial rights, and ultimately to his emancipation. The freedom of the individual, the moderation of absolute power, the limitation of burdensome exactions were by-and-by seen to be favourable to industry, and consequently to better cultivation and a larger revenue, and it was on the plea of the utility of emancipation both to the proprietor and his land that emancipation became more and more common, and ultimately, in some countries at least, general. Even the claims of humanity found an occasional vindication during the centuries when serfage was in full vogue. In spite of a social order so unfavourable to the appreciation of the rights of man, voices were heard proclaiming, on grounds of religion and reason, the gospel of humanity. They were for long, however, voices crying in the wilderness of feudal caste, for feudalism, in spite of all that may be adduced in favour of its utility for the time being, meant degradation and oppression for the mass. If it did not create serfage, which was to some extent inherited from earlier times, the anarchic centuries, from which it sprang, greatly increased the proportion of the unfree. The slave might rise, but the freeman sank in large numbers to the position of the serf. Serfage might be a refuge to many—the only refuge of the weak from the violence of the marauder. The strong man who could protect the inhabitants of a district from some plundering and murdering band of Normans, Saracens, Hungarians might be a benefactor, but his protection was only the lesser evil, and it is certain that the strong man, as represented by the feudal lord, came to be detested by the people as a taskmaster, a usurper. "The feudal *régime*," says M. Guizot, "has always been repulsive, odious; it has weighed upon the destiny of men, but it never reigned over their souls." The principle of feudalism was in itself, as far as it affected the masses, detestable. The proprietor was not merely the owner of the land; he was practically the owner of the peasants who cultivated it. The system reserved all privileges, rights for the members of the feudal hierarchy, for the aristocratic caste; for all outside, for the unfree mass there was nothing but burdens, subjection. "Between the seigneur and the cultivators of his domains," to quote M. Guizot once more, "there were no rights, no guarantees, no society . . . there was only the power of one individual over another, the domination of the capricious will of one man." Nor did the abuse of privilege, right tend to make this radically vicious system more palatable. The proneness of these feudal lords to quarrel with one another, their right of private warfare, placed the peace of a district in constant jeopardy. Their fightings and their forays, carried on in accordance with the brutal code of the age, turned all too frequently the domain into a desert, and exposed the masses to the miseries incident to the *régime* of a host of petty, quarrelsome tyrants. The chronicles of the period are full of tales of savage strife in which the violent instincts of human nature found full scope. Society might be best described by calling it an active volcano. On the imagination of the time the most incredible horrors imprinted themselves as sober history, and though we may not take the stories of wholesale cannibalism retailed by a Raoul Glaber too seriously, it would not be easy to exaggerate the real sufferings of the masses from war, famine, pestilence. Sober history is in these feudal centuries to a large extent the chronicle of the quarrels, the barbarous wars of these feudal lords, a chronicle of contention and bloodshed, in which the peaceful intervals, under the auspices of some strong ruler, are all too rare. "The kingdom was a prey to perpetual broils and wars," laments Abbot Guibert de Nogent, whose autobiography covers the period from 1053 to 1124. "One heard only of brigandage perpetrated on the highways, homesteads blazing, war raging on all hands, without other cause than an insatiable cupidity. Men devoured by greed respected no property, and delivered themselves over to pillage with unbridled license." "The nobles," complained Peter the Venerable to St Bernard, "are not content with the services which are their due in virtue of usage; they claim without mercy both persons and goods. In addition to the ordinary rents, they pillage three or four times in the year the gear of their serfs, and impose on them innumerable *corvées*, intolerable burdens. The greater number are in consequence anxious to desert the country, and seek refuge in neighbouring lands."

Against this oppressive system reaction was inevitable, and this reaction produced, as we shall see, a general movement of emancipation from feudal trammels. In France, in particular, the idea of the State revived in the person of the strong monarch, and it will not be surprising if the masses should be found on the side of the strong monarch against the magnate. In the Roman empire the State overshadowed the individual; in the feudal kingdom the individual, in the person of the magnate, overshadowed the State. In the revival of the State, in a limited form at least, lay, therefore, the hope of the masses, and though this revival ultimately led, in France and some other countries, to the establishment of absolute government of the old imperial type, it was at first favourable to the cause of liberty. Feudalism has indeed been lauded as a stage in the progress of liberty. It substituted, we are assured, the sovereignty of the individual for the despotism of Rome, and it bequeathed the germs of liberty to modern times. It represented the *régime* of contract between individuals instead of the submission to an absolute central authority. Let us not forget, however, that the individual was confined to the members of an aristocratic caste, and that the mass was exposed to the despotism of this caste. There was no liberty, there were no rights for the mass as against the caste. The *régime* of contract was in fact the elaborate formula of the sovereignty of the few over the many. The sovereignty of the few might, if you will, be a necessary product of an age of anarchy, though I, for my part, have no liking for the word "necessary" as applied to systems which involve the oppression, the degradation of the mass of a people in favour of a privileged class. In the dissolution of society, the state of war, the vortex of anarchy from which this necessary product sprang, the main thing is the creation of some kind of order, and order can only be created in these circumstances by the mailed fist. The mailed fist uplifted in resistance to the marauding bands of Normans, Saracens, Hungarians, Huns was the only guarantee of protection, subsistence to the helpless population of a district. Protection, subsistence being indispensable to bare life, any expedient that ensured these must be credited with a certain efficacy. But the mailed fist was also uplifted in usurpation of the rights of those it professed to protect, and while it checked anarchy for the time being, it disintegrated the State, and led in turn to anarchy and oppression. To credit the system with philanthropy, as its champions do, is, in view of this fact, to take too sanguine a view of feudal human nature. There is no philanthropy in the mailed fist, apart from the orders of chivalry who assumed the noble mission of protecting the oppressed, the weak. Its benefits have to be bought with the surrender of liberty, or property, or both. If it ensured protection, it blighted progress for centuries to come, and depressed the masses to a condition of servility which it took centuries more to efface. There was little enough philanthropy in the origin of this caste, and, if we may trust the chroniclers, there was as little in its operation, except perhaps incidentally.

There was, in truth, little scope for individuality under the feudal *régime*, except within the narrow limits of the privileged class. The mass of individuals was cramped by a set of hard and fast institutions as rigorously as it was by the compress of the State in imperial times. The organisation, the corporation is a distinctive mark of mediæval society, and its origins may be traced to an imperial source. It received its widest expression in the idea of a universal empire and a universal Church. Within this wider organisation society is graded, bound in well-defined groups or associations like the gild, and the attempt to assert rights that have been lost, or to claim new ones, was certainly not easier under feudal than it was under imperial auspices.

There was not even the hierarchical symmetry which the feudists admire. Feudalism might range society into two categories, based on the tenure of land, the relation of lord and vassal, and this society might form a caste as exclusive, as rigid, as the old patrician order whose privileges the plebeians swept away at Rome and Athens. All outside it—the mass of the people—were subject to disabilities, burdens of a more or less servile character. But this caste did not form a strictly graded hierarchy superimposed on every domain in the kingdom. The lord of a vassal might be the vassal of another lord. A holder of a fief might indeed be the vassal of more than one lord. The relation of lord and vassal intermingles, becomes confused, in accordance with a variety of accidents. Here and there, too, in Southern France, in the Pyrenean and the Swiss mountains, in Friesland, the free peasant proprietor, independent of a feudal lord, and subject only to the sovereign of the region, survived in greater or lesser number all through the Middle Ages. The mass of the population, the serfs and tenants, were, moreover, not vassals in the strictly feudal sense, for vassalage was, as a rule, confined to the possession of a fief, and the holder of the fief, the vassal, was of noble rank. The mass was bound up with the system, but only as a drudge is bound up with the household. They could not be members in any real sense of this aristocratic household, and even in their case it is the diversity rather than the symmetry of usage that strikes the contemporary observer. "The variety of persons," says Beaumanoir, "is so great that it would be difficult to find in the kingdom of France two estates which, in many particulars, make use of the same customs."

This caste system might be an ideal system for the few; there was very little of the ideal to the masses in it. If we ask what generation after generation of toiling human beings thought of it, the answer, judged from the repeated attempts of the peasantry to free themselves from its despotism, is certainly not very complimentary. The scientific historian may find ample reasons for justifying its utility, its necessity, and may be disposed to reproach its critic with a lack of the historic sense. But, after all, to explain any system historically, to show its historic utility or necessity, is not to justify it. Nor is the historian bound to look at a system or an age solely in its own light, though he should beware of looking at it merely in the light of his own ideas. He may exercise the right of criticism and comparison, and he should not leave out, in his judgments, the question of right or wrong. If he does so, his judgment may be historic; it must also be narrow and inadequate. It is not sufficient to say that, because a certain state of things prevailed, this state of things is, therefore, even historically what should have been. Judged by its effects on the generations that lived under it, and the irresistible reaction that it aroused, the feudal system was, to a large extent, neither historically nor morally beneficial.

SOURCES.—Salvian, De Gubernatione Dei; the chronicles mentioned in the list affixed to Chapter I., and in addition, Raoul Glaber, Chronique; Helgaud, Vie du Roi Robert (II.); Vie de Bourchard, Comte du Melun; Chronique de Hugues de Fleury; Histoire de Monastère de Vézelai par, Hugues de Poitiers; Vie de Guibert de Nogent par, lui-même (Abbot of Nogent in the diocese of Laon)—all in Guizot's Collection. The last two are interesting for the emancipation of the communes of Vézelai and Laon. See also the editions of Glaber by M. Prou, and of the Vie de Bourchard by M. Roncière in the Collection de Textes pour servir à l'Étude et à l'Enseignement de l'Histoire; Luchaire, Le Régime Féodale, in t. ii. of

Sources of Chapter II.

Histoire de France, edited by Lavisse; Seignobos, Le Régime Féodale, in t. ii. of Histoire Générale (1893); Berthelot, chapters 6, 7, and 8 on the Merovingian and Carolingian Institutions, in t. i. of Hist. Gén. (1893); Langlois et Luchaire, Le Royaume de France in *ibid.;* Flach, Les Origines de l'Ancienne France (1886-93); Luchaire, Manuel des Institutions Françaises (1892); Gasquet, Precis des Institutions Politiques et Sociales de l'Ancienne France (1885); Rambaud, Histoire de la Civilisation Française, t. i. (1893); Roth, Geschichte des Beneficialwesens (1850), and Feudalität und Unterthanenverband (1863); Waitz, Deutsche Verfassungs-Geschichte (1880-85); Hallam, Europe in the Middle Ages.

CHAPTER III.

The Emancipation of the Italian Communes and the Italian City Republics.

The growth of the feudal system was as fatal to free municipal institutions as it was to the rights of the free rural population. The cities, like the small free proprietors, passed under the domination of lay or ecclesiastical lords, of the bishop, the count, or other feudal magnate. They were subject to this feudal lord as the domain was subject to the feudal proprietor, though some trace of the old municipal constitution survived in their administration. To this subjection is largely due that stagnation of civic life which is one of the sombre features of the earlier Middle Ages. Its revival, on the other hand, produced the great emancipation movement which resulted in the restoration of the ancient right of municipal self-government, and dealt a serious blow to the power of the feudal magnate. In Italy and Southern France this movement is discernible as early as the eleventh century; it became general and irresistible in the twelfth and the thirteenth.

The decline of civic life is already apparent in the latter days of the empire. Under imperial auspices the cities enjoyed a very large measure of self-government. They were subject to the supervision of the provincial governors and their agents who collected the taxes due to the imperial treasury, but they were ruled by magistrates, elected by the free citizens, and by a senate, or council, or curia, chosen from the decuriones, or richer class of the inhabitants. Their population embraced a number of classes—slaves, freedmen, freemen— and among the freemen there was a further distinction between the inferior, or plebeian, and the superior, or wealthy, class. The distinction was, however, not a rigid one. While the slave and the freedmen were debarred from municipal office, the plebeian might rise to a place in the magistracy and council, if he became rich enough to be eligible for such an honour. In the period of imperial decline a change for the worse is observable in the cities, as in the provinces. Social progress and material prosperity were alike blasted. The election of the magistrates by the people ceased. Municipal office became a burden instead of a prize, and exemption from it was accounted a privilege. The decuriones, who now appear as the curiales, were responsible for the taxes to the imperial exchequer, and taxation became exaction in spite of the appointment of a Defensor Civitatis by Valentinian in 364 to check the oppression of the fiscal officials. To escape the rapacity of these officials the curiales became the clients of powerful patrons, lost their social position and their independence, sank even, in many cases, into serfdom. The plebeians suffered, too, in their personal freedom as well as their political rights. They were formed into gilds according to occupation, and membership of these gilds, formerly voluntary, now became compulsory, and even hereditary. The free citizen class thus degenerated into a sort of urban serfage. It was as much bound to the gild as the rural serf was to the glebe, with this difference, that while the rural serf was the dependant of an individual proprietor, the urban serf was the dependant of the State, which, in organising labour, obliterated industrial liberty. In return for a fixed allowance, the State exacted from the artisan certain services, as the proprietor exacted certain dues, services from the servile or semi-servile cultivators of his domain.

The history of the ancient municipia of Italy and Gaul is wrapped in obscurity for several centuries after the irruption of the barbarians. Most of them seem to have dwindled into insignificance. The invaders had not reached the civic stage of civilisation, and settled, as a rule, on the lands which they took, or acquired, as the result of conquest. Their kings, indeed, chose a city as their capital. The great Theodoric established his headquarters at Ravenna, the Visigothic Wallia at Toulouse, Clovis at Paris, the Lombard Alboin at Pavia. Their followers preferred to reside on the domains of which they took possession as their share of the spoil of conquest. The domain rather than the city thus became the social centre in the new order of things, and the village that grew up around the stronghold of some great proprietor or some wealthy abbey, only gradually swelled into the town of the future. Of the five hundred towns of modern France, for instance, scarcely eighty can trace their origin from Gallo-Roman times. Some of the cities of Gaul and Italy—Marseilles and Lyons, Milan, Pisa, Genoa, Florence—loom out of the ruins of the old civic life of the empire as important centres of commerce. Some of the forms of municipal government, too, survived, but this link of continuity, which writers like Raynouard and Savigny sought to forge out of these forms, is very feeble, and the theory of the survival of Roman municipal institutions has accordingly been discarded as untenable. In general the city relapsed under the domination of some powerful individual—the bishop whose episcopal seat it formed, the count who governed the district of which it was the centre. Between the government of this powerful individual and his assessors, or scabini, and the old *régime* of elective magistrates and council, the resemblance is faint indeed. "The municipal *régime* of the empire," conclude Giry and Réville, "vanished completely."

It was not till the eleventh century that the torpor of the towns began to relax. The crusades, first in Italy and then in France, instilled new life into these languid communities. The call to the holy war set the nations in motion, and the revival of commerce was one of the fruits of the universal quickening of the age. The mariners of Genoa, Venice, Pisa not only carried the crusaders to the East; they established commercial relations with the ports of the Levant and the Black Sea, the coasts of Syria and Africa. The cities of Southern France followed their example, and as the result of this spirit of enterprise, the products and manufactures of the East found their way to the west and the north of Europe. The mariner, the merchant became the pioneers of a new era, not only of commercial, but of industrial activity; for the revival of commerce led to the revival of industry. The towns became hives of industry as well as centres of busy fairs and markets. Where before the sleepy community had sufficed for its own rude, solitary existence, supplying its simple wants by the tillage of the ground and the exercise of the more elementary crafts, a vigorous life developed with the development of commercial intercourse, the growth of some special branch of industry. This development of commerce and industry contributed in turn to the revival of municipal life, and in this revival the merchant association or gild, in particular, was, as shall be amply apparent in the sequel, a most important factor. The gild appears originally to have embraced the artisan who both made and sold his goods as well as the merchant proper, and the organisation of both capital and labour, commerce and industry in the gild led to the creation of common interests on the part of the community, and ultimately to the constitution of the municipality. The gild was not indeed, as we shall see, synonymous with the municipality, but it led to the "conjuration," the association of the community, as a civic body, in vindication of municipal self-government.

The emancipation movement in Italy has, however, a wider interest than that which attaches to the revival of municipal life in other countries. It was a national, a political as well as a civic movement. The cities of Lombardy and Tuscany not only asserted their right to municipal self-government against the feudal magnate, whether bishop or count; they asserted their right to sovereign independence against the despotic supremacy of the emperors of the house of Hohenstaufen. The revival of the Italian municipality was, indeed, virtually the revival of the ancient city State of both Greece and Italy which Rome had absorbed within her universal sway. Not only does the free municipality of the old empire reappear; it develops into the sovereign republic, and these sovereign republics, like those of Greece, unite in antagonism to an alien power. The struggle for supremacy between pope and emperor gave them their opportunity. In that struggle both pope and emperor had to reckon with the cities whose material prosperity rendered their alliance a matter of the highest political consideration. Both were alike eager to disarm their hostility, or buy their assistance by concessions or promises, and it was the accumulated hatred of an alien domination that turned the scale in favour of the pope in the case of the larger number. Northern Italy rose at last against her conquerors from beyond the Alps after five centuries of impotent submission, and vindicated the republican spirit as well as the independence of a former age.

Unfortunately, independence did not bring unity in its train. It produced a number of city republics, which, in spite of Lombard and Tuscan leagues on emergency, hardened into a number of petty States, whose jealousies and factious feuds ultimately led to the establishment of a number of petty tyrannies. In mediæval, as in ancient Italy, we find the aspiration of liberty without the ability to conserve it. There is the same fatal tendency to factious strife, for which the dictator was the only remedy in republican Rome of old. This dictator reappears in mediæval Italy, not in the person of a Cæsar, who, if he destroyed liberty, welded the broken State into a powerful empire, but in the petty despot, who, while crushing liberty, transformed the small republic into a hereditary duchy. Liberty and unity were the ideals of the political dreamer; their realisation was the despair of the present, the secret only of the remote future.

The emancipation movement in Italy, though it gave rise to long and terrible conflict with the imperial power, had not to contend with so fierce an opposition on the part of the feudal magnate as in France. Feudalism was weaker in Italy than in France, and the frequent broils between lord and vassal nurtured a spirit of self-assertion within the cities, which, in the eleventh century, were both populous and strongly walled. The movement began at the end of the eleventh and the beginning of the twelfth centuries with the substitution of supreme magistrates, known as consuls, for the bishop or the count. Though these consuls were elected only for a year, they were invested with extensive powers, which included the command of the city militia and the administration of justice as well as the government of the city and its territory. Their jurisdiction was, however, controlled by a small council (*concio della credenza*), and both consul and council were, again, subject to the control in all important affairs of the general assembly of the citizens (*concio publica*). Though the constitution was thus democratic in form, the city did not really form a fully fledged democracy. As in the case of the Roman municipia, the wealthier class predominated, and the plebeians were not only excluded from office, but in some cities from political rights. Even where they shared in the rights of citizenship, power was the monopoly of the richer families, the wealthy merchants, and the nobles who had migrated from the surrounding country into the city, and the exercise of this monopoly by wealth and rank was far from creditable to the intelligence and public spirit of either. The population was the victim of the family and faction feuds which rent the dominant class and filled the city with riot and bloodshed. Every nobleman's house was a fortress, every quarter a camp in which ambition, revenge, faction gave scope to lawless passions. This contentious spirit infected the masses, which resented the class domination of their rulers, and strove to win for the artisan gilds, in which they were organised, a voice in the government. It displayed itself, too, in the rancorous hatreds of the cities towards one another, and in the savage wars in which they vented their ungovernable fury towards a rival or a neighbour.

In spite of this chronic state of intestine strife, the revival of municipal life had a quickening effect on both the industrial and political activity of the cities, many of which, notably Milan and Florence, increased rapidly in wealth and population. It is apparent, too, in the united energy of the leagues which the common danger of imperial despotism forced them to form, and which stayed for a time their mutual and internecine feuds. The autocratic policy, the aggressive temper of Frederick Barbarossa, to whom their independent spirit was an offence, provoked the conflict which first forced upon those of Lombardy the necessity of union. Frederic not only attacked and reduced Milan, the most powerful and defiant of their number; he encroached on their municipal autonomy by appointing an imperial podesta to control, and, in many cases, supersede, their consuls. He visited the revolt of Milan, which a second time threw defiance in his face, with savage retribution, and its destruction (1162) after a heroic defence, as well as the oppressive *régime* of his podestas, drove them to adopt the expedient of concerted resistance. His quarrel with the pope (Adrian IV., and, after his death, Alexander III.) over the old question of supremacy, played into the hands of the league during the war which ended in his crushing defeat at Legnano (1176). Pope Alexander refused to desert his allies in the negotiations at Venice which followed this decisive victory and ended in a six years' truce, and Frederick was ultimately compelled to guarantee them a large measure of autonomy (Treaty of Constance, 1183), including the right to nominate their consuls, to exercise their regalian rights without as well as within their walls, to build fortifications, to wage war, and to maintain and renew their league for the defence of common interests. On the other hand, the emperor exacted an oath of fidelity, renewable every ten years, and retained the right of investing the consuls by means of his legates, of levying the usual tribute of purveyance and maintenance during his residence in Italy, and of appointing a judge in each city to decide appeals in civil causes. The cities, it is evident, had the best of the transaction, which legally transformed them into sovereign communities, with a general organisation in defence of their common rights, and reduced the imperial supremacy to the level of suzerainty.

They failed, however, to take advantage of their success to transform their temporary association into a permanent federation, in spite of the imperial recognition of the league. During the stress of the struggle for their common rights the ideal of a common fatherland had kindled a transient enthusiasm. "We desire peace with the emperor," remarked their delegates to the pope at Venice, " provided the honour of Italy is secured and our liberty remains intact." This profession of devotion to the interests of Italy was, however, but short lived. Peace concluded, the league broke asunder on the rocks of mutual hatreds, selfish ambitions. Instead of a confederation based on a national policy, it split into a number of small leagues, which owed their ephemeral existence to the dominant influence of the moment. Aggression or resentment thus proved too strong for the enthusiasm begotten of the struggle with the despotism of Barbarossa. League fought against league, and union was only forged in hatred. When not linked in this way, individual cities strangled their energies in conflict with each other, and their mutual dissensions were aggravated by the partisan rancour of Guelf and Ghibeline, which divided the inhabitants of each city into bitter factions. These distinctions, originating in a dynastic quarrel in Germany, came to differentiate in Italy the adherents of the pope or the emperor. In general the Guelfs were the party of the pope, the Ghibelines the party of the emperor, but these party names were often the specious cries of local factions which fought for the mastery of the city. The party allegiance of the city was thus a changing quantity, according as the mastery within its walls passed from Guelf to Ghibeline, or from Ghibeline to Guelf. Generally speaking, the ascendency of the Ghibelines represented the predominance of the aristocratic, that of the Guelfs the predominance of the popular party, which resented the monopoly of power by the rich. Its attitude was influenced, too, by its hatred of some neighbouring city. If one city became Ghibeline, that was a sufficient reason for its enemy to profess adherence to the political creed of the Guelfs. In these feuds the opponents of the dominant party in one city, are even found allying themselves with the faction of the same political creed in another, with which that party might be waging war. The Ghibelines of Florence, for example, take the side of the Ghibelines of Siena in their contest with the Florentine Guelfs.

This party strife drew into its vortex the cities of Tuscany, which, during the minority of Frederick II., leagued themselves together under the patronage of the redoubtable Innocent III., to secure their rights and champion those of the pope. Here, too, these party shibboleths nurtured endless dissension, gave scope to the virulence of deadly passions. The irreconcilable enmity of pope and emperor, of Gregory IX., Innocent IV., and Frederick, the fury of factious rancour, blasted the promise of national independence and unity which might have developed out of the germs of these leagues of free cities. As in Greece of old, liberty was merely the synonym for license, anarchy, factious strife within, for aggression without. As in Greece of old, too, these Lombard and Tuscan republics were merely working for a master, tempting ultimate doom with the blindness of infatuation. The future had indeed no Philip of Macedon, no Roman proconsul as the castigator of the mediæval city State. Frederick II., the last of the great mediæval emperors, was not the master destined by fate to snatch this artificial liberty from the hands of its unworthy champions. The master lurked in the meantime in the form of some petty tyrant like Ezzelino da Romano, master of Verona and Padua.

Frederick threw down the gauntlet to the Lombard cities, and the league was renewed in spite of the relapse of some of its old members, of Cremona, Bergamo, Parma, &c., to the imperial or Ghibeline standard. This time it was the emperor who triumphed, who avenged Legnano on the leaguists at Cortenuova (November 1237), who destroyed the Genoese fleet off the coast of Elba. But Pope Gregory IX. threw himself into the breach, excited revolt in Naples, of which Frederick was king, excommunicated his enemy, and roused the monks to preach the crusade against the impious aggressor of the Holy See. Gregory's successor, Innocent IV., fugitive though he was, not only excommunicated this impious aggressor a second time, but solemnly deposed him at the Council of Lyons (1245). In Italy, meanwhile, Ghibeline and Guelf, leagued in hostile associations, waged inhuman war against each other, and though the Guelfs formed the majority, their opponents were strong enough to render the struggle bloody and desolating enough. Death at last surprised Frederick whilst hurrying from Naples to chastise rebellious Lombardy, and nullified the hope of vindicating a supremacy which he, like Barbarossa, had fought for in vain.

To the Lombard and Tuscan republics was reserved a humbler fate than that of being mastered by one who, whatever his faults, was one of the great actors on the stage of mediæval history. Where the great emperor had failed, the petty despot succeeded. Lassitude tended to produce a disposition favourable to despotism, and made it easy for some powerful noble, like the Romano and the La Scala at Verona, the Azzos of Este at Ferrara and Modena, the Carrara at Padua, the Gonzaga at Mantua, to step in between rival factions and seize the government, with or without the consent of the people. The institution of a podesta was the expedient in which this weariness of intestine feud and external war generally took refuge. Its adoption was a virtual confession of the failure of self-government, a sure sign of the complete declension of public spirit. What a descent from the days of Barbarossa, when the establishment of this agent of imperial despotism roused these cities to a heroic and concerted resistance to arbitrary rule! As at Rome of old, the dictator was the only remedy for the factious anarchy which rendered self-government an intolerable abuse to the mass of the citizens. Under stress of necessity the mass of the citizens, therefore, welcomed the revival of an office which they formerly detested and fought so energetically to overthrow. They entrusted that office to some person of note, who could not be a native of the city and was thus a stranger to its factions. The extent of his functions varied in the different cities, but he was bound in all by strict regulations to preserve neutrality as between contending parties and uphold order by an impartial administration of the laws. In spite of such precautions, the expedient proved an ultimate failure. The podesta, in many cases, paved the way for the tyrant, who took advantage of his position to obtain the mastery of the city; or he proved impotent to repress the spirit of faction, the war of family against family, of class against class, of aristocracy against democracy, which ended in the domination of some powerful local magnate. In these struggles the old party names of Guelf and Ghibeline survive, but the real struggle is for the possession of power by rival chiefs of rival followings. At Milan, for example, it is the Visconti and the Torriani, at Bologna the Lambertazzi and the Giremei who dispute the predominance, and this predominance finally resolves itself into the absolute rule of the victor. "Italy," cried Dante, bitterly, "is full of tyrants."

Most of these city States in Lombardy and Tuscany, in losing their republican institutions, dwindled into political insignificance. Some of them, like Ferrara, became famous as centres of the new culture which heralded the dawn of the Renascence. Art and literature throve where liberty had been stifled, for the despot was often a patron of poets, artists, scholars. Milan, which became a hereditary duchy first in the family of the Visconti and then of the Sforza, alone maintained in Lombardy the political eminence which it had long enjoyed as the greatest of the Lombardic cities. Its dukes extended their rule over the greater part of Lombardy, and were powerful enough to hold their own with Venice for predominance in the basin of the Po. Florence, which preserved its republican constitution till well into the fifteenth century, not only succeeded in absorbing Pisa, but in acquiring a predominant position in Tuscany, comparable to that of Milan in Lombardy. Milan and Florence thus emerge in the fourteenth century as the two most powerful remnants of the old leagues, and share with the maritime republics of Venice and Genoa the predominance of the northern half of Italy. Florence, in particular, occupies, along with Genoa and Venice, a front place in international history as well. The naval and commercial predominance of the two maritime republics, the industrial and financial supremacy of Florence, raised them to a pitch of greatness altogether incommensurate with their territorial extent.

The secret of this prosperity is ascribable, in the case of Venice at least, to the stability of the government. At Venice supremacy gradually passed into the hands of the commercial aristocracy, which succeeded both in limiting the power of the doge and of depriving the people of participation in the government.

"This wealthier class," says Dr Brown, "gradually drew together and formed the nucleus of a plutocracy. The policy of this powerful class, embracing, as it did, all the leading citizens, naturally pursued the lines along which Venetian constitutional development consistently moved. This policy had a twofold object—first, to curtail the ducal authority; secondly, to exclude the people, and to concentrate all power in the hands of the commercial aristocracy. The history of the Venetian constitution is the history of the way in which the dominant party attained its ends." The old popular Concione, or General Assembly, fell into abeyance as the State expanded and the lack of a more centralised government made itself felt. The evolution of this government is merely an object-lesson in the evolution from democracy to oligarchy. It began in 1172 with the establishment of a Council, subsequently known as the Great Council (*Maggior Consiglio*), which virtually displaced the older General Assembly and largely absorbed the internal government, while the conduct of foreign affairs was entrusted to the Senate (*Consiglio dei Pregadi*—those "summoned" by the doge to assist him). The people were thus gradually ousted from the control of the government, and ultimately by "the

Closing of the Great Council" in 1297—a measure which limited its membership to those who could prove descent from at least one paternal ancestor who had sat in the Council—the domination of the oligarchy was complete. Of this oligarchy the Council of Ten, instituted shortly after, became the mainstay. The Ten effectively employed their extensive powers to preserve the oligarchic *régime* from conspiracy and reaction. The republican government, in fact, practically narrowed into the terroristic *régime* of this redoubtable council of public safety, whose power was felt in every department. The doge himself, though representing the majesty of the State, was not permitted to embody its powers. He was controlled by a small Council, and was practically, as Dr Brown puts it, "a symbol, not a factor of the constitution—the outward and visible sign of all that the oligarchy meant."

In Florence, on the other hand, the triumph of the Guelf or Black faction over the Ghibeline or White faction, lent the constitution a popular character. In spite of aristocratic opposition, the rich middle class asserted its supremacy; but while excluding the nobles from the government, it denied the plebs a voice in the administration by confining the election of the magistrates, or Priori, to the members of the major gilds (*Artes majores*). This middle class oligarchy was, however, exposed to frequent attacks both of nobles and people, and was forced at times to reckon with the popular demands. It was, as we shall see in a separate chapter, the adroitness with which the Medici, originally a plebeian family, took advantage of these intestine broils to gain the ascendency, that at length led to the domination over this middle class oligarchy, first of Cosimo, and then of Lorenzo de Medici.

Like Florence, Genoa contained an active democratic party, and was the scene of frequent conflict against the dominant aristocratic factions. Here, too, party spirit ran riot under the watchwords of Guelf and Ghibeline, but the interminable dissensions of the leading nobles—the Grimaldi, the Fieschi, the Doria, the Spinola—who pursued their ambitious designs under cover of these distinctive party cries, preserved the republic from permanently falling under the despotism of an aristocratic caste, as at Venice, or the individual despotism of some local magnate, as in the case of the neighbouring Milan. During one of these popular commotions in 1339, the people indeed saluted Simon Boccanigra as its tribune or abbot, under the title of duke, but the office, while checking aristocratic domination for the time being, did not imply the establishment of a hereditary tyranny. The institution of an elective doge did not, however, suffice to curb the spirit of faction, and for the next two hundred years the republic was more than once compelled to resort to the expedient of seeking a temporary respite from faction feud in the protection of France or Milan.

In Rome itself, which had not been uninfluenced by the revival of republican institutions in the north, the attempt to substitute self-government for the temporal supremacy of the pope was equally futile. Here the republican ideal took a higher flight, contemplated nothing less than the restoration of the ancient republic, which should once more rise from the ruins of her crumbling edifices as mistress of the world. The ideal seemed to stand a fair chance of realisation as far as the Eternal City itself was concerned. The measure of power possessed by the pope at Rome was in marked contrast to the vast pretensions of universal supremacy which seemed so terrible, on the lips of a Gregory, or an Innocent, to the nations beyond the Alps. His authority as temporal sovereign was frequently set at defiance by the turbulent nobles, who interfered in the papal elections, and drove more than one obnoxious occupant of the chair of St Peter from the city. There was frequent strife, too, between the nobility and the people, and it was during one of these crises of anarchy in 1143 that the republic was solemnly constituted on the Capitol, in an attack on which Pope Lucius II. was mortally wounded. A Senate of fifty-six members was elected. A "Patricius" displaced the papal prefect as head of the executive, and "the Senate and People of Rome" pompously entered on its sovereign functions after the abeyance of many centuries. It was in this emergency that Arnold de Brescia, who had already been excommunicated and driven into exile by the pope, appeared on the scene towards the middle of the twelfth century. A disciple of Abelard, he preached the trenchant reform of the Church, and his denunciations of the worldliness of the clergy made his heresy all the more offensive to pope and prelate. He applied the rationalist spirit of Abelard to politics as well as morals. He not only damned bishops, priests, and monks, who owned the broad lands of the Church; he denounced the temporal power of the pope, the temporal jurisdiction of the bishops. He coupled the demand for a return to primitive Christianity with a passionate advocacy of the institutions of ancient Rome, and his eloquence gave him a dominating influence over the popular movement. Arnold and his abettors among the people and the lesser nobility strove to gain the support of Conrad III. by professing fealty to the emperor, as the successor of Cæsar and Justinian, and thus rendered their republican profession of faith still more fantastic. They renewed their offer in less submissive terms to Barbarossa, who preferred the more solid advantage of being crowned by Pope Adrian IV. (June 1155) to the dubious experiment of receiving his crown from the Roman people, and poor Arnold ended his vision on the gallows. "It is not," said Frederick, "for the people to give laws to the prince, but to obey his command." Arnold was none the less, as Emerton has aptly called him, "the first in the long series of martyrs to liberty, whose blood stains the records of the triumphant Church." The first of the martyrs to liberty has, needless to say, no place in the calendar of the Church triumphant.

The Roman republic survived in more or less shadowy form until the Babylonian captivity of the popes at Avignon, and the horrors of faction strife gave another tribune, Nicolas di Rienzi, a Roman of the fervid, antique type, an opportunity of repeating Arnold's experiment. Rienzi rekindled by his eloquence the old enthusiasm for the traditions of the past, and as tribune of the people succeeded for a time in establishing an effective government. His success seems to have turned his head, and he gravely proceeded to summon to his bar the two rivals—Ludwig of Bavaria and Charles of Bohemia—who disputed the title of emperor in Germany. His arrogance and his pretentious grandeur were not supported by a strong will, and before the revulsion of feeling which his fantastic vagaries excited, he lost courage and fled to the Abruzzi (1347). The anarchy which he left behind him led to his recall seven years later. It also proved his destroyer, and after two months' trial of his dictatorship, the mob caught him, while attempting to escape a second time, and tore him in pieces. A hundred years later a similar effort made by Stephen Porcaro ended even more summarily in the sacrifice of the would-be restorer of the republic.

From these mediæval Italian republics modern liberty has little to learn, and the lesson, such as it is, is mostly of a negative character. It may learn from mediæval Italy, as from ancient Rome, how liberty may be but a stage on the road to despotism, how democracy may be a failure as an essay in self-government. It will not learn how liberty may be allied with order, how order may be the best guarantee of liberty. The cause of this failure does not lie in liberty, but in its environment. Temperament and circumstances were both unfavourable to its development. Party spirit dominated within these city States, and party spirit is only compatible with freedom, if tempered by the self-control that nurtures compromise and respect for opponents. Self-control, compromise were, however, impossible to these mediæval Italians. Every party struggle is a war to the knife, which ends with the exile or the destruction of the vanquished. The old Greek device of ostracism is the only expedient for dealing with an opponent. Revenge, reprisal, ambition, class predominance, rather than public spirit, are the incentives of public action, and the play of these passions fans the eternal feud of individuals, families, factions, classes. It is unfair to democracy to class these city republics as democracies at all. They are rather, for the most part, aristocracies, either of birth or wealth, of nobles or middle class. The people in the larger sense play but a subordinate part in all of them—the part chiefly of striking the blows which take the place of argument in the ceaseless strife of faction or class. Equilibrium of rights, of interests is impossible where power is the monopoly of a class, a faction, which uses it to the destruction of another class or faction, and without this equilibrium there may be a republic, there can be no democracy in the true sense, no liberty in any sense. Republic, democracy, liberty, are constitutional terms, but they are, as a rule, pretexts for the tyranny of an aristocratic Council of Ten at Venice, or of a so-called democratic Consiglio di Comune at Florence. When most of these republics had relapsed into formal despotisms, they were only assuming a character which they had in practice for long possessed. Some excuse may be found in the circumstances of the time for this tendency to faction violence that outraged liberty in the name of liberty. Feudalism might be, as some historians assert, a safeguard against the universal tyranny of emperor or king, but it was the nurse of anarchy, and exerted an evil influence in this respect on the generations that came under its sway. It is the *régime* of the mailed fist, which does not argue with an opponent, but knocks him down if it can. Force is the main remedy, and this expedient of the feudal magnate becomes the expedient of the faction, which wields the government for the time being in the city State. Its operation is patent enough in the attitude of one city State towards another. To be a neighbour is, as a rule, to be an enemy, and for the enemy there is nothing but oppression or extermination in case of victory. A city that has the misfortune to be reduced by another is frequently razed to the ground, and its inhabitants, if they are not massacred, are dispersed to seek refuge where they can. It is war to the death with the enemy, whether within or without the city, and liberty has only too good cause to veil its face at the spectacle of passionate hatreds that are only sated with the blood alike of the beaten faction and the vanquished city.

The great duel between pope and emperor tends, too, to aggravate the spirit of violence inherited from feudal anarchy. The political atmosphere is charged with the deadly electricity of papal and imperial contention. Here again we may see a palliating, or at least an explanatory circumstance in the situation of these republics. Guelf and Ghibeline are stung by the political rabies of the times, and it is not from the pope that they may learn a lesson in Christian forbearance. The popes, in their hatred of the Hohenstaufens, in their arrogant lust of domination, stir the embers of party hatred into conflagration all over Italy. Their partisans are the bitterest of foes, and it is a melancholy spectacle that of the vicars of Christ, pretenders to the supremacy of a kingdom that is not of this world, flaunting the fiery cross and calling into play the most barbarous passions in the service of their own arrogance. Patriotism might have something to say in defence of their action, if their action had been less self-seeking, for the struggle is in some degree a struggle for the independence of Italy from an alien *régime*. Italy against Germany is the cause that stands behind the cause of the pope against the emperor. It was a noble cause, the cause of liberty against tyranny, and as far as the Italian republics fought for this cause, their history is honourable and even glorious. Unfortunately, it is almost their only title to the admiration of posterity. Their intestine feuds, their barbarous wars against one another, their parody of liberty under the specious phraseology of self-government, render their political history petty, sanguinary, and often repulsive. It is only in the history of art and literature that they gained an imperishable renown.

SOURCES.—For the Roman municipia—Pelham, History of Rome; and more particularly for those of Gaul—Coulanges, Institutions Politiques, t. i. For the Italian cities of the Middle Ages and the political history of the time, in its bearing on the subject—Muratori, Scriptores Rerum Italicarum (1723, and the new edition edited by Carducci and Fiorini, in course of publication), and Annali d'Italia, vols. ii., iii., iv.; Otto von Freisingen, Chronicon, and the continuation by the Chronicle of St Blaise (Continuatio Sanblasiana) in Monumenta, vol. xx.; the same, Gesta Frederici, continued by Ragewin; John of Salisbury, Historia Pontificalis; Sismondi, Histoire des Republiques Italiennes; Hallam, Middle Ages, vol. i.; Bayet, La Papauté, L'Allemagne, et L'Italie, in t. ii. of Histoire Générale (1893); Horatio Brown, Venice, in vol. i., Cambridge Modern History (1902); Giesebrecht, Geschichte der Deutschen Kaiserzeit, vol. iii. (1869); Prutz, Kaiser Friedrich I. (1871-73); Hegel, Geschichte der Städteverfassung von Italien (1847); Haulleville, Histoire des Communes Lombardes (1857); Hausrath, Weltverbesserer im Mittelalter—Arnold von Brescia (1895); Guibal, Arnaud de Brescia et les Hohenstaufen (1868); Guerzoni, Arnaldo da Brescia (1882); Vignati, Storia Diplomatica della Lega Lombarda (1866); Lanzani, Storia

Sources of Chapter III.

dei Communi Italiani (1881-84); Gregorovius, Geschichte der Stadt Rom im Mittelalter (1875-82); Winkelmann, Geschichte Kaiser Friederichs des zweiten und Seiner Reiche (1863-65); Perrens, Histoire de Florence (1877); Emerton, Mediæval Europe (1894); Oscar Browning, Guelfs and Ghibelines (1893); Bent, Genoa (1881).

CHAPTER IV.

Republican Florence and the Medici.

During the thirteenth century Florence, like other Italian cities, was torn by the party feuds of Ghibelines and Guelfs—imperialists and anti-imperialists. Between these parties, the wealthy members of the Greater Arts enhanced their influence, and at length in 1282 they were successful in asserting themselves against the tyranny of the triumphant Guelf nobility. They vested the government in six elected representatives or priors. These priors—subsequently increased to eight—formed the Signory or executive power of the republic, with a Gonfalonier of Justice, who had at his disposal an armed force to maintain order. This middle class government, from which the nobility was by the ordinance of 1293-94 excluded, did not, however, bring a cessation of strife. The old noble families did not relish their loss of power, and would not renounce their factious spirit. The republic was harassed by their intrigues, their family feuds, their attempts to absorb the government. The Cerchi fought with the Donati, the Whites with the Blacks, as their adherents were respectively called, and their factious fights perpetuated under a new name the old feud of Ghibeline and Guelf, and made Dante an exile. In its impotence to restrain the excesses of faction, the Signory even tried the experiment of transferring the sovereign power to a foreign potentate. It placed the republic in subjection to King Robert of Naples for five years. But this move only produced new party divisions in the form of the friends and the enemies of the king, and new miseries in the oppression of his viceroys. "Great city truly, but most miserable," exclaims Machiavelli, "which neither the memory of past divisions, nor the fear of Uguccione (sometime lord of Pisa and Lucca, an aggressive neighbour), nor the authority of a king had been able to hold in union, so that she found herself in a very evil plight." The conflict with neighbouring tyrants like Uguccione and Castruccio aggravated the evil and led the hapless Signory to seek a new protector in Duke Charles of Calabria, King Robert's son. Charles sent them the Duke of Athens as his viceroy. This adventurer succeeded in 1342, with the aid of the mob, in getting himself proclaimed sovereign of the city "for life," and in playing the despot pure and simple for a year. His oppression and cruelty united all classes and parties, and in July 1343 the whole city rose and expelled him, and tore two of his minions in pieces. In ridding herself of her tyrant, Florence also lost her subject towns, which threw off their allegiance, and thus, as Machiavelli says, " she rid herself at one stroke of both her tyrant and her territory." But, adds our historian, " for every tyrant dethroned, there sprang up a thousand." That is to say, the nobility, for once united with the people for the common good, took to their old trade of intrigue and tumult anew. With the help of the discontented lower class—the plebeians, in contrast to what Machiavelli terms the people, the *popolari*—they made a determined effort to overthrow the *régime* of the dominant commercial class. For several hours the city was the scene of a pitched battle. At the end of this battle victory remained with the "popular" side, and the vanquished paid for defeat with the destruction of their palaces and castles, and the revival of all the laws against their order.

Even this signal victory of democracy so-called did not stamp out the bane of faction, that noxious bacillus that preyed on the vitals of the Italian republics. The party shibboleths of Ghibeline and Guelf continued to tear the city in twain, though they might now signify distinction of interests, ambitions, not the antagonism of imperialist and anti-imperialist, might, for instance, distinguish the party of the Albizzi from that of the Ricci. The nobility of wealth (the *nobili popolari* of Machiavelli) who had overthrown the nobility of rank, proved equally factious and selfish. Thus the Ricci are found in 1356 demanding "the admonition" or proscription of the Albizzi, and these admonitions kept the republic in a state of perpetual broil, the exiles seeking to return by force or craft, and fomenting dissension within the city to this end. In 1372 we find an assembly of the citizens complaining to the Signory of the prevailing "hatred, animosities, quarrels, frictions, resulting in death, banishment, affliction to all good men and the advancement of the most unprincipled. While the leaders of parties deck their ambition with the name of liberty, they are the enemies of liberty and of the common good. The city is governed by parties, not by laws, and even if one party becomes dominant, it must needs divide against itself and disturb the public repose. The Florentines can neither agree to live in freedom, nor suffer a ruler like the Duke of Athens. The bane of all republics—the contention of rival families for power—is as fatally active as of yore." Such is the burden of their complaint, reported by Machiavelli in his "History of Florence."

To aggravate this chronic anarchy, there was feud between the Greater Arts who monopolised the government, and the Lesser who strove for a share of political power, while the discontent of the mass—the Labour Gilds, and the proletariat—added its fuel to the combustion of party and class animosities.

This complicated friction of class and faction culminated in 1378 in the revolt of the Ciompi. It was heralded by a war with Pope Gregory XI., whose legates plundered many of the Italian cities for the benefit of their holy master at Avignon. The war under the direction of the Eight of War, as the Committee entrusted with its prosecution was called, was successful, but it gave the "Guelfic" faction of the Albizzi an opportunity of trying its strength with the Signory. The Albizzi determined to seize the government and "admonish" or banish their opponents. It was in this contingency that Salvestro de Medici succeeded in getting himself appointed Gonfalonier of Justice. Salvestro proposed to revive the former restrictions on the power of the nobility and recall the "Ammoniti," the victims of the Albizzi tyranny. He enforced his demand by a speech in which he accentuated the honesty of his purpose, demonstrated the necessity of putting down once for all the factious tyranny of the *Parte Guelfa* which was ruining the republic, and threatened to resign. The city was thrown into ferment at the news. The Arts, Greater, Lesser, and Labour alike, assembled in force under their banners, forced the Signory to issue a *balia*, or mandate, to various officials, including the syndics of the Arts, to reform the government, and plundered and burned the houses of the obnoxious Albizzi and their adherents. This commission ordered the relief of the Ammoniti, annulled the tyrannic laws made at the instigation of the Albizzi, and outlawed their leaders. These measures failed to satisfy the Lesser Arts and the Labour Gilds. They determined to seize the opportunity to redress their own grievances and force the oligarchy of the Greater Arts to yield them a share in the government. The rising was actuated, too, by economic as well as political motives. While the Lesser Arts pressed for a share of political influence, the Labour Gilds demanded higher wages. " In the time of Charles I.," explains Machiavelli, "when the city was divided into arts, a head or governor was appointed to each, and it was provided that the individuals of each art should be judged in civil matters by their own superiors. These arts, as we have before observed, were at first twelve; in the course of time they were increased to twenty-one, and attained so much power that in a few years they grasped the entire government of the city; and as some were in greater esteem than others, they were divided into major and minor; seven were called major and fourteen the minor arts. From this division and from other causes, which we have narrated above, arose the arrogance of the Capitani di Parte; for those citizens who had formerly been Guelfs, and had the constant disposal of that magistracy, favoured the followers of the major and persecuted the minor arts and their patrons; hence arose the many commotions already mentioned. When the companies of the arts were first organised, many of these trades, followed by the lowest of the people and the plebeians, were not incorporated, but were ranged under those arts most nearly allied to them; and hence, when they were not properly remunerated for their labour, or their masters oppressed them, they had no one of whom to seek redress except the magistrate of the art to which theirs was subject, and of him they did not think justice always attainable. Of the arts, that which always had and now has the greatest number of these subordinates, is the woollen; which being both then and still the most powerful body, and first in authority, supports the greater part of the plebeians and the lowest of the people."

The rising became in fact a trial of strength between the wealthy oligarchy and the artisan and proletariat democracy, who, to judge from the speech which Machiavelli puts into the mouth of one of their orators, talked of equality in the spirit of the French Revolutionists. "Our opponents," cried the democratic orator in question, "are disunited and rich; their disunion will give us the victory, and their riches, when they have become ours, will support us. Be not deceived about that antiquity of blood by which they exalt themselves above us; for all men, having had one common origin, are all equally ancient, and nature has made us all after one fashion. Strip us naked and we shall all be found alike. Dress us in their clothing and them in ours, we shall appear noble and they ignoble, for poverty and riches make all the difference. . . . God and nature have thrown all human fortunes into the midst of mankind, and they are thus attainable rather by rapine than by industry, by wicked actions rather than by good. Hence it is that men feed upon one another, and those who cannot defend themselves must be worried. Therefore we must use force when the opportunity offers; and fortune cannot present us one more favourable than the present, when the citizens are still disunited, the Signory doubtful, and the magistrates terrified; for we may easily conquer them before they can come to any settled arrangement. By this means we shall either obtain the entire government of the city, or so large a share of it as to be forgiven past errors, and have sufficient authority to threaten the city with a renewal of them at some future time."

The populace rallied in its thousands at the call of the fervid orator, and the sight of these thousands in the great Piazza paralysed the Signory. The terror of the Signors was heightened by the renewal of pillage and conflagration, "for it was enough," says Machiavelli, "to secure its destruction if a single voice in the mob called out, 'To the house of So-and-so.'" They not only yielded the demand for the creation of three new arts, representing the artisans and the proletariat, and the inclusion of their representatives in the Signory; they abdicated at the bidding of the mob, which took sovereign possession of the signorial palace. "You see the palace is now ours, and the city is in your power," said the wool-comber,

Michael de Lando, their leader, "what do you think ought to be done?" Their reply was to proclaim him Gonfalonier, and invest him with the supreme power at discretion. Michael began by setting up a gallows in front of the palace, from which Ser Nuto, one of the most obnoxious of the Albizzi functionaries, was suspended by the foot and torn in pieces by the mob. After this terrible object-lesson in intimidation, Michael had it all his own way in creating a new Signory, four members of which were selected from the Labour Gilds, two from the Greater and two from the Lesser Arts. This decree was not radical enough for a section of his followers, who threatened a new revolution, but the doughty Gonfalonier set upon the malcontents with the more moderate of the revolutionists and slaughtered them out of the city. His reform was, however, short-lived. In 1381 the Greater Arts succeeded in depriving the Labour Gilds of the political power they had won, and in reducing that of the Lesser Arts to a minimum. "Thus the nobles of the people and the Guelfi," says Machiavelli, "resumed the government, and the plebeians lost it, after having wielded it from 1378 to 1381, when these changes took place." The defeat of the populace did not, however, give stability to this patched-up constitution, and the old see-saw of class and faction feud continued to shake the foundations of the republic, and pave the way for the future despot. The revolution, if it failed to vindicate popular rights in the democratic sense, had at least discovered the friend of the people. Salvestro became a popular hero, had in fact been dubbed a knight by the popular sovereignty, had supported Lando in his reforming efforts, and the Medici family was to reap in the not distant future the reward of his services to the popular cause. "Not Salvestro, but Salvator," exclaimed the poet, Saccheti. "Salvestro," says Machiavelli, "was among those who became almost princes of the city."

These Medici had long been conspicuous in Florentine politics; they were erelong to become supreme over their rivals, the Albizzi, in the struggle for the monopoly of power. In 1394, for instance, we find the citizens appealing to Veri de Medici, the head of the family after Salvestro's death, to free them from the tyranny of Maso degli Albizzi, and offering him the supreme power. If Veri had had more ambition than integrity, he would, according to Machiavelli, have become prince of the city. Veri, in a patriotic speech, declined to encroach on the liberty of the republic for his personal advantage. His moderation only increased the reputation of his family, and the banishment by Maso of two of its members, Alamanno and Antonio, invested it with the halo of suffering for the popular cause. The tyranny of the Albizzi faction overshot its mark and worked into the hands of its enemies. Of these the Medici reaped the greatest advantage. "The popular or new nobility (in contrast to the old)," remarks Machiavelli, "committed two errors, which eventually caused the ruin of their faction. In the first place, by long continuance in power, they became insolent; in the second place, by the envy they cherished for one another, and by long possession of power, they relaxed their vigilance over those capable of doing them injury. Thus by rousing daily the hatred of the mass of the people, and not taking measures to check the danger, they gave an opportunity to the family of the Medici to recover its influence. The first to take this opportunity by the forelock was Giovanni de Medici, who, being one of the richest of men, and of a benign and humane disposition, obtained the supreme magistracy by the consent of those in power (1420)."

The advent of Giovanni was hailed with acclamation by the people, who saw in the favourite the champion of their rights, in spite of the warnings of Niccolo da Uzzano as to the danger of giving so much power to one already so powerful. Giovanni, however, showed no disposition to abuse his position. He cared more for commerce and finance than for politics, but the vast financial power which he wielded was more efficacious than political craft in securing the supremacy of his house. His influence as a financier extended far beyond Florence; his name was a power in Europe. He had the knack of hitting the right medium in matters political, "took just such a share in public affairs," as he told his son on his deathbed, "as the laws and his countrymen bestowed, and thus escaped both risk and envy." His generosity with his money certainly helped him to retain the popular goodwill, which passed at his death to his son Cosimo. While Cosimo inherited his father's generosity, he developed a far keener political spirit, and his self-assertion brought him into collision with Rinaldo Albizzi, son of Maso, and leader of the faction since his father's death. Rinaldo was strong enough to drive him from the city, but the heavy taxation (*castato*) necessary to maintain the wars with Duke Philippo Visconti of Milan and with Lucca soured the richer members of his party, who had to pay for this bellicose policy equally with the other citizens, and in the reaction against his *régime*, Cosimo was borne back from exile to power (October 1434).

The long personal domination over a so-called free city, which commenced with Cosimo, was the natural result of its anarchic history. Machiavelli's "History of Florence" is one long tale of strife, proscription, bloodshed, from which it appears that, while aspiring to liberty, the Florentines did not understand how to preserve it, and merely used it as a cloak for selfish factious ends. It was the innate spirit of faction that prevented Italy from leading the way to modern democracy and turned so-called republics into unofficial despotisms. The free popular institutions of a Florence existed only on paper, and fell a victim, first to the oligarchy, and then to the despot. To talk of liberty in a small city State which was at the mercy of every intriguing magnate, and in which freedom was often merely another name for faction, is sheer pretence. Anarchy is the rightful term. Liberty meant merely the right of one faction, which happened for the moment to dominate the Signory, to proscribe another, not the right to live in freedom under the laws. Besides, political rights, even after the rising of the Ciompi, were not for all. The mass was in a state of subjection to the class, and the class again was dominated by the oligarchy of a few families for the time being. "With the nobility and the people alike," remarks Machiavelli, "only the name of liberty is held in estimation, for both alike do not desire to be subject to laws and magistrates." It is, therefore, somewhat singular to find modern writers mistaking this Florentine republic for a democracy. Mr Harford, the accomplished author of a well-written life of Michael Angelo, Hallam, Sismondi, even so erudite and recent a writer as Villari, seem unconscious of the fact that the *régime* of "the people" was not identical with what we understand by this term in these modern days of democracy. If we might invent a word we should call the Florentine government a poplocracy—the rule of the "*popolari*"—as distinguished from the democracy. The "*popolari*" of Florence did not include the mass of the inhabitants; they embraced only the qualified citizens. The rule of the people in the wider sense it was not. The republic was no more a democracy than the Reform Bill constituency of Great Britain in 1832 was a democracy. It was simply the rule of the upper and lower middle class, in which the upper predominated.

The only apparent remedy for such a state of things lay in the advent of the master who understood how to take advantage of the situation. I do not reckon this political aptness so highly as historians, who judge merely from the practical point of view, usually do. It is but a matter of dexterity, but this dexterity may conduce to the public weal, and though usually not a thing to arouse enthusiasm, it has historically proved its utility for the time being often enough. For this utilitarian *rôle*, then, Cosimo was admirably fitted. He knew Florence, and Florence had learned that it could not do better, in the circumstances, than submit to his dictation. He knew how to hold the rein without tightening it unduly. He cared for the substance, not the emblems of power, was content to direct the State from the counting-house rather than the palace. He professed equality, while possessing superiority. He was, moreover, in full sympathy with the genius of the age, the patron of art and literature, of a liberal, intellectual culture, which was a powerful bond of union in the midst of disunion. As a financial magnate he was, too, just the man to become the leading representative of the powerful commercial class, while his generosity to the lower classes made him, though no democrat, what, for want of a better name, we might call a "popular" leader. He patronised in his own astute fashion the Lesser Arts, whilst disintegrating the gild system and depressing the Greater, and thus undermined the power of the oligarchy. In this way he created a large *clientèle* devoted to his *régime*, and by his finesse, his shrewdness, succeeded perfectly in his policy of keeping his thumb on the magistracy without apparently violating its rights.

Cosimo was not officially the ruler of Florence. The forms of the constitution existed as before, but while constitutionally a republic, it was a republic in leading strings. He concentrated in his own person that power over the Signory which faction after faction successively wielded. More recently that power had lodged in the Albizzi; for nearly sixty years it was absorbed by Cosimo and his successors.

It is a curious spectacle, that of a nominal republic whose machinery is manipulated for several generations in the service of a personal despotism. The Gonfalonier of Justice, and the Eight Priors who constituted the Signory and held office for two months; the two colleges of the Twelve Buonomini, and the sixteen Gonfaloniers of the Companies—the town militia—elected by lot for three and four months respectively; the Ten of War; the Eight of Watch and Ward; the Six of Mercanzia, or commercial court; the Councils of the People and the Commune, of 300 and 250 members each; the Pratica, or occasional deliberation of the chief citizens at critical emergencies; the Balia or Reform Commission, with its sub-committee the Accopiatori; the Parlamento or General Assembly of the citizens; and sundry officials of high-sounding title—the Podesta and the Capitano del Popolo, for instance, whose offices had shrunk into insignificance—still exercised the executive, legislative, and judicial functions. To this complicated machinery Cosimo in 1458 added a new council—the Council of the Hundred—composed of his chief adherents, and fitted to give him the control of the cumbrous machine at will. The Balia by which the manœuvre was carried through, in the face of the growing opposition of the constitutional party to his rule, was an additional proof of his power. Whenever he wished some special measure carried, he could get a Balia nominated to do his will; and in the tug-of-war which took place in 1458 over the question whether the consent of the Signory and the colleges, and the approval of the Councils were necessary to its appointment, the constitutionalists found themselves on the vanquished side. When such diplomatic means failed to cow opposition, he could have recourse to the old method of proscription. He was by no means scrupulous or merciful when his power was threatened, though very politic in the pursuit of his objects. He could strike an intractable opponent like Baldaccio da Anghiari from his path by means of the assassin's knife. "Better to injure a city than ruin it;" "Two yards of rose-coloured cloth can make a gentleman;" "You cannot direct a government by merely counting your beads," were some of his practical maxims. They bespeak the cynic and the ruthless politician, and Cosimo could be both. Nevertheless, at his death, the Florentines solemnly decreed him "The Father of his Country," and Machiavelli, banished republican though he was, is profuse in his laudations of his character.

And Florence and its historian had some reason for their encomiums. Under his *régime* the republic became a great power, politically as well as commercially, and in alliance with Milan and Naples checked for a time the ambitious growth of Venice. Its fame as a centre of culture was enhanced by his prodigal patronage of art and letters. The parallel between Cosimo and Pericles, often drawn, is in some respects an apt one. If faction did not entirely disappear—there was friction at times within the Medici "caucus," restiveness under the sceptre of the uncrowned monarch—it was not allowed to rend the republic. The travesty of republicanism was more tolerable, because less injurious, under Cosimo than the travesty of republicanism under the Albizzi and the factions of old. Yet his *régime* was demoralising. The dependence of the State on a commercial magnate, whose liberality was only another name for corruption, was not favourable to civic virtue. Cosimo bribed and bought, while he ruled the republic; and the Florentines unfortunately submitted with little demur to be corrupted into subjection. "The city for sale, if it can find a purchaser," materially contributed to the success of the corrupter, and for what of odium there is in such a career of political craft, the Florentines certainly deserve their share of censure. Corruption which bends to the master has no right to complain of the yoke, nor is the historian tempted to do so for it.

Corruption, demoralisation, veiled by the luxury, the splendour, the intellectual activity of the age of Lorenzo, is the dominant note of the republic's internal history till the advent of Savonarola. With Cosimo's death, the rule of his grandson, Lorenzo, practically began, for Lorenzo's valetudinarian father, Piero was unfitted for the active direction of affairs, and died five years after Cosimo. This short interval witnessed an attempt, not to vindicate republican institutions against the Medician despotism, but to gratify, under the pseudonym of the public interest, the resentments of a malcontent party in the Medician "caucus" against its chief. The conspiracy was, therefore, no evidence of a welling up of public spirit against corruption, was in truth rather an evidence of the prevailing demoralisation, since the conspirators, with the exception of Niccolo Soderini, a respectable character, were pure opportunists. The chief plotter, Diotisalvi Neroni, led Piero artfully on to the ice by advising him to call in his debts, and thus rousing the anger of the numerous debtors of his father. The ice, however, broke under Diotisalvi's feet, not under Piero's. At the decisive moment, Piero threw off his lethargy and completely outwitted the Mountain, as the discontented faction was called. This counter *coup* saved the fortunes of the family at a crisis when the debility of the father and the youth of the son exposed it to the risk of premature eclipse. During Lorenzo's twenty-five years of supremacy, its brilliance reached the zenith. On the other hand, corruption became even more foul. Piero, in the speech to the chief men of the "caucus" which Machiavelli reports, had rebuked the abuse of power of which his adherents were guilty. "You plunder your neighbours of their wealth; you sell justice; you evade the law; you oppress the timid and exalt the insolent. Throughout all Italy there are not so many and shocking examples of violence and avarice as in this city." Under Lorenzo corruption reached high-water mark, though Machiavelli and Guicciardini pronounce the conventional eulogy on the corrupt despot. Machiavelli, for example, bewails the declension of virtue, while mentioning the efforts of the more respectable citizens to counteract it by sumptuary laws. The fashionable youth gave themselves up to gambling and debauchery, and displayed the vacuity of their minds by the immoderate indulgence of their passions. Inclination and policy alike impelled Lorenzo to encourage this libertinism. He had none of his grandfather's commercial spirit. He left the management of business affairs to his agents, who ruined his fortune. He was himself a poet of considerable merit, and his ballads were the rage of the city.

He had fine artistic as well as literary tastes, and his palace was a sort of shrine where all the *élite* of art and literature worshipped. Critic, scholar, philosopher, he not merely patronised the Platonic Academy which his grandfather had founded, he took part in its discussions. Intellectually, he was the worthy equal of men like Marsilio Ficino, Angelo Poliziano, Pico Mirandola. His versatility was extraordinary. To his *rôle* as poet and Mæcenas, he added that of Maître de Plaisir to the citizens at large. He kept them in good humour by masquerades, tournaments, carnivals, and wrote the obscene ballads which the ribald young nobles sang for the delectation of the multitude. For the decent he could build a church or a monastery, and could even listen with admiration to one of Fra Mariano's sermons. Nay, he could write hymns or lauds. With all this, he was the busy practical politician, the compeer of kings and dukes, whose influence was a factor in international as well as Italian politics, and who perfected the system of personal government which Cosimo had inaugurated by the institution of the additional Council of the Seventy. Even captious, factious Florence became a fairly orderly State under his rule. The Pazzi conspiracy which did his brother Giuliano to death in the cathedral, and just missed taking his own life, was but a sputter of malcontent egotism. Florence might not altogether relish its master, but it was content to be amused and corrupted into good-humoured acquiescence. The moral effects of this fascination, wielded by the Magnificent, were bad enough. In spite of its intellectuality, its neoplatonism, Florence was sunk in a moral lethargy which sorely needed the awakening voice of the prophet to rouse it to a life that intellectual culture had tended to sap, rather than quicken. "Culture," says Signor Villari, "was generally diffused, . . . but artists, men of letters, statesmen, nobles and people, were all equally corrupt in mind, devoid of public and private virtues, devoid of all moral sense. Their religion was either an engine of government or a base hypocrisy ; they were without faith of any kind, whether civil, religious, moral, or philosophical ; they were not earnest even in scepticism. Their dominant feeling was utter indifference to principle. These clever, keen-witted, intellectual men were incapable of real elevation of thought, and, despising all enthusiasm for noble and generous ideas, showed their contempt by coldly compassionate smiles. Unlike the sceptic philosophers, they neither combated nor threw doubt on such ideas; they simply regarded them with pity. And this *vis inertiæ* was more hurtful to virtue than a declared and active hostility. It was only in country places and among the lowest classes, removed from all contact with politics and letters, that any germ of the old virtue was still to be found. And even this was not visible on the surface." Villari lays no small share of the blame for this state of things at Lorenzo's door, and his mastery of the period makes it difficult to dissent from his judgment, harsh though it is. "Gifted by nature with a brilliant intellect, he had inherited from Cosimo a subtle astuteness, rendering him—although by no means a statesman of the first rank—very swift of resource, full of prudence and acumen, dexterous in his negotiations with other powers, still more dexterous in ridding himself of his enemies, and equally capable of daring and cruelty whenever emergencies called for bold strokes. He was alike regardless of honesty and honour; respected no condition of men; went straight to his ends, trampling over all considerations, whether human or divine. The cruel sack of unfortunate Volterra, the robbery of the funds of the Monte delle Fanciulle, in consequence of which many dowerless girls fell into bad courses; and his rapacious appropriation of public property are all stains that even his blindest worshippers are unable to ignore. His countenance was a true index to his character. It was a dark skinned, unpleasing, sinister face, with a flattened, irregular nose, and a wide, thin-lipped, crooked mouth, suited to the accents of his nasal voice. But his eyes were lively and penetrating, his forehead lofty, and his manners marked by the most perfect finish of that cultured and elegant age; his conversation was full of vivacity, wit, and learning, and he won the genuine affection of all who were admitted to his intimacy. He encouraged all the worst tendencies of the age, and multiplied its corruptions. Abandoned to pleasure himself, he urged the people to lower depths of abandonment, in order to plunge them in the lethargy of intoxication. In fact, during his reign Florence was a continuous scene of revelry and dissipation. It is true that in the midst of this corrupt, pleasure-loving society, a mighty transformation of the human mind was already in progress. But it seemed to grow spontaneously by the natural force of things, uncared for and unnoticed. What was most visible at the time was the general passion for pleasure, the pride of pagan learning, the increasingly sensual turn, both of art and literature, under the fostering hand of the man who was master of all in Florence."

Such was the city in which Savonarola's trumpet call to repentance before coming judgment was heard in the waning years of the Magnificent's career. A most unlikely place surely for the message of the prophet who was inspired by a childlike simplicity of belief in visions, spirits, portents. In a city of philosophers there was presumably not much chance of a hearing for the austere monk, the impassioned visionary who set himself to stem the floodtide of immorality and cynicism. Yet Florence was ripe for Savonarola; there were points of contact between its corruption and indifference and the gospel of the new John the Baptist. In spite of the culture and scepticism of the age, men were easily moved by superstitious fancies. They had dethroned the mediæval saints to set up the gods, the spirits of antiquity. They believed in alchemy and astrology, in the occult influence of the stars above them, of inanimate objects in the world around them. In such an environment portents and miracles are rife enough. Even Machiavelli believed the world to be full of spirits who gave warning to mortals, with sinister auguries of the evils about to supervene. They were oppressed with the forebodings of these calamities, and predisposed to listen to the prophet. The prophet himself was in this respect the man for his time. His impressionable soul drew from that atmosphere, surcharged with sinister inspirations, his mandate and his mission. Being a man of intense faith and wild eloquence, it is not surprising that he succeeded in such an environment in revolutionising even sceptic, sensual Florence, in making it virtuous, earnest-minded, for a time at least, in spite of itself.

It was in 1481 that Savonarola migrated from the Dominican monastery at Bologna, where he had begun his novitiate in 1475, to that of St Mark at Florence, which Cosimo the elder had founded in connection with the Lombard congregation of the Order, and which was celebrated for its learning and its philanthropy. In refined, intellectual Florence the uncouth, fervid preacher failed to make an impression. The Florentines were spellbound by Fra Mariano's artificial and highly polished eloquence; they only smiled at Savonarola's rugged perorations. His success, it may be said, began in failure, for his failure only made him the more determined to succeed in his divinely ordained mission. These critical, cultured Florentines who flocked to hear sermons that Cicero or Plato might have preached, that breathed the spirit of Ficino and the Platonic Academy, must be taught to relish a different doctrine; they must learn to hear the voice of the prophet instead of the rhetorician, the prophet crying to a godless generation, " Repent, and return to the Lord." The visions that came of vigils and fastings, and revealed to him the judgments in store for the Church and the world, confirmed him in his prophetic mission. It was not at Florence, however, but at San Gimignano that he really began his crusade as prophet, and here his less refined hearers were thrilled by the voice that denounced the corruptions of the Church, and foretold its punishment and regeneration in the near future. At Brescia, too, he electrified the crowds that pressed to hear him by the vivid picture of coming woes as reflected in the Book of Revelation. The degenerate state of Italy seemed to invite the scourging foretold by the preacher, and the public mood, as well as his own whirlwind oratory, helped to make his reputation. The fact is evident from his recall to Florence in 1489 by Lorenzo de Medici at the instigation of Pico della Mirandola, one of the humanist prodigies of the day, who had learned to appreciate Savonarola at a chapter of the Dominicans which he attended at Reggio in 1482. Pico was a man of wide, though superficial, learning, and had brought on himself the papal threat of excommunication for a series of nine hundred propositions, which he offered to defend against all the world. He submitted to the pope's censure, but would not retract, and in the midst of his quarrel with the infamous Innocent VIII., bethought him of Savonarola. Savonarola saw in this summons the call of God. His ecstatic mind received the divine impression at every important turn of his life. The divine messenger appeared to him as he lay exhausted by the way near Bologna, took him to an hospice, and bade him go forward and do the work that God had sent him to do.

The second arrival at Florence of a man of such force of character, whose soaring purpose was inspired by the divine afflatus, proved to be an epoch-making event in Florentine and Italian history. Men who move their age are made in strangely different moulds, and visionaries like Savonarola, who are also highly intense moral natures, have produced startling results at times on the world. His appearance in the pulpit of St Mark, on the 1st August 1489, now drew a crowd to listen to his fulminations from the Apocalypse of speedy doom for a godless generation. The Platonists even took to discussing Savonarola, and, naturally enough, some of them could not relish the fiery friar. The friar was, nevertheless, no mere ignorant ranter, though he courted the opposition of the philosophers by dilating on the vanity of philosophy. He had had a dialectic training, and while teaching the novices at Bologna and Florence, he had, as Villari has shown, treated some points of the scholastic philosophy in an acute, independent spirit. "Even from early childhood," says his biographer, Burlamacchi, " he would not judge authors according to the greatness of their fame, nor follow any opinions solely because they were in vogue, but always had his eye on truth and reason."

This note of bold independence soon made itself disagreeably felt in his sermons as well as in his writings. In Lent, 1491, he began to preach in the Duomo, Santa Maria del Fiore, to the crowds whom the chapel of St Mark could no longer contain. Such a preacher, with his self-imposed divine mission to reform the world, as well as the Church, must needs trench on social abuses. He thundered against the greed of the clergy, and against the gambling and usury of the rich; nay, he struck boldly at Lorenzo and his administration. His temerity was startling, even to himself, and he questioned himself whether it were not wiser to practise more self-restraint in his language. But a vision would suffice to stifle such a passing doubt in his mission, and a voice would ring in his ears as from God, Fool, dost thou not see that it is God's will that thou shouldst continue in the same path? "All the evil and all the good of the city depend from its head," he cried in a sermon delivered before the Signory, "and, therefore, great is his responsibility even for small sins, since, if he followed the right path, the whole city would be sanctified. . . . Tyrants are incorrigible, because they are proud, because they love flattery, and will not restore ill-gotten gains; they leave all in the hands of bad ministers; they succumb to flattery; they hearken not unto the poor, and neither do they condemn the rich; they expect the poor and the peasantry to work for them without reward, or suffer their ministers to expect this; they corrupt voters, and farm out the taxes to aggravate the burdens of the people."

The preacher was repeating in the pulpit what was being said of Lorenzo and his government in the street, and such public declamation was both dangerous and exasperating. Lorenzo, nevertheless, bridled his resentment, and strove to win the goodwill of the potent orator, who was elected Prior of St Mark in July 1491, by presents of game and money to the monastery. Savonarola received his overtures coldly, and when he sent five of the principal citizens to remonstrate against his sermons, he curtly bade them tell him to do penance for his sins, "For the Lord is no respecter of persons, and spares not the princes of the earth." Even the threat of exile only called forth a volley of judgments to come, including the prediction of the speedy death of Lorenzo himself. Lorenzo tried another tack. He set Fra Mariano da Genazzano a preaching against the unconscionable Dominican prior. The rival friar denounced the false prophet. His outrageous attack only added to Savonarola's admirers, and he merely discomfited himself by his personal violence. Needless to say, he became henceforth Savonarola's enemy, while Lorenzo gave up further opposition. He was suffering from a fatal disease, was in truth a doomed man, and had no need of a Savonarola to tell him the fact. On his deathbed he summoned the prior to confess him at Careggi. "You must do three things," demanded Savonarola. "Have faith in God's mercy; restore all your ill-gotten gains; and restore liberty to the people of Florence." At this last stipulation Lorenzo turned himself in his sick-bed away, with a look of anger, from the eye of the stern confessor, who departed without granting him absolution. He died on 8th April 1492. Such is the story related by Cinozzi, and it appears to accord better with the stern preacher's character than the tamer version of the scene given by Poliziano.

After Lorenzo's death Savonarola became the central figure of the opposition to his son Piero. This Piero had inherited none of his father's gifts except the art of versification. He was as violent, reckless, harsh, as his father had been courteous, astute, refined. While he had the craving for political power, he was destitute of any skill in the art of the political trickster. He affected the *rôle* of the master; he neglected the means by which his predecessors had attained it. His passion was to excel all Italy as a boxer, a footballer, a tennis player. He forgot that these things do not make a statesman, and he speedily lost all the prestige which his father and his great-grandfather had won for his family. With such a weakling to support it, the Medician system must have crashed to the ground, even if there had been no Savonarola to undermine its foundations.

Savonarola does not seem to have entered on a set crusade from the pulpit against the son of the man who on his deathbed had turned his back on him, and—what in his eyes amounted to the same thing—on the Lord. He concerned himself at first with preaching, not with politics. But his preaching became increasingly militant in tone; it fanned the general reaction which Piero's infatuated foolery quickened; it gave a powerful handle to the competitors for place and power. New visions steeled the daring of the Puritan preacher in the pulpit of the Duomo. During the night before his last Advent sermon in 1492, a hand grasping a sword suddenly gleamed in the sky with the words " The sword of the Lord that cometh speedily and suddenly," inscribed on it. Then the hand that held it turned it towards the earth, and amid a terrible thunderstorm fire, swords, and arrows shot downwards and smote the world with destruction. The vision ended as usual with the command to proclaim the judgments of God. At another time, it was a black cross rising above Rome, with the inscription *Crux Iræ Dei* upon it, whose arms overspread the whole earth, while the lightning gleamed and the thunder rolled and the tempest raged upon a doomed world.

These thunderings and lightnings certainly lost none of their terror when translated into the wild oratory of the excited pulpiteer. Savonarola launched them straight at the heads of the rulers in Church and State. "These wicked princes," he cried, "are sent to chastise the sins of their subjects; they are truly a sad snare for souls; their courts and palaces are the refuge of all the beasts and monsters of the earth, for they give shelter to ribalds and malefactors. These wretches flock to their halls because it is there that they find ways and means to satisfy their evil passions and unbridled lusts. There are the false councillors who continually devise new burdens and new taxes to drain the blood of the people. There are the flattering poets and philosophers who, by force of a thousand lies and fables, trace the genealogy of those evil princes back to the gods; but, and worse than all, there are the priests who follow in the same course. This is the city of Babylon, O my brethren, the city of the foolish and the impious, the city that will be destroyed of the Lord."

In his oratoric fury Savonarola became the sworn revolutionist, the defiant adversary of all constituted authority wrongly used. He swore divine vengeance on all wrong-doers in high places. "I am like the hail," he said, in reference to these denunciations of secular and ecclesiastical authorities, "which pelts every one who is out in the open air." The deluge is at hand, and the burden of the discourses on Noah's ark, begun in 1492 and concluded in the autumn of 1494, is, Let all haste them to enter the ark of the Lord.

The political situation was destined to give a startling fulfilment of the preacher's prognostications of doom as far as Piero de Medici was concerned. Many a fervid pulpiteer before and after Savonarola has indulged in such impassioned denunciation of divine judgment on a godless world, and the world has not been a hairbreadth the worse in consequence. Such preachers have often shouted themselves black in the face to no purpose. This tendency to see visions and curse mankind in general is as often an index of spiritual pride and fanatic fancy as of moral prescience. But Savonarola had wittingly or unwittingly gauged the general political situation as well as the will of Heaven in predicting woe upon woe to Florence and Italy. Whilst he was thundering retribution from the pulpit of the Duomo, Charles VIII. of France was on the march across the Alps to the conquest of the land of the Renascence. Here then was the avenger of Heaven, the sword of the Lord that should smite quickly and suddenly. A strange hand truly to wield the sword that Savonarola had seen in the angry sky. The dissolute, crack-brained Charles VIII., the commissioner of Heaven to execute righteous judgments on earth! King Charles came not, in fact, in the spirit of the crusader to do the will of Heaven. The motives of his expedition were mundane enough. He came at the instigation of that blackest of tyrants, Ludovico Moro, in order to filch the kingdom of Naples for France from the hands of Ludovico's enemy, King Ferdinand. The alliance between Naples, Florence, and Milan, which Lorenzo had striven to maintain, had snapped in Piero's inexperienced hands, and Charles, with Ludovico to prompt him, saw the chance of aggrandising France at Italy's expense. It was, then, as Ludovico's ally and the champion of the claim of the House of Anjou to Naples, not as the Lord's knight-errant, that Charles and his mighty host poured from the heights of Monte Ginevra down on the Lombard plain in the autumn of 1494. Nor was he altogether an unwelcome intruder to others besides Ludovico. Pope Alexander VI. as well as Duke Ludovico saw in him an ally against his enemy of Naples, and every city with a grievance to redress hoped for salvation at his hands. "Indeed, by a strange anomaly," says Villari, "the French invasion, fated to bring so many woes on our country, was, at that moment, fervently desired by almost all Italians, and only opposed by the French." Florence, in particular, in its aversion of Piero de Medici, was ready to acclaim his approach, even though its nerves were kept in a state of acute tension by the friar's terrible sermons. Nevertheless, the news that Charles was across the Apennines in full march on Tuscany, and his flying columns were burning and massacring all before them at Rapallo, Fivizzano, and in the Romagna burst like a thunder-bolt on the city of Savonarola. The maladroit Piero, after a despairing attempt at resistance, resorted to Charles's camp to surrender the fortresses that barred the French king's advance, and make an abject submission.

This madcap act sealed Piero's doom. The report of his humiliating submission sent a paroxysm of fury through Florence, and the cry of "People and Liberty" resounded from the Piazza. "Behold," cried Savonarola to the throng in the Duomo, "the sword has come upon you, the prophecies are fulfilled, the scourges begun. Behold, these hosts are led by the Lord, O Florence! The time of singing and dancing is at an end; now is the time to shed floods of tears for thy sins. Thy sins, O Florence! thy sins, O Rome! thy sins, O Italy! They have brought their chastisements upon thee. Repent ye then!" At that moment Savonarola had it in his power to launch the city into the horrors of a bloody revolution, for among his congregation were many who only needed a word from him to take instant vengeance on the rich family oligarchy which had participated in Medician misgovernment. Many of his hearers were indeed armed and ready for the bloody work. It is to the credit of the fiery friar that the revolution which drove Piero from the city was a bloodless one. On the 4th November Piero Capponi, one of the few men who had preserved the old republican spirit, rose at the sitting of the Signory to demand his expulsion. "Piero de Medici is no longer fit to rule the State; the republic must provide for itself; the moment has come to shake off this baby government." Let them, he continued, receive the French, but as an independent State with arms ready to maintain its liberty. While ambassadors, among whom was Savonarola, were sent to invite Charles to Florence, Piero, who had returned and made a vain attempt to assert his authority, was hounded, along with his brother, Cardinal Giovanni, the future Pope Leo X., into exile at Venice.

Shortly after Piero had fled, Charles entered, and though he had not definitely declared his intentions to the ambassadors, he received a magnificent welcome in the splendidly decorated and illuminated city. He was inclined to play the conqueror and recall Piero on his own terms, but changed his tactics and moderated his demands in the face of the firm attitude of Capponi. A rupture was in fact only averted by Capponi's determination to stand up to the overbearing potentate. When Charles' secretary read his ultimatum, and the syndics of the Signory demurred, "Then we will sound our trumpets," burst out the irascible monarch. "And we," retorted Capponi angrily, snatching the document and tearing it in pieces, "will ring our bells." Capponi's determination settled the question, and rid the city of its dangerous guest at the cost of recognising him as restorer and protector of its liberty, paying him a contribution of 120,000 florins, and leaving its fortresses in his hands for two years. Charles would fain have protracted his stay, but was finally persuaded to move by Savonarola's solemn objurgations, and on the 28th November left the city to solve its constitutional problems as it best might. The divine castigation was after all comparatively mild, except for Piero de Medici, but the advent of Charles seemed to have fulfilled Savonarola's prognostications, and the fiery friar was now unquestionably master of the situation. He had played the prophet with success; he was now to essay the part of the politician. The task of rehabilitating the republic on the spur of the moment was by no means easy. The first expedient was to call a Parlamento. The clang of the palace bell summoned the people to the Piazza on the 2nd December, and to the old popular assembly the Signory proposed a Balìa for the reform of the government. The proposal was received with acclamation by the Parlamento, and approved by the Councils of the People and the Commune; and a board of twenty Accopiatori with power to nominate to all great offices, was forthwith appointed. These twenty thus took the place of the Council of Seventy, in which Lorenzo's personal government had latterly lodged. They selected a new Signory to carry on the executive, and a War Council of Ten to maintain the authority of the republic against its enemies. The advance of the French had not only overthrown the Medici; it had snapped the allegiance of Pisa, Arezzo, Montepulciano, and other towns, which had seized the chance of regaining their independence. It was, therefore, indispensable to formulate a constitution applicable to the situation, and the Conclave or Pratica in the Palace was soon racking its brains to find the most feasible constitutional expedient in the circumstances. The problem was how to secure stable, effective government while avoiding tyranny. The wealthy patricians, led by Vespucci, were, of course, in favour of government limited by oligarchy. But Florence, it was evident, liked the Medicean oligarchy as little as it relished the Medicean tyrant, and the popular party, championed by Antonio Soderini, demanded a constitution which would ensure all qualified citizens at least a share in the government. Soderini, who had been an ambassador at Venice, advocated an experiment on the Venetian model. There was heated debate in the palace between Vespucci and Soderini; there was agitation in the streets where the artisans, instead of working, took up the debate and threatened to settle the question in their own forcible fashion by massacring the whole Medicean faction. It looked as if the disputants in the palace and the disputants in the streets would debate the republic to perdition.

In this emergency the extraordinary powers of the friar once more proved themselves. Savonarola, strange to say, began to preach moderation from the pulpit. He did not show any originality; he was no apostle of new and epoch-making political truths. He expounded the politics of Aquinas, but as he proceeded in his discourse the schoolman was gradually lost in the practical politician, and the preacher threw the weight of his influence into the scale in favour of Soderini's scheme. This fiery prophet is a strange mixture of fancy and practical sense, and it is a striking proof of his practical sense that, in this critical emergency, he did not attempt to foist on the city a visionary constitution drawn from the Old Testament. He spoke to the magistrates and the male citizens, whom he summoned to the Duomo, as the practical politician, not as the theologian, though he of course improved the occasion to moralise in his own peculiar fashion. It is for the salvation of men's souls that he feels called on to intervene in these mundane matters. Monarchy, he insisted, might be suitable for the nations of the north or the extreme south, but it was unsuited to the keen-witted, mobile Florentine temperament. Tyranny is fatal to the well-being of the city. But having overthrown the tyrant, let them begin by reforming their lives, spiritual being higher than material things. Let them then establish a government conformable to the will of God and *the will of the people.* " Let this be the basis or model of pure government, that no man receive any benefit save by the will of the people, who must have the sole right of creating magistrates and enacting laws." To realise this principle the best expedient is a Grand Council on the Venetian model. Let the people assemble under their sixteen Gonfaloniers and declare their will. The suggestion of the preacher sounds like a pure democracy, but aristocratic Venice was rather a strange place to seek a pure democracy, and Savonarola's scheme, which the Councils of the People and the Commune voted unanimously, was, in practice, by no means democratic. The Grand Council (*Consiglio Maggiore*), on which now devolved the supreme power, was only open to those who had themselves held one of the great magistracies, or one of whose immediate ancestors had done so. Only in exceptional cases was this cardinal qualification dispensed with. The sovereignty of the republic thus passed, not into the hands of the people in the wider sense, but into those of the 3,200 individuals whom the scrutiny found duly qualified in accordance with this artificial test of citizenship. This proportion out of a population, variously computed at 90,000 and 128,000 souls, shows clearly enough that Savonarola's rule, "by the will of the whole people," was no anticipation of Rousseau, but a purely mediæval idea with a modern aspect. The plebs at Florence still, in the prophet's view, form no part of the people, and democracy is still a misnomer as applied to the republic; nay, the Parliament, the only institution which had given the people a voice in affairs under the old *régime*, was swept away along with the Councils of the People and the Commune. The only check on the middle class rule of the Grand Council was the Council of Eighty, and even this body, which was intended to act as a senate, was nominated by the larger Council.

The rest of the old republican machinery—the Signory, the Colleges, the Ten of War, the Pratica, &c.—was left intact, and together with the two councils made up the legislative and executive powers of the republic. Savonarola was the sworn foe of the Parlamento. He was afraid to trust the plebs with political power, and the Parliament had in the past often enough lent itself as the instrument of faction and tyranny. It might easily be made the tool of a Medician reaction, and therefore was to be eschewed as the most dangerous of contingencies. He preached one of his fieriest sermons on the subject. "See," he cried, "that no parliament be called unless thou wouldst lose thy government. Let the Signory swear to summon no parliament, and if any member of it do so, let his head be cut off; if not a member of the Signory, let him be proclaimed a rebel, and all his goods confiscated. Likewise let all the Gonfaloniers swear on taking office that on hearing the bell ring to parliament, they will at once sack the houses of the Signory, and let the Gonfalonier who doth direct the sack receive one-fourth of the spoil, and the remainder be distributed among his comrades. Yea, should the Signory seek to call a parliament . . . all may cut them to pieces without sin." This savage outburst, unworthy of the man who posed as the moralist of his age, sealed the fate of the old popular assembly, which was formally abolished on the 13th August 1495. Its suppression might, in the meantime, be a necessary precaution against tyranny and anarchy, but it was none the less a strange travesty of the principle of ruling "by the will of the people." The measure might be efficacious for the time being, but it could hardly fail ultimately to defeat its own purpose. What if the middle class *régime* should, in its turn, play the tyrant as against the mass? Might not the mass remember its parliament in spite of pains and penalties, and ring its bell and flock to the Piazza, in its sovereign capacity, for the struggle with class egotism, or open its arms to receive the tyrant as the redresser of its grievances? Savonarola, political opportunist though he appears, did not understand that to leave the body politic without a safety valve for popular grievances is to run the risk of political explosion. In settling the constitution of the rejuvenated republic, he did nothing to solve the mighty problem of the future. He failed to see that the stability of a State depends on the just recognition of the political rights of all—of the plebs as well as the populus— and his republic does not take us one step further away from the Middle Ages to modern times. No wonder that in twenty years it had ceased to exist. In this matter the friar thought only of expediency, not of justice or injustice—a strange thing for the friar to do—and even expediency might have suggested some consideration of the claims of the poor man. He certainly had not had too many champions of his cause in this Florentine republic, and Savonarola was strong enough at this juncture to have accomplished something on his behalf, besides bidding him return to his work, and his master give him alms. The "democratic monk" of Villari is not easily recognisable.

In spite of the truculent tone of his sermons against the Parliament, the preacher strove to infuse a humane and equitable spirit into the new government, and raised his voice in favour of equitable taxation, a general pardon, and a fair trial to accused persons. It was largely due to his summons, "Florence forgive and make peace," that so little blood was shed in retaliation on the agents of Piero's *régime*. It was equally his merit that a check was put upon the arbitrary judgments of the Tribunal of Eight on political and criminal offenders. This court could by six votes (the Six Beans) imprison, exile, confiscate, sentence to death without possibility of appeal. Henceforth, it was decreed, after hot debate, that such appeal should be permitted to the Great Council within eight days of sentence, though not to the Senate, as Savonarola would have wished.

With the sequel of Savonarola's career we have little concern. It was a series of stages to a great tragedy. The reformation of Church and society was far more important in his eyes than the deliverance of the republic from political tyranny. He succeeded for a short interval in stemming the tide of depravity. Florence became in appearance a holy city under his puritan auspices. Gambling was put down; bands of young people—"the children of the friar"—paraded the streets burning "the vanities," the indecent books and pictures in vogue under the Medician supremacy, and chanting hymns and collecting alms for the poor. "It was a holy time," noted Luca Landucci, "but it was short." It certainly was not a happy one. Florence was not minded to become a puritan city, and its corruption was only scotched, not killed. Whenever the friar withdrew, the gambling hells and brothels were filled to overflowing by the dissolute youth of the Compagnacci, who would fain have taken the life of the puritan reformer, and scoffed at his denunciations of vice, when they dared. Worse still, faction threatened to upset his political system, for the Medici had still their adherents in the Bigi or Palleschi, and the Arrabbiati, or party of the *nobili popolari*, who resented the supremacy of the Great Council, grew restive and rebellious under the *régime* of the Piagnoni or Frateschi, as they dubbed the dominant puritan party.

The failure of Charles' expedition against Naples and his ignominious retreat left the friar in an awkward, nay, dangerous, position. Milan, Venice, the emperor allied themselves against the intruder, and the intruder was driven out never to return. The allies then united their strength against the republic. Florence and its prophet were left in isolation to struggle against rebellious Pisa and her allies, and the struggle became ever more disastrous and hopeless. "Believe now in your friar," cried the scoffers, "who declared that he held Pisa in his fist." To save the situation for Savonarola, it was imperative that the French should return, but the French came not, and when Pope Alexander VI. at last shot his bolt of excommunication against the prophet, and plague and famine ravaged the city, the situation became desperate. Savonarola spiritedly set the depraved pope at defiance, would not admit the right of the infamous politician who wore the tiara to dictate to his conscience, and appealed to a General Council, as so many reformers had done before him, against the dictum of the base usurper of the name of Christ. Had he been more prudent, he might have succeeded in his appeal. But he was foolish enough to risk his reputation on a miracle, and then when the confidence of the Signory and the people was being shaken by the calamities which were overwhelming the republic, he accepted the challenge of his enemy, the Franciscan Francesco da Puglia, to prove the truth of his doctrines by the test of fire, or rather Fra Domenico accepted it for him. The miserable fiasco of the trial by fire in the Piazza, and its terrible finale of the rising of the Compagnacci and Arrabbiati, sealed the prophet's fate. He had played into the hands of his enemies, and in the mad revulsion of the moment, the people, who had crowded to hear his sermons in the Duomo, now cursed the false prophet and crowded to the Piazza on the morning of the 23rd May 1498 to gloat over the spectacle of his degradation and death, and that of his fellow-sufferers, Fra Domenico and Fra Silvestro.

Savonarola's republic outlived him but fourteen years.

In 1512 the Spanish general, Ramon da Cardona, marched on Florence and forcibly restored Giuliano and Giovanni de Medici. In that short interval the castigation which he had foretold was meted out to Italy with a vengeance. It became the battleground of French and Spanish ambition, the scene of ravage and slaughter, whose terrors were but the beginning of half a century of woes which fulfilled all the prophet's worst premonitions many times over. Rome itself was destined to a terrible atonement for the sins of its rulers. Many of his persecutors lived to witness the judgments that a degenerate age had invited. The worst judgment of all is the fact that for three centuries to come Italy was crippled morally, intellectually, politically. The dooms of the prophet had been fulfilled; his forecast of a regenerated republic—the Jerusalem of a new age—proved the mere fancy of an overheated brain. Florence played out its *rôle* as a political and intellectual force when it swung its prophet from the gallows and threw the ashes of his burned body into the Arno. Savonarola fell because moral force in such an age was not sufficient to maintain a political position. The masses had no reason to see in him a political benefactor, and if he lost his moral influence over them, he had nothing to fall back on in the hour of emergency. Had he given them some share of political power, he would not have been reduced to trust to a miracle for deliverance. The populace would have furnished him with an army to foil the designs of his enemies and overawe them into impotence. His visionary confidence in Providence, his faith in visions and prophecy, inevitably tended to make a martyr of the political reformer. From the practical point of view he appears, in fact, as the victim of religious mania, and it is not surprising that a Machiavelli could only see the lunatic in this side of his character. His lack of saneness in this respect unfitted him to be what Villari calls "the leading spirit in a great political drama." But if he mistook his vocation in attempting to direct a political revolution, he must still be regarded as a great force in his true sphere—that of a preacher of righteousness in an age of surpassing wickedness. This was his true calling, and from this point of view he appears even to Machiavelli as a truly great figure.

His career is but an episode in the history of a small Italian State; yet it is important as the expression of the *Zeit Geist*, the active, impatient, inquisitive spirit of an age antagonistic to traditional authority. It would be erroneous to regard him as the pioneer of Luther in his denunciation of the traditional hierarchy. He professed allegiance to the pope and the schoolmen, was and remained a mediævalist rather than a modern, and Luther erroneously included him among the Protestant martyrs. Nor have Protestant historians succeeded in the attempt to make a Protestant of the great friar. He was a reformer within the Church, was concerned with moral, not with doctrinal reformation. Yet his attitude towards the pope shows that he was at least half a Protestant, or better expressed, an unconscious Protestant. In his teaching, too, he lays stress on the spirit rather than the letter, and his insistence on spiritual religion must have made it difficult at times to preserve allegiance to the traditional hierarchy. Inwardness, spirituality, not the performance of ceremony, is the mark of the true Christian. He did not, indeed, dispense with rite, but with him, as with Christ, rite is not religion. "The true worshipper," he insists, "shall worship the Father in spirit and in truth." The multiplication of rite is, in fact, the sign of the decay of real religion. "All fervour, all internal worship is dead. Therefore are we come to announce to the world that external worship must give way to internal, and ceremonies are nothing but means to excite the spirit." In this respect we may place him among the heralds of a new age, though his place is not exactly beside Luther and Calvin.

SOURCES.—Le Istorie Fiorentine de Niccoló Machiavelli, edited by Nicolini (1857); English translation in Bohn's Standard Library (1847); Villari, The Two First Centuries of Florentine History, trans. by Linda Villari (1894-95); Perrens, Histoire de Florence (1877), and Histoire de Florence depuis la Domination des Medici (1889); Von Reumont, Lor. de' Medici, translated by Harrison (1876); Armstrong, Lorenzo de Medici and Florence in the Fifteenth Century (1896); Roscoe, Life of Lorenzo de Medici, edited by Hazlitt (1883) (antiquated); Gardner, Florence (Mediæval

Sources of Chapter IV.

Towns Series) (1902); Hyett, Florence: Her History and Art (1903); Villari, La Storia di Ger. Savonarola e de' suoi Tempi (1882), English translation by Linda Villari (1889); Guicciardini, Storia d' Italia, edited by Rosini (1874); Clarke, Savonarola (1878); Armstrong, Florence: Savonarola (in Cambridge Modern History, i.) (1902); Harford, Life of Michael Angelo Buonarotti (1857).

CHAPTER V.

The Emancipation of the Communes in France.

In Provence, as in Lombardy, the emancipation movement was inspired by the revival of commerce and industry, which quickened civic life and lent strength to the reaction against feudal oppression. From Provence it spread to the north, and though its political effects were not so far reaching as in Italy, they were, nevertheless, of capital importance in the social and political progress of the people. In Italy, as we have seen, the movement became hostile to the emperor, was actuated by a republican and nationalist spirit, and contributed to the decline of the imperial power south of the Alps. In France it was the ally of the crown in the struggle with the feudal magnates, and though it is incorrect to say that the earlier Capetian kings, like Louis VI., systematically befriended the communes in the conflict with their feudal superiors, some of their successors, such as Louis VII. and Philip Augustus, were shrewd enough to adopt the policy of emancipation in the interest of the crown, if not of the people. The political effects of the movement were not, however, limited to the aggrandisement of the monarch at the expense of the nobility. The communes erelong emerged as the Third Estate, and in this capacity became, as we shall see, a recognised political power in the nation. Their emancipation was thus the first step in the political as well as the social progress of the people. The commune did not, indeed, attain the same high level of power in France as in Italy. It did not develop into the republic, for the power of the monarch was greater in France than the power of the emperor in Italy. The grand enemy of the monarch was not the commune, but the feudal magnate, and the growth of the monarchic supremacy was at first favourable both to liberty and order. It was the most potent factor in the reaction against feudalism, and it made for the unity of the nation. It saved France from the calamity of republican anarchy which desolated Lombardy and Tuscany, and which, but for its powerful action, would have aggravated the disintegration of the feudal kingdom. In the long run, however, this monarchic supremacy proved as fatal to liberty as the despotisms to which republican anarchy exposed the Italian republics. The time was to come when the monarch should deprive not only the feudal lord, but the Third Estate of all political power, and play the despot as unrestrainedly as any petty Italian prince.

If the feudal system destroyed the municipal autonomy of the Gallo-Roman cities, it favoured the formation of new clusters of population. Many of the villages that grew up around the feudal donjon, the wealthy abbey, swelled into towns— Montpellier, Montauban in the south for example; St Denis, St Omer, Bruges, Ghent, Lille in the north. In the eleventh and twelfth centuries a large number of new towns thus emerged into prominence in addition to the old cities of Roman Gaul. Some of these new centres of population probably owed their rise to the need of security, which drove the peasants to seek the shelter of some neighbouring stronghold from the ravages of Norman marauders. The attraction of a wealthy abbey, where the conditions of serfage were often more tolerable, the means of subsistence more abundant, than on the secular domain, swelled, in other cases, the aggregate of settlers into a large community; or the institution of a fair sufficed to transform the village into the nascent town.

While population tended to centralise under the action of such causes, this centralisation only very gradually led to the revival of a vigorous civic life. With the decline of commerce, the difficulty of communication, these communities seem to have languished for centuries in a state of social comatose. They grew up under the shadow of feudalism; it was long before the rays of liberty penetrated that dank atmosphere and quickened that growth into maturity. Civic freedom could not thrive under a system which diminished the number of freemen and subordinated individual rights to the rights of the feudal superior. The inhabitants of the towns were as much the dependants of this superior as the villeins of the rural domain. They were subject to his jurisdiction, and owed him a variety of dues, services. They were exploited for the benefit of a master, in many cases of several masters, for the same city might have two, or even, as at Amiens, four feudal superiors—the king, the bishop, the count or viscount, the chatelain. In some cases, as at Marseilles, Toulouse, Tours, Arles, Narbonne, the old Gallo-Roman city was subject to the bishop; the "burg" which had grown up around some baron's stronghold, or some great abbey, was under the jurisdiction of the count, viscount, or abbot. Even the various quarters of the city might be subject to different superiors, and in such cases constituted separate, and often hostile, communities.

The *régime* of this superior was absolute enough. It was within his right to tax the inhabitants at pleasure, transfer them to another superior, summon them to follow him in arms. The arraignment of his *régime*, which the people drew up at a later period, in support of their demand for a charter, shows that it gave unlimited scope for terrible abuses. This oppression sometimes led to revolt, but in the absence of an active civic life, revolt only rarely led, before the end of the eleventh century, to the concession of some measure of liberty. Nevertheless some of the elements of self-assertion were there, and in the cities of the south, in particular, the wealthier part of the community seems to have made its influence felt on its affairs. From its ranks the superior, with the professed assent of the people, nominated the officers—the advocate, the *scabini*, or *échevins*—to whom he entrusted the administration of justice. The custom of associating for commercial, industrial, charitable, or religious purposes was, in itself, a certain check on the exercise of arbitrary power. It only needed the revival of commerce and industry to endue these corporations with the vigour necessary to transform the defence of interests into the demand for rights.

The revival came, as we have seen, in the wake of the crusades, and in the wake of this revival came, in its turn, to France as to Italy, the emancipation movement. Once fairly launched, its progress was irresistible, in spite of the obstacles in the way of progress. To break down the social tyranny which had deprived the great mass of men of their rights as freemen, might well seem a Quixotic enterprise. Prestige prejudice, privilege, power, were all arrayed against it. But the mighty factor of numbers was in favour of the cause of liberty, and as in the case of all popular movements, success was primarily a question of the organisation of numbers. Its strength lay in the principle of association for a common object, for whose operation the merchant gild, the artisan corporation, the religious and charitable fraternities paved the way. The great feature of the movement is "the conjuration," which united the people in the determination to force the amelioration of their condition. All through the Middle Ages the conjuration is the device of the miserable. Here and there the people is found taking counsel together, holding its secret assemblies, calculating its numbers, and making trial of its strength in spasmodic rising. In the "Roman de Rou" some peasant, bolder than the rest, bids his fellows bethink themselves that they are a thousand to one, and are men with arms and souls as well as any mailed baron. Why, then, submit to be miserable? Why not be men and fight the oppressor? Thus the thought of rights to champion, of collective force to vindicate them, gleams at times, in furtive fashion, like a sun-ray of hope into the gloom of omnipresent wretchedness. Alas, such spasmodic attempts to force the amelioration of their material lot were speedily nipped in the bud. When the Norman peasants thus took courage, about the beginning of the eleventh century, to assemble together and deliberate on the reform of feudal usage, the soldiers of Duke Richard II. swooped down on their assembly, cut off the hands and feet of the popular deputies, and thus gave a bloody object-lesson in the duty of submission to their miserable constituents.

Though the "conjuration" had thus hitherto been impotent enough against oppression, the awakening vigour of civic life now transformed it into a powerful instrument of attack. While the people became formidable by the organisation of numbers, its enemy was weakened by division. Whatever its formal harmony, feudalism was lacking in cohesion. Its spirit was pugnative; it wasted its strength in petty warfare, and even when the crusades unified it in the general enterprise of a Holy War, they exhausted its strength at the very time that the cities were experiencing the quickening effects of the crusading spirit. The multiplicity of jurisdictions, in many of the towns, likewise played into the hands of the emancipationists. While the people associated, their local seigneurs continued to quarrel and fight, and in order to gain popular support against a rival, championed the popular demands. Moreover, the hostility of lay lords towards the ecclesiastical magnates, the intervention of the greater barons against the oppressive *régime* of the lesser, similarly stood the popular cause in good stead at times. The Count of Amiens, for example, is found, from ostensibly philanthropic motives, interposing on behalf of the people, against the viscounts of his county; and the Count of Nevers, in his hatred of the monks, exhorts the inhabitants of Vézelai to revolt against the jurisdiction of the Abbot of St Madeleine, and even offers them his alliance. " I am profoundly afflicted by the miserable condition to which you are reduced," quoth the count to an assembly of the men of Vézelai, " for, possessing many things in appearance, you are in reality masters of nothing. Nay, you do not even enjoy in any fashion your natural liberty. At the sight of these beautiful lands (belonging to the abbey), these superb vineyards, these fertile pasturages, these fruitful fields, these shaggy woods, these trees heavy with fruit, these splendid buildings—all these things which, by their situation even are within your resort, whilst you are deprived of the possibility of enjoying them—I cannot but feel for you a very tender compassion. . . . If, therefore, you will conclude with me a sworn treaty of mutual alliance, and if you will remain faithful to me, you will enjoy my protection, and I will strive to deliver you from every oppressive exaction, from all obnoxious rents and services, and will also defend you from all the ills that threaten to overwhelm you." Such philanthropic professions might be actuated by self-interest, but the protection of such magnates, who had quarrelled with the ecclesiastical dignitaries, or coveted their broad possessions, was none the less helpful to the cause of emancipation.

In spite of incipient antagonism on the part of the feudal superior, the movement spread with the force of fate over France. It was one of these periods when human society undergoes a transformation which obliterates the landmarks of centuries. Sometimes these crises are born of great principles which overmaster the minds of men and call forth the highest faculties of soul and mind. In this civic reaction against feudalism there is little of this heroic devotion to ideal principles. There are no impassioned theorists who dilate on the rights of man, the sovereignty of the people. The world does not resound with the battle-cries of freedom which were to stir future generations with a sort of religious fervour. The profession of high doctrines of natural equality, of human solidarity, are indeed found in the preambles of charters and ordinances, but it is merely the stereotyped phraseology of the lawyers. It is found, too, in an occasional sermon, but the preacher is no impassioned prophet of a general movement in favour of ideal verities, no Peter the Hermit with a popular mission. It appears in the "Roman de Rou," where the poet puts into the mouths of his rustics some reflections on the dignity and rights of mankind, but Wace was probably making his rustic orator speak merely his own sentiments. It is not in such professions that the principles of the movement are to be sought. The movement was born of lowlier aspirations, had no higher ideal than the amelioration of the accumulated misery of the centuries. The complaint of the ordinary man is concerned with the facts of his daily existence. It is the interest of his vocation, whether as peasant, artisan, merchant, that stirs him to action. His object is merely to strike a bargain with his oppressor, and the bargain relates not to verities of a transcendental order, but to the affairs of common life. He will have liberty to keep body and soul together, with some measure of security from the petty tyrannies that make life a wretched struggle with adversity. He will, in particular, have a charter which will enable him to protect himself from the arbitrary abuse of power, will regulate dues and taxes, will define usage, will substitute law for license, will guarantee him some measure of control over the affairs of the community. There is no flourish of transcendental rhetoric in these modest stipulations, yet to the ordinary man they meant much. They assured the improvement of his material lot, and to realise what this improvement involved, it is only necessary to turn to some of the charters and the chronicles. Charters and chronicles are very explicit as to the general misery of humble mankind in these ages. Wherever the advocates of the social system, known as feudal, get their facts in support of their belief in the beneficence of that system, it is certainly not from contemporary records. Extortion, private war, pillage, famine, pestilence, doom the people to an existence of suffering, for which purgatory is the only fitting name. This existence is only tolerable in virtue of the fact that death mercifully intervenes to put an end to its torments. Death, in truth, is the great philanthropist in these feudal-ridden centuries. The Church is sometimes a refuge for the miserable, and the episcopal device of the truce of God affords an occasional respite from the rampant brutality, but generally speaking, the world is a place of torment for the mass of miserable humanity. "Reflecting how miserable is the people in the county of Amiens," begins the charter granted by the count in 1091, "that it is crushed by the viscounts with new and unheard-of calamities, oppressed as was the people of Israel in Egypt by the taskmasters of Pharaoh ... we have been moved by the zeal of charity; the cry of the churches, the groans of the faithful, have touched us with sadness." This pathetic strain is by no means exceptional. The demand or the concession of a charter is usually based on the clamant necessity of deliverance from local oppression, and it is amply enough confirmed by the chroniclers. Open for example the "Life of Louis VI.," by Abbot Suger, his minister and intimate friend; or the "Life" of the abbot himself by William of St Denis; or the "Life of Louis VII.," by the same author. Almost every page is a picture of brutal lawlessness and violence, of which the following snatch must suffice as an example:—"It is the duty of kings to repress with a strong hand the audacity of the tyrants who dislocate the State by their endless wars, take pleasure in pillage, desolate the poor, destroy the churches, and give themselves up to a license, which, if not arrested, would inflame them with an ever-increasing fury. ... Of this, Thomas de Marle affords an apt example. This Thomas, a consummate scoundrel, whom the demon favoured ... like a furious wolf ravaged and devoured the territories of Laon, Reims, Amiens, with such severity that he was not debarred by fear of ecclesiastical penalties from attacking the clergy, or by any sentiment of humanity from cruelly oppressing the people. Massacring and destroying, he took from the Convent of St John, at Laon, two rich domains. He fortified the high towers, the strongholds of Crécy and Nogent, as if they had belonged to him, and made of them veritable caves of dragons, dens of robbers, and from thence desolated cruelly almost the whole country with fire and pillage." "It is impossible," writes Ives de Chartres, one of the counsellors of Louis VI., "to read with a dry eye the record of the violences inflicted on the inhabitants of Beauvais, the pillage of the houses, the devastation of the fields. Lay and cleric have outvied one another in their pride and their passions." "So terrible was the misery that hung over this city," notes Guibert de Nogent, *à propos* of the situation at Laon, "that no one feared God or any other power, and according to his ability and caprice, filled the republic with murder and rapine. . . . And what shall I say of the state of the people? No peasant could enter the town, no one could even approach it, who was not thrown into prison and forced to ransom himself, or cited to trial without any real cause and under the first pretext that presented itself. . . . The magnates and their minions committed publicly robbery and brigandage with armed hand; there was no security for any one who ventured by night into the streets; to be held up, seized, or killed — such was the fate that awaited him." This, be it remembered, is the testimony of an inveterate enemy of the emancipation movement, of one who denounced "the new and execrable name of Commune." The testimony of another enemy is equally conclusive. "The race of Saracens" (the feudal nobility), cries Adalbéron, Bishop of Laon, "always ready to strike rude blows, occupies, sword in hand, the kingdom of the Franks, and holds it bowed under its yoke. On all hands, blood moistens and reddens the earth; the streams are swollen with the blood of horrible carnages. . . . Alas, there is no limit to the tears and groans of the serfs." "These men," laments an anonymous preacher, in speaking of the tyranny of the barons, "have claws, and study how to tear their subjects. They live with the wild beasts, that is to say, they associate with accomplices as cruel and savage as themselves. They devour their subjects, as the wolf the lamb, by their oppressions, their exactions." The

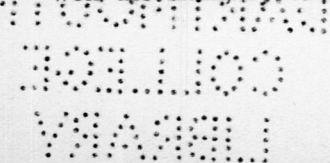

Hostility of Bishops and Abbots. 93

following refers to a later period, and is taken from the " Life of Philippe Auguste," by William the Breton. "Count Renaud" (of Boulogne), he tells us, "oppressed the churches of God, for which cause he was almost continually under excommunication. He robbed the poor, the widows, and orphans, and pursued with his hatred the neighbouring nobles."

The bitterest enemies of the emancipation movement were, however, not the lay superiors, but the bishops and abbots, who clung tenaciously to their rights of jurisdiction. The loss of these meant the diminution of both their power and their revenues, and the ecclesiastical spirit, which invested both the power and the property of the Church with a divine sanction, resolutely withstood all considerations of utility contrary to its own advantage. The popes were equally opposed to any curtailment of the feudal jurisdiction of the higher clergy, which materially increased the papal income. The Church is not even entitled to the merit of systematically championing the enfranchisement of the serf, though it has till lately been credited by the historians with the consistent and unvarying advocacy of the rights of the humble masses. The more enlightened of the clergy professed indeed the doctrine of natural equality and Christian brotherhood, and advocated by precept and example the humane treatment of the oppressed. "In the presence of Christ," insisted Ives de Chartres, "there is neither serf nor free. All men admitted to the sacraments are equal." The worldly minded prelate of the day by no means shared such humanitarian sentiments, though they might be in accord with the gospel he professed to preach. He preferred to emphasise the scriptural dogma of obedience, and exercise his ingenuity in demonstrating that the serfage of the masses was part of the divine order. "Serfs," we read in one of these characteristic episcopal harangues (that of an Archbishop of Reims), "be submissive at all times to your masters, and take not, as a pretext of revolt, their harshness or their avarice. The canons of the Church declare anathema those who excite the serfs to disobedience." "Enfranchisement," to quote M. Fournier, whose investigations have thrown new light on this subject, "had for its object the lessening of every tie between the Church and its bondsmen. The Church, therefore, eager to conserve on its lands and under its authority as large a number of dependants as possible, looked on emancipation with an unfavourable eye, and strove to limit its effects by onerous conditions, which practically nullified them." Its phraseology was benevolent, its practice was tyrannic enough. The clergy in general acted as proprietors, not as philanthropists, *i.e.*, in accordance with the interests of their order. They might favour the enfranchisement of the serfs of lay landowners, and, by offering an asylum to these freedmen, attract them to their own domains; but they assumed jurisdiction over those to whom they gave domicile. They did not encourage emancipation on principle, and only enfranchised their own serfs in return, as a rule, for some compensatory advantage. They are, for instance, found emancipating a serf, or a serf's children in return for a sum of money, or for the piece of land which he cultivated. They took care to be paid for their generosity. They rarely accorded full freedom, but reserved certain rights, restrictions intended to retain the freedman under their patronage, their jurisdiction, and revoked the freedom accorded if the conditions were not fulfilled to the letter. These conditions were usually more onerous than in the case of the emancipations conferred by laymen, and it is more correct, generally, to say that they modified, rather than abolished, serfage in their domains.

The emancipation movement, whether of the serf or the commune, was, I repeat, a social and economic, not a political or philanthropic movement. It has, nevertheless, a higher signification than that attaching to the amelioration of the material lot of the people. It brings the people into prominence as a social, if not, as yet, as a political factor. It is a sign of reviving life after centuries of stagnation. It represents the rising protest against a caste domination largely based on usurpation and force. The small freeman regained his place in the social system, and secured protection against arbitrary oppression as a member of the community. He could assert himself where his interests were concerned, and if these interests were limited to the smaller matters of his circumscribed life, the assertion of them led to higher things, afforded a training for a larger and loftier destiny. The descendants of the merchant, the craftsman who stood up to petty local oppression, and learned to participate in the administration of his town, will be found one day standing up to the oppression of the monarch, and claiming a voice in the administration of the State.

The movement, however limited its aspiration, has, too, its heroic side. It did not achieve success without a struggle in many towns. M. Thierry, the historian of the Third Estate, has, indeed, exaggerated its violent side. It did not develop into a regular Jacquerie, like that which accompanied the democratic movement of the fourteenth or the eighteenth century. The incipient antagonism of the feudal superiors relaxed in face of the general demand for a charter, and consented to come to terms. Many of the communes, profiting by the pecuniary embarrassments of their superiors, bought their privileges, and, in such cases, the revolution was little more than a monetary transaction. In some cases the superior freely co-operated in the establishment of the commune. In others, on the contrary, the movement only triumphed at the point of the pike, and in such cases victory was dearly bought, particularly where victory only came as the result of repeated failure. Even in the south, where the community seems to have preserved and gradually increased some of the elements of municipal life, the people sometimes, as at Toulouse, Montpellier, Nismes, Béziers, had recourse to violence in order to quicken the concession of a larger measure of liberty. At Béziers, for example, the citizens, in spite of the entreaties of their bishop, murdered their viscount and his followers in the church of La Madeleine (1167). The struggle was most severe in the north—in Champagne and Vermandois—where the victory seems at the same time to have been most complete. It was in the towns along the Oise, Aisne, Somme, that the greatest degree of municipal liberty was secured, and it was here, especially in the episcopal cities, that the most heroic and also tragic scenes were enacted. In these scenes the selfish and barbarous conduct of some of the bishops, who acted the tyrant with the words of Christ on their lips and the passions of the savage in their hearts, is as repulsive as the brutal excesses of the people who knew not how to temper fury with mercy. Both sides indulged in and suffered terrible brutalities, according as either gained or lost the mastery for the time being. At Laon, in particular, passion sated itself in terrible ferocities. In the absence of the bishop, Gaudri, who kept a negro as his hangman and maintained his authority by the excesses of terror, the people established the commune in 1106. After swearing to recognise it, the bishop bribed the king, Louis VI., to abolish it in 1112. In their fury the people closed their shops and rallied in their thousands at the cry of "Commune" for the attack on the episcopal palace. The overweening contempt of Gaudri, who had nothing but disdain for the threats of the rabble, cost him his life. The "rabble" burst into the castle and tore its episcopal tyrant, who hid himself in a wine cask, in pieces. It meted out the same cruel fate to every cleric or noble who was not fortunate enough to escape, and gave the finishing touch to its triumph by pillaging and burning their houses. Its triumph was short-lived. Louis marched on the doomed city, massacred the victors of yesterday, and abandoned it to the pillage of his brutal soldiery and the peasants of the surrounding district (1114). The movement was only checked, however, and a few years later the commune was partially re-established with the assent of both king and bishop.

Amiens, Sens, Vézelai, Beauvais, Cambrai were likewise the scenes of bitter conflict. These afford, indeed, the worst examples of the mingling of the heroic, the tragic, the brutal element in the struggle, but in many other towns the popular cause only triumphed at the point of the sword. Other heads fell besides that of the episcopal tyrant of Laon. At Sens, at Vézelai, for example, the abbot superior paid for his resistance with his life, and fierce must have been the popular rage that in such an age did not scruple to strike down the sacred, if obnoxious persons of refractory ecclesiastical dignitaries.

It is impossible to range these communities under one category. The measure of liberty varied with the charter. Some of the cities of the south secured a large measure of autonomy, were in fact little behind those of Lombardy and Tuscany in their vindication of self-government. Arles, Marseilles, Béziers, Narbonne, Montpellier, Toulouse, Perigueux, where the power of the feudal suzerain was reduced to a minimum, were almost sovereign republics. In the north, on the other hand, emancipation from the jurisdiction of the superior was, as a rule, less extensive, and in what it is usual to term the burgher towns (*villes de bourgeoisie*) the rights of the community were still more restricted. The lowest in the scale was the rural community, whose charter, whether it applied to a single village or to a confederacy of villages, was couched in much humbler terms than that of the large and thriving city. No greater mistake, therefore, than to imagine the communes as all of one type. They varied both with the locality and the circumstances of their emancipation. The only common feature is the charter, but the charter varied greatly in scope and character, except in cases where one city or town or village merely copied the constitution of another. We should be equally mistaken if we were to conceive of their organisation as uniform. The number, names, mode of appointment of the magistrates were by no means of one pattern. In the south they often appear under the name of consuls, councillors, capitols; in the south-west, instead of consuls, we hear of a mayor and a jury (*jurati*), or syndics. These officials, as a rule, governed the commune in co-operation with a council, and in some of the cities we light upon the parliament or general assembly of the citizens which elected the magistrates, and appears to have been occasionally consulted on important affairs. Office, however, seems to have been the privilege of the nobles and the wealthier citizens, and we even meet occasionally, as in Italy, with the *podesta*. Municipal organisation in the south in fact closely resembles that of the Lombard cities. In the north, on the other hand, the members of the municipal council appear as *échevins*, aldermen; in the north-west as jurymen (*jurés*) or peers, with a mayor or chief magistrate. They were not in many cases elected as in the south, but appointed by the feudal superior, or were merely the representatives of an oligarchy of wealthy families, " *les grands*," as Guibert de Nogent calls them.

It is only a singular partiality that has seen in these self-governing communities fully fledged democracies of the modern municipal type. The people helped to win the charter; they did not, in many cases, obtain a voice in the administration. Self-government frequently meant the government of the richer classes, of a *bourgeoisie* aristocracy, which in some communities contracted into an oligarchy of wealth. It would be a still greater mistake to infer that these mediæval municipalities leaped at a bound out of their mediæval environment. The commune did not emancipate itself from the feudal system. It merely obtained a legal position in that system. It acquired a certain measure of independence of the feudal superior—greater or less, as the case might be; it did not shake itself free from the feudal institutions of the age. It weakened the jurisdiction of the feudal lord by regulating, reducing, appropriating part of it. The city became a collective fief, and as the holder of a fief it attained the status of a vassal. As the vassal was both a dependant of a superior and at the same time the superior of those domiciled on his fief, the city was the dependant of a suzerain, and at the same time invested by charter with certain rights of jurisdiction within its walls. The characteristic result of this revolution is the fixation of rights and obligations on the model of those of lord and vassal. The city obtains a recognised place in the feudal hierarchy. It advances from absolute dependence, virtual serfage, to the modified independence of the vassal, and its share of autonomy is proportionate to its obligations towards the superior on the one hand, and its rights of jurisdiction over the inhabitants on the other. The revolt against feudalism thus does not destroy the system, but only weakens the power of the feudal caste by limiting its tyranny. The town or city is emancipated from direct submission to a single superior, or a couple of superiors, and passes under the jurisdiction of a collective superior in the person of its municipality. This might be a great reform, and its greatness varied according as the municipality was elective and thus responsible to the citizens, or not; but it was not a revolution in the sense of sweeping away root and branch the institutions of centuries. The destruction of the feudal system in France was the work of the king, not of the towns, and though the king was already at work, we are still a long way from the days of Louis XI. and Richelieu. As a vassal, the commune still owed its superior homage, dues, aids, military service, though its obligations were henceforth strictly regulated. On the other hand, its magistrates acquired administrative and, in some cases, sovereign rights within the area of their jurisdiction. They could wage war and make peace with more or less independence; could, especially in the south, contract alliances, form leagues with other cities in defence of their interests; could acquire lands, and thus, as the superiors of a fief, receive the homage of their vassals. They exercised legislative, judicial, and executive powers more or less extensive, levied taxes, commanded the town militia, made use of their own seal, had their *beffroi*, belfry, fortified donjon, like any feudal magnate, where the charter and the archives were jealously guarded, and whence the town bell, the deep-voiced Roland, gave the alarm in case of danger, or summoned the people to the public assembly. In many cases these powers represented virtual, if not absolute, autonomy; in others there were considerable reservations in favour of the superior, lay or cleric, and these reservations were the source of much future quarrel and conflict, especially in the north, where they were more extensive. The prelates long remained their most inveterate enemies, for the communes were not minded to respect either their pretensions or their immunities. The mitred superior of those days was certainly not conspicuous for forbearance or self-sacrifice in regard to the things of this world, and the unedifying spectacle frequently presents itself of the ministers of Christ engaged in fomenting strife and bloodshed, as well as repelling attacks against themselves. Harmony was often lacking, too, within the commune itself. In France, as in Italy, the exercise of power became the monopoly of a few rich citizens, and the oppressive *régime* of this corrupt *bourgeoisie* class led to conspiracy and sedition, of which the confraternity or secret society was the focus. In France, too, as in Italy, social antagonism was aggravated by the spirit of faction begotten by the rivalries of leading families. These intestine feuds afforded a handle, if not for the elevation of some local despot, as in Italy, for the intervention of the monarch, who, while repressing abuses, took advantage of the situation to increase the power of the crown at the expense of municipal independence. The monarch pursued, in fact, the same policy towards the feudal commune as towards the feudal magnate—that of limiting its jurisdiction in favour of the royal authority

It is not easy to define the initial attitude of the French monarchs towards the communal movement. It was lacking in consistency, and was certainly not, even in the case of Philip Augustus, uniformly favourable. It was governed by policy, and this policy was subject to variable influences. The supremacy of the crown was the great aim of the Capetian monarchs from Louis VI. onwards, and as the weakening of the power of the feudal magnate was indispensable to the increase of this supremacy, the monarch appears at times ready enough to aid in the emancipation of the towns on the domains of the turbulent nobles. In episcopal cities the motive for co-operation was still stronger, for emancipation transformed the commune into an immediate fief of the crown.* Within the royal domains, on the other hand, the royal attitude towards the movement before the reign of Philip Augustus was distinctly conservative, for here complete emancipation would have lessened the feudal power of the monarch over his immediate dependants. These facts help to explain the vacillation from co-operation to resistance on the part of a Louis VI., a Louis VII., and even a Philip Augustus. The position of the king, too, rendered it difficult to observe a uniformly friendly attitude, even if he were personally inclined to do so. If the diminution of the power of the feudal nobility was beneficial to that of the crown, it was at the same time part of the task of the monarch to maintain the general interest, to preserve the peace, and suppress outrage. The outbreak of popular violence, as at Laon and Amiens, demanded the energetic intervention of the central power, and as between the two contending parties, whose mutual hatred rendered an enforced truce necessary, it was not possible always to champion the popular side, and yet ensure public order. The time had not yet come when the monarch could afford to beard the power of feudalism with impunity, though a Louis VI. is seen in Suger's biography

* The bishop or abbot held his fief, his temporalities, from the crown, and his tenure was only provisional. At his decease the fief returned to the king, and was administered by him till another nomination was made. In case of emancipation the commune became directly subject to the crown, and the abolition of the episcopal immunity thus favoured the direct exercise of the royal authority over the city.

manfully bringing some of the recalcitrant barons to bay. Other motives of a less reputable stamp sometimes underlay the royal action. The king in the person of a Louis VI. and even of a Philip Augustus, appears willing at times to help the side that would pay most. "The covetousness of the king" (Louis VI.), says Guibert de Nogent, "inclined him to take the side that offered most." It is only as we take into account this complexity of motive that we can form an adequate idea of the royal attitude towards the movement. To regard it, with M. Thierry, for example, as purely opportunist would be one-sided. To see in it, on the other hand, the evidence of democratic patronage, or pure benevolence, is equally visionary. The fact seems to be that the policy of Louis VI., Louis VII., and to some extent Philip Augustus, was actuated by a mixture of motives derived from considerations of the increase of the royal authority, the maintenance of the public interest, and, more or less, the pecuniary advantage of the moment. It was to a certain extent opportunist. Witness the mercenary conduct of Louis VI. and Philip Augustus in the case of Laon, for instance, or the frequent refusal of emancipation within the royal domains, while favouring it at the expense of the feudal magnates. It was nevertheless influenced by larger considerations. Witness the frequent appeal to the king to act as arbiter, the efforts of Louis VI., Louis VII., Philip Augustus, Louis IX., to bring to bear on the strife the demands of justice and the public interest.

This appeal is important in view of the sequel. It gave the king a handle not only for intervention, but for claiming and exercising jurisdiction in the internal affairs of the communes, which proved fatal to their independence. The pretext became a right, and the anxiety of the commune to obtain the royal sanction of its charter, and thus increase its validity as against the local superior, greatly accelerated the process. It was the exercise of this right of interference that led to the curtailment of their liberties and their virtual suppression in the fourteenth century. The maladministration of the local oligarchy, the popular conspiracies and revolts against its oppressions, the appeal for justice to the Parliament of Paris, to the Chamber of Accounts against its corrupt financial *régime*, contributed to undermine its autonomy by transferring the administration into the hands of the royal officials. "The king (through these officials)," says M. Lavisse, in reference to the municipal history of the fourteenth century, "exercised the supreme jurisdiction, and his authority was necessary for every important measure." Instead of the mayor and jury, we find the royal provost appointed by and representing the king, and though the community retained some of its privileges and liberties, it lost its seigneurial jurisdiction, its internal independence. In view of the abuses which inhered in the *régime* of the collective as in that of the single feudal superior, the loss was not a calamity to the people, though the exactions of the royal officials did not render the royal *régime* by any means an unmitigated boon. Emancipation is a noble word, but in too many cases it meant merely the transfer of the mass of the people from the jurisdiction of a single superior to that of a corrupt oligarchy, meant rather the emancipation of the city than of its inhabitants. The imperfect reform of one age may be the abuse of another, and this emancipation within feudal limits shows how little reform the feudal system was capable of. It was too much steeped in the spirit of caste to be the nurse of progress for the people at large.

SOURCES.—Poème d'Adalbéron sur le Regne de Robert; Histoire du Monastère de Vézelai, par Hugues de Poitiers; Vie de Louis le Gros (Louis VI.), par Suger; Vie de Suger, par Guillaume, Moine de St Denis; Vie de Louis le Jeune (Louis VII.), also attributed to Suger; Vie de Guibert de Nogent, par lui-même; Vie de Philippe Auguste, par Rigord, continued by Guillaume le Breton—all in Guizot's Collection (Suger's works have found a recent editor in M. Aug. Molinier); Vie de Louis le Gros, suivie de la Vie du Roi Louis VII.; Joinville, Histoire de St Louis, edited by Wailly; Luchaire, Les Premiers Capetiens, in t. ii. of the Histoire de France, edited by Lavisse; Flach, Les Origines de l'Ancienne France, t. ii. (1893); Giry et Réville, Emancipation des Villes, le Commerce, et l'Industrie au Moyen Age, chapters 8 and 9 in t. ii. of Histoire Générale (1893); Gasquet, Précis des Institutions, t. ii. (1885); Giry, Documents sur les Relations de la Royauté avec les Villes en France de 1180 à 1314 (1885);

Sources of Chapter V.

Fournier, Les Affranchisements du Ve au XIIIe Siècle, Revue Historique (1883); Pirenne, L'Origine des Institutions urbaines au Moyen Age, Revue Historique (1893 and 1896); Lavisse, Le Pouvoir Royal au Temps de Charles V., Revue Historique (1884); Thierry, Essai sur l'Histoire du Tiers Etat, which, however, should be compared with the researches of more recent writers.

CHAPTER VI.

THE THIRD ESTATE AND THE STATES-GENERAL IN FRANCE.

WHILST the king suppressed the feudal commune, he created the Third Estate, and the creation of the Third Estate was a more important act than the emancipation of the commune on feudal lines. In the Third Estate the people attained some measure of political power, and expanded once more into the collective body of freemen. As yet, however, it by no means represented the people in the larger modern sense, the mass of the nation. It merely represented the communes, and the communes, as we have seen, were far from being municipal democracies. They were made up, for the most part, of the *bourgeoisie* notables. As for the rural population, it does not seem to have been represented to any large extent, though a few village communes seem to have sent delegates to the assembly of 1308. The States-General, in which the Third Estate took part, were composed of nobles, clergy, and deputies of towns. In fourteenth-century France, as in the republics of ancient times, there was still an inferior, unfortunately a very large inferior, element, which was denied political rights. Nevertheless, this emergence of the people, such as it was, in a political capacity from the political nullity of many centuries, is sufficiently startling by its novelty, and is of great prospective importance. The fact that an order, nominally, if not really, representative of the nation, takes its place beside the dignitaries of Church and aristocracy, reveals the transformation that has taken place in the feudal State. It shows that, with the growth of the royal power, the people already count politically for something. The commune has at least organised the middle class, made its corporate influence felt. It was the preparation for the States-General, and it is during the period when the feudal commune begins to disappear that the States-General heave in sight. Though the States-General were by no means the assembly of the sovereign people, they were, in spite of limitations, to play a great *rôle* at times in the history of France. In fifty years from the period of their organisation, we shall find them, for instance, during a temporary lapse of the royal authority, playing the part of the sovereign power in the nation.

Philip IV. is generally regarded as the creator of the Third Estate as a political factor, and the States-General of 1302 are cited as evidence of the fact. There were, however, assemblies in which representatives of the communes took part, before this date. Philip's immediate predecessors, Philip III. and Louis IX., summoned consultative assemblies before taking some important step in policy or administration. The "Parliament" of the nation * never quite fell into abeyance, however shadowy its form, since the establishment of the Franks in Gaul. Even before their advent, the representatives of the Gallic cities were occasionally found meeting in general session to review the administration of the Roman officials and transmit their grievances to the emperor. Throughout the Merovingian and Carolingian periods the political assembly of the magnates, at least, subsisted, though its function appears, under the stronger monarchs, to have been consultative rather than legislative. It was not always a subordinate factor, however, and one memorable example of its self-assertion we have seen in the memorable assembly of the magnates of Church and State which met at Senlis to substitute the monarch of its choice for the last of the Carolingians. After the election of Hugh Capet these assemblies became more frequent under the name of Councils or Curiæ. But they, at the same time, became narrower, and at length contracted into the Royal Council, whose members were chosen by the king. Still, the larger assembly is occasionally perceptible, and it is certain that, after the emancipation of the communes, representatives of the towns took part in some of them.

Before the reign of Philip IV., however, such reunions were merely the germ of the States-General, and it is the

* In applying the terms "nation" and States-General to mediæval France, we must be careful to discriminate. The French nation hardly existed as yet in the modern sense.

distinctive merit of this king that he systematised an irregular practice into a constitutional institution. It is only in his reign that the Third Estate appears as a distinctly constituted order alongside those of clergy and nobles, summoned to give advice at some crisis of affairs, and express its approval of some important measure. The frequency of these assemblies, whether national or local, reveals the fact that they possessed a distinctive function in the State. In 1290, 1302, 1303, 1308, 1314, the king sought, and acted by, the advice of the Estates. The work of government had become more complex with the growth of the monarchic power, and the king, however anxious to play the master, could not afford to ignore the nation. Though tending towards absolutism, the feudal monarchy, even under a Philip IV., was by no means independent of the age, and there was still ample room for the hammer and anvil policy of a Louis XI. and a Richelieu. The increase of the monarchic power rendered, for example, an increase of revenue indispensable, and though the agents of the king did not scruple, on occasion, to browbeat the taxpayers into submission, it was sometimes necessary to obtain the general assent for extraordinary fiscal measures. Hence the assembly of 1314. Again, the struggle with Pope Boniface VIII., in an age of superstitious devotion, could not be carried to a victorious issue unless national sentiment was pitted against superstition, alien usurpation. Hence the assembly of 1302. Or, the attack on some mighty corporation, some semi-secular, semi-religious Order of Templars, whose ramifications covered the kingdom, and whose wealth was so tempting to royal impecuniosity, demanded some share of vindication as a national act to hide its real character of covetous tyranny. Hence the assembly of 1308. Thus the royal astuteness, in order to justify or render more effective its drastic expedients, systematised the appeal to the nation, drew the nation into closer association with the crown.

We should be guilty of a glaring anachronism, however, were we to see in these assemblies the type of the modern parliament, or even of the Council of the earlier Capetians. The assembly summoned by Philip IV. to Paris or Tours in the fourteenth century differed as widely from the assembly at Senlis in the tenth, as it did from the assembly at Versailles at the end of the eighteenth. Hugh Capet was merely the figure-head of the feudal hierarchy; Philip IV. was its master. It was not as the elected head of the State that he summoned or addressed the barons, clergy, and Third Estate. He speaks in tones of authority comparable almost to those of the Roman Cæsar. The deputies are summoned not to debate or criticise, but merely "to hear, approve, and do what shall be commanded them by the king, without recourse to their constituents." Royalty since the days of Hugh Capet has become not merely hereditary; it has become relatively absolute. Legislation is merely the command of the king given in the presence of the representatives of the nation. Very different, in all essential respects, from the assembly either of 987 or of 1789. The only resemblance to the latter consists in the fact that the three orders meet and consult in separate chambers.

This transformation from Hugh Capet to Philip IV., though apparently revolutionary, was the result of the natural trend of things during the intervening three hundred years, and Philip only embodied this result. In spite of its cast-iron system and pride of power, feudalism lent itself to subordination and disintegration. It was pervaded by the spirit of division, and inevitably tended to dissolution, as a political, if not as a social system. It had no organisation capable of resisting attack if a monarch of energetic personality studiously and steadily set himself to undo it, and the more forceful men of the direct Capetian line knew how to take advantage of its weak points to subvert it by force or diplomacy. A Louis VI., a Philip Augustus, even a Louis IX., were not slow to make use of this double weapon to assert their power over the feudal baron, the feudal ecclesiastic, the feudal commune, and finally the mediæval pope himself. As warriors they are found energetically pursuing the turbulent magnates, sword in hand, and compelling them to observe some measure of moderation in their feuds and oppressions, or join them as their leaders in the defence of the kingdom against the kings of England or the emperors of Germany. The sword of the strong king is his best ally in the struggle for predominance against both internal and external enemies. As justiciaries their striving was to assert the jurisdiction of the royal court— the incipient parliament of later times, with its skilful jurists—

over that of the feudal superior. The king's justice was indeed a boon in an age of multitudinous petty tyrannies and fist right, and was eagerly sought by the weak against the strong. The jurist was the next most potent ally of the king —the man cunning in the law, who strove to give a legal basis to the royal encroachments, and, ignoring the elective origin of the Capetian crown, exalted the royal dignity as a divine right. "The king," insisted the jurist in the "Établissements" ascribed to St Louis, "holds only of God and his sword." Even the earlier Capetians of the less sturdy type of a Henry I., or a Philip I., claimed to be the vicars of God, to govern by divine right, though their ancestor was but yesterday elected king by the suffrages of the magnates. The consecration to their office tended to nurture this idea, and the bishops and abbots, whom they took as their councillors, lent the sanction of theology to the subtleties of the jurists. These anointed kings acknowledged neither pope nor emperor as their superior. They were heads of the Church as well as of the State, as Pope Boniface learned to his cost. As diplomatists, too, they and their councillors were exceedingly clever men. It was mainly by their diplomacy that they ceased more and more to be merely the grand feudal superior, and become more and more the sovereign. Their policy was to accentuate the sovereign under the guise of the superior. The ordinances, the administrative measures, which as superiors they drew up for their own domains, they extended to the domains of other superiors. Louis IX., for example, not only suppressed the judicial duel within the royal domains; he interdicted private war throughout the whole kingdom (1258), and Philip IV. is found repeating the experiment in 1304. Both Louis and Philip profited greatly, too, from the growing practice of "avowals," which withdrew any person avowing himself the subject of the king from the jurisdiction of his local superior. The appeal from the court of the superior to that of the king tended to the same result. A still more effective device was the extension of taxation beyond the feudal aids which the vassal owed to the sovereign. A large revenue was the best guarantee of effective sovereignty, and the revenue of a Philip IV. was swelled by these special or "extraordinary" assessments, as well as by loans, maltôtes (taxes on commercial transactions), and subsidies or income taxes (10ths, 20ths, 50ths, &c.). If resistance showed itself, as it did occasionally, it was disarmed by a skilful combination of craft and force, of cajolery, threats, and executions.

This supremacy, which Philip IV. so energetically exerted in Church and State, the crown henceforth maintained and gradually increased, in spite of temporary relapses in the face of aristocratic and even democratic, or at least middle class, reactions. France never won a magna charta on the strength of these reactions, though they became periodic throughout the long agony of the Hundred Years' War. Charles V. and Charles VII. maintained and continued the work of Philip IV. and his predecessors in spite of seasons of grave danger to the monarchy. Even Philip's insignificant sons, Louis X., Philip V., Charles IV., the last of the direct Capetian line, managed to disarm by vague assurances and promises, never seriously meant, never practically observed, the leagues of feudal magnates, who demanded the restoration of their old rights, and who, unlike the English barons, neither exacted nor secured constitutional guarantees. Even Philip VI., the first of the Valois, who owed his crown, like Hugh Capet, to the suffrages of the magnates, was not minded to be a mere feudal king, and laid a merciless hand on conspiracy and revolt in high places. At the same time, the frequent appeal to the nation, systematised by Philip IV., proves that if the king was master of the magnate, he had become more and more subject to public opinion. Henceforth it was usual to summon representative assemblies, general or provincial, not only in days of grave crisis, but to strengthen some important administrative measure with their approval. They were frequent under the sons of Philip IV., they continued fairly frequent under Philip VI., and they were frequent enough to nurture the spirit of self-assertion in the Third Estate. While the nobles lost more and more prestige and independence as against the crown, the Third Estate came more and more into prominence as a political factor. The city politician of the communes developed in less than a hundred years into the politician of a large and important national order, with some experience of national affairs, and a growing appetite for the exercise of power.

Which fact appears very prominently in the reign of King John, when a veritable storm of reactionary aspiration threatened for a few years to deprive the crown of its acquired prerogative, and transform the monarchy into a middle class republic. The disaster of Poitiers coming in the wake of the disaster of Crécy; the crushing discomfiture of the nobility by the English yeomen; the captivity of the king; the devastations of the brigand bands that pillaged friend and foe alike; the repeated ravages and pestilence; the horrors of brutal war, prolonged from decade to decade, and spreading carnage, pillage, ruin over many a fair region of France; the bankruptcy of the State, in spite of a variety of expedients invented by an oppressive government,—such were the miseries and horrors that bred the revolutionary spirit of 1356-57. Since the king cannot rule, and the nobility cannot fight, let us put our hands to the work and see whether we cannot rule and fight better for ourselves. So reasoned Étienne Marcel and his fellow-members of the Third Estate of Languedoïl, who, along with nobles and clergy, met in session at Paris on the 17th October 1356, a month after the battle of Poitiers. They were in no mood to temporise longer with the administrative abuses that aggravated, and were deemed responsible for, the miseries of the war. They were determined, now that King John was a prisoner in the hands of the Black Prince, to take the administration out of the hands of his corrupt and incapable ministers, and assume the government themselves under the Duke of Normandy as lieutenant of his father. They had already in the previous year (December 1355), in according a subsidy for the maintenance of 30,000 men-at-arms, wrested from the embarrassed monarch the avowal of their right not only to grant, but to collect the taxes by means of a commission chosen from each of the three orders (*élus*). With the king a captive, they could now step into his place and establish something like parliamentary government, if we may use so modern a term. Nothing less than this would satisfy Étienne Marcel, the energetic provost of the Parisian merchants; Robert le Coq, the eloquent and fiery Bishop of Laon; Robert de Corbie; Charles Toussac; Jean de St Aulde; Jean de Pecquigny, and other sworn antagonists of King John's oppressive and corrupt *régime*.

The motives of these popular leaders have been impugned as self-seeking and seditious. Marcel in particular has been accused of using his position as provost to play the *rôle* of demagogue, Le Coq of acting the turbulent part of the disappointed candidate for high political office. They doubtless compromised their cause by the excesses of popular violence, by intrigues with the oppressor of their country, Edward III., by truckling to the personal resentments and ambitions of that questionable personage, Charles the Bad, King of Navarre. Such aberrations from an honest, patriotic course are hard to avoid in a revolutionary crisis of this kind, when the popular leader is at times as much the victim as the director of events. On the other hand, the appalling evils of the time are sufficient to justify their antagonism to the incapacity and extortion that were ruining France, and to explain the resort to drastic measures in order to circumvent their reactionary enemies. In view of this fact, the Third Estate had no reason to be ashamed of the champions who threw themselves into the breach with reckless energy, perhaps, but with the heroism of intense earnestness of purpose. To look for ulterior motives for political action when ruin is staring the country in the face is a rather superfluous task.

The Estates of the north assembled, 800 strong (those of Languedoc met on the 15th October at Toulouse), and set to work to arraign the abuses of administration in support of their drastic demands. They found matter enough for declamation and legislative remedy in the misery of the people, in whose name they professed to speak and act. They did not directly arraign the king, but they showed no mercy to his advisers. Their corruption and their incapacity had exasperated the nation as much as the outrages of the English invader and the brigands, and remedy must forthwith be had if the nation was not to be annihilated by misgovernment as well as by English victories. Not only must these corrupt and incapable ministers be brought to justice, but a committee of the Estates must take their place as the advisers of the crown. Only on these conditions would a subsidy be accorded, and the collection and application of this subsidy must be controlled by them. The importance of these demands is evident. They involve some of the root principles of modern parliamentary government, though the principles are only as yet vaguely expressed—responsibility of ministers, participation of the Estates in the administration, control of taxation. The Estates mean henceforth to conduct the government in co-operation with the king, but some of their spokesmen even hinted that they might dispense with the king in case of necessity. "To demand the deposition of the chancellor is not a very great matter, for in times past the Estates, as history testifies, have deposed the King of France."

From this embarrassing situation the Duke of Normandy meanwhile saved himself by evasion. Under the pretext of consulting his father and his uncle, the Emperor Charles IV., he prorogued the session and hied away to Metz. The Estates were not to be evaded, however, and in February 1357 the duke was forced to convoke them anew. The result was the Grand Ordinance of March of that year, which transferred the constitutional claims of the Estates and their demands for trenchant reforms out of the arena of parliamentary debate into the statute book for the time being. Unfortunately, to incorporate them in the statute book was, as the sequel was to prove, to consign them to the lumber room. The ordinance is merely a monument of an enthusiastic, but transient devotion to the public welfare, begotten of the misery that drove men to despair, and suggested measures that were centuries before their time. The conditions of parliamentary government in France were not yet in existence. The Estates might postulate government by a Council composed largely of members of the three orders, decree the general reform of the State by means of a reforming commission responsible to them, and posit their frequent convocation for legislative purposes. The machine was too disjointed, and, therefore, too weak, to stand the strain of this sudden outburst of parliamentary effort. The orders did not understand how to work harmoniously in the pursuit of common ends. Their jealousies, their divergent aspirations and aims, produced friction within the machine which could only end in its collapse. The two higher orders submitted with reluctance to equality of burdens and representation with the Third Estate, and there was no organised and forcible public opinion behind it to second the energy of its leaders. None of the measures of the Estates had, therefore, the slightest chance of realisation. Even the subsidy, which they resolved to assess and apply by means of their own commissioners, proved a failure. In the exhausted state of the country few had anything left to give. Taxation by parliamentary ordinance was thus as obnoxious as taxation by royal decree, and King John added to the difficulties of the commissioners by declaring the action of the Estates null, and interdicting payment of the subsidy. Still more ominous, the nobility abstained from attending a new session in April, and the clergy would on no account submit to be taxed. Even the representatives of the towns, the Third Estate itself, were by no means unanimous. The essay in parliamentary government thus proved a failure from the outset, and no amount of intrigue or eloquence on the part of Marcel and Le Coq could lend it efficacy.

In these unpropitious circumstances Marcel and Le Coq had recourse to the assistance of the King of Navarre, whom John had thrown into prison at Arleux in Artois, and whom they now summoned from his dungeon to the rescue. Navarre, like Le Coq, was a born orator, and "preached" to the people of Paris for hours at a stretch, from a platform at the Pré aux Clercs, on the abuses of the time, and the necessity for their reformation. He was not a patriot of the transcendental type, however. He had his own wrongs to right, his own ambitions as a claimant to the throne to realise, and his intervention only complicated the difficulty of the situation for Marcel and his coadjutors, as well as for the Duke of Normandy. The reconciliation of Navarre and the duke—the fruit of the popular enthusiasm excited by these "sermons"—proved but a makeshift. The duke tried in vain to nullify their effects by himself "preaching" to the people in their thousands in the market hall (*les Halles*), and inveighing against the futile interference of the Estates in the work of government. They had talked, innovated, decreed subsidies which nobody would pay, and left him meanwhile without a penny to carry on the administration, or defend the country from its enemies. To parry this onslaught, the popular leaders held counter-demonstrations and "preached" themselves hoarse in vindication of the Estates, and in attack on the duke and his creatures. The storm of recriminating oratory only intensified party rancour, and ultimately the duke determined to make an end of it by force. He snubbed the popular leaders who ventured to renew their complaints and remonstrances, quietly gathered an army in the environs of the capital, and prepared to assert himself with its help at a favourable moment. The favourable moment did not come, however. While the brigand bands were ravishing the country far and near, from the Loire to the Seine and beyond, Paris was starving, and it is an evil day for the powers that be when Paris takes to talking politics on an empty stomach. Why does the duke not take action against the brigands, instead of keeping his army idle in the environs and feeding it at the expense of the capital? Why will he persist in listening to evil counsellors and refusing the advice of honest men like the provost of the merchants and the Bishop of Laon? Since no satisfactory answer to these questions was forthcoming, Marcel, profiting by the fury aroused by the execution of the murderer of the duke's treasurer, who had refused to pay a debt owing to his assassin, marched to the royal palace at the head of an armed mob, bent on vengeance (22nd February 1358). There should be an end to this trifling with the demands of the people, and the heads of these evil counsellors, whom the Estates had arraigned in vain, should atone for its sufferings. One of these obnoxious officials, the advocate-general, Regnault D'Aci, had the misfortune to run amuck of the mob on its way to execute its mission of atonement, and was beaten to death in the shop in which he sought refuge. Other victims of higher rank, Jean de Conflans, marshal of Champagne, Robert de Clermont, marshal of Normandy, succumbed to its pikes in the palace itself— Conflans at the very feet of the duke, Clermont while frantically trying to escape. Charles tremblingly supplicated the provost to spare his life, and Marcel, handing him the red and blue bonnet of the popular party, bade him trust to his protection. It is the scene enacted by the *sans culottes* in the Tuilleries before Louis XVI., on the 10th of August 1792, in anticipation. "This has been done by the will of the people," said Marcel, and the abject regent even went the length of formally recognising the justice of the bloody deed and exonerating its perpetrators. " The good of the kingdom demanded the blood of these false traitors," further explained the stern tribune to the crowd on the Place de Grève.

This brusque and bloody species of justice in the name of the people was none the less a mistake as well as a crime. It not only rendered compromise henceforth impossible, as soon as the regent should recover from the terror inspired by the mob; it estranged and embittered the nobles, and made harmony of action by the Estates more hopeless than ever. While Amiens, Rouen, and other towns donned the red and blue bonnet as a mark of their alliance with the Paris *bourgeoisie* in the work of violent reform, the duke slipped out of Paris, summoned the States-General of Languedoïl to Compiegne, and obtained the condemnation of Marcel, Le Coq, and their accomplices, and the nullification of the Grand Ordinance of March 1357, from the angry nobles, who formed the large majority of the assembly. Thus heartened, he seized the fortress of Meaux which commanded the valleys of the Seine and the Marne, and enabled him to cut off the food supply of Paris from the east, as the preliminary to an attack on the capital. In this emergency, Marcel cultivated the King of Navarre still more assiduously, strengthened the fortifications of the city, exacted loans from the wealthier citizens, confiscated the gear of the regent's partisans, and held the opposition in check by a reign of terror. The forceful provost was evidently the prototype of the Dantons, the Robespierres, and other men of terror of a remote posterity, as the movement of which he was the soul is in some respects the exemplar of the modern revolutionary spirit. The attack on the royal palace might in fact, as I have hinted, pass for an anticipation of the attack on the Tuilleries.

The analogy is strengthened by the sudden trend of events in the southern provinces. While the nobles backed the regent, and offered their swords in defence of the established government, the peasants rose in revolt against aristocratic privilege and offered their alliance to the Paris democrats and the King of Navarre. This opportune diversion promised to paralyse the aggressive measures of the regent and the aristocratic party of reaction. The peasants had more excuse for taking the law into their own hands than the Parisian mob. In spite of partial emancipation from serfage, their lot was still that of the burden-bearer of a privileged caste, which exploited them with a heartless indifference to their sufferings, a supercilious disregard of their murmurs. The peasant was fleeced to support his lord's dignity, pay his debts, cater even to his vices. In addition to the pinch of local tyranny he was exposed to the depredations of the English invader, and the temporary respite from invasion merely exposed him in turn to the excesses of the brigand "companies," who roved the country burning, plundering, outraging, murdering at will. Among these brigand chiefs might often be seen the lords whom the rampant lawlessness had transformed into marauding *condottieri*, and whom he had learned, since Crécy and Poitiers, to despise as well as hate. The horrors of the time had driven many a hapless wight literally to seek refuge among the wild beasts, in caves, in pits, in woods, in marshes, in the islets of the river beds, and it is not surprising that he should have issued from these lairs more beast than man, bent on vengeance for the children which hunger or brutality had snatched from him, for his blackened hut, his wasted fields. There were memories, too, of risings against the misery of oppression which had occasionally, all through the later Middle Ages, driven his forefathers to challenge the inhumanity of the strong toward the weak, memories of those bands of Pastoureaux who ever and anon suddenly sprang out of the chaos of misery and swelled into a vast army under the standard of some sturdy rustic leader, and wandered far and near in search of Elysium, until they lost cohesion, and their fragments were crushed by the rally of king and noble. With king and noble in disrepute, why not make trial of our united strength once more? Why not kill these seigneurs, extirpate the whole race of *gentilhommes,* these cowards and traitors who cannot fight, will not protect us from the brigands, have even, many of them, turned brigands themselves? So spoke one gaunt rustic, whose eye burned with the fury of despair. "Truly said, truly said," answered a chorus of approving voices. "A curse on him who would spare one of them alive." Suddenly, towards the end of May, the country round Beauvais and Clermont on the Oise was startled by the appearance of a band of wild, haggard men, armed with bludgeons tipped with iron, knives, hatchets, plough-socks, anything that would batter out the brains of a lord, and generalled by a native of the village of Mello named Calle or Karle, intent on the destruction of the châteaux and their hated owners. The patient, docile creature, whom pillage and murder had driven into the woods, burst forth from his hiding place a wild beast—"like enraged dogs," says Froissart. The excesses of this outburst may have been exaggerated as to details by the chronicler. Froissart is fond of improving a vague report and curdling the blood of his readers by some grim touch of savagery. But even making allowance for exaggerations, artful or credulous, it is certain that many châteaux were burned, those of their owners who were unable to save themselves by flight, tortured and killed, their wives and children, in some cases at least, murdered, and their property confiscated for the benefit of the starving hordes of insurgents. This revolutionary fury spread from district to district like an epidemic, all over the north of France from the Yonne to the Somme, and beyond, where the country had been most harried by the brigands. In the stupor and consternation of the first weeks, there was no attempt at combination and resistance by the nobles, and the itinerant bands swelled to thousands in consequence. Jacques Bonhomme promised to do Marcel's work for him and crush the party of reaction before it could lift a finger in self-defence.

The dictator of the capital saw his advantage and entered into an alliance with Calle, the King of the Jacques, while striving to moderate the savage spirit of his followers. Detachments of Paris militia joined the insurgents, on condition, however, that the atrocities of the first few days of the rising should cease. One of these confederate bands of *bourgeoisie* and peasants laid siege to Meaux, which opened its gates. The fortress (the Marché), however, in which the Duchess of Orleans and over three hundred ladies of noble rank had sought refuge, held out long enough to enable Gaston, Count of Foix, and the Captal of Buch, who were returning from a crusade in Prussia, to hurry from Châlons to the rescue. A single charge of a handful of trained warriors sufficed to scatter the ill-armed rustics in hopeless rout, and several thousand of them were either killed or drowned in the Marne. A terrible retribution now overtook the misguided Jacques as the result of this successful rally of their enemies. The nobles, emerging from their hiding places, banded themselves together in their turn, and attacked the villages, slaying, torturing, burning as they went. The capture and execution of Calle by the King of Navarre, who inveigled the credulous leader to his doom, followed by another butchery at Montdidier, where Navarre attacked and slaughtered 3,000 of them, broke the spirit of his followers. The remnants of the horde were hunted down like so many packs of wolves. Before the end of June 20,000 had perished—a terrible vengeance for the murder of a handful of nobles, some of whom were not free of grave crimes, and the destruction of over a hundred castles.

Though disapproving and condemning the excesses of the Jacques and seeking to moderate their fury, Marcel accepted their alliance. They had the same enemies in the nobles, and the triumph of the one would have been the victory of the other. The defeat of the Jacques consequently meant the defeat of their ally. There was still the King of Navarre to fall back on, and Navarre came to Paris at Marcel's summons to discourse in his facile, patriotic vein to the assembled citizens at the town-house on the necessities of the situation. The main necessity of the situation, the regent having by this time blockaded the capital with 30,000 men, resolved itself into his nomination as captain-general. Another expedient, still more dubious, was to admit within the walls the Anglo-Navarese brigand bands, by whose assistance Navarre hoped to maintain his commanding position, and Marcel to raise the blockade. The presence of the brigands only aroused the alarm and anger of the people, and instead of marching against the foe, people and brigands took to fighting in the streets and in the environs. The odium of the bloodshed fell on the head of the hapless provost, who sent imploring messages to the Flemish cities for assistance. The Flemings would not move, while Navarre withdrew his cutthroat followers to St Denis. His departure did not restore the confidence of the people in its tribune, and for Marcel the outlook was now palpably desperate. The fateful moment had come in the history of revolutions, when the revolutionary leader has reached the end of his resources and at the same time lost command of the situation. On the one hand, the populace, estranged by his maladroit measures, turned against him; on the other, the agents on whom he was reduced to rely were not to be trusted. Navarre, for example, was at one moment overturing the duke, and making terms with an eye chiefly to his own advantage; the next, conspiring with the English to sell his country to Edward III., in return for solid acquisitions of territory for himself. Even in the closer circle of his ostensible supporters there were traitors ready to serve the regent's cause and play him false. As a last desperate resort, the doomed tribune seems to have resolved to give up the city to Navarre and consign the future to his mercies, come what might. Charles the Bad might be King of France under Edward III. and France take the consequences, if a well-meaning patriot could not otherwise extricate himself or it from an impossible situation. It was the last straw of the desperate man, and it failed to keep him from sinking under the billows of fate.

On the night of the 31st July 1358, Navarre with his brigands should, therefore, be admitted within the city as potential King of France. Towards midnight Marcel repaired with a small armed following to the gate St Denis, and ordered the guard to deliver the keys to Josseran de Mâcon, the King of Navarre's treasurer. The guard refused, and it was stiffened in its refusal by Jean Maillart, one of the regent's secret agents, who upbraided the provost in abusive terms. After a hot altercation the disputants separated in flaming anger—Maillart to gallop to the Halles to raise the city with the cry of "Montjoie and St Denis, to the King, to the Duke," Marcel to seize the gate St Antoine. Here, too, the guard demurred to the demand for the keys, and during the debate Maillart appeared on the scene with a motley crowd of armed men. "Show us the letters which you have received from the King of Navarre," demanded he. Marcel refused, and the cry of treason greeted his refusal. "We are betrayed and undone by the provost," shouted an angry voice from the midst of the scowling crowd, and with levelled pikes the mob pressed in upon the hapless tribune and his small following. A desperate struggle, and Marcel and two of his staunchest supporters lay prostrate on the ground. "Why do you me harm?" gasped the luckless reformer, as the blows rained on his prostrate body. "What

I have done, I did for your welfare as well as for my own. Before I began this enterprise you made me swear that I would maintain with all my power the ordinance of the Estates." The mob paid no heed to this dying declaration, and, mingling brutality with rage, dragged the mangled bodies of its victim and his friends through the streets and hung them on a gibbet in front of the church of St Catherine. When Navarre arrived from St Denis, he found the gates barred in his face and the walls mounted by the royalists, who repulsed an attack on the Bastille St Antoine and compelled the would-be king to retire. Charles of Normandy returned to his palace in triumph, two days later, to receive the submission of the cowed city, after the axe of the executioner had prepared the way. Marcel and his scheme of a patriotic parliamentary government had disappeared in the abyss of conflicting and selfish interests, leaving the legacy of faction and civil war to aggravate the horrors of two years of abortive revolution.

The attempt at revolution is notable as, in some respects, an anticipation of the future. There is a distinctly modern note in both the demands of the Estates and the forcible efforts on the part of Marcel and his abettors to realise them. The play of events and influences, which complicates the situation and renders failure inevitable, resembles to some extent the factors at work in the great revolutionary drama of the future. There is the same reactionary tendency on the part of the privileged class, which gravitates in support of the government; the same outburst of insurrection on the part of the peasants; the same revulsion from its leaders, under the influence of terror and intrigue, on the part of the populace of Paris, to the undoing of the would-be reformers. Only, the revolution stopped short at the stage of incipient failure. It does not get the length of universal anarchy. Marcel slain, the duke regained his authority, and the popular movement was nipped in the bud before it could develop into a general upheaval. Paris was cowed, the Jacques were slaughtered, the government was reinstated. *Voila tout.* That is all. Nothing more came of it for another half-century, when the revolutionary outburst proved equally abortive. Time, the mother of revolutions, is tardy in bringing to maturity the aspirations of the ages. It is usual to conclude, therefore, that such a movement, being doomed to failure, should not have been attempted, and its authors are decried accordingly as crack-brained enthusiasts or designing adventurers. The movement was, nevertheless, a necessity of the situation, if only as the safety-valve for the despair of the age. Nor should we forget that the party that triumphs is not therefore the party that has right on its side, or the party that fails the party that is therefore in the wrong. Failure or success in revolutions may be a matter of accident, not of right or wrong, and the blame for the evils incident in such a movement lies frequently at the door of the victors as much as of the vanquished. It is the cause, not the consequence of the revolutionary movement that is mainly responsible for its excesses. In this case the movement was undoubtedly a patriotic attempt on the part of the Third Estate and its leaders to save the people from the intolerable misery of misgovernment, defeat, anarchy. Marcel is the representative, not of a class, but of the people, and there is a ring of sincerity, sympathy, patriotism in his letters to the Flemings in vindication of his cause. "We have indeed need of your help, and of that of the Lord, and all our good friends. Those who will lend a hand in the defence of the good people, the labourers and merchants, without whom we cannot live, against these murderers, robbers, and cruel enemies of God and the faith, will acquire greater merit in the eyes of our Lord than if they went on crusade against the Saracens." His denunciation of the brutal excesses, perpetrated by the nobility in the repression of the peasant revolt, breathes an equally fervid spirit of humanity. To decry such a leader as a visionary, a demagogue, is to ignore the clamant necessities of the situation, to judge the man apart from his environment. If ever antagonism to the government was legitimate, nay, imperative, it was so in the case of the corrupt, crapulous *régime* of King John and his creatures. They were impotent either to rule the country or to defend it. Their incapacity was only too palpable in the crushing defeats which threatened to dismember France, in the anarchy which assigned many of the provinces to the tender mercies of hordes of marauders, in the oppression which drove the maddened peasants to revolt, in the paralysis of authority which could neither devise nor apply a remedy. The misery of the people, exposed to the accumulated horrors of war, famine, pestilence, pillage, exaction, was probably greater than at any time since the Hunnish or Norman invasions. The situation undoubtedly demanded drastic measures. Unfortunately, the situation which invited revolution made its failure inevitable. As well try to sow in the midst of a whirlwind as venture on constitutional experiments at a time when the very existence of the nation is menaced by the foreign foe. Nay, there is as yet hardly a nation to reform, for the feudal state is only being slowly unified in the mould of suffering, and has not reached the stage of a vigorous nationality. There are two parliaments instead of one: the States-General of Languedoïl—the north—which meets at Paris; those of Languedoc—the south—which assembles at Toulouse. North and south are, as yet, in language, in civilisation, in sentiment, almost alien countries, are only just beginning to coalesce for national ends. Besides the lack of national unity, there is a lack of harmony between the orders, whether at Paris or Toulouse. Both clergy and nobility look askance at the Third Estate as an intruder within the privileged hierarchy, and between democratic aspirations and ancient privilege there is an impassable gulf. Moreover, there is no adequate force of public opinion to strengthen the action of the Estates even if harmony could be infused into their deliberations. To reform in accordance with certain ideas, practical or theoretic, is sufficiently difficult at all times. In such circumstances it is utterly futile. The reformer must be content to be the martyr, to atone for his mistakes and forswear the merit of his intentions, to let posterity vindicate his memory and achieve his work. He may account himself happy if he attain to even this species of immortality.

SOURCES.—Chronique de Guillaume de Nangis, edited by H. Géraud for the Société de l'Histoire de France; Isambert, Recueil Général des anciennes Lois Françaises, tt. iii., iv., v.; Thierry, Recueil des Monuments inédits de l'Histoire du Tiers Etat (Documents inédits)—only four vols. published; Chroniques de Jean Froissart (Luce's and Lettenhove's editions); Chronique des Quatre Premiers Valois, edited by

Sources of Chapter VI.

Luce; Les Grandes Chroniques de France, edited by Paulin Paris, tt. v. and vi.; Chronique Normande du Quatorzième Siècle, edited by Molinier; Boutaric, La France sous Philippe le Bel (1861); Perrens, Étienne Marcel (1860); Secousse, Memoires pour servir à l'Histoire de Charles le Mauvais; Flammeront, La Jacquerie en Beauvaisis, Revue Historique (1879); Coville, Les Premiers Valois et la Guerre de Cent Ans, in t. iv. of Histoire de France, edited by Lavisse (1901); Luchaire et Langlois, Extension de l'Autorité Royale, t. iii. of same work; Luchaire, Le Royaume de France, chap. vii. of t. ii. of Histoire Générale; Gasquet, Precis des Institutions; Dufayard, La Reaction Feodale, sous les Fils de Philippe le Bel, Revue Historique (1893-94); Mackinnon, The Growth and Decline of the French Monarchy, chap. ii. (1902).

CHAPTER VII.

The Third Estate and the States-General in France — Continued till the End of the Fifteenth Century.

The victory of the Duke of Normandy was a victory for the monarchy as well as the government, though the monarchy remained for some years longer in sore plight until the duke's accession, in place of his father, as Charles V. As king, Charles did not give the Estates a chance of disputing his authority. He contented himself with convoking the notables of the three orders for financial reasons in view of the renewal of the war with Edward III., and though these assemblies are sometimes spoken of as meetings of the States-General, they hardly merit the name. He played the part of absolute king both wisely and well for the most part, in spite of renewed English invasions. The tide of misfortune turned at last, and after seven years of warfare, Edward lost to Du Guesclin all his conquests except Calais. With this turn of the tide to help him, Charles strove to undo the mischief wrought by his predecessors both to the monarchy and the people. He was no soldier, but he was a conscientious and laborious administrator, and tried hard to restore some measure of prosperity and order by eschewing the oppressive fiscal expedients of his father and his grandfather, and repressing the excesses of armed anarchy. His short reign was, however, but a transient respite from these abuses. His premature death in 1380 exposed the nation to the misery of a long reign of folly and madness. To perpetuate his work Charles V. should have reigned forty years longer, so as to have outlived his lunatic son, known as Charles VI.

Charles VI. was only twelve years of age when he succeeded, and though crowned king at Reims, the government was entrusted by the will of his father to his uncles, the Dukes of

Anjou, Berry, Burgundy, Bourbon. This division of authority did not tend to strengthen it, and the popular restiveness at the heavy taxation of the previous reign, which the firm hand of Charles V. had crushed, broke out in riot and revolt all over the kingdom. At Paris, Rouen, St Quentin, Orleans, Nantes, Laon, Reims, Soissons, Béziers, and other towns, the people demonstrated arms in hand against the tax-collectors and the Jews. At Paris in particular the Maillotins—men of the iron mallet—battered out the brains of the obnoxious fiscal officials and Jewish usurers. At Rouen and Béziers the mob was equally defiant and aggressive. The democratic spirit burst over France, Flanders, England like a whirlwind, disputing the right of government or class to oppress the people, and vindicating with blows as well as arguments the claim to resist the abuse of power. The widespread revolutionary spirit, which threatened a general upheaval, gave a momentary fright to kings and magnates. The Kentish peasants who marched in their thousands on London, the Flemish democrats who drove the army of their oppressive Count Louis de Mâle into rout at Bruges, the Paris Maillotins who struck down the royal officials in the street, seemed the champions of a universal crusade on behalf of the rights of man. The spirit of democratic self-assertion filled the air, and in this atmosphere royalty and aristocracy did not breathe freely. Listen, for instance, to the speech of one of these Parisian Maillotins, a leather dresser, who voiced the aspirations of the masses for some share of protection against the abuse of power and privilege: "Shall we never enjoy the sweets of repose and ease? Shall we never see an end of the increasing cupidity of the nobles, who crush us without respite with unjust exactions, constantly multiplied, and reduce us to such a state of exhaustion that, saddled with debts, we are forced each year to pay beyond our means? Do you realise, fellow-citizens, in what contempt you live? They would deprive you, without doubt, if they could, of your portion of the light of heaven. They are indignant that you breathe, that you speak, that you have human figures, and that you appear in the same public places with them. Why, say they, thus mingle heaven and earth? Doubtless these men to whom we render a forced homage, for whose welfare we are ever awake, and who live from our substance, have no other thought than to shine in their gold and jewellery, and surround themselves with a great train of domestics, build superb palaces, invent taxes in order to ruin the capital. The patience of the people has too long borne this pest of oppression. If we are not speedily delivered from this insupportable yoke, certain am I that the whole city will rush to arms, for we should rather wish death than submit to such misery."

In its momentary plight authority put on a conciliatory, philanthropic mien until it found the opportunity to avenge itself on these unconscionable orators with mallets in their hands. Charles' uncles convoked the States-General of Languedoïl, and promulgated at their behest another reforming ordinance (January 1381)—so much waste parchment as far as the fulfilment of the demands of the popular orators was concerned. It merely served to gain the royal uncles' time to crush the Flemish democrats at Roosebeke (27th November 1382), and this victory enabled them to set the executioner to work to crush the democrats of Paris, Rouen, and other cities without trial, suppress their municipal privileges, exact enormous fines, extort oppressive taxes as before, and generally rule by the drastic expedients of martial law. France sank back under the domination of king and feudal aristocracy, which the people, in its improvised revolutionary organisations, was as impotent as its representatives in the States-General to shake off.

Charles VI. was not the man to profit by this lesson, as his father had profited by the lesson of 1356-58, to pursue an enlightened policy. He had the sense to throw off the tutelage of his uncles and recall his father's ministers, showed, too, some kindly, benevolent traits of character which endeared him to the people. But his debaucheries disordered his brain, and his frequent fits of madness gave scope to the designs of factious magnates, like his uncle (the Duke of Burgundy), his brother (the Duke of Orleans), who intrigued against and fought with each other for the mastery. Their selfish rivalry plunged the country once more into the abyss of civil war, and in spite of spasmodic fits of reforming zeal on the part of the victor for the time being, the misery of the people grew more harrowing year by year. It seemed as if these factious substitutes of the mad king, who only occasionally recovered a gleam of reason sufficient to recognise himself and his wife and children, were bent on ruining France in the interest of their own egotism. They succeeded at least in conjuring another revolutionary hurricane, which well-nigh proved fatal to the monarchy, and brought upon the nation once more the misery of English conquest.

The assassination of Orleans in 1407, by intensifying party passion, was the prelude to the tragic drama played by the Armagnacs, the royalists, and the Cabochiens, or democrats. The deed had been done at the instigation of John Without Fear, son and successor of Philip of Burgundy. Hence the sworn feud between Orleanists and Burgundians, or Armagnacs and Cabochiens, as their partisans were respectively called. Orleans had been deservedly unpopular as the queen's reputed paramour and the profligate patron of extortion. John Without Fear, on the other hand, like his father before him, professed himself the enemy of the duke's oppressive measures, and the friend of the people. Consequently, in spite of his avowal of the murder of his antagonist, the Paris populace rallied to his side, and even the university compromised itself, in the person of some of its members, notably Dr Jean Petit, by defending the assassin as the avenger of the people. The son and widow of the murdered duke were by no means content to sit still under the vilification of father and husband, and acquiesce in the whitewashing of the murderer. The young duke, married to a daughter of the Count of Armagnac (hence the name Armagnacs adopted by the Orleanist party), could count on the adhesion of most of the princes of the blood and a large amount of support in the country, against the capital, where John the Fearless was supreme, and where the Armagnacs were hunted and beaten to death like stray dogs. Both sides appealed for aid to Henry IV. of England, and thus their party rage gave fatal scope for the intervention of the traditional enemy, who finally espoused the side of the Armagnacs. In the civil war which once more desolated the kingdom, Burgundy could pose as its patriotic defender against the rebels and their English allies, and the temporary accommodation negotiated at Auxerre (July 1412), saw his reputation greatly augmented.

As in 1356, the States-General should now bring its wisdom to bear on the situation and undo the mischief which misgovernment and failure had sedulously worked for thirty years past, and take measures against the foreign invader. The States-General was the last desperate remedy of the charlatans who exhausted the body politic by their administrative quackery, and, as in 1356, the States-General of Languedoïl found the condition of the patient past recovery. Their demand for trenchant reforms, accompanied by the refusal of a subsidy, which the miserable people could not possibly pay, was a purely academic device. The States-General with their long-winded grievances and academic remedies, were clearly impotent, and the reactionary attitude of the court in favour of the Armagnacs suggested the necessity of drastic measures to Caboche and his butchers and skinners of the Burgundian party (hence the name Cabochiens). The Cabochiens, led by Caboche and Dr Jean de Troyes, donned the white hood of their party, attacked the Bastille, burst into the Hôtel de Guyenne, the Dauphin's residence, and carried away a number of Armagnac dignitaries as pledges of the concession of their demands (28th April 1413). Masters of the city, they hunted down, seized, maltreated their opponents, with merciless energy. Even the king, in a moment of sanity, was forced to don the white hood in order to humour Dr Jean de Troyes and his rough-fisted allies, and promulgate the ordinances drawn up under the inspiration of the bludgeons of the butchers. The general drift of this bulky document was to secure an effective administration by constituting elective bodies in place of irresponsible officials throughout the whole administrative hierarchy. Its authors desired to reform, not to revolutionise the nation. They would not substitute the States-General for the king, as in the days of Étienne Marcel, for the intervention of the States-General had proved a fiasco, and was evidently discredited for the present. The nation should help itself, in co-operation with the monarch, by means chiefly of the Parliament and the Chamber of Accounts, controlled by a system of election, meant to guard against corruption and maladministration. This is all, and with the experience of past grand ordinances, it is not surprising that the Cabochiens were sceptical of its reputed millennial effects.

The butchers had more faith in their bludgeons than in the political wisdom of the doctors of law and theology, who penned the ordinance, and resorted to their terroristic methods. These excesses produced the inevitable reaction on the part of the exasperated Armagnacs, which destroyed both them and the ordinance. The ordinance was promulgated on the 25th May 1413; it was revoked on the 5th September following. The triumph of the Armagnacs was in turn blasted by the terrible disaster of Agincourt, which gave the oppressed Cabochiens an opportunity of wielding their bludgeons once more with such terrible effect that fifteen hundred of them, the count himself among the number, were massacred.

Agincourt and its sequel were the beginnings of forty years of fresh calamity for France. Party passion even stooped to recognise Henry V. as the successor of Charles VI., and, on the death of Charles in October 1422, some weeks after his would-be English successor, to acknowledge Henry VI. as King of France and England. Charles VII. had indeed an uphill task in vindicating his title to the crown against his English rival, and in rehabilitating the Valois monarchy from the impotence to which faction and civil war had reduced it. He was, in the earlier part of his reign, at least, a very poor king to fight for, but the electric influence of a highly imaginative peasant girl, fired with devotion to France and its divinely appointed monarchy, endued him with a spirit of energy, and rallied the people to his cause. The relapse into lethargy that followed this premature attempt to play the man, and the capture and martyrdom of Jeanne D'Arc only temporarily checked the patriotic movement, and the growing influence of its champions at last recalled Charles to a sense of his duty as its leader, and gave scope to the talents of men like the Constable Richemont, the Count de Dunois, and the merchant statesman, Jacques Cœur. With their co-operation Charles amply earned the title of "The Victorious," by wresting back all the English conquests on French soil, with the exception of Calais. To this result the States-General of Languedoïl, which met at Orleans in 1439, powerfully contributed by taking the initial step towards the establishment of a standing army, which acquired definite shape by the military ordinance of 1445. The measure was more than it professed, or was intended to be—the safeguard of the nation from the lawless, undisciplined soldiery that pillaged friend as well as foe. The standing army, unlike the feudal array which marched and fought under its feudal chiefs, was controlled, paid, disciplined, directed by the king, and bound to yield him obedience. As the master of this standing army, Charles VII. was a far more formidable ruler than any of his predecessors, if not so strong a man as some of them. In thus strengthening the monarchy the Estates neglected to ensure their control over the standing army by giving away their right to grant the taxes necessary for its maintenance. Not only did they vote a subsidy for this purpose; they allowed the king to continue to raise it without their mandate. And if the king might levy a *taille* for the maintenance of the army without the intervention of the Estates, why not other *tailles* as well? Charles did not hesitate to draw this conclusion under the plea of State necessity, and in spite of protests against his arbitrary procedure, ended by claiming and practising the right to raise taxes at will, and taking the assessment out of the hands of the people, and entrusting it to officials appointed by himself. He was the first king to do so as a matter of right, for hitherto the king was theoretically dependent for any revenue beyond the proceeds of the royal domain and the feudal aids, on the consent of the taxpayer. Though the States-General continued to protest against this usurpation when they got the chance, which was but very rarely, the usurpation passed into the category of royal prerogative. The only remaining check on royal absolutism, in matters of taxation, was the right of the provincial Estates to deliberate on and diminish the quota of the *taille* demanded by the king. As head of the Church (in virtue of the Pragmatic Sanction), chief of a permanent army subject to his exclusive control, arbitrary assessor of taxes, Charles VII. was practically unlimited master of France. He was thus the founder of the modern French monarchy—absolute king *de facto*, if not *de jure*—and his crafty successor Louis XI. was not the man to let slip the advantages gained by his father.

By a series of astute diplomatic moves, followed by a series of terrible blows at recalcitrant magnates, Louis crushed the reaction which found expression in the Ligue du Bien Public, or Association of the Commonweal, in alliance with Charles of Burgundy. France probably did not lose much from the discomfiture of the League, which, in spite of its popular professions, was essentially a caste movement, a conspiracy of the barons against the crown. The Bishop of Lisieux reasoned most plausibly to prove that it was a laudable reaction against tyranny in the interest of liberty and the people, but in the final treaties of accommodation, by which Louis disarmed the hostility of the League, while waiting the opportunity to smite its more powerful members, the Leaguists forgot all about the public weal, and remembered only their individual interests. The commission of thirty-six reformers, whose appointment they formally stipulated, was as useless as the commission of 1357, and was but a pretext for saving appearances. A second spasmodic revolt, engineered by Charles of Burgundy, succumbed to Louis' military and diplomatic talents, and its collapse left him at liberty to deal out terrible retribution to its leaders. After the execution of the Count of St Pol, the Count of Armagnac, and the Duke of Nemours, not a prince of the blood or a feudal magnate dared to measure himself against the royal craft, or risk exposure to royal retribution. Till his death in 1483, Louis XI. was as absolute as Domitian or Diocletian. He eschewed the advice of Commines to rule in co-operation with the States-General, and preferred to encrust himself in his own egotism. In spite of his proficiency in the subtle art of overreaching his opponents—domestic and foreign—and the consequent success of his efforts to strengthen the crown and consolidate the State, his government was far from popular, and it was especially obnoxious to the feudal magnate. He was both feared and hated, and his demise was the sequel for a violent rebound against the man and his system.

Once more the States-General were proclaimed to be the saviour of the situation. Let the States-General, demand the magnates and the fervid spirits of the capital, blot out the abuses of the tyrant's *régime*, and inaugurate the reign of justice and liberty. This sounded democratic enough, but democratic appeals on the lips of the feudal magnates should not be taken too seriously, especially as they appear, from the report of the proceedings of the Assembly which met at Tours in 1484, to have clung tenaciously to their rights, jurisdictions, prerogatives, liberties, privileges, and what not, on which Louis had laid so heavy a hand. There is, nevertheless, a distinctly modern note in the speeches delivered on these occasions by orators of the various orders. The sovereign people is much in evidence. The people, as represented by the Estates, ought to take the administration into its own hands pending the majority of Charles VIII. Thus argued the democratic orators of the Assembly in answer to the question, What are the powers of the Estates? Others claimed the sovereignty for the princes of the blood, and relegated to the Estates only the right to control taxation. This claim was strenuously rebutted by Philippe Pot, Lord de la Roche, and one of the Burgundian deputies, whose oration might pass for a harangue of Robespierre in the Assembly of 1789. According to Philippe Pot, who spoke in the name of "the sovereign people," by whose suffrages kings were created, the supreme power in the case of a minority devolves on the Estates, who elect from their members those best fitted to carry on the administration. In ancient times when men began to form societies, they elected the most enlightened and honest men to govern them. Those who took possession of the supreme power without election were tyrants, not kings. To whom, then, in such a case as the present, can the right of government belong but to the people, who created kings, and in whom the supreme power fundamentally resides? The State, the government, is merely the public interest, and the public interest is the affair of the people. The people embraces the totality of citizens, and to them, as represented by the States-General, belongs the right of administration during the minority of the king, in accordance with the principle of the French constitution, historically exemplified over and over again. The States-General are the depôt, the guardians of public liberty, and ought not to surrender their charge to the princes of the blood. These remarkable words were received by the Assembly, according to Jehan Masselin, the reporter of its proceedings, "very favourably and very attentively." They are at least an indication that democratic theories were floating about in fifteenth-century France, and demonstrate, if such demonstration is needed, that the democratic idea is, to a great extent at least, a product of mediæval as well as of modern times. And yet M. de la Roche was no democrat in the modern sense, no anticipation of Rousseau; was, there is reason to suspect, merely the champion of the court against the princes, though he played his part very skilfully. His argument was good as against the assumption of the princes and the magnates to control the nation. It sounded democratic enough, but the States-General did not yet in reality represent the people, the body of the nation, and the Lord de la Roche merely uses the name of the people as a specious plea for defeating the intrigues of the magnates against Anne de Beaujeu, regent for her brother. After much haranguing *pro* and *contra*, the debate ended in a compromise. The council during the king's minority should be composed of the princes of the blood, the chief magnates, and a number of less notable members selected from the Estates. In spite of their democratic professions and their reforming zeal, the States-General of 1484 failed completely to make a permanent impression on the fortress of the monarchy, and its members, after two months' hot debate, vanished as empty-handed and as impotent as previous reforming Assemblies. So far the attempt at parliamentary government in mediæval France had been a misadventure, and after the reign of Louis XI. the prospect of any effective reaction in this direction was by no means promising. During the sixteenth century the States-General flit across the stage of French history as a sort of apparition in times of storm and stress, and during the seventeenth and eighteenth centuries even the apparition ceases. We have reached the epoch of the absolute king, and in spite of an occasional fit of parliamentary aspiration in the stormy period of reformation and counter-reformation, the absolute king was to reign supreme in France for three hundred years.

At this stage of their history the States-General were not a sufficiently homogeneous body to wage successful war with absolute authority. The jealousies and antagonism of the three orders, especially of the nobles and the Third Estate, the undue influence of merely provincial and local, as distinct from national interests, rendered their Assemblies impotent in opposition to the concentrated power of the crown. As to the people, though nominally represented by the Third Estate, it was largely a negligible quantity, and it is only too apparent that at this period it was unfit to wield political power. It was, in truth, too ignorant to take an intelligent interest in political affairs, and as long as it was fairly prosperous, it had no political aspirations. It regarded the king with a superstitious reverence, and if the government did not harass it to excess, it had nothing to fear from popular movements. Starvation alone goaded it into enterprises dangerous to authority, and of such popular outbreaks France, as well as Germany and England, was to furnish at least one memorable example during the sixteenth century. Religious passion, too, was to find expression in France, as elsewhere, during the century of the Reformation, in a convulsion as threatening to the monarchy as to the Church.

SOURCES.—Isambert, Recueil Général, tomes vi. to x.; Chronicon Karoli Sexti, or Chronique du Religieux de St Denis (1380-1422), edited by Bellaguet (Documents inédits); Mémoires de Pierre de Fenin, edited by Mdlle. Dupont (Soc. de l'Hist. de France); Froissart, Chroniques (from 1380 to 1400), edited by Lettenhove; Chroniques de E. de Monstrelet (1400-1445), edited by Douët D'Arcq (Soc. de l'Hist. de France), and in Buchon's Collection; Choix de Pièces inédites relatives au Règne de Charles VI., edited by D'Arcq (Soc. de l'Hist. de Fr.); Chronique de Mathieu D'Escouchy (1444-61), edited by Beaucourt for *ibid.*; Mémoires de Jacques du Clercq (1448-67), in Petitot's Collection, t. xi.; Journal d'un Bourgeois de Paris (1405-49), edited by Tuetey; Mémoires de Philippe de Commines, ed. by Mdlle. Dupont (Soc. de l'Hist. de Fr.), and in Petitot's Collection, xi.-xiii.; Lettres de Louis XI., edited by Charavay and Væsen (Soc. de l'Hist. de Fr.); Bazin, Bishop of Lisieux, Historiarum de Rebus a Ludovico XI., edited by Quicherat for *ibid.*; Chronique or Journal de Jean de Troyes or le Roye, in Petitot's Coll., xiii. and xiv.; Mémoires d'Olivier de la Marche, in Petitot, ix. and x.; Journal des États Généraux ténus à Tours en 1484 par J. Masselin, edited by Bernier (Docts. inéd.); Coville et Petit Dutaillis, La Guerre de Cent Ans—Les Debuts de la Royauté Moderne, t. iv. of Histoire de France, edited by Lavisse (1901); La Clavière, Origines de la Revolution Française au Commencement du XVIe Siècle; MacKinnon, The Growth and Decline of the French Monarchy (1902), chaps. ii., iii., iv.

CHAPTER VIII.

The Emancipation Movement in Germany, and the German Free Cities.

The constitutional history of mediæval Germany is, in some important respects, the reverse of that of mediæval France. In France, the power of the monarch from Louis VI. onwards steadily increases; that of the feudal magnate steadily decreases. In Germany, the power of the emperor, in spite of occasional bursts of self-assertion, steadily decreases; that of the feudal magnate steadily increases. The imperial power was at first far greater than that of the early Capetian kings; it became ultimately far less than that of their successors. In France, the sovereignty of the feudal magnate was absorbed by the crown; in Germany, the crown was overshadowed by the sovereignty of the feudal magnate. In explanation thereof, it must be remembered that, whereas the French monarchy was a native plant of vigorous growth, the empire was an exotic that would not flourish in German soil. The imperial dignity was in fact an anachronism. After the failure of the experiment of Charlemagne, it was impossible to rehabilitate the empire of the west. It was really little more than a pretence, a political creed which Italy and Germany might profess, but which both Italy and Germany found it impossible permanently to embody. Even if Italy and Germany could have coalesced in one imperial State, the pope and the rest of the western potentates would not consent to subordinate themselves to the imperial crown. The pope claimed to be the superior, the kings of England, France, and Spain the equals, of the emperors. From a very early period France repudiated the imperial claim to supremacy over its kings. "We have followed the custom of France," replied Archbishop Foulques of Reims to the Emperor Arnulf, who remonstrated against the election of Charles the Simple, "and this custom demands that, the king once dead, the magnates of the kingdom should choose another of the blood royal, without asking the agreement or the opinion of any one." And thus it came to pass that the imperial title was but a dignity without real authority, a tradition without efficacy, a pretence without substance. Not that it was devoid of a certain fascination, but it was a fascination that had no practical effect in arresting the disintegration of the West, and only lured the emperors into the fatal policy of wasting their strength in the pursuit of an impossible ideal. While they strove to be masters of Italy, they became less and less masters of Germany. The struggle to maintain this mastery against the popes and the Tuscan and Lombard cities ended, as we have seen, in failure, and this failure weakened their attempts to maintain their authority north of the Alps. While the French kings strengthened the monarchy by adopting and pursuing a practical national policy, the emperors sacrificed the monarchy to the impracticable dream of a universal dominion, which had become an anachronism and an impossibility. In spite of a pompous title, the Germanic Imperator Augustus by-and-by sank into the impotence of an elective figure-head of the State, from which the Capetians had gradually emerged. Occasionally, indeed, the strong men among the emperors of the Saxon, Franconian, and Hohenstaufen dynasties bade fair effectively to assert their imperial power both north and south of the Alps. The Saxon Otto the Great, the Franconian Henry III., the Hohenstaufen Frederick Barbarossa and his grandson Frederick II. were men of great force of character, sturdy warriors, able rulers, who, for the time being, made the imperial title the symbol of energy, if not always of success, in war and administration. But it was, in the circumstances, beyond the range of possibility for even a Barbarossa or a Frederick II. to master both Italy and Germany, and their dramatic and futile attempts only gave scope for the aggrandisement of the feudal magnates at the expense of the imperial sovereignty. The policy of depressing the greater magnates of an earlier period, the dukes of Franconia, Bavaria, Swabia, Saxony, had indeed been successful, but the dismemberment or diminution of the duchies was accomplished to the advantage of a host of lesser magnates—counts, markgraves, landgraves, not to mention the lesser dignitaries of baronial or knightly rank. The imperial officials of an earlier time grew into an hereditary aristocracy, the owners of extensive domains, the possessors of practically independent jurisdictions, and these hereditary domains, these independent jurisdictions were due, not to the policy, but to the weakness of the central power. While, in France, the king encroaches on the rights of the feudal magnates and reduces them to the status of crown officials, in Germany the crown officials encroach on the rights of the emperor and develop into feudal magnates. The duchies that survived (Saxony, Bavaria), if shorn of much of their territory, became hereditary possessions, and their dukes local sovereigns. The prelates, who profited so largely from the generosity of the earlier emperors, similarly grew into great feudal princes. Everywhere the emperor was thus confronted by the local sovereign, who was ready to throw defiance in his face whenever the embarrassment of his impotent superior gave him the opportunity of pursuing his ambition, or gratifying his turbulent passions. Most significant of all, the greatest of these local sovereigns ultimately arrogated to themselves the right of filling the imperial throne itself, of electing the imperial figure-head of this phantom of a Holy Roman Empire of the German nation, and even of deposing him for his incapacity to rule, as mad, drunken Wenzel found to his cost, or for his hostility to their interests. It was their policy to choose an insignificant or weak candidate, or even a foreigner like Richard of Cornwall, Alphonse of Castille, Edward III. of England, in order the better to pursue their scheme of self-aggrandisement.

Thus from the extinction of the House of Hohenstaufen till well into the fifteenth century, when the imperial crown found at last a permanent resting-place in the Habsburg dynasty, the constitutional history of the empire presents the melancholy spectacle of disputed elections, civil war, and ruthless anarchy, compared with which the energetic rule of a Philip IV. or a Charles V. of France might almost pass as the golden age in things political. Numerous are the laments of the chroniclers over the misery of these anarchic times. "The princes and rulers," complains one of them, "are making us the laughing-stock of the world by their incessant quarrels. Incendiarism and pillage are laying waste the land. The princes are to blame that the empire, once so mighty, has become powerless. In Italy and Germany there is no longer any respect for the Roman empire of the German nation." The Magna Charta of this anarchy is the Golden Bull, wrested from Charles IV. in 1356, which confined the right of election (*prætaxation*), formerly the prerogative of all freemen, and subsequently of their representatives, to seven magnates—three ecclesiastics, the archbishops of Maintz, Trier, and Köln, and four laymen, the Count Palatine of the Rhine, the Duke of Würtemberg, the Margrave of Brandenburg, and the King of Bohemia. It clothed them at the same time with sovereign rights within their dominions, and constituted any attempt on their life high treason. As territorial sovereigns, their power was in reality far more substantial than that of the holder of a splendid but empty dignity. With the alienation of the imperial domain, the imperial tolls and customs to magnates and cities, the emperor had practically no revenue, and without a revenue his high-sounding titles were purely ornamental. His power and prestige were gone, absorbed by the seven electors in the first place, and by the host of magnates of lesser rank who, while deprived of a vote, and owning perhaps but a robber castle and its immediate environs, were practically a law unto themselves. An elective monarchy meant in such circumstances the domination of an aristocracy, and while this aristocracy professed allegiance to the imperial head of the State as sovereign by divine right,* every petty elector or markgraf was no less sovereign by God's grace in his own territories.

The growing debility of the central power, the growing ascendency of the feudal magnate is thus the trend of the constitutional history of mediæval Germany. In France the tendency of authority is concentric; in Germany it is centrifugal. The former produces the national monarchy, the latter

---

* In spite of their election, the emperors professed to hold their office by divine right, and the electors recognised that the sovereignty which they were instrumental in conferring was derived from God. The electors, it has been well said by Mr Bryce, selected the sovereign; they did not create him.

a multiplicity of petty sovereignties. The triumph of feudalism was, however, by no means absolute. Germany did not in the thirteenth century become the feudal State that France had been under the earlier Capetians. If the weakening of the imperial power favoured the growth of the local feudal sovereignty, it was equally favourable to the growth of local liberty. The extension of the feudal system had indeed been fatal to liberty in Germany, as in France. The freeman largely disappeared in the bondman. In the ninth and tenth centuries liberty was a rare privilege among the rustic population. But the freeman did not totally disappear. The peasant communities of the Frisian marshes of the north, of the Alpine valleys in the south, struggled, as we shall see in another chapter, to maintain their ancient rights, and the struggle resulted in an ever-memorable vindication by the brave Swiss mountaineers of the free institutions of the old German Volk, though even among the Swiss mountains serfdom was not unknown. The German cities, too, threw down the gauntlet to their feudal superiors, and were still more successful than those of France in their struggle for emancipation. For while the French communes lost to the crown what they had gained from the feudal magnates, the German Freistädte not only retained the autonomy they had won from their feudal superiors, but developed into local sovereignties of a more or less democratic character. The emancipation movement was thus more far-reaching in Germany than in either France or Italy. While in France the communes were suppressed by the monarch, in Italy by the tyrant, the free cities of Germany both retained and increased their internal independence, and became a powerful political order in the State. The struggle thus produced in Germany, as in France, a memorable revolution in the very citadel of feudalism, and ultimately dotted the map of the empire with a multitude of municipalities from the Scheldt to the Danube, from the German Ocean and the Baltic Sea to the Alps.

In mediæval Germany, as in mediæval Italy and France, the communal movement came in the wake of the revival of commerce. Singular fact though it be, civic life reached a higher stage of political development in Germany, where it was an innovation, than in France where it was as ancient as the age of the Greek colonies. In Roman Gaul, as in Roman Italy, the city was the ancient centre of a vigorous municipal and commercial life, the nurse of an advanced civilisation. In ancient Germany, on the other hand, the city, according to Tacitus, was unknown. The barbarians looked askance at the Roman cities on the fringe of their forest solitudes, on the thriving commercial centres of the Rhine and the Danube. Cologne, Maintz, Strassburg, Ratisbon, Augsburg, Worms, Spires, were the objects of their wonder, perhaps, but not of their liking. The great city with its towers and walls, suggested to them the idea of a prison. They were monuments of slavery (*munimenta servitii*, as Tacitus phrases it) in which men, like the caged beast, grew accustomed to restraint and forgot their liberty. They were no fitting abodes for the wild freeman, whose home was the rude hut which stood apart from, though in the vicinity of that of his neighbour, in its setting of sombre forest that bordered the clearance cultivated by the *gemeinde* or village community in common. Only in times of danger did he seek refuge in the forest or hill stronghold, the burg, the Teutoburg, for example, which was for the time being the citadel of the tribe. When these wild freemen burst over the Roman *limes* in fierce, expansive flood, they sacked and destroyed many of these frontier Roman cities which the empire was too weak to defend. And when their wanderings came to an end, and the tribe struck root in some region of Gaul or Italy or Spain, it was not, as a rule, in the city, but in the country that its members took up their abode. The barbarians were, however, as I have already pointed out, quick to adapt themselves to Roman institutions, and by-and-by the Roman cities on the Rhine and Danube frontiers, which they had sacked and left behind them in the first headlong rush of invasion, reappear under German names as centres of a new population of largely Germanic origin. The descendants of the wild freemen of the forest clearance became citizens on or near the sites of the old cities. Argentoratum became Strassburg; Taberna, Zabern; Nemeta, Spires; Vangiona, Worms; Moguntiacum, Maintz; Agrippina, Köln; Castra Regina, Regensburg; Augusta, Augsburg, and so on. Thus the old Roman cities on the Rhine and the Danube rose again from the ruins of the migratory period. Not only so, but in barbarian Germany itself, from the times of the Carolingians onwards, town after town sprang up to the east and the north around the palace of the emperor, or the seat of the bishop, or the burg of the duke or count, or the abbey of the missionary monk, until the country as far as the Elbe and even beyond was dotted with what we might more correctly denominate large villages, but what were the germs of future cities.

The growth of this germ was in most cases very slow. Centuries elapsed before the village or the hamlet became the walled city. We speak of Aachen, for instance, as the capital of Charlemagne, and we are apt to figure under this high-sounding term a second edition of Rome itself. In reality, Aachen was but a village or villa clustering around the imperial burg, and only became a walled town in 1172. Frankfurt, Ulm, Zurich, and other royal or imperial residences similarly remained, for a longer or shorter period, mere villages, and some of them, like Ingelheim, Salzburg on the Saale, never grew into towns. Charles and his immediate successors are nevertheless spoken of in the chronicles as builders of cities. Magdeburg, Wurzburg, Halle, for example, are mentioned as cities as early as the ninth century. The number increases in the tenth, and this increase is explained by the necessity of fortifying some village or hamlet at certain strategical points against the attacks of Slavic or Hungarian invaders. Henry I. the Fowler (919-936), first of the Saxon line of kings and emperors, was the active promoter of this policy, and transformed a number of villages (Meissen, Merseburg, for instance) into walled and garrisoned towns, capable of withstanding the attacks of the invading hordes which pressed westwards in many a devastating raid. His Saxon successors, the Ottos, and the rulers of the Franconian and Swabian dynasties continued the policy from the additional motive of finding in the towns a source of revenue, and a counterpoise to the power of the great nobility. It found equally ardent champions in the emperors of miscellaneous extraction (notably in Rudolf of Habsburg, Ludwig the Bavarian, and Charles IV. of Bohemia), who wielded the imperial sceptre in the latter half of the thirteenth and the first half of the fourteenth centuries. The emperors were, however, by no means the only founders or patrons of cities. A large number of villages owed their transformation into walled and market towns to the secular and ecclesiastical magnates, though previous to the Diet of Worms in 1231, the imperial consent was deemed necessary to these creations by duke, markgraf, bishop, abbot, not to speak of the lesser dignitaries of the feudal hierarchy. Such towns were subject to the jurisdiction of their local superior, while those which were under the immediate jurisdiction of the emperor were governed by the imperial burggraf or burgvogt, and were known as imperial towns.

Thus it came to pass that the land of the ancient Teutonic tribes, whose forest solitudes were broken here and there by the village clearance, became by the thirteenth century a land of cities, of great and growing centres of commerce and industry, not merely along the Rhine, as in Roman times, but along all the great rivers and roads from the Oder to the Maas, and the Scheldt. It is a striking transformation, figurative of the great social and economic revolution that had taken place in the interval. This transformation from the village to the town, subject to the jurisdiction of emperor or feudal magnate, is plain enough. The origin of the municipality which emerges, in the thirteenth and fourteenth centuries, as the governing body in all these cities, imperial or non-imperial, is far less luminous, and has given rise to hot controversy among German antiquaries and historians. It is a question of rival theories, and the see-saw between these theories has gone merrily on for the last fifty years, according as Von Maurer or Below is up, and Arnold or Nitsch or Hegel is down. That equilibrium has not yet been reached is evident enough, though it should be remembered to the credit of the contending theorists that their speculations have thrown much light on special points of an obscure subject. The older view, countenanced by Savigny, which saw a Roman origin in the German mediæval municipality, has long passed out of fashion. In Roman Germany, as in Roman Gaul, the municipality seems to have been effaced by the feudal system, and there is no reason for holding that its mediæval successor was formed after the earlier type. In such of the old Roman cities of the Rhine and the Danube as were not destroyed or depopulated, the administration passed to the episcopal or secular superior. In Roman Germany, as in France, the towns thus remained for several centuries in subjection to a lord, whether this lord were the emperor, or the emperor's deputy, the prelate, the duke, the markgraf, or their representatives. Where, then, are we to look for the germ of the future municipality? In the bishop's court of the episcopal cities, at least, answers Arnold. The bishop's court embraced a number of free burghers, who succeeded during the period of the struggle between the empire and the papacy in ousting the bishop's men—the *ministeriales*—and substituting a burgher council representing the free inhabitants, and invested with supreme administrative functions. Nitsch, on the other hand, finds the germ of municipal autonomy, not in the self-assertion of the ancient free burghers, whose existence he denies, but in the *ministeriales* or episcopal functionaries, who gradually became an aristocratic class and governed the city through an oligarchy, composed exclusively of members drawn from this patrician order. The former derives the municipality from public law (*Staatsrecht*), the latter from domanial law (*Hofrecht*). Starting on another tack in the wake of Wilda, Gierke sought an explanation, and at the same time a confutation of his predecessors, in the merchant gild; but this theory was in turn attacked by Gross, who showed that the gild was not a municipal, but a mercantile corporation, and did not originate, though it influenced, the development of municipal rights. In Hegel it encountered a more decided antagonist, who denied any political influence whatever to the gild. If not then, in the gild, or the Roman *municipia*, or the episcopal court, why not in the ancient Germanic institution of the *mark*, the village community? This was the alternative which suggested itself to Von Maurer, who contended that when the village became a walled town, the old administrative system simply perpetuated itself in a feudal form. Von Maurer based his theory on certain analogies between the mediæval municipality and the ancient village community, and it was not difficult for his numerous assailants to show that the municipal constitution of a great city like Cologne, Hamburg, or Lübeck, was, in most essential respects, very different from the primitive constitution of the ancient *mark* or *gemeinde*. The identity was palpably fanciful, but the idea set Von Below to work in elaborating the proposition that the mediæval rural community (the Burding) was at least the type, if not the origin, of the urban commune; the two were identical in function, though they differed in mechanism. Unfortunately, there is no trace of this village autonomy before the rise of the mediæval municipality, and instead of the rural commune being the model of the mediæval municipality, it would seem as if the mediæval municipality were the model of the mediæval rural commune. Von Below accordingly raised as many objectors as Von Maurer, and the most recent of these theorists, Sohm, has been no more successful in conjuring unanimity than his predecessors. His ingenious contention that the municipality sprang from the market (*Marktrecht*) has by no means ended the debate.

The theorists, though thus harping too much on one string, have at least directed attention to the various possible factors that were at work in the development of urban rights throughout the empire. Probably all these factors, for each of which their respective champions claim the exclusive instrumentality of creating the municipality, contributed something—here less, there more—to the grand result. The theorists err chiefly in trying to explain by a single principle what is a complex movement.

Very important is the economic factor, which in Germany, as in France and Italy, lent the chief impulse to the emancipation of the cities. During the period in which the theorists seek the operation of their respective principles, civic life was in a languishing state in the eastern, as in the western Frankish kingdom. Commerce and industry were probably more stagnant to the east than they were to the west of the Rhine. Charlemagne, as his capitularies show, was indeed the vigorous patron of both, but under his decrepit successors, and in spite of the efforts of the great Otto to reinvigorate his policy, the merchant was but a sort of vagabond, who ventured along the highways with his mule or his pack at the risk of being robbed and murdered by the robber bands, lurking in wait for the luckless wayfarer. The penalties of the emperors, the excommunications of the bishops notwithstanding, the highways were as unsafe, as uninviting to enterprise as feudal anarchy could make them. Moreover, the economic conditions of the age were equally unfavourable to commercial and industrial enterprise. In feudal Germany, as in feudal France, the domain, not the town, was the chief social factor. The land was the only source of wealth, of power; the possessor of the land the only owner of either. The small freeman became as a rule the serf, though the degree of serfage varied. In the ninth century liberty was a rare privilege among the rural population. The town was, as a rule, but a walled village, and this village was the domain of some superior or superiors. It had little industry or commerce beyond what was created by the needs of its scanty population. Its inhabitants were agriculturists, rather than traders or artisans. They cultivated the land attached to the town; they plied in addition the crafts necessary to supply their simple wants, and unless situated on the banks of a large river, or along a main road from north to south, east to west, like Cologne or Worms, communication with the outer world was both rare and risky. Even in the case of those thus favourably situated, commerce and industry developed but slowly, and civic life was consequently in an enervated state. Nor, indeed, could the forces, which nurture the civic spirit, develop under a social system which deprived the freeman of his liberty. The only energy that disturbed the lethargic monotony of existence was the energy of the turbulent magnate who usurped all rights, especially the right of breaking the peace by his feuds and his greed, and eschewed commerce as a degradation of his caste. People lost the very remembrance of the busy city of the Roman frontier lands.

It is, therefore, futile to grope about in the earlier Middle Ages for the origins of municipal institutions in Germany, as elsewhere. Its conditions are not there. There is no spirit of self-assertion in these serfish centuries to aspire to self-government; no spirit of enterprise to nurture commercial activity. In order to create these, a social and economic revolution was indispensable, and this revolution came to Germany, as to France, in the wake of the commercial and industrial revival of the twelfth century. Land ceased to be the only source of capital; liberty was no longer the privilege of a few individuals in the community; the world was no longer limited to the domain. Hamburg, Cologne, Magdeburg, Worms, Strassburg, Frankfurt, Basle, Liège, Ghent, Bruges, Ypres, felt the new impulse that stirred the dry bones of centuries, equally with Lyons and Marseilles. Where the geographical situation of a town marked it as a centre of commerce and industry, thither commerce and industry irresistibly gravitated, and the municipality sprang sooner or later into existence.

The merchant, then, is the chief author of the new life that begins to pulsate with increasing strength in the veins of the body politic from the eleventh century onwards. Slowly but steadily the dormancy of these centuries of clair-obscure disappears as commerce and industry make their influence felt in the feudal world. They supply the means, they furnish the skill, to build the great cathedrals. They extend and beautify the fortified agglomeration of huts and booths lying around some burg or abbey, hitherto dignified with the name of town or city. At some favourable geographical point, the busy mart swells the population from hundreds to thousands, as the vagabond merchant of an earlier time settles in colonies at some centre suited for his operations,—in the towns on the Rhine, Elbe, Maas, Scheldt, and other great waterways,—and the activity of the town attracts a multitude of workmen seeking freedom from serfdom, protection for their industry, bread for their labour. Cologne, for instance, the city of splendid churches, of stately merchant palaces, boasts as many as six hundred wealthy merchants as early as the eleventh century. To the class of merchant belongs not merely the trader proper, but every one who exercises a craft and sells his wares. Naturally the members of this class—the trader and the artisan who is also a trader—associate together in the confraternity, the general gild, in order to protect their interests against the feudal superior. This association is by no means the municipality, however. It is voluntary, and though it has its own regulations, it has no public jurisdiction, which still remains in the hands of the superior and his agents. But its tendency is to break the feudal bonds that shackle its development, and thus it helps to prepare the way for the commune, the municipality, the Freistadt. It is a training for the "conjuration," the sworn union for public purposes, and in Germany, as in France, it is from the conjuration that the municipality directly springs, though the municipality, when once formed, doubtless owed something to the pre-existing administrative elements which the theorists emphasise. It is the conjuration in Germany, as elsewhere, that gives strength, victory to the resistance to tyranny. In the dormant community, which the merchant rouses out of drowsy stagnation, men combine in sworn confederation to assert themselves and vindicate their demands. Thus we light in Cologne on such a sworn union as early as 1112, the *conjuratio pro libertate*, in opposition to the hostile tactics of the archbishop. And Cologne is only one example among many. In Trier, Maintz, Spires, Worms, and other cities, the burghers are found similarly uniting during the next hundred years for purposes of defence and aggression. For, while the emperors were, as a rule, favourable to the emancipation of the cities, at least as far as civil liberty was concerned, as a counterpoise to the rebellious or aggressive feudal magnate, the ecclesiastical and secular superiors were at first as hostile to the movement as in France. As in France, too, the ecclesiastics were especially inimical, and the cities could not always rely on the imperial support against their antagonism. Thus, when the Bishop of Worms appealed to Frederick II. against his refractory burghers, emperor and diet, assembled at Ravenna in 1232, declared dissolved and null all municipalities established without the consent of the archbishops and bishops. Frederick's sweeping condemnation was, however, the fruit of the embarrassment of the situation, and the burghers, as the renewed episcopal complaints show, treated this solemn deliverance as so much waste paper. Thus the conjuration, in many cases, only triumphed in Germany, as in France, after a hard struggle. At Liège, Cologne, Worms, Trier, Maintz, Passau, Augsburg, Spires, Cambrai, blows as well as angry words were exchanged before the ill-will and hostility of the mitred opponents of the burghers were overcome. In Germany, too, the bishops had the worst of the struggle in the long run, in spite of ecclesiastical thunderings, of the resort on occasions to more forcible expedients and of the appeals to the emperor, to which Barbarossa, as well as Frederick II., is found at times responding. Worsted by the determination of the burghers to oppose force to force, they had to be content in some cases, as at Strassburg and Worms, with a compromise; in other cases, as at Maintz, with the reluctant recognition of the new order of things. The opposition of the secular superiors was less obstinate, for the secular superior was more ready to strike a bargain with the conjuration, and either sold the coveted charter, or found it to be to his interest to grant a concession, which the changed economic conditions of the time rendered it both impossible and inadvisable to withstand.

What, now, was the texture of these municipal constitutions, thus extorted or conceded in the thirteenth-century Germany? The universal feature is the municipal council, the Stadtrath, with a mayor or Bürgermeister as president. In a large number of cities the Schöffen or aldermen—the officers of justice under the feudal *régime* with their president, the Schultheiss,—may have been the model of this Stadtrath and its Bürgermeister, though the assertion has been hotly contested by writers like Von Maurer. If it is easy to dogmatise, it is difficult to generalise, where local variety is infinite. It seems incontestable at least that the merchant corporation or gild was an influential factor, in all the larger commercial cities, whether imperial, princely, or episcopal, in the formation of the municipal council. For the merchant corporation included at first, as has been noted, both the merchant proper, and the craftsman who sold as well as made his wares. This corporation tended, however, to become a close association— the gild *par excellence*—from which the artisans were gradually excluded, and the Stadtrath accordingly became the monopoly of an oligarchy of wealth. Municipal autonomy was thus originally far from synonymous with self-government by the citizens for the citizens. It meant merely the domination of a patrician order of wealthy merchants (*die Geschlechter*)— represented by the Richerzeche of Cologne, for example—with whom were associated the knights who settled in the cities. Election to the municipal council was, too, subject to the approval of the superior, and in some cases the superior retained the right of nomination. This noble, or would-be noble, class was as jealous of its power as any member of the feudal hierarchy—formed, in fact, a new feudal caste within the city, and kept the inhabitants of its dependent territory in a state of vassalage and even of serfdom. Its domination inevitably produced a reaction in Germany, as in France, on the part of the excluded mass, though the result of the struggle of the mass against the class was widely different in Germany. While in France dissension and conflict gave scope to the intervention of the monarch and brought about the suppression of the communes, the struggle in the imperial cities ended in the triumph of the mass and the establishment of something like democratic self-government in a considerable number. Mere wealth and patrician prejudice succumbed to numbers. For with the development of trade and industry, the population of the cities swelled enormously. Cologne, Aachen, Strassburg, for example, could each place 20,000 able-bodied burghers and dependants (*Pfahlbürger*, suburbans) in the field. But mere numbers, without organisation, could not have wrested a share in the municipal government from the privileged oligarchy, and this organisation was supplied by the craft gilds (*die Zünfte*) in which the artisans, following the example of the merchants, erelong associated. Each trade thus represented the serried army of its members—graded in apprentices, partners, masters, living as a rule in one quarter or street, and subject to strict regulations both as to conduct and work. It is to these craft gilds that the perfection of mediæval handicraft is due; to them, too, the vindication of political rights within the city for the whole body of organised labour. Long and fierce was the struggle that ensued during the thirteenth and fourteenth, and even into the fifteenth centuries between this disciplined army of craftsmen and the privileged aristocracy and their dependants. The abuses of oligarchic rule, which stooped to extortion and oppression to maintain its privileges, provoked the pugnative spirit of its opponents. The feuds of the dominant class played into their hands, and these artisan and aristocratic malcontents are often found united in the attempt to break down the oligarchy. As in the case of the battle against the bishops and other feudal superiors, the conjuration played an important part in the struggle. The members of the crafts confederated with one another and with the enemies of their common enemy, and if concession could not be had by persuasion, the confederates did not hesitate to resort to force. There was bloodshed as well as hot controversy, hard fighting as well as angry words in the streets of Strassburg, Cologne, Spires, Worms, Maintz, Frankfurt, Augsburg, Nürnberg, Ulm, Constance, Basle, Zürich, Regensburg, Bremen, München, Magdeburg, Halle, &c. As the result of the battle, the aristocratic faction was sooner or later overpowered, and in many cases driven out of the city.

This revolution was, however, not identical in every city. Here, the aristocratic element was simply wiped out of the council, and its place taken by the elected representatives of the trade gilds, as at Strassburg. There, the government of the city was divided between a small council, consisting of members of the burgher aristocracy (*die Alten*), and a large council chosen from the gilds, whose co-operation was imperative in all the more important affairs, as at Cologne and Nürnberg. Or, the administration might be confided to three councils, representative of both parties, each to hold office for a year, and then demit it the two following years, as at Spires. Or, there was but one council embracing so many aristocratic members and so many gild members, who deliberated and administered in common, as at Maintz. The type thus varies; the result is usually the same—the subversion (especially in the southern cities) of the oligarchy by the craftsmen, who attain the dominant influence in administration and legislation. The patrician families were either banished, or ultimately, as a rule, lost in the ranks of the mass of the citizens.

This triumph of the craft gilds is an important fact in the history of advancing liberty. In the atmosphere of the city, to breathe the air of which is to be free, we feel as if we had left the feudal world behind and were launched into a new era. Not that the individual enjoys untrammelled freedom; the individual has no political rights except as a member of a corporation, and thus the word democracy can only be used in a qualified sense. If he is not an artisan, he must, *pro forma*, enrol himself in some gild, industrial or political, in order to qualify for political rights. The corporation, the gild, is, then, the condition of citizenship, and in this sense the individual is as much under constraint as if he were the dependant of a superior. The industrial democracy embodies the conception of corporate, not of individual liberty, and individual liberty had still centuries to wait for its vindication. In spite of this limitation, however, the gild performed a great service to the cause of liberty. The individual could have made little impression on the solid phalanx of privilege which pressed so hardly on the mass of the citizens, could not have broken down the power of the oligarchy. Organisation, concentration was the only successful weapon of attack, and the gild admirably fulfilled this function. It was inimical to free labour, free exchange, free initiative, and might easily become an instrument of tyranny, the focus of narrow, pedantic, selfish, class interests. It developed in the future all these objectionable features, became, in its turn, an abuse to be swept away. In these later mediæval centuries, it nevertheless fulfilled a great purpose in training masters of the various crafts, whose workmanship has been the admiration of later times, in concentrating the energy of the age in a marvellous burst of industrial activity, securing the public against the abuse of scamped work and inefficient training, nurturing in the craftsman an inspiring consciousness of the dignity of his calling, serving the purpose of the modern benefit society and the modern union, and lastly, and by no means least important, bringing the collective power of the community to bear on the struggle for self-government as against an oppressive oligarchy.

The emancipation of the towns had important constitutional results. It gave the free imperial cities a recognised place in the imperial Diet from about the end of the thirteenth century onwards, if it did not secure this privilege to the towns which did not hold immediately of the emperor. Even these non-imperial towns, however, had their share in provincial legislation and administration as members of the *Landesstände,* or territorial assemblies of their respective princes, and exercised, till the end of the fifteenth century at least, a far more effective control over both than fell to the lot of the more privileged representatives of the imperial free cities in the Diet. "As the princes have brought the emperor to a state of dependence," says Pierre Froissart, "and allow him only certain superior rights, so, in turn, are they dependent on the pleasure of the provincial estates."

Though the representatives of the imperial free cities did not cut a very great figure in the imperial Diet (the Diet being, as far as practical legislation was concerned, a merely academic body, to whose measures the magnates paid little heed), their municipality was a sovereign body within their own walls. Its powers were far more extensive than those of the modern town council. It resembled, in miniature, the government of a State rather than of a town, for it was as independent of any external jurisdiction as the prince or markgraf in his principality or his markgraviate. Like the prince or markgraf, or other petty ruler, it was, indeed, subject to the imperial supremacy, but apart from this subjection as a member of the empire, it was sovereign in its own domain, independent of any feudal superior. It recognised the emperor as head of the State, not as superior of the city, for the emperor alienated, in many cases sold, his sovereign rights in its favour. This sovereignty resided, however, in the people, and the municipal council only wielded an authority delegated by the citizens. It was bound to consult the citizens in all important affairs and act in virtue of their mandate. The people was the source of all legislative measures, of all executive authority. The assembly of the people—the Conventus Civium—was, therefore, an indispensable feature of the constitution, though in practice the function of this assembly fell in many cities to the great Council (the Grosser Rath), or Burgher Committee (Bürgerausschuss), which was directly or indirectly elected by the citizens and controlled the smaller or executive Council. In virtue of this delegated authority it maintained, in the city militia, an armed force, which was bound to assemble at the sound of the tocsin for defensive or offensive service. Each gild was, in fact, a battalion of this burgher army, and though formerly bound to respond to the imperial summons, it eventually became an independent force, whose participation in the imperial service depended on the consent of the Council. The Council possessed, moreover, the right of declaring war and concluding peace, of making alliances with other cities. It had its own banner, its own mint and customs, its own code of laws (*Stadtrecht*), courts, and judges, its torture chamber, as at Nürnberg, and its prison, and possessed supreme civil and criminal jurisdiction over the citizens. Even its ordinary administrative functions gave scope for more interference with social life than is deemed tolerable in these modern days. It controlled, for example, the commercial relations of the citizens with those of other towns. It maintained municipal taverns for the reception of travelling traders and artisans. It supervised the industrial activity of the gilds, and exercised the right to change their constitutions. It kept a sharp eye on the bakers, butchers, millers, brewers, &c., in order to ensure against the adulteration of food and drink. It even busied itself with the cut of a man's coat, and the style and material of a woman's dress, and gravely legislated the colour and length of the shoes which each class of the citizens should wear. The clothes and shoes question gave rise, in fact, to one of the most solemn of the sumptuary laws of the period. Nay, the quantity of wine which might lawfully be consumed on festival occasions, the number of guests to be invited to a marriage, and the value of the presents to be given were regulated with the same grave minuteness.

As virtually sovereign bodies the cities entered into alliances or confederacies with one another for the mutual protection of their interests. The gild, which organised the citizens in the struggle with a privileged class, was the forerunner of the league, which organised the towns in the struggle with the territorial aristocracy. These leagues did not, as in the case of the Lombard and Tuscan republics, lead to the establishment of independent States, except ultimately in Switzerland, where Berne, Zürich, Basle, became the members of a confederacy which at last threw off allegiance to the empire. The cities of the Rhine, Swabia, the northern provinces remained within the imperial pale, but their leagues invested them, in the fourteenth century at least, with a political and military importance comparable to that of independent States. Unfortunately for the unity and political efficacy of the crumbling empire, these leagues failed to fulfil the promise of the great things which they imagined in their own interest as well as that of the empire.

Jealousy, ill-will, mutual grievances produced inevitable friction between the territorial magnates and the great city corporations. The magnates, whether feudal prince or mere knight, envied the city its prosperity, and resented the protection afforded by it to the runaway peasants who sought a refuge from local tyranny within its walls, and were welcomed as Pfahlbürger or dependants. The cities in turn complained of the outrages of the Raubritter, the robber knights whose castles commanded the highways from their rocky heights on the Rhine, the Main, the Necker, the Moselle, and who swept down and plundered the merchant caravan, or extorted heavy tolls as passage money. It was primarily for such protective purposes that they banded themselves together, but they were actuated by political motives as well. They sought to secure a more influential part in the government of the empire against the increasing prerogative of the princes, and to preserve their civic rights from aggression, and the general peace from disturbance by their quarrelsome aristocratic neighbours.

The great factor of the league, as of the municipality, was the conjuration, and this form of the conjuration was, as we shall see, exemplified at an early date by the Bund of the Forest Cantons. It became common in the thirteenth century in other parts of the empire, and especially in the Rhine country and in Swabia, where such larger or smaller town alliances were formed in 1247, 1254, 1265, 1273, 1278, 1285. It culminated in the fourteenth century in the formidable Rhenish and Swabian League, which maintained a bitter and bloody struggle with Eberhard of Würtemberg and the princes and nobles until, after an alternation of successes and reverses, it was broken by the overthrow of the cities at Döffingen and Worms in 1388. Its discomfiture was due partly to the maladroit policy which neglected to make common cause with the Swiss mountaineers in their struggle with Leopold of Austria, partly to the lack of cohesion arising from local jealousies and dissensions in the League itself. The aim of the confederates was laudable, the execution of their plans faulty. "The League was formed," to quote a contemporary, "in a spirit of greatness and liberality, but it was turned to a bad account. In the first great 'town war' in 1388 the power of the burghers succumbed to the superior might of the princes, and thenceforward the burgher element has always occupied a subordinate position in the government." Apart from their local importance as industrial and commercial centres and their representation in the imperial Diet, they thus lost the opportunity of turning their strength to account in the vindication of the unity of the empire from the domination of a host of petty territorial sovereigns. While they continued to be a power in the State in virtue of their wealth and population, and appear occasionally in some imperial complication, their political *rôle* was limited, compared with what it might have been had a larger spirit of patriotism lent greater efficacy to their union.

More important was the Hansa League of the north, which, though mainly commercial, exerted great political influence not only within, but without the empire. It was under the auspices of the Hansa, which united Lübeck, Bremen, Hamburg, and other great commercial centres of the Baltic and the North Sea, rather than of the Swabian League, that the cities attained the maximum of power and prosperity. These cities carried on an extensive oversea commerce with the Netherlands, Norway and Sweden, Russia, England, Scotland, France. As the commercial caravans of the interior were exposed to the outrages of the robber knights, the ships of these northern merchants were constantly attacked by the pirates that swarmed in every strait and estuary. To protect their commerce by sea and land, these merchants united in the Bund which by-and-by swelled into the vast combination known as the Hansa, and embraced the cities of the four quarters or divisions under its jurisdiction. Lübeck was the capital of the Wendist quarter, and city-in-chief of the whole confederation as well, Brunswick of the Saxon, Cologne of the Lower Rhenish, Dantzig of the Prussian-Livonian quarters. The extent of territory embraced by these divisions show the vast power of the combination, which, at its prime in 1367, included seventy-seven cities. It maintained a fleet of warships to protect its large merchant fleets. It concluded treaties with foreign powers, and held the monopoly of the commerce of the northern seas and lands. It made war on the pirate chiefs of the Baltic and the North Sea, waged war, too, with King Gerard of Denmark in favour of Waldemar, and subsequently with Waldemar himself in alliance with Sweden, Holstein, and Mecklenburg. It assembled in diets, and legislated for the general interests of the confederacy. It had its fortified settlements at London, where the Hanseatic colony was known as the Steelyard, Wisby in Gothland, Novgorod, Bergen, Schonen, Bruges, Antwerp, which were subject to a strict, semi-monastic discipline, and their own code of laws. It practically possessed a monopoly of all the articles in which it traded—furs from Russia, herrings from Schonen, wood from Norway, hemp and flax from Germany, wool from England. The period of its glory is coeval with the period of industrial and commercial enterprise in the fourteenth and fifteenth centuries which made Germany the supreme commercial power in North Europe—the period of the splendid town halls (Rathhauser), churches, merchant palaces, whose spacious architecture and artistic adornment are the admiration of posterity. The Hansa just missed transforming the north into a mighty political confederacy, as the Swabian League had the south. So powerful did it become, in virtue of its energy and its wealth, that its alliance was courted by foreign potentates, and the Emperor Charles IV. proposed to put himself at its head. The brilliance of this period was, however, by-and-by eclipsed by the shadow of decline that began to creep over it in the fifteenth century, and extinguished its glory in the sixteenth. Both as a political and as a commercial power, it flourished only to wane and sink into obscurity. For this decline the lack of an adequate organisation, the dissensions which frequently lamed its policy and its activity, the growth of competition on the part of England and Holland, the revival of Denmark under Margaret and Eric, who reunited Scandinavia, were mainly responsible. Its organisation was so loose that individual cities were at liberty to secede or accede at pleasure, without further penalty than that of liability to the Hansa ban—a penalty entirely insufficient to prevent frequent disintegration. Moreover, the lesser organisation of the four quarters tended to disjoint the general confederation, and this spirit of particularism eventually brought about the rupture of the Osterlings and the Westerlings—the eastern towns of the Baltic, and the western towns under the hegemony of Cologne. The hostility of England in the latter half of the fifteenth century forced it into a great naval effort against the navy of Edward IV., but the Peace of Utrecht in 1474, which ratified all its privileges, was the last triumph of the mighty association. It had thenceforward to contend with the commercial revolution that opened up new markets and new trade routes, and left its splendid cities isolated amid the ruins of their former grandeur.

SOURCES.—For the constitutional history of the German empire—Giesebrecht, Geschichte der Deutschen Kaiserzeit; Lamprecht, Deutsche Geschichte (1892-94); Prutz, Staatengeschichte des Abendlandes im Mittelalter (1885-87), in Allgemeine Geschichte, edited by Oncken; Janssen, History of the German People at the Close of the Middle Ages, English translation by M. A. Mitchell and A. M. Christie (1896); Bryce, The Holy Roman Empire (1889); Fisher, The Mediæval Empire (1898); Henderson, Select Historical Documents of the Middle Ages (1892), and A Short History of Germany, i. (1902); Mathews, Select Mediæval Documents; the chapters on Germany by MM. Bazet and Blondel in tt. ii. and iii. of Histoire Générale; Pütter, An Historical Development of the Political Constitution of the Germanic Empire, translated by Dornford (1790); Menzel, Geschichte der Deutschen, i. and ii. (1872); Hallam, Middle Ages, ii. For the German cities—Von Maurer, Geschichte der Städteverfassung in Deutschland (1869-70); Arnold, Verfassungsgeschichte der Deutschen Freistädte (1854); Nitsch, Ministerialität und Bürgerthum im XI. and XII. Yahrhundert (1859); Heusler, Ursprung der Deutschen Stadtverfassung, (1872); Wilda, Das Gildenwesen des Mittelalters (1831); Gross, The Merchant Gild (1890); Gierke, Das Deutsche Genossenschaftsrecht; Hegel, Städte und Gilden der Germanischen Völker (1891); Von Below, Die Entstehung der Deutschen Stadtgemeinde (1889), and Der Ursprung der Deutschen Stadtverfassung (1892); Sohm, Entstehung der Deutschen Städtewesens (1890); Pirenne, L'Origine des Constitutions Urbaines au Moyen Age, Revue Historique (1893 and 1895).

CHAPTER IX.

Religious and Social Revolt in Bohemia and Germany in the Fifteenth Century.

HITHERTO the main factors of the emancipation movement had been economic and social. From the fourteenth century onwards, the religious factor becomes active as well. Throughout the Middle Ages voices might indeed be heard appealing to the gospel against the oppression of humanity. But these voices were few, and their message had small effect in breaking the shackles of feudalism. From the age of Wicklif and Hus, however, this appeal becomes ever more audible, ever more forcible, and it at length took shape in a series of popular outbreaks, in vindication both of religious and social reform, in Germany and other lands. The movement owed its origin, as we shall see more particularly in another chapter, to the writings of John Wicklif. Wicklif was pre-eminently a religious reformer. So, too, was his Bohemian disciple John Hus. But Wicklif's doctrine of "lordship" tended, as we shall see, to fan the spirit of social revolution, and from the fourteenth century right onwards throughout the Reformation period, its influence may be discerned in the fact that the demand for religious, went hand in hand with the demand for social, reform in Central and Western Europe. Wicklif and Hus inaugurated a mighty reform movement against social as well as religious abuse, which in Bohemia produced the first dramatic attempt at reaction on the grand scale in modern history, and whose effects, even after the overthrow of the Taborites, continued to be felt, till the advent of Luther, over the length and breadth of the empire in quasi-religious, quasi-social insurrection.

Bohemia had been prepared for the doctrines of Wicklif and the evangelical activity of Hus by a series of fervent preachers—Conrad Waldhauser, Milic, and Mathias of Janov

—who, in the latter half of the fourteenth century, laboured to achieve a moral, if not a doctrinal reformation of the Church. It was from these men that Hus inherited his reforming spirit. It was from Wicklif that he drew his reforming teaching. The works of Wicklif were already being read and discussed in Bohemia at the end of the fourteenth and the opening years of the fifteenth centuries, when Hus, who was born in 1369, was rising into prominence as a master of the University of Prague and a popular preacher in the Bethlehem chapel of that city. The close connection between England and Bohemia, through Anne, daughter of King Wencelaus and queen of Richard II., favoured the importation of the English reformer's books. Travelling scholars who, after the fashion of the time, wandered from Prague to Heidelberg, Paris, and Oxford, disputing and learning by the way, brought back copies of the "De Ecclesia," the "De Dominio," and other treatises of the great master. Certain it is that the University of Prague in 1403 condemned forty-five propositions extracted from these treatises as heretical, and inhibited any one who had not taken a master's degree from reading them. Seven years later (June 1410), Archbishop Zbynek ordered Wicklif's works to be publicly burned, and though Hus, who headed the opposition, protested against this sentence as too sweeping, burned they accordingly were to the number of two hundred. By this time Hus had taken up a resolute attitude as a religious reformer, as well as a patriot, in the struggle, which resulted, in May 1409, in the secession of the German element in the university to Leipzig. The burning of Wicklif's books was in fact a blow aimed at his Bohemian protagonist who had shortly before been denounced in a petition to the archbishop as a heretic. At the archbishop's instigation he was excommunicated by Pope John XXIII. (March 1411). He was, nevertheless, determined not to be silenced by such tactics, and boldly inveighed against the papal Bull (December 1411) directing the sale of indulgences in Bohemia for a crusade against Ladislaus of Naples, who supported the antipope Gregory XII. He would, he protested, obey the pope only in so far as his commands were in harmony with those of Christ and the apostles. In reply, John XXIII. not only excommunicated him anew, but placed Prague under an interdict (1412). With the connivance of Wencelaus, who had hitherto protected him from his enemies, he retired from Prague to Austi to write his "De Ecclesia." In this work, which is simply a compression of Wicklif's treatise on the same subject, he represents the Church as the body of predestined believers, and repeats his doctrine of conditional obedience to the pope. Ultimately in 1414 he determined to lay his case before the Council of Constance, which the Emperor Sigismund, at the pope's instigation, summoned to end the papal schism.

He went to Constance voluntarily in the expectation of vindicating his position. He was cruelly disillusioned. In spite of the imperial safe-conduct, he was thrown into prison and arraigned as a heretic on a variety of charges. He was accused, *inter alia*, of refusing to condemn the works of Wicklif as heretical, of expressing the wish that his soul might be with that of the English reformer and consequently of sharing his heresies, of denying that the pope and the hierarchy constituted the Church, and asserting that the Church consists of the whole body of believers (the *predestinati*), of teaching that no obedience is due to pope, priest, or even king in mortal sin, and that the tithes are alms to be used for the benefit of the poor, not the property of the clergy, of denying transubstantiation, of inciting the people to rebellion and spoliation, of bringing about the forcible expulsion of the Germans from the university, of questioning the right of the Church to put heretics to death, &c. Some of these charges he denied point blank. Others he endeavoured to explain. Some he defended by appealing to the Bible as the supreme arbiter of faith. He had, he bluntly asserted, again and again, never denied the real presence. Nor was he concerned to defend the opinions of Wicklif or any other man, but he could not subscribe to the deliverance that every proposition in his works was heretical. He saw no heresy in the pious wish that his soul might be with that of so noble and pure a man. He was not prepared to submit unconditionally to the authority of the pope, for Christ, he contended, is the real head of the Church, the pope only His representative, and His commands are supreme. A pope in mortal sin has no authority, is indeed Antichrist, and from Antichrist he was entitled to appeal to Christ. By what right have you deposed John XXIII., demanded the bold prisoner, if the power of the pope is absolute? Heretics, he maintained, should be instructed rather than put to death. Though he did not deny that an obstinate heretic might be subjected to corporal punishment after every means to instruct him had been exhausted in vain, he bade his judges remember Christ, whom the scribes and Pharisees in their mad zeal delivered over to Pilate to be crucified.

Thus he reasoned and appealed for several days in the face of a prejudiced assembly against the demand for unconditional retraction. His appeals and his reasonings availed him nothing against the tactics of his enemies, chief of whom was his former reforming associate, Stephen Palec, and the German priest Michael de Causis, one of his opponents at Prague. Even Gerson and the Paris doctors entered the lists against him with twenty articles drawn from the "De Ecclesia," and the very suspicion of Wicklifite sympathies was sufficient to damn him in the eyes of the English members. So strong was the prejudice against him that it would not be baulked of its prey even by the imperial safe-conduct.

And yet Hus was, at worst, but a very mild heretic, compared with a Luther or a Calvin. We can hardly reckon him a reformer in the later sense of the term. The man who held the doctrine of transubstantiation and was willing to recognise the authority of the pope on certain conditions, might have sat as a member of the Council which was determined to burn him. But, if no reformer of the later type, he had at least given unequivocal expression to one of the great principles of the later reformation. He claimed the right to appeal from pope, or even Council, to the Bible. He championed the right of the individual conscience against tradition, mere constituted authority, papal or conciliar. He emphasised the democratic as against the hierarchic conception of the Church. He refused to limit the Church to its external organisation; he equated it with the whole body of the faithful, and thus attacked the monopoly of rights which the pope and the hierarchy had usurped. He would recant if the Council would convince him from Scripture. He would not surrender his beliefs merely because the Council proclaimed them to be heretical, and reserved the appeal to Christ and conscience. It was this appeal to conscience, this refusal to submit to corporate authority *per se*, that steeled the animosity of his judges against him. They shouted him down, jeered at him, cursed his presumption and obstinacy. He never had a chance of a fair hearing, and day after day his examination was simply a riot of bigotry and prejudice. To the reformers of Constance the appeal to conscience and Christ was but another name for rebellion, and for persisting in this rebellion they committed him to the devil and the flames. In so doing they immortalised their own barbarous intolerance as well as the memory of the first of the great martyrs of one of the greatest of modern causes.

His sympathisers among the Bohemian nobles addressed a scathing protest to the Council against his murder and against the slanders which had been heaped on their native land. Hus, they maintained, was the victim of the malignity of his enemies. Neither they nor their revered teacher were heretics, and the doctrines for which he had been condemned they would maintain with their blood, despite "all human statutes enacted to the contrary." They not only vindicated Hus, they refused to submit to the decree of even a representative Council as final, if it outraged justice and humanity.

The defiance of the Council was the prelude of the modern Reformation. It was a distinct intimation, not merely of a solitary reformer like Wicklif or Hus, but of a body of men who claimed to speak in the name of a whole people, that they would not submit to traditional authority *per se*. It was a plea for fair discussion of matters of controversy, and a protest against the principle of stifling inquiry and dissent by such authority. The Council must not merely dictate; it must convince. Otherwise the reason and intelligence of the inquirer will revolt in the name of conscience, justice, religion. The martyrdom of Hus' disciple, Jerome, intensified the indignation, and stiffened the defiance of their followers. They treated the citation of the Council to appear and answer for their adhesion to a condemned heretic with defiant contempt. They not only defied the Council and its decree of extermination against all Wicklifite and Hussite heretics; on the death of Wencelaus in 1419 they refused to accept his brother, the

Emperor Sigismund, who had basely abandoned Hus at Constance, as king, without explicit guarantees of reform in both Church and State. Sigismund, who relied on the adherents of the Council among the Bohemians and the German part of the population, refused to deviate from the traditional Church as represented at Constance, or to conciliate the Bohemian national spirit at the expense of the German element. His refusal plunged the country into the first of the great modern religious wars. In that war, which began with Zizka's seizure of Prague, in November 1419, and lasted for fifteen years, the more advanced reformers who rallied round Zizka and Nicolaus de Husinec on Mount Tabor, and were known by the terrible name of Taborites, played the leading part. The more moderate section, the Calixtines and Utraquists, who co-operated with them, would have been content with the concession of the Four Articles of Prague (July 1420). These articles stipulated the free preaching of the Word of God throughout Bohemia, communion in both kinds, the exclusion of the clergy from secular office and possessions, in accordance with apostolic practice, and the suppression of gross sins in clergy and laity alike. The Calixtines had no desire to break away from the traditional Church. They made no serious attack on its doctrine, government, ritual. While they demanded the cup for the laity, which Hus was prepared to waive, they did not expressly include in their demands his dogma of conditional obedience to the pope, or insist on the democratic conception of the Church as the community of believers. They were aristocratic, not democratic, in their views, and the reformation which they championed was in this respect more moderate than that of the leader they professed to follow.

Very different was the spirit of the more advanced party. The Taborites not only outran Hus, they anticipated, and, in some respects, even went beyond the later reformers of the type of a Luther or a Calvin. They denied the doctrine of transubstantiation; they smashed images and relics; they hated the monks as drones and devotees of superstition, and sacked monasteries and even churches. They were puritans of the straitest sect, denounced the ornate ceremonial of the Church, despised mere human learning, and observed a Spartan simplicity in worship and life. Life for the vast multitudes that thronged to Mount Tabor was one continual conventicle, with endless preaching, praying, singing of psalms and hymns, frequent communion in both kinds. Their moral code was severe, and counted even the amusements of the children among sins.

Nor did their revolutionary zeal exhaust itself in the uncompromising attack on the traditional Church. They aimed at the same time at revolutionising the State. They sought to carry Wicklif's doctrine of lordship to its practical issue. That doctrine had evidently made a deep impression on the Bohemian people. It might remain a mere academic speculation in England—might, as we shall see, exercise little influence on the great social revolt of 1381. In Bohemia, on the other hand, it bulks very largely both in the controversy that led to the condemnation of Hus, and in the revolution which his condemnation conjured. It occurs among the forty-five articles condemned by the University of Prague in 1403. "No one is a civil lord, or a prelate, or a bishop, whilst he is in mortal sin" ("Nullus est dominus civilis, nullus est prælatus, nullus est episcopus, dum est in peccato mortali"). It was again condemned by the university as "false and erroneous" in 1412. Gerson denounced it at Constance, and Hus defended it by quoting a text from the prophet Hosea. "Of all the errors of Hus," we find Gerson writing to the Archbishop of Prague, "that proposition—it notably came down from Wicklif—is the most perilous, that a man who is from eternity reprobate, or who is living in deadly sin, ought to have no dominion, jurisdiction, or authority over other Christian men." It may be traced among the extravagances of the fanatic preachers on Mount Tabor, and on the lips of these fiery preachers it became a trumpet call to social and political revolution. Wicklif and Hus might protest that it should not be held to justify the forcible redress of grievances, and rebut the charge of fomenting sedition and revolution. It was open to their Bohemian followers of the Taborite camp to accept the doctrine and ignore the caveat against its revolutionary application. Bohemia was ripe for social revolution as well as religious reform, and though Hus was no prophet of revolution, his death was the signal for an upheaval in which racial, religious, and social elements intermingled with startling results. The national antagonism between Slav and German, the widespread reaction from a pampered, worldly Church, the covetousness of the nobles, who saw their opportunity to lay hands on the Church lands, the restiveness of the peasantry against the oppression of their lords—all these elements contributed to the revolt which Hus initiated, but which he did not live to control. " Religious in its origin, its aim, its character," says M. Denis, " the Hussite revolution touched the whole life of the people. It grew out of all the passions that then agitated Bohemia, and absorbed in its flood all the particular currents of the time. To the idea of a religious regeneration was added, in the first place, the rancours of race, then political interests. If the nobles saw their opportunity of increasing their domains at the expense of the lands of the Church, and extend their privileges, the peasants, irritated by oppressions, so much the more odious that they were a violation of the charters and the laws, hailed in the re-establishment of the gospel the return of a *régime* of liberty and equality."

The recluse doctor of Oxford or Prague might plausibly discourse on the sinfulness of using force to rid the world of a dominion founded, not in grace, but in unrighteous usurpation. To the bellicose Zizka, the born leader of men, and his peasant army, whose zeal was inflamed by the fiery preachers on Mount Tabor, the kingdom of God could only be established on earth by a more masculine Christianity than that which would merely preach and pray against injustice. Is not the Church corrupt by reason of its overgrown wealth and the immorality of the clergy? Are not the masses of God's people, in whom the Church consists, the victims of a social order that militates against the divine law as well as against all equity? Is it not sin against God to suffer these things to exist, a duty to God to make an end of the reign of Antichrist in the Church and the world? The knell of Antichrist in Church and State has sounded, the cup of his iniquity is full to overflowing with the abuses, the wrongs of centuries. The last days of the apocalyptic vision have come; the reign of Christ, the Christian theocracy, in the view of extremists like Martin Loqui, the fieriest of the fiery preachers of retribution, shall replace the *régime* of the usurper and the oppressor. It was one of those crises when the consciousness of right in the human breast is overwhelmingly stirred, the silence of centuries, the dumb endurance of many generations (of which the chroniclers tell us little) finds utterance and demands a reckoning from the misgovernment, the oppression, the wrongdoing which the present has inherited from the past. In this theocracy in which the oppressed masses see the fulfilment of the visions of the men of God of old, there is no room for king, noble, or wealthy clerical dignitary, for any title—even an academic degree—for any inequality of class or property; there shall be no taxes, no feudal dues, no privileges, no law but that of God. Nay, sin itself shall ultimately vanish; Christ Himself will descend; the dead shall rise, and a paradisaic state of innocence and bliss shall prevail. Zizka was too shrewd a leader to share in these vagaries, but he was shrewd enough to tolerate them, and allowed Martin Loqui and the wilder pulpiteers to nurture the military fervour of his followers, which his military skill made invincible on many a bloody battlefield. He only stopped short at the practical anticipation of this chiliastic phantasmagoria, and summarily exterminated the Adamites—the most extreme section of the extremists—who taught that men should return to the state of nature pure and simple, eschewed the wearing of clothes, and practised, according to their enemies, community of wives.

In spite of this medley of radically divergent notions, Calixtine and Taborite united (though with frequent intervals of friction) under the heroic personality of Zizka, and after his death in 1424, under "the great" Procopius, in militant opposition to the traditional Church and its patron, the Emperor-King Sigismund. Even if they had been minded to bow to the irenic teaching of Wicklif and Hus, the attitude of emperor, Council, and pope left them no alternative but to fight or be exterminated. Let God arise, therefore, and let His enemies be scattered. In this appeal to the sword they were only answering the challenge of the enemy. The Council had burned Hus, and fulminated a decree of extermination against heretics. Pope Martin V., whom it enthroned on the seat of John XXIII., had denounced confiscation and fire against them in the outrageous Bull in which he gave separate utterance to its corporate fury and bigotry. For centuries the popes had adopted this barbarous policy of preserving the unity of the Church by brutal methods, of maintaining a colossal tyranny by the stake and the dungeon. And if the sword might be used by divine command to preserve the Church, might it not be used by divine command to reform it? Thus the hosts of a Zizka took up their terrible threshing flails to smite the armies of Antichrist and his secular abettor, the false Sigismund. And terrible enough was their exemplication of this doctrine of force in the service of reform —religious, social, political—by which the reign of Christ on earth should be established. The record of their exploits is a record of battles and sieges, of marchings and invasions, of bloodshed and brutality, of rapine, cruelty, and desolation, in which the heroic, the religious mingle with the excesses of the fanatic, the savage. It was the first clash on the grand scale of the warring tendencies of tradition and emancipation in these modern times, and it was not to be the last, though the champions of emancipation ultimately had the worst of the encounter. For years Zizka's tactics and the fervour of his rustic hosts made the popular armies invincible. Time and again the mere appearance of these peasant levies, with their omnipotent flails, drove the armies of Sigismund and his allies into panic-stricken rout. Even after Zizka's death the imperial and papal crusaders were beaten again and again, and would have been permanently worsted but for the inevitable breach in the ranks of the sectaries, which ended in war between the moderates and extremists, and in the overthrow of the Taborites at Lipany, where Procopius died a hero's death in May 1434. For fifteen terrible years, however, the cause of the common man seemed a winning cause, and feudalism, as well as traditional orthodoxy, trembled for its supremacy, not only in Bohemia, but in every land where its iron despotism prevailed. The victory put an end to the *régime* of the men of God who had gone forth from Mount Tabor to establish the new earth and the new heaven. It paved the way for a compromise on the basis of the Compactates of Basle, which conceded to the Calixtines the four articles in a slightly modified form. Happily the remnant of the defeated sectaries, chastened by the experience of war and defeat, survived to become the Bohemian Brethren, and to preserve, in spite of persecution, the simpler creed and worship which had shed their crudest excesses in these terrible years of revolutionary fanaticism.

With the defeat of Lipany, Europe had, however, by no means heard the last of the revolutionary creed of the Taborites. The prophets of Mount Tabor contemplated an international as well as a national revolution. All Christendom should rise and destroy, sword in hand, the tyranny of Antichrist over the nations. Their manifestoes were carried as far as England and Spain. Their missionaries roamed about the empire, and one of them, Paul Craw, whose evangelical zeal carried him as far as Scotland, was burned at St Andrews in 1431. In South Germany in particular their influence made itself felt through the "Waldensian" sectaries and "The Friends of God," who had gained numerous adherents among the people, and seem to have maintained sympathetic relations with their fellow-heretics in Bohemia. Even after the discomfiture at Lipany, this influence was perpetuated by the fugitives whom persecution drove across the frontier into Germany. About 1446 we hear of a Hussite congregation at Aischgrund and Taubergrund in Franconia. Some years later another had planted itself in the bishopric of Eichstädt. Though the propaganda of these missionary fugitives was directed against the Church rather than against society, the doctrine of the nullity of all law and all rights that militated against the law of God still formed part of their teaching. Nor did the doctrine fall on deaf ears, as the numerous peasant risings in South Germany in the latter half of the fifteenth and the first quarter of the sixteenth centuries show. "To John Hus and his followers," complains a contemporary scribe, "are to be traced almost all these false principles concerning the power of the spiritual and temporal authorities, and the possession of earthly goods and rights which before in Bohemia, and now with us, have called forth revolution and rebellion, plunder, arson, and murder, and have shaken to its foundations the whole commonwealth. The poison of these false doctrines has been long flowing from Bohemia into Germany, and will produce the same desolating consequences wherever it spreads." From the Alps, too, blew the breeze of freedom that fanned the revolutionary aspiration into flame, for the example of the stout mountaineers across the Lake of Constance, who had struck such mighty blows for liberty, was not lost on the oppressed peasants of Swabia, Baden, Franconia, Alsace. Swiss and revolutionist were indeed synonymous in the eyes of the dominant classes of society in those parts. Had not the men of Appenzell but recently risen against their feudal oppressors, both lay and clerical, and added one more free State to the Swiss confederation (1411)? Thus the infection of revolt spread from south to north, as from east to west, and showed itself in sporadic outbreaks of the revolutionary fever among the peasants of Swabia and Upper Rhineland in 1423, 1449, 1459. Eastwards in Tyrol and Carinthia in 1462 and 1478 there were similar outbursts of the popular hatred of worldly priests and tyrannic lords, who lived on the fat of the land which the peasant cultivated in the sweat of his brow for their profit. The nemesis of feudalism in Church and State seemed to have come. Beat priests as well as nobles to death, burn the abbeys as well as the castles, was the fierce cry of these peasant banditti. The Appenzeller, in whose spirit these outrages were perpetrated, were, complained the Reichstag in 1427, worse enemies of the Church and the nobles than even the Bohemian heretics.

These outbursts were for long merely local, sporadic. But with the advance of the century the revolutionary spirit was embodied in widely ramified conspiracy. The peasant, as represented in the popular literature of the time, became self-conscious, aggressive. He might be ground down under the accumulated burden of social abuse, and give angry expression to the misery that made his lot so wretched. Yet was he not the sinew of society? Was it not from his labour that all lived? Was not the dignity of labour superior to that of worthless priests, lords, knights, who supported a vain pomp at his expense? "Work," says Rosenplüt in the "Miracle of the Drop of Sweat," "is the divinest law on earth. Work is serving God, and the industrious man has a great advantage over the idle and voluptuous, whose lives are full of care and anxiety." "God and the labourer," says Werner Rolewinck, "are the true lords of all that serves for the use of man." "The peasant," we read in a "Christian Exhortation," "must in all things be protected and encouraged, for all depend on his labour, from the emperor to the humblest of mankind, and his handiwork is, in particular, honourable and well-pleasing to God." Said the knight in the popular song, "I am born of a noble race." "I cultivate the corn," retorted the peasant, "that is the better part. Did I not work, you could not exist on your heraldry." "The peasant," we read in the "Book of Fruits," "loves his work, and holds his calling in high esteem, for God Himself instituted it in Paradise." Hence the figure of "the noble peasant," whose self-esteem the popular scribes nurtured, while lashing the vices, the luxury, the pride of the upper classes. He was no longer the clown whose antics lent zest to the popular tale. He is introduced to us as the ideal of human nature, the nearest to Christ in his life of faithful, fruitful activity, infinitely superior in moral worth to the artificial, ornate, degenerate *noblesse*. For the noble peasant had evidently arrived at the conclusion that the inequality and injustice of the age had passed the limit of human endurance, and must be mended or ended. The idea of a great revolution had become a fixed idea—revolution of society, revolution of the Church, for the two usually went hand in hand, though the peasant was, of course, more immediately concerned with the amelioration of his miserable lot. Ominous prophecies, elaborate schemes of this great transformation pass from lip to lip, nay, are written down like any party programme of the present day. A deliverer shall appear (for long it was the resurrected Frederick II. who should put his mighty hand to the task of a radical reform of empire and society), and the outline of his work is ready to his hand. Such an outline is "The Reformation of Kaiser Sigismund," to whom, when the great Frederick came not, the popular expectation eagerly, but vainly turned. Another—"The Reformation of Kaiser Frederick"—pinned the popular faith to Sigismund's successor, the third Frederick; and then the hopes that Frederick III. disappointed sought their realisation in his son, the chivalrous Maximilian. But the peasants were doomed to discover again and again that, in spite of the favourable omens which the astrologers read in the movements of the planets, each prospective reformer on the imperial hrone would not, or could not rise to the height of his humanitarian mission. The peasant, it was patent, must help himself, must be his own benefactor, and to this end must unite in a great Bund or union, and secure by his own brawny arm the reformation which kaiser, prelate, prince, refused to grant.

Thus, with the advance of the century, South Germany appears honeycombed with secret societies, composed of peasants and the proletariat class of the towns, which conspire for the forcible redress of their grievances. Such a secret society we find busy concocting revolution in the Hungersberg, near Schlettstadt in Alsace, in 1493, under the guidance of Hans Ulman and Jacob Wimpfeling. Another was hatched by Joss Fritz and others at Untergrombach, in the bishopric of Spires in 1502. In 1512 the village of Lehen, near Freiburg in Breisgau, where the redoubtable Joss Fritz had settled, was the centre of another widespread conjuration. About the same time the peasants of Würtemberg united themselves in the society of "The Poor Conrad," and in 1517 Baden and Alsace were again seething with the revolutionary propaganda. There were similar movements in Hungary, where George Dozen headed a terrible crusade against the nobles, and among the Styrian and Carinthian mountaineers, who rose in 1514 against their feudal taskmasters.

The method and object of these rural conspirators were more or less the same. Mayhap the popular restiveness took on the colour of a religious movement, as at Niklashausen, in the diocese of Würzburg, in 1476. Some ecstatic rustic like Hans Böheim (his name suggests, as some believe, a Bohemian origin) would take to preaching the gospel of deliverance from human misery for the poor peasant. Popular preachers were numerous in Germany in the fifteenth century, and when they took as a text the social ills that pressed so hardly on the everyday lives of their humble listeners, they were never at a loss for a congregation. Such a preacher was Hans Böheim, cowherd or "pauker," drummer, some say bagpiper of Niklashausen, and seer of visions of the pure white Mother of God. The kingdom of God on earth which he heralded in ecstatic Taborite fashion should bring emancipation from injustice and oppression. It should inaugurate the age of human brotherhood at last, as shadowed forth in the gospel, ecstatically preached. No more feudal burdens to grind the poor people in the dust. All things free to all. No man, be he emperor, pope, prince, baron, or bishop, should henceforth lord it over the free Christian community. "The emperor," cried the preacher, "is a miscreant, the pope a nonentity. It is the emperor who gives to princes, counts, and knights authority to tax and burden the common people. Alas! for you, poor devils. Princes, civic and ecclesiastical, ought to possess no more than common folk, and then all would have plenty. The time would come when princes and nobles would have to labour for a day's wage. Every one would then be his neighbour's brother. The fish in the water, the game upon the land ought to be common. Tolls, road-money, servitudes, rents, taxes, and tithes to spiritual or temporal superiors were to be wholly done away." More especially should the judgments of God descend on an ungodly priesthood. "The clergy have too many benefices. They ought never to have more than one. If they do not forthwith amend their lives, judgment will come upon the world." But woe be then unto these evil living, greedy priests. "They shall be slain, and erelong it will be seen that a priest will put his hand upon his shaven crown, that it may not be known what he is." Such was the gospel preached at Niklashausen, and it was plainly an echo of the democratic, communistic sermons preached on Mount Tabor. From far and near the people resorted to hear and welcome, in the impassioned rustic, the expected Messias, came, too, at length, arms in hand, to inaugurate the reign of righteousness and equality. Apostle Hans raved a great deal, and the fantastic ravings of an ignorant rustic could only lead to delusion and disaster. Yet there was a practical vein in his ravings which caught the crowd and threatened serious enough consequences, if the Bishop of Würzburg had not taken time by the forelock by seizing poor, ingenuous Hans and burning him as a heretic, in spite of a forlorn attempt by the peasantry of the countryside to rescue their apostle. The axe and the dungeon put an effective period to the promised millennium in that part of the empire for the time being.

In most cases the crusade against feudal oppression took on a more mundane aspect. No inspired apostle would appear to harangue the people into ecstatic revolt. That was too dangerous. The kingdom of God on earth could only come by stealth, and accordingly the more resolute and restless spirits, like Joss Fritz, who would stand the injustice of their lot no longer, would steal out of the village or small town in the hour of "gloaming" to some forest glade near, and hold council how to bring about the amelioration of their misery. To this end the social institutions of the time must be fundamentally altered. First of all, every man must be free, and in order to be free, all traditional authority—that of the emperor and the pope, which Hans Böheim would have destroyed, excepted—must be swept away, all social inequality rooted out, the ecclesiastical and territorial courts, all dues and services abolished, lands, woods, pastures, fishings be free to all. In some cases princes, nobles, priests, monks, who withstood the popular crusade must be killed; in other cases compelled to give back the rights they had usurped, and cease oppressing the people and waging their interminable feuds at the people's expense. It was to secure such far-reaching social reforms that Jacob Wimpfeling, or Joss Fritz, or Hans Ulman furtively deliberated at the trysting-place outside the village or the small town, and carried on their intrigues throughout the district, with the result that whole provinces were imperceptibly drawn into the conjuration, and tens of thousands of brawny arms were ready to strike at the decisive signal. Joss Fritz proved a veritable cobold who sprang into activity where he was least expected—now as priest, now as pedlar, pilgrim, beggar. Thus the Bundschuh was furtively hatched into a vast organisation, arranged in "circles," whose leaders kept up an active correspondence. Its emissaries—pedlars, beggars, wandering musicians, or cunning spirits disguised as such—moved from village to village, scheming, exhorting, enrolling in secret, giving the watchword. Each of these rustic movements had its programme on behalf of "the Justice of God" (*Gerechtigkeit Gottes*) and the rights of man, of which all swore acceptance. Each had its mottoed banner—a peasant's shoe, emblazoned on a piece of silk—to which all swore to rally. The reaction against the rampant injustice of the age, against the historical development of society, which seemed to have violated all innate human right, is clearly discernible in the Bundschuh. The great revolution should change all this, should vindicate the divine righteousness on earth, and restore to man his pristine rights.

At the decisive moment the people would hasten to the general rendezvous and begin the revolution. But at the decisive moment something would go wrong. The Swiss, to whom the peasants looked for help, would not move. The oligarchy which ruled most of the Swiss cantons were not the men to espouse a cause which threatened the *régime* of rank and wealth, and the Swiss democrats had work enough to do in the struggle with their aristocratic rulers. Moreover, a traitor would warn the enemy, and the enemy would swoop down on the deluded rustics before they had time to gather in large masses, and seize, torture, kill, quarter them alive in detail. Fortunate those who managed to escape into Switzerland to await the opportunity of another venture. Needless to say, each successive venture, in spite of cunningly laid plans, was as hopeless as its predecessor.

In spite of the revolutionary mood of the German peasant at the close of the Middle Ages, Johannes Janssen, who is, however, evidently actuated by the striving to make things look as well as possible for the old ecclesiastical *régime*, quotes from contemporary writers to show that in the fifteenth century the German peasant had very little to complain of. Jacob Wimpfeling (not the popular leader) declares, for instance, that "Germany was never more prosperous than she is in our day, and she owes it chiefly to the untiring industry and the energy of her citizens—artisans as well as merchants. The peasants, too, are rich and prosperous." In view of the scale of wages and the mode of living, Janssen further opines that the agricultural population was exceedingly well off. Among the rural population serfdom, we are further assured, existed only in Pomerania; in the rest of Germany the peasant was practically free. True, there were grades of freedom—the small freeholder or peasant proprietor, the leaseholder who paid rent in money or kind, the villein who rendered personal service as well as paid rent. "It *might* be said," concludes our optimistic author, "that at the close of the Middle Ages most of the land was virtually in the hands of the tenants, the lords of the soil merely receiving rent or service for it. By degrees the possessions of tenants became as independent as those of free peasants." He, nevertheless, admits that "those who paid rent for their land either in money or personal service could not leave the holdings confided to them without the permission or knowledge of their lords," though, it seems, "they had personal liberty, and their leases were for the most part perpetual." He further sees "in this species of tenure right over tenants, personally free, the evidence of a care for the peasant on an hereditary basis." He lays stress on every regulation of the "Manor Rights," on every passage of the chronicles that will make out a case in favour of the feudal-ecclesiastical organisation of society which he admires. Further quotations seem to make it absolutely certain that peasant life in the fifteenth century under this organisation was an idyll of happy contentment, and if the peasant rose against this blissful order of things it must have been, we are to infer, that he had grown rich and insolent under it.

The picture has, however, a reverse side, and we must look at the reverse if we would understand why the peasants periodically conspired and rebelled. It is not sufficient to quote the flattering testimony of an occasional eyewitness, or refer to the "Oracles or Manor Rights" in proof of the beneficial *régime* of the feudal lord, ecclesiastical or secular. If the peasants of large areas were not satisfied with this *régime*, we may reasonably conclude that the actual state of things was in accordance neither with the judgments of a Wimpfeling, nor with the spirit of the customary law as reflected in the "Oracles." Of course there were good superiors and contented tenants, whether free or semi-servile, in this revolutionary age, and Dr Janssen deserves credit for emphasising the fact, but if we study the origin of these risings attentively, it is difficult to get over the impression that the good landlords and contented tenants were, in large areas in the south at any rate, the exception rather than the rule.

The increasing luxury of the age had indeed reacted on the peasants. They wore better clothes than formerly, affected a better style of living, showed a spirit of independence towards their betters unheard of in the good old times. "We hear the peasant nowadays addressed as Gracious Sir (*gnädiger Herr*)," cries Geiler indignantly in one of his sermons. "Why not?"

retorts the peasant, "I have money enough and clothes like any gracious lord." "The prosperity of the peasants here (in Alsace), and in most parts of Germany," notes Wimpfeling, "has made them proud and luxurious. I know peasants who spend as much at the marriage of their sons and daughters, or the baptism of their infants as would buy a small house and farm or vineyard. They are extravagant in their dress and living, and drink costly wines." The testimony of Wimpfeling receives confirmation from the ordinances passed in 1497 prohibiting "the common peasant to wear cloth costing more than half a florin the yard, silk, velvet, pearls, gold, or slashed garments."

But if times had changed for the peasant, they had also changed for his lord, and for the lord there was an increasing temptation to make the peasant pay for the luxury which had become fashionable on the agricultural domain, as well as in the wealthy commercial city. He had pretexts in plenty at hand for sucking his rustic dependants, traditional rights which might be twisted to his advantage in spite of the prescriptions of time and custom, and in general he was not slow to apply the screw of oppression. In spite of the improvement of the peasant's status from serfdom to tenancy, "there remained," to quote Dr von Bezold, "a terrible remnant of oppressive burdens which, just in an age of economic development, and by reason of its rampant luxury, pressed doubly hard on the peasant." The aspiration from below is met by the harsh antagonism of oppression from above, and "the oppression of the poor man" is the burden of the cry that frequently rises from the home of the peasant. Against these recalcitrant peasants the jurists were ready to adduce the rules of the Roman law, which was gradually subverting the old customary law of the land. They justified with texts from Justinian not only the claim of the princes to sovereign rights, but the right of the lords to harass the peasant, on the plea that the lord was absolute proprietor of his lands. Hence the rampant oppression on the one hand, the growing spirit of antagonism on the other, which could lead only to revolution. The peasant claimed the abolition or the modification of his semi-servile status; the lord strove to press him back into a condition of serfdom by means of legal chicanery very hard to bear. No wonder that the peasant hated the jurist, as he hated the Jew or the Raubritter. Because the peasant is found wearing gaudy garments, unworthy of the good old times, we are not to infer that he had no grievances, and the impatience with which he bore them increased in the ratio of the economic progress of the age, and the exactions which it brought in its wake. Hence the widespread restiveness which found expression in conspiracy and revolt. Naïve indeed is the idea that just in an age when the discontent and defiance of the masses were seething towards the inevitable explosion, the lot of the common man was a heaven on earth. Instead of the patriarchal idyll of a mutual benefit society, we see in fifteenth-century Germany a State not only politically disorganised, but undermined with social conspiracy, disintegrated by class antagonisms, ripe for social cataclysm.

Given, in addition, the revolutionary impulse born of the hatred of a degenerate and oppressive priestly caste, which every official attempt had failed to reform, and we have a sufficient diagnosis of the revolutionary spirit of the age. For the social movement wore more or less a religious aspect. It concerned itself with the Church as well as with society. The common man was the enemy of the clergy, and now that the day of reckoning seemed to have come, the common man was evidently in a mood to strike at priest as well as lord. The radical reform of ecclesiastical abuses, in practice if not in doctrine, must be taken in hand by the people, to whom the divine inspiration has come. Nay, without such radical reform, the movement must be in vain, for the existing Church is as great a stumbling-block, in the way of the social millennium, as the existing social order. There is no room in the Christian commonwealth, that the people has resolved to establish, for a hierarchy of worldly prelates and abbots, who are also feudal magnates under the guise of a pseudo-Christianity, and whose scandalous lives belie their religious profession so shockingly. Thus the religious element coalesced with the economic and social elements to fan the revolutionary spirit. Let priests and lords beware of the *dies iræ* that is surely dawning out of the mists of mediæval darkness.

With the agrarian movement was contemporary, and sometimes combined, a democratic movement in the towns.

Throughout the last two decades of the fifteenth century and the first two of the sixteenth, the civic population is found in state of ferment closely analogous to that of the country people. The proletariat of the towns join hands with the peasants in the forcible attempt to redress their grievances. These attempts become widespread and simultaneous as the revolutionary spirit is intensified, and in the years 1512-14 a veritable tidal wave of insurrection swept over town as well as country, from Constance to Aachen. Cologne, Aachen, Düren, Neuss, Andernach, Göttingen, Brunswick, Worms, Spires, Ratisbon, Stuttgart, Tübingen, Ulm, &c., blazed into revolt.

How had things come to such a pass? The emancipation of the towns from the domination of the feudal lords, secular and ecclesiastical, was coequal, as we have seen, with an extraordinary development of industry and commerce. The hardly won autonomy of the German town was at once the offspring and the nurse of an economic revolution which, in spite of the political decline of the empire for several centuries, made Germany the leading industrial and commercial State of Europe. The German city, with its busy looms, its great fairs, its gild hall, its skilled artisans, its thriving merchants, was the admiration of the world. German art and industry challenged comparison even with those of Italy or Flanders. "When any one wishes to have a first-rate piece of workmanship in bronze, stone, or wood," wrote Fabri of Ulm in 1484, "he employs a German craftsman. I have seen German jewellers, goldsmiths, stone-cutters, and carriage makers do wonderful things among the Saracens." The gild system at its best, as it existed in these mediæval German cities, was certainly conducive to the thoroughness and finish of all manner of handiwork. It was to her skilled workers, thus organised and trained, that Germany owed her industrial pre-eminence among the nations in the fourteenth and fifteenth centuries. And industrial activity went hand in hand with the commercial development which culminated in the mighty organisation of the Hansa, whose mercantile sway extended, as we have seen, far and near — over Russia, Denmark, Norway, England, Scotland, France, Spain, and Portugal. "England itself at the close of the fifteenth century," as

Janssen remarks, "stood in the same position to Germany in regard to trade as Germany later, up till within a short time, stood to England." Moreover, in virtue of its gold and silver mines, the empire, in the words of another modern writer, "was formerly the Mexico and Peru of Europe." "Germany," boasts a chronicler in 1493, "is rich through her commerce and industry. In mineral wealth she is second to no country on earth, for all nations—Italian, French, Spanish, or other— get nearly all their silver from Germany." "Our rich merchants," notes Wimpfeling, "circulate the gold and silver of our country over all Europe."

Numerous, therefore, are the encomiums of these hives of German industry and trade in the fifteenth century. German and non-German writers break into ecstasy at the spectacle of the proud cities on the Rhine, the Main, the Weser, the Elbe, the Danube. Compared with any stately modern city, they would indeed cut but a poor figure, for even in the proudest of them the scavenger and the sanitary inspector seem to have been unknown. Relative to the time, however, their splendour and opulence were superlative, if the squalid offensiveness of their streets would have disgusted a modern visitor. "Cologne," exclaims Wimpfeling, "is the queen of the Rhine, through its riches and extensive commerce. What shall I say of Nürnberg, which holds commercial relations with almost all the cities of Europe, sending forth its priceless works of gold, silver, copper, bronze, and stone? It is difficult to estimate its wealth, and the same may be said of Augsburg. Ulm, which is much less important than these cities, estimates its annual trade revenue at half a million of florins." From Venice to Novgorod, from Muscovy to Scotland and Portugal, the merchants of Strassburg and Cologne, Augsburg and Nürnberg bargained, sold, bought. The "Findaco" of Venice, the great German trading establishment, was one of the wonders of the mercantile world. "I saw there," notes the pilgrim knight, Arnold von Harff, in 1497, "merchandise of all kinds exported every day in all directions; the merchants of Strassburg, Nürnberg, Augsburg, Cologne, and other German cities had their respective booths." But the pæans of all the panegyrists, national or foreign, are faint in comparison with the high-flown rhetoric of Æneas Sylvius, that keen observer and future pope. "The kings of Scotland," he assures us, "would have wished to be as well housed as the simple burghers of Nürnberg. Without exaggeration it may be said that no country of Europe has better or more beautiful cities than Germany; they look as fresh and as new as if they had been built but yesterday, and in no other cities is so much true freedom to be found. The inhabitants of the so-called free States of Italy are really bondsmen; in Venice, Florence, Siena, even the burghers, with the exception of the few who are connected with the government, are treated like slaves; they do not dare use their own property as they please, nor to speak as they think, and are subject to the most onerous taxation. Among the Germans all are free and joyous, none are deprived of their rights, each one keeps his inheritance to himself, and the government interferes only with those who annoy others."

There is, however, a discordant note in this chorus of admiration. Relatively these panegyrics might be true, but we should err greatly if we were to infer from these flattering passages that the economic and social condition of the German towns in the fifteenth century was superlatively satisfactory. Quotations might be culled in plenty to show that, with all this glitter of splendour and opulence, all this activity and wealth, there was much that was wrong in the State of Denmark. Not only are we surprised to learn that most of those cities, which bulk so largely in contemporary eyes, were relatively small and insignificant and shockingly filthy. The conditions of permanent prosperity were lacking. In spite of the material efficacy of the gild system, it was evidently not incompatible with a vast amount of poverty and discontent among the masses. As in the country, so in the town there were frequent conspiracies, revolt, and bloodshed against the dominant class of incorporated burghers. The large proletariat which had accumulated from the surrounding territory, and had no share in the privileges and benefits of gild membership, was nursing the revolutionary spirit, equally with the peasants beyond the walls, and even within the gilds there were frequent quarrels between the masters' gilds and the journeymen gilds (*Gesellen*) about wages and hours of labour to threaten the dominant order of things. The gild system might be, as Dr Janssen contends, a truly Christian organisation of labour, admirably fitted to advance the material and moral welfare of the worker, but it was evidently only partial in its philanthropy. Luxury on the one hand, poverty on the other, showed the glaring contrast between the higher and the lower classes. The Ehrbarkeit, or patrician class of the "Geschlechter," swelled by the new men whom trade and industry had raised in the social scale, since the emancipation of the industrial gilds from the old patrician tyranny, was confronted by the mass of workers, gildsmen and non-gildsmen, who had grown restive under their corrupt *régime*, and demanded an account of their stewardship in the government of the city. The quasi-democratic revolution which had given the craft gilds a voice in its government bade fair to be followed by a really democratic upheaval which should realise the aspirations of the artisans and the proletariat. The sovereignty of the people, for which the gilds had fought, was not synonymous with popular sovereignty in the modern sense. It meant merely the *régime* of the qualified burgher, and the burgher qualification, which involved gild membership, was by no means a simple matter, and kept a large element of the population outside the pale of civic rights.

There was much outcry in particular against the monopolist companies, which absorbed the trade in certain articles and raised prices at will. The result was the selfish accumulation of wealth in a few hands in many of the great commercial towns. The wealthier merchants were thus enabled, according to a decree of the Reichstag in 1522-23, to cripple the small trader by manipulating prices. They sold goods to the small trader at a high price, and then, by lowering their own, ruined him. Competition, continues the decree, was impossible where a few men commanded the market and demanded what price they pleased even for the necessaries of life. Hence the chronic discontent on the part of the poor man, " which if timely measures be not taken will grow more formidable." To obviate this discontent the amount of stock of such companies should not exceed the limit of 50,000 gulden, prices should be fixed, loans by wealthy merchants to poor peasants, on the security of their land or produce, be forbidden, &c.

Worse still, these rich monopolists have turned money-lenders, usurers. The Welsers and Höchstetters of Augsburg, the Imhofs, Ebners, Volckamer of Nürnberg, the Rulands of Ulm are worse sinners in this respect than the Jews. Geiler von Kaisersberg curses them in his sermons as "greater extortioners and deceivers of the people than even the Jews. They not only plunder and possess themselves of foreign goods, which indeed may be dispensed with, but they monopolise the necessaries of life such as corn, meat, and wine, and bring up the prices to suit their greed and avarice, and glutton on the hard toil of the poor. These bloodsuckers, corn and wine usurers, injure the whole community; they should be driven out of towns and parishes like packs of wolves; they fear neither God nor man; they breed famine and thirst, and they kill the poor." "It has become a by-word in the nation," complains Kilian Leib, "that merchants of this sort commit, unpunished, deeds which in former days robbers only dared at the risk of their lives—they rob men and women of their money." In these diatribes it is the poor man in town and country that is in the most pitiable plight, and evidently the poor man sees no remedy for the ruin that threatens him but in his own stout arm. "The law of mercy does not extend in our land to the poor and the labourers," we read in a devotional book of the period, "yet it is much needed by them, and the authorities are very remiss in the matter." The Diet might well decree: the gold of the greedy monopolist, who bribed even in the highest circles, was stronger than the Diet. "Many of the town councillors," complain the inhabitants of Ulm, "were members of the trading companies, and among the imperial councillors many were open to bribes . . . or had secret shares in these enterprises." "The emperor's councillors are swindlers," roundly declares a chronicler; "they nearly all grow rich while the empire grows poor." When the price of food is artificially raised to satisfy the greed of the few, and extravagance and luxury convey the fact to the popular eye, it is not surprising that democratic discontent is seething in town as well as country. Add to this the rampant vagabondage of the time—beggars by profession, broken men of every kind, artisans, peasants, even knights and merchants; swarms of mercenaries in the service of emperor, prince, prelate; strolling players, musicians, quacks, men of no occupation, who play the thief in the town, the highway robber in the country; crowds of moral and social wrecks, the dregs of mediæval society. Add, too, the fact that in these times of violence, when the Raubritter lurked on the roads and plundered and murdered at will, men were accustomed to give and receive blows on the slightest provocation, were strangers to our modern way of settling disputes by argument or arbitration, were hardened to scenes of brutality, were taught by example that force is the great remedy, whether the cause be just or unjust. Add, further, the fact that authority is relaxed, that the central power is a mere figure of State, and each magnate is a law unto himself. Add all these things to the social and economic forces that make for revolution, and it will not be surprising if the age of the Reformation in Germany should witness an onslaught, not merely on the mediæval Church, but on mediæval social and political institutions. To this attack all along the line of mediævalism, the Lutheran reformation contributed, as we shall see presently, its own quota of inspiration.

SOURCES.—Palacky, Documenta Mag. Joannis Hus, Vitam, Doctrinam, Causam in Constantiensi Concilio Actam, 1403-1418 (1869), and, Geschichte von Böhmen, vols. iii. and iv. (1845-57); The Works of Wicklif as noted under Chap. XIV. vol. i. of the present work; Gillet, The Life and Times of John Huss (1864); Loserth, Wicklif and Hus, translated by Evans (1884); Bonnechose, Letters of John Huss, translated by Mackenzie (1846); Wratislaw, John Hus (1882); Lechler, Johann von Wicklif und die Vorgeschichte der Reformation (1873); Maurice, Bohemia (1896); Denis, La Revolution Hussite, in tome iii. of L'Histoire Générale (Lavisse et Rambaud); Weber, Geschichte des Mittelalters (1870), and, Geschichte der Völker und Staaten im Ubergang vom Mittelalter zur Neuzeit (1873); Bezold, Geschichte der Deutschen Reformation (1890), particularly the introduction, Deutschland am Ausgang des Mittelalters; Janssen, History of the German People at the Close of the Middle Ages, English translation by Mitchell and Christie, vols. i. and ii. (1896);

Sources of Chapter IX.

Ulmann, Reformers before the Reformation, i., translated by Rev. R. Menzies (1853), Clark's Foreign Theological Library ; Maurer, Geschichte der Städteverfassung in Deutschland (1870-71); Ranke, Deutsche Geschichte im Zeitalter der Reformation, translation by Sarah Austin (1847) ; Bax, German Society at the Close of the Middle Ages (1894).

CHAPTER X.

The Swiss and the Frisians.

The Alpine land, known as modern Switzerland, was divided, throughout the Middle Ages, between Burgundy and Swabia, or Alemannia. The western portion was Burgundian, the eastern, Swabian. These divisions dated from the break-up of the Western Empire, when the Alemanni and the Burgundians shared the possession of ancient Helvetia. Both divisions formed part of Charlemagne's empire, and the great emperor, if tradition may be trusted, loved to take up his abode at his *pfalz* or mansion at Zürich. After the dissolution of the Frankish empire, the old division ultimately reappeared and perpetuated itself for several centuries, in spite of the vicissitudes of both the Burgundian kingdom and the Swabian duchy. In the twelfth century, the Swabian dukes of the Zaeringen dynasty obtained the upper hand over the greater part of this Alpine region, but on the extinction of their house in 1218, it fell under the rule of a number of magnates, of whom the Counts of Kyburg, Savoy, and Habsburg were the most powerful. During these changeful centuries, feudalism struck root in Switzerland, as in the rest of the empire, and the anarchy of the thirteenth favoured its growth. In Switzerland, too, the small freemen dwindled in numbers in virtue of the necessity of seeking the protection of a superior. Nevertheless, in this mountain land the spirit of liberty had by no means died out. The wild glens, where sprang the Rhine and the Rhone, nurtured a sturdy independence which would not bend to the usurpation of force. Nature, while nurturing the spirit of liberty, gave these freemen the means of asserting it against the aggressor. As the feudal magnate maintained his independence behind the strong walls of his castle, the Alpine herdsman maintained his birthright as a free man amid the giant precipices of his mighty mountains.

The feudal bully, spiritual or temporal, found his match in the hardy peasant of Valais or Schwyz, who defied his threats or his excommunications, and knew how to defend his rights against aggression.

This, Duke Berthold IV. of Zaeringen found to his cost when in 1180, as superior of the bishopric of Sitten, he crossed the Grimsel to reduce the defiant peasants to submission. The hardy mountaineers of Valais rushed to arms under their valiant Bishop Warin, and drove Berthold's horsemen into flight back across the pass, and just missed taking their ducal aggressor himself prisoner. These valiant herdsmen of the upper Rhone valley still governed themselves, as of yore, in their local assemblies at Combs, Brieg, Visp, Leuk, Syders, Sitten, and elected their own leader in war time. Equally forceful were the men of Schwyz, Uri, Unterwalden in the Reuss valley on the other side of the mountains that form the watershed of these rivers. There was, indeed, an inferior or serfish element in the population, for there were Church lands and feudal domains within this region, as elsewhere in Switzerland; but the freemen seem to have predominated, at least in Schwyz, and even the dependants of ecclesiastical and secular superiors enjoyed certain political rights. Though the men of Schwyz placed themselves under the local jurisdiction of the Counts of Lensburg and owned the supreme jurisdiction of the Dukes of Swabia, they managed their own affairs under their Landamman and their local elective officials. This liberty they stoutly defended against the encroachments of the Abbots of Einsiedeln who claimed their alps as part of the abbey lands, in virtue of a charter granted by Henry II. They refused to submit to canon law or to appear for judgment at the abbot's summons, defied the judgment of the emperor (Henry V.), to whom the abbot appealed, in his favour, defied even the imperial ban and the excommunication of the Bishop of Constance, compelled their priests to celebrate divine service notwithstanding, and earned from Frederick II., by their staunch support of the Hohenstaufen against pope, prelate, and magnate, the generous recognition by charter of their "Reichsfreiheit" (1240). These Schwyzers appealed to the emperor against these pretensions in the capacity of a free community (*tamquam homines liberi*); it was their glory that Frederick solemnly recognised the fact, and placed them by charter under his immediate suzerainty. They showed themselves equally resolute to resist the violation of their charter by the Habsburg counts, to whose arbitration and protection they had appealed in the course of the struggle with the Abbot of Einsiedeln, and who strove to increase their territorial power at their expense, and refused to recognise the imperial edict. Though they seem on the death of Frederick to have lost the boon of their "Reichsfreiheit," and to have owned the jurisdiction of the Habsburg, they continued to regard themselves as a free community (*liberi homines*), to manage largely their own affairs under their Landamman, or chief judge, and their Amman, or district officials, and to nurture the aspiration, at least, of complete self-government. "Meeting in general assembly," says Rilliet, "the Schwyzers assessed the taxes, and imposed them on the monasteries of their territory in spite of the inhibitions of their superiors. They intervene as guarantors in private transactions, and accord recompenses to those employed in the service of the community—a fact which denotes the exercise of self-government. They possess a common seal, the sign, if not of absolute political liberty, at least of complete municipal autonomy; they assume in their public acts the title of *universitas* and *communitas*, and they preserve that of *liberi homines*. They seem, in a word, to have enjoyed an independence equal to that which their neighbours of Uri had acquired."

These men of Uri, though subject like those of Schwyz, in part at least, to the *régime* of individual feudal superiors, such as the Abbess of Our Lady of Zürich, the barons of Rapperswyl, the Maison Dieu of Wettingen, were no less actuated by the aspiration of freedom. "The firmness," says M. Rilliet, "with which they maintained, in the face of the pretensions of their superiors, or the encroachments of their neighbours, what they regarded as their legitimate and hereditary possessions, denotes at once a fundamentally independent spirit, and a very lively sense of common interests. In these traits we recognise the future founders of a free confederation." They, too, had secured the privilege of "Reichsfreiheit" from Frederick, and though they lost it in 1218 by an imperial decree which placed them under the dominion of Count Rudolf the Silent of Habsburg, they succeeded in recovering it in 1231 at the hands of Frederick's son, King Henry, regent of Germany during his father's absence in Italy. It is in Uri, in fact, that we discover the permanent germ of the future free Confederation of the Forest Cantons. These Uri mountaineers were more successful than those of Schwyz in maintaining their "imperial" freedom, and though we find Count Rudolf III. of Habsburg intervening as arbiter in the strife which, in 1257 and 1258, rent them into bitter factions, he seems to have acted in his capacity as imperial deputy, not as feudal superior. This Count Rudolf, in fact, who became Roman king in 1273, confirmed in 1274 the decree of his predecessor, Henry, which granted them "Reichsfreiheit." During his long reign (1273-91), Uri was a self-governing community under its Landamman, who was at once the king's representative (the imperial title was in abeyance for the time being), and the head of the "Gemeinde," which met for common deliberation. A danger to the self-governing community lurked, however, in the fact that the Habsburg head of the empire was also a great territorial magnate—Count of Aargau and Zürichgau—and in the striving of the Habsburgs to increase their territorial jurisdiction at the expense of local rights and privileges. The danger was to prove a real menace under Rudolf's successors.

In the more lowland district of Unterwalden, where the Habsburg counts were the largest owners of the soil, the number of freemen seems to have been more limited than in Uri or Schwyz. Nor do these freemen seem till a later period to have attained the corporate organisation which made the Schwyzers, and in particular the men of Uri, self-governing communities. But the part they played in the coming struggle for complete independence shows that they bore the feudal *régime* with impatience and were as ready as their neighbours to rise against oppression.

The beginning of that united struggle may be definitely dated from the year 1291, the year of Rudolf's death, when the men of Uri, Schwyz, Unterwalden entered into a sworn confederation to maintain their rights against attack from without and oppression within. It was not the first time that they had done so, though, historically, we know little or nothing beyond the fact that in 1291 they were but renewing the old league which the anarchy of the previous fifty years had forced them more than once to conclude. The League or Bund of 1291 was a precautionary measure, in view of the accession of Duke Albert, Rudolf's successor, to the hereditary Habsburg possessions. Rudolf, as Roman king, might respect the "Reichsfreiheit" of Uri, though even under his auspices there was apparently a tendency to encroach on their rights for the sake of family aggrandisement. Duke Albert, whom the electors refused to invest with the royal dignity in preference to Adolf of Nassau, had not, as Count of Habsburg, the same inducement to do so. Nay, it was to be feared that he would seek to enhance his territorial jurisdiction as a neighbouring magnate at their expense. Hence the eternal *Bund* or confederation.

The spirit of this "Bund," which is written in Latin and preserved at Schwyz, is by no means revolutionary. The confederates do not throw off allegiance to the empire and found an independent State. They inculcate, in fact, the duty of obedience on the part of all who are under the jurisdiction of a superior, emphasise the feudal relation in the case of those who are amenable to it; but the spirit of independence is all the same unmistakably present. It appears in the sworn determination to maintain their rights against oppression from without, to resist the oppressive *régime* of any non-native officials whom the Habsburg may attempt to place over them. "Let it be known to all that the men of the valley of Uri, the commune of Schwyz, and the community of Unterwalden, in view of these evil days, have leagued themselves in good confidence, and have promised to maintain one another in their lives, goods, and rights with all their power, both within and without the valleys, against all who would do violence to them, or to one of their number." To this end they swear anew to observe their ancient alliance. "We have agreed not to receive in these valleys any judge (*judex, amman*), who is not a citizen and an inhabitant of this region, or who shall have obtained his office by money" They undertake, moreover, to administer public justice themselves, and to refer to arbitration any discord within the communities. This is the cardinal portion of the document, and it is replete with the stern, free spirit of men who regard their right to govern themselves as their highest good. In these Forest Cantons, as in the cities of Italy and France, it is in the conjuration (the confederates call themselves *conjurati*), the sworn confederation, that the champions of liberty find their remedy and prove their strength.

And in this peasant conjuration, this sworn "Bund" of the Rütli mead, lies an important political significance. These Schwyzer peasants not only taught their compatriots of the wider Alpine land that they had but to unite and strike to be free; they gave to Europe the first example of a free State founded in resistance to tyranny, and preserving its freedom in spite of seasons of internal friction and trial. It was an example which the Italian republics and the French communes failed to give, and which only the Dutch were able effectively to imitate after an interval of several centuries. The league of these freemen of the Forest Alps is, therefore, a most notable fact of mediæval history. It is a harbinger of modern liberty that does not prove to be a false prophet, and to the student of the parched waste of feudal history, with its monotonous record of anarchy, war, and tyranny, it comes like the refreshing midsummer breeze from the sunny Alpine heights. There is something peculiarly impressive, too, in the spectacle of a handful of hardy mountaineers throwing defiance in the face of the insolent feudal oppressor. Here is the spirit born of the wild Alpine land, where to be a slave seems so evidently to be out of harmony with nature, where man's environment is the nurse of bold self-reliance which disdains danger and hates slavery, where to be weak seems so palpably to be unworthy to live in communion with nature's gigantic forces. It was meet, therefore, that tyranny should find its invincible foe in the land of the avalanche and the mighty mountain flood, under the shadow of the Uri Rothstock and the Bristenstock, the Frohnalpstock and the Mythen.

The traditional sequel to this solemn conjuration has been picturesquely told by the chronicler, Tschudi, and immortalised in Schiller's stirring drama. It is the story of the beginning of the heroic age of Swiss history, of William Tell and the three confederates, Fürst, Melchthal, and Stauffach. It has given rise to violent controversy; has had its bitter opponents, who have discredited it as pure fiction; its ardent champions, some of whom have upheld its literal accuracy, others its historic value as a mixture of fact and fiction. Its spirit, at all events, is certainly in keeping with that of the *Ewiger Bund*, the eternal alliance concluded in 1291 at Schwyz. "We shall not submit to an alien oppressive rule, and we shall unite and fight in resistance to it," is the resolute tenor of this *Bund*, as quoted above. Tell may be wholly or largely a myth; the spirit that created the Swiss Confederation is no myth. It is embodied in the resolute language of an historic document, still preserved as the precious heritage of a free nation.

The chronicler's circumstantial story has, however, failed to stand the test of hostile criticism, and it certainly challenges criticism, even if we admit that it is not wholesale fiction. Very supicious at the outset is the fact that, while the historic evidence becomes ever more meagre the nearer we approach the period of the traditional struggle for independence, as described by the later chroniclers, it gradually expands with the centuries into the coherent, detailed, and picturesque narrative of Tschudi. The earliest chronicler who notices the revolt which culminated in the battle of Morgarten in 1315, is the Abbot of Victring in Carinthia. The abbot flourished during the first half of the fourteenth century, and was, therefore, a contemporary, if not an eye-witness of the events to which he all too briefly refers. His silence may be partly explained by his remoteness from the scene of action. From such a writer we should only expect a very general knowledge of what was passing in the remote and sequestered region around Uri Lake. He says nothing of the oppression of King Albrecht's local officials, and merely notes the innate love of freedom which nerved these high-spirited mountaineers of Uri, Schwyz, and Unterwalden to resist the demands of Duke Leopold of Austria, Albrecht's successor, and transformed them into the heroes of Morgarten. Assuming that the Abbot of Victring did not know, or did not wish, as a Habsburg subject, to make known the facts discreditable to the Habsburg *régime* in the Forest Cantons, which a later tradition has preserved—what are we to make of the silence of other fourteenth-century chroniclers—of Mathias of Neuenburg, of the anonymous chronicler of the town of Zürich, of Jean de Winterthur—who lived near the scene of the drama of which Tell and his confederates form the heroic figures? They too seem to have known nothing of the heroic exploits of Tell and his fellow-patriots, or of the precise outrages which made them at once the avengers of wrong and the founders of a free State. It is not till fully a hundred years after the battle of Morgarten that Conrad Justinger, Secretary of the Council of Bern, who, about the year 1420, wrote an account of the origin of the Swiss Confederation, ventures some general observations on the tyrannic Habsburg *régime* which made these Alpine freemen of Uri, Schwyz, Unterwalden its implacable foes. Justinger, however, places the outbreak of the struggle for independence much earlier than the later traditional account. The attempt to maintain their ancient liberties against the Habsburg oppressor lasted, in fact, according to the Secretary of the Bern Council, with little intromission throughout the thirteenth century right on to the battle of Morgarten, in the middle of the second decade of the fourteenth. Justinger's testimony is of considerable weight, as that of a writer who specially investigated the subject, in contrast to his predecessors, who merely notice the Forest Cantons in passing. He emphasises the fact that these Habsburg counts, especially of the older line, were guilty of usurpation and oppression in their dealings with the men of these cantons, that this oppression continued under the later Austrian line, and that the men of Uri, Schwyz, and Unterwalden maintained a long feud in defence of the rights which the officials of these grasping Habsburgs ignored and strove to suppress. But even Justinger deals only in generalities, and evidently knows nothing of the three confederates, of the Rütli assembly, of the Tell episode. It is difficult to believe that if he had known the picturesque details of the later heroic tradition, he would have passed them over in silence. His tone is, in fact, that of a writer who had only a vague and general knowledge of what he was writing about.

The details are, however, supplied in increasing instalments by the later chroniclers and popular songs of the fifteenth century. They grew in bulk, in fact, with the lapse of the generations. Hemerlin, canon of Zürich, for instance, gives the names of the local tyrants whose excesses conjured the storm of popular wrath in the three cantons. Before the end of the century, the Rütli and Tell episodes appear in the ballad story, which delighted the popular ear. Melchior Russ of Lucerne improves on Hemerlin, and incorporates the Tell ballad in his chronicle in the form of a chapter entitled, "What happened to Tell on the Lake." Only, he places the episode in the middle of the thirteenth century, instead of the beginning of the fourteenth—the period, that is, of the conflict between the Schwyzers and the earlier Counts of Habsburg. We get a step further, on turning to the "White Book of Sarnen," the work of an anonymous chronicler, written about 1470. The Sarnen author professes to give quite a circumstantial account of the events that led to the formation of the confederation, and, moreover, advances these events to the end of the thirteenth and the beginning of the fourteenth centuries. The story, as thus embellished and chronologically fixed, was reproduced with some small variants and additions by the chronicler Etterlin, Secretary of State at Lucerne, whose book appeared in 1507. It received its final form at the hands of the indefatigable Tschudi of Glarus—the Swiss Herodotus as he has been called—and in this form it long passed for sober history in the eyes of posterity.

Here it is in brief *resumé* from Tschudi. Duke Albrecht of Austria (who, be it remembered, succeeded to his father King Rudolf's hereditary possessions in 1291, and became himself German king in 1298 by the victory of Göllheim over King Adolf of Nassau) proved a very taskmaster of these Alpine freemen. He instructed his agents, Beringer von Landenberg, governor of Unterwalden, and Gessler, governor of Schwyz and Uri, to disregard the liberties of the people and treat them with the utmost rigour if they demurred. Many were the outrages committed by these men and their subordinates, and to the remonstrances of their victims Duke and King Albrecht paid not the slightest heed. Landenberg, for example, sent a servant to seize the two best oxen of Henry of Melchthal in Unterwalden in punishment of some trifling misdemeanour on the part of his son Arnold. In answer to the old man's remonstances, the insolent valet retorted that it was the opinion of the governor that the peasants themselves should draw the plough. In a moment of passion, young Arnold struck the valet with a stick and broke one of his fingers. He escaped to Uri, but Landenberg in revenge tore out his father's eyes. To Uri, too, had fled Conrad of Baumgarten, likewise of Unterwalden, who had cleft the skull of Landenberg's bailiff, Wolfenschiess, with his axe in revenge for the attempted outrage of his wife. On learning the tragic fate of his father, young Arnold took secret council with the more trusty men of the district as to how to avenge his wrongs. Thither also came Werner Stauffach of Steinen in Schwyz, who hated and had reason to fear the tyranny of Gessler, the governor. This tyrant had built a fortress on a height above Altorf, which he called Zwinghof or Zwing Uri (Uri's prison), and stuck the ducal hat on a pole in the market-place of the village, to which he ordered the passers-by to do obeisance in token of their servitude. He further vexed the people by his insolent and overbearing language, menacing in particular this Stauffach, who was one of the richer peasants and had built himself a handsome house at Steinen. "To whom belongs this house?" demanded he, in passing on his way to Schwyz. "My lord," replied the cautious Stauffach, "it belongs to my sovereign lord the king, and is your fief and mine." "I will not suffer peasants like you to live in such lordly houses," cried the tyrant angrily; "I will teach you to resist." Stauffach's prudent wife, foreseeing trouble, advised her husband to go to Uri and take council with the malcontents there against the governor's tyranny. Stauffach accordingly departed to visit his friend, Walter Fürst of Attinghausen, in whose house Arnold of Melchthal lay in hiding. These three men resolved to concoct a rising of the inhabitants of Schwyz, Uri, and Unterwalden, and at a meeting on the night of 8th November 1307, at the sequestered spot called the Rütli, below the Seelisberg, on the Lake of Uri, they and their confederates resolved to deliver their fatherland from the tyranny of the Habsburg oppressor, and fixed the 1st January following for the rising.

Thus, according to our chronicler, the basis of the union and deliverance of this Alpine land was laid by these three peasant patriots and their fellows. Among their confederates was a certain William Tell, a native of Bürglen, and son-in-law of Walter Fürst. On Sunday the 18th, Tell was in Altorf, and passed the hat without doing obeisance. The sequel is too well known to be retold. The story of Tell's master-shot which split the apple on his darling boy's head and earned him a reluctant pardon, of the avowal of his intention to shoot the tyrant with the second arrow in his quiver, in case the first had transfixed the head of his child, of his renewed seizure and doom to life-long imprisonment in the tyrant's dungeon at Kussnacht, of the storm on Uri Lake on the way thither in the governor's barge, of his release in order to make trial of his skill as a boatman in the midst of the howling tempest, of his escape at the Tellenplatte, and the second master-shot which struck the tyrant's heart in the narrow way near Kussnacht—this dramatic tale has been told again and again since old Tschudi, culling chiefly from the "White Book of Sarnen" (1470), wrote it in his chronicle in 1570, and Schiller embodied it in the most telling of his dramas. Tell's resolute deed fired his confederates with the courage to strike the meditated blow for their common deliverance. On New Year's Day 1308 they seized, by a series of ruses, the strongholds of their oppressors at Rotzberg and Sarnen in Unterwalden, Gessler's Uri prison at Altorf, and Lowerz in Schwyz, took Landenberg prisoner, and compelled him and his fellow-tyrants to swear never to set foot again in the Forest Cantons. Whereupon these forcible patriots met at Brunnen and swore anew an eternal *Bund* in defence of their liberties.

Such is the tale which the patriotic chronicler fashioned together fully two and a half centuries after the events in question. Is it romance or is it history? is the question over which the controversialists have fought so fiercely. The tendency has for some time been towards scepticism. Some of these hostile critics emphasise the striking resemblance of the Tell episode to the story of the Danish Toko, the assassin of King Harold, and regard it as the transplantation of the northern tradition to Swiss soil. The identity of the two episodes is certainly suspicious, in the absence of contemporary historic proof of Tell's exploits. Resemblances between historic episodes, otherwise unconnected, are common enough, and mere similarity may be no reason for denying that both actually happened. But indubitable historic evidence, in support of the recurrence in Switzerland of such an episode as that said to have taken place in Denmark, is indispensable, and in the case of the Tell Saga, this evidence is lacking. We cannot be sure even of the existence of Tell, not to speak of his traditional exploits, since we cannot be certain that the testimony of the 140 men of Uri, who in 1388 averred that they had known him in bygone days, was not the fabrication of a later time. More serious is the chronological difficulty inherent in the tale. It assumes that the confederation owed its rise to the events said to have happened in the year before King Albrecht's death. This is clearly an anachronism, for the confederation, as a permanent union, was at least as old as 1291, and the cantons are even found temporarily allied fifty years earlier. It assumes, further, that Albrecht was a grasping autocrat, and his agents in the Forest Cantons harsh and heartless instruments of his greed and his high-handed ways. On the other hand, some of the hostile critics minimise the oppression of the Habsburg officials; some deny it altogether as the poetic and patriotic invention of a later time, and ask for proofs of Gessler's existence. Whatever may be adduced in mitigation of Albrecht's *régime*, his reputation still remains as that of a hard, violent man who showed no mercy to opponents, and sought to aggrandise his house, as well as strengthen his power and put down anarchy in the empire. At the same time it is but fair to remember that authentic contemporary history, as far as it touches on this remote region—and it does so but very intermittently—has taken no notice of the traditional misdeeds of Albrecht's tyrannical representatives in the Forest Cantons.

That at all events there slumbered in the hearts of these Alpine freemen an invincible hatred to the Habsburg *régime* is evident from the fact that they petitioned and obtained the confirmation of their Reichsfreiheit from Albrecht's enemy and predecessor King Adolf in 1297, and that after the short reign of Henry VII. of Luxemburg, the murdered Albrecht's successor, they clave to the Bavarian Ludwig against the Habsburg Frederick as their imperial head, and resorted to arms to resist the three armies with which the Habsburg Duke Leopold determined, once for all, to crush their sworn antagonism to his house. It was one of these armies led by Leopold himself, and composed of the *élite* of Habsburg chivalry, that these sturdy peasants cut in pieces at Morgarten, on Aegeri Lake, eight years after the traditional Rütli episode (15th November 1315), while the other two fled in dismay at the news of the crushing disaster. And Morgarten was but the first of a series of decisive victories, won in the same cause, which lend such an heroic grandeur to the incipient history of this little free State among the Alps. It was the precursor of Laufen and the prowess of Rudolf von Erlach (1339), of Sempach and the heroism of Arnold von Winkelried (1386), of Naefels and the doughty deeds of Ambühl and his men of Glarus (1388), of Stoss and the noble champion of the Appenzell peasants, Graf von Weidenberg (1405), of the equally heroic struggle which resulted in the gradual emancipation of Wallis from Savoy, and Graubunden from Austria. It was the precursor, too, of the wider confederation of the eight cantons to which the little State had swelled by 1368, and of the still larger union of the thirteen cantons and their subject or allied lands (*zugewandte Unterthane*), which at last, at the end of the fifteenth century, cut themselves clear of the empire, as a sovereign federal republic with its general diet, or Tagsatzung. Some of these federated cantons were city States, such as Bern, Lucerne, Solothurn, Freiburg, in which the government was exclusively aristocratic; or like Zürich, Basle, Schaffhausen, where it was more democratic. Uri, Schwyz, Unterwalden, Glarus, Appenzell, Zug, were democracies where the sovereign people met and legislated in Landesgemeinden, or district parliaments, and thus perpetuated the popular assembly of the old Germanic tribe. This sovereign assembly still remains as a relic of a hoary antiquity in certain sequestered spots of this Alpine land, at Trogen in Appenzell, Glarus, Bozlingen in Uri, Sarnen in Unterwalden, for instance. Hither the people flock, as a rule, on the last Sunday of April, to engage in common worship, listen to an address from the Landamman, elect their magistrates and other officials, accept by holding up the right hand the proposals presented by the Landrath, and finally instal the Landamman for the year. This simple and impressive scene takes us back far beyond the Middle Ages, to those primitive times when the *Volk*, the people, was supreme, and presents an object-lesson in the liberty which the freemen of the Forest Cantons had preserved and knew how to vindicate from the encroachment of the oppressor.

From the snow-clad mountains that feed the sources of the Rhine, the scene now changes to the marshy flats in which it loses itself in the northern ocean. Here, too, freedom found a refuge, struggled hard to preserve itself from feudal encroachment, and finally, though in more modern days, achieved a triumph still more important than that won by the brave freemen of the Alpine land at the far south extremity of the Rhine River. On these flats dwelt the Frisians, and in the days of Charlemagne they are found occupying the coast lands from the mouth of the Scheldt to the mouth of the Weser, and divided by the Zuyder See—the Almeer—into the East and the West Frisians.

Till comparatively recently the historians taught us to believe that these men of Friesland, particularly East Friesland, were a race of freemen who had never bowed their necks beneath imperial or other yoke, who retained throughout the wild mediæval centuries the pristine liberty and the characteristic institutions of their Teutonic ancestors, who formed a republic, consisting of seven federated States under a supreme popular assembly, which met at the Upstalboom, near Aurich. Friesland, or what portion of it remained unsubdued, constituted, in fact, a purely primitive democracy, unalloyed by Roman or Romano-German imperialism, uninfluenced by the feudal system, and presenting the most perfect system of popular government known to the world before the days of modern parliaments. Such, in general, is the picture presented by patriotic writers like Emmius (the Frisian Tschudi) in the sixteenth and Wiarda in the eighteenth centuries, and reflected in the German erudition of an Eichhorn in the nineteenth. Alas! as in the case of the primitive Alpine republic, the remorseless scepticism of the historic critic has dashed the picture of primitive Frisian democracy in pieces. The iconoclast is a German *savant* of the most ponderous and painful type—Professor Dr Freiherr Karl von Richthofen, of Damsdorf, bei Striegau. Von Richthofen has written one of the most unreadable of these terrible productions of the critical historical school. He calmly tells us, indeed, in his preface, that he is concerned solely with his subject, not with his reader. Nevertheless, the student of Frisian history cannot afford to eschew his shaggy volumes.

According to Von Richthofen, then, the idea of a popularly governed Frisian republic dating from the days of Karl the Great, and taken by him under his protection, is a pure myth. In the "Lex Frisionum," of date 785, and its Additio (802), there is no trace of such a republic. Karl gave law to the Frisians as subjects of the empire, and like other subjects of the empire, they were under the jurisdiction of imperial counts. Various parts of Friesland were, in fact, successively subjugated by Pepin Heristal, Charles Martel, and the great Charles himself. The so-called "Privilege" by which Charles conferred on the Frisians self-government in return for their services to the empire, more especially in the Saxon wars, is a palpable forgery of a much later time. According to this document, they were to remain perpetually free, and absolved from any proprietary servitude. No lord should rule over them except by their freewill and consent. They were empowered to elect their own podesta, consuls, and judges, &c. All this is palpably unhistoric. There were no podestas, no consuls in Friesland for hundreds of years after the reign of Charlemagne. The "Privilege" is a forgery of some patriotic scribe of probably the thirteenth century. The so-called privileges of King William (1248) and King Rudolf have equally vanished into the realm of romance before the critical eye of the acute, if ponderous Von Richthofen, who, if no master of style or literary arrangement, has certainly mastered the records of Frisian law and history as no writer had done before him.

It behoves us, then, unfortunately, to discard the idea of a free Frisian people, maintaining the continuity of pristine freedom and republican self-government from the pre-Carolingian period right through the dark ages into the fifteenth century. The fact is that the Western Frisians living between the Sinkfal, near Bruges, and the Zuyder See were subjugated by Pepin Heristal in 689. Charles Martel extended Frankish rule in 734 over that portion of the Eastern Frisians dwelling between the Zuyder See and the Laubach. Charlemagne completed the conquest of the remainder as far east as the Weser, between 775 and 785. The western and part of the eastern divisions were placed by him under the ecclesiastical jurisdiction of the Bishop of Utrecht, the remainder under that of the Bishops of Bremen and Münster. For both divisions Charlemagne promulgated the Lex Frisionum in 785, and the addition to it in 802. Moreover, the people thus subdued and incorporated into the empire did not consist exclusively of freemen—an assumption of a much later time. In Friesland, as among other German tribes, there were nobles, freemen, lites, and slaves. Nor were they allowed to retain the exclusive right of self-government, as the pseudo-Privilege of the great Karl would make believe. Each "Gau," or county, embracing a number of "pagi," or minor territorial subdivisions, was in secular matters subject to the jurisdiction of an imperial count, or "Graf," and as in the other parts of the empire, these imperial officials gradually became feudal lords, holding their fiefs of the Kaiser or the bishop. The feudal system penetrated here as in most other parts of the empire. It would seem, however, that these feudal lords did not succeed in superseding all the old customs of the land. The noble proprietors and the freemen of each county retained, or claimed, in spite of feudal pretension, the right to assemble under the presidency of the count or his intendant, to deliberate on the affairs of the community, to give judgment in accordance with the old Assega Book of Frisian law, and the infringement of their right appears to have been vigorously resented. At all events we find traces here, as in the Forest Cantons and in the German cities, of the "conjuration" or sworn union in defence of old rights, or for the purpose of securing new ones, throughout the twelfth, thirteenth, and fourteenth centuries.

Thus a league or confederation gradually developed, which welded the provinces, or Seelanden of East Friesland (the number varied with the occasion) for common purposes of defence against feudal aggression from within or without. The elected representatives of these confederate provinces (*conjurati*, *deputati*) met in general assembly at the Upstalboom, near Aurich in Brokmerland, and Von Richthofen admits that these assemblies are as old at least as the twelfth century. Our critic admits, too, that this elected assembly did, when in session, exercise legislative and executive functions. As evidences of its legislative activity he prints the *Vetus Jus Frisicum*, which, he thinks, is not older than the middle of the twelfth century, though it professes to be enacted by Charlemagne himself; the *Ueberküre*, or *Supreme Laws*, as the word may be translated into English, which have survived not in the original Latin, but in an old Frisian text, and date from the beginning of the thirteenth century; and the *Leges Upstalboomicæ*, which belong to the beginning of the fourteenth (1323). He will, however, not allow that this confederation had existed from the days of Charlemagne, or that it represented an organic free State, a fully fledged republic, with permanent sovereign authority over its members and a permanent central administration. The assembly at the Upstalboom was neither the general assembly of the people, nor the representative parliament of a homogeneous nation. "It was merely a reunion of the representatives of various Frisian districts, between the Zuyder See and the Weser. The deputies of these districts came together for definite objects—in the earliest times for the preservation or restoration of the peace, for the punishment of those who had broken it, for the defence of the existing laws, for the maintenance of the common security against those feudal lords who possessed certain traditional rights, and sought to enforce them." And though the powers of this assembly seem to have grown with the centuries, and its acts were passed "with the common consent of all Frisians," and were sealed with the seal of "all Friesland," it only exercised these powers at long intervals, and finally collapsed in the latter half of the fourteenth century. The attempt to establish a federal republic, which succeeded in the Alpine valleys, failed in these Frisian flats. That attempt was only to triumph as the result of the mighty religious conflict, two centuries later, when East Friesland, or at least part of it, became one of the provinces of the great free State founded by William of Orange.

What we have in this East Frisian land from the twelfth to the fourteenth century is, as I apprehend, the germ of a free State, rather than an actual free State. The spirit of freedom is strong in the people; the will to defend it, the effort to incorporate it in a general confederation are there. The freemen, as in Brokmerland, have preserved, or recovered and developed a system of self-government. Each of the four subdivisions of Brokmerland, for instance, is found in the thirteenth century under the jurisdiction of four annually elected consuls, Gretmanni or Redjeven (Rathgeber, Councillors), and these sixteen form an executive and judicial Council for the whole territory. The same phenomenon appears in the other provinces, where the freemen have similarly succeeded in asserting complete self-government against the feudal superior. From these elected councillors the deputies to the general assembly, or Thing, at the Upstalboom were in turn chosen. We have here a system of local and general representative government, which only lacked the touch of the statesman to transform into an organic free State. Unfortunately the touch of the statesman was lacking till the days of William of Orange. The East Frisians never got beyond the embryonic stage in State formation. Their union did not constitute a republic, for, according to Von Richthofen, the phrase "conspiratores contra rem publicam" refers to the community (*Gemeindewesen*), not to a regularly constituted State. It was only a league for certain purposes, and this league was renewed as occasion happened to dictate. The assembly at the Upstalboom was fitful, intermittent. The only indisputable historical instances occur in the first half of the thirteenth (1216, 1224, 1231) and the fourteenth centuries respectively. The attempt of Groningen to renew the league and its assembly in 1361 proved abortive.

These tentative efforts of the men of East Friesland deserved a better fate. The glimpses we get of their history in the chronicles show them to have been a mettlesome race, ever restive under the feudal bit, ever ready to rush to arms, when the blazing pitch barrel spread the alarm from village to village, and repel attack by sea or land. During the tenth century the Western Frisians came under the domination of the Counts of Holland, but their insurrectionary proclivities gave their rulers no end of trouble before they gradually developed into the industrious citizens of the towns which sprang into thriving municipalities two hundred years later. The Eastern Frisians likewise acknowledged the feudal supremacy of various magnates, like the Dukes of Oldenburg and the Archbishop of Bremen, but they were quick to resent aggression, and ultimately secured what was practically self-government. Thus when Duke Bernhard of Saxony, and Adalbert, Archbishop of Bremen, marched a mighty host into their fens in 1060 to break their defiant spirit, the sturdy inhabitants met their aggressors in pitched battle, drove them into flight, and sacked their camp into the bargain. Henry the Lion, who attempted to reduce the men of Groningen to obedience about the middle of the next century, was equally unsuccessful. Towards the end of it, the Stedingers, the Frisian inhabitants of the tongue of land at the mouth of the Weser, are found in bitter feud with the Counts of Oldenburg, whose castle they razed to the ground. Excommunicated by the Archbishop of Bremen, and denounced by the pope as heretics, they were exposed to the terrible visitation of a crusade, organised by Conrad of Marburg, and after suffering the horrors inflicted by the brutalised religious spirit of the age, were overwhelmed in the battle of Altenersch in 1234. In spite of this bloody triumph on their eastern flank, the Bremen archbishops were never able to enforce their will on these redoubtable freemen, who showed their contempt for one of these mitred Bremen dignitaries, John Fursat, by thrashing him with their sticks and forcing him to flee to Avignon.

Their would-be conquerors of Holland and Guelders, on the western side, had no better success. Reinhold of Guelders, who presumed to claim their allegiance, paid for his rashness by the defeat of Vollenhoven in 1323. A still more crushing disaster overtook Count William II. of Hainault and Holland, who in 1345 sailed across the Zuyder See, with a mighty flotilla, to settle old scores once for all with these redoubtable freemen. Not only was the greater part of his fleet destroyed by a storm, but William himself was slain in the encounter that followed his landing at Staveren. Fifty years later the attempt to crush their resistance was repeated by William III. at the head of a second great army. The Frisians were temporarily subdued, but the invader was unable to hold what he had won by force of numbers, and was compelled, in the face of repeated risings, to acknowledge their independence in 1402, and driven, twelve years later, from Staveren, the old outpost of these Holland Counts on the eastern side of the Zuyder See. More or less independent they continued to be for another century, in spite of internal dissensions between Schieringers and Vetkoopers, when they fell under the dominion of the Duke Albert of Saxony, whom the Emperor Maximilian created their Podesta in 1498, and by whose successor, Duke George, they were transferred in 1515 to the sceptre of the Habsburg Charles. It was during this period that the towns of Emden, Norden, Leeuwarden, Groningen rose in importance as trade centres.

Evidently a mettlesome folk were these men of East Friesland, whose indomitable spirit was steeled by the constant struggle with the ocean floods that frequently devastated their swampy fens, as was that of the Alpine freemen in the presence of the gigantic forces of their mountain land. Amid the dunes by the northern sea, where the floodtide beat its wild music and nerved the strong man to devise his preservation, as on the wild slopes, where avalanche and torrent taught a hardy race the virtues of daring and resolute toil, freedom was equally in its true element. And thus the story of their heroic resistance to aggression has in it many points of similarity—the same deeds of prowess against overwhelming numbers, the same tough determination to oppose force by force, the same contempt of danger, whether from the mountain torrent or the ocean wave.

The mettlesome spirit of these free and hardy men has imprinted itself on the Frisian laws as well as exemplified itself in Frisian history. The oldest of these laws, with the exception of the *Lex Frisionum*, cannot claim a higher antiquity than the twelfth century. The *Vetus Jus Frisicum*, the *Ueberküre*, the *Leges Upstalboomicæ*, the Brokmer Briefs (latter half of the thirteenth century), &c., belong to the period of the reaction against feudalism. Whatever their exact date, their spirit is that of freemen conscious of the right to govern themselves, and jealous for its maintenance. "The Frisian shall be free as long as the wind blows out of the clouds and the world stands." This generous sentiment must indeed be received with considerable reservation. It trespasses, as is usually the case in such generalisations, beyond the real state of things. All Frisians were evidently not free, for not only feudalism, but serfdom struck root in this fenland as elsewhere. But it expresses a very general aspiration which the Frisian freemen were not slow on occasion to exemplify against their aggressors. " If any prince, secular or spiritual," decrees the first article of the *Leges Upstalboomicæ* of 1323, "of whatever name or dignity he may be, attack us Frisians, or any of us, with intent to reduce us under the yoke of slavery, we shall, with common concurrence, and armed hand, mutually defend our liberty." These Frisians would not submit to dictation, whether from their own officials or their would-be conquerors. " The Frisians claim free speech, and free answer, and a free judgment-seat." They would accept no law that they themselves had not willed. " So will the Brockmen ; so have the people decided." " This is the first law of all the Frisians," we read in the *Ueberküre;* "we come together (by representatives, that is) once a year at the Upstalboom " (the annual meeting proved, however, abortive) " on Tuesday in the Whitsun week in order that we may then and there consult as to the laws which the Frisian is to hold. And if any man knoweth how to amend a law, then may we set aside the lighter law and hold to the better law."

Each one shall be assured the unquestioned right of his property, unless deprived by law, and no violence may rob him of his rights. " This is the supreme right of all Frisians," we read in the *Vetus Jus Frisicum*, " that each man possess his own goods." Only in case of dire necessity—that of the fatherless child, for instance, in danger of perishing from starvation—may property be alienated. "If the child is stark naked and houseless, and exposed to the dew and the mist or the winter cold, when every man goeth to his garden, or into his house, or to his own corner, as the wild beast seeks the hollow tree and the shelter of the mountain to protect its life, while the fatherless child cries and weeps, mourning its nakedness and homelessness, and its father, who should have screened it from hunger and the winter's cold damp, lies deep and dark under four nails and under oak and earth, concealed and covered, then must the mother sell and dispose so much of her child's possessions and watch over it as long as it is young, so that frost and hunger may not destroy it."

Equally sacred is the duty of defending the land against the invader. The Frisian freeman must be ready at any moment to risk his life "against the southern Saxon and the Northman, against the tall helmet and the red shield, and the unrighteous might, with the aid of God and St Peter." He must fight, too, against the treacherous foe that daily beats against his low and feeble coasts, "with the spade, and the fork, and the hod." Within he is equally jealous for his birthright of freedom, and will not permit his fellow, at least before the fourteenth century, to entrench himself in a stone house and play the master, as nearly everywhere in the world lying outside his fens. Only the house of God may be stone built, and the same wariness of tyranny is perceptible in the law that sought to frustrate the interference of the clergy in political affairs. So deeply was the love of freedom engraved in their hearts that the epithet of free sprang from heart to lip in common salutation. *Eala fria Fresena*, "Hail, free Frisian!" was the greeting which conveyed the sense of a common dignity from one freeman to another.

Thus in the Frisian fens and the Alpine glens the old free institutions of the German Volk maintained, or reasserted themselves in defiance of feudal aggression. There were other districts within the empire where the peasant proprietor had not been quite enveloped by the meshes of feudal servitude— in Saxony, Franconia, Swabia, the Rhinelands, Bavaria, Tyrol —and where the peasant retained sufficient self-respect to turn occasionally on his oppressors. Such risings did not succeed, however, in attaining or perpetuating the liberty lost from earlier times. Only in the Scandinavian lands of the rugged north did the peasantry or Bonden, after long battling to preserve their individuality against the growing power of king, nobility, and priesthood, finally succeed in asserting their rights as the Fourth Estate in the national Council. To this privilege the German peasant never attained in mediæval times. Nay, he remained a serf, for the most part, till the era of the French Revolution, in spite of the great insurrection in the days of Luther.

Sources of Chapter X.

SOURCES.—For the origin of the Swiss confederation—The Chronicle of the Abbot of Victring, in Böhmer, Fontes Rerum Germanicarum, vol. i. ; The Chronicle of Mathias de Neuenbourg, edited by Studer (1867); Jean de Winterthur, ed. by Wyss, in Archiv für Schweizerische Geschichte, xi. ; The Chronicle of Justinger, ed. by Stierlin and Wyss (1819); Hemmerlin, De Nobilitate et Rusticitate Dialogus, in Thesaurus Historiæ Helveticæ; Eidgenössische Lieder-Chronik vom XIII. bis zum XVI. Jahrhundert, ed. by Rochholz (1842); Melchior Russ, Chronicle, ed. by Schneller (1834); The White Book of Sarnen, edited in 1856 by Wyss under the title of Die Chronik des Weissen Buches im Archiv Obwalden ; The Chronicle of P. Etterlin, edited by Spreng (1752); Tschudi, Chronicon Helveticum, edited by Iselin (1734-36). Among modern books, see especially Kopp, Geschichte der eidgenössischen Bünde (1847-62); Rilliet, Les Origines de la Confederation Suisse (1869); Dierauer, Geschichte der Schweizerischen Eidgenossenschaft (1887); Menzel, Geschichte der Deutschen, vols. i. and ii. (1873); Hug and Stead, Switzerland (1890); Freeman, Growth of the English Constitution, chap. i. ; Müller, Histoire de la Suisse, is in part antiquated. For the Frisians see especially Richthofen, Untersuchungen über friesische Rechtsgeschichte (1880 - 82); Schwartzenberg, Charterboek van Friesland, vol. i. (1768); Telting, Het Oudfriesche Stadrecht (1882); Hegel, Städte und Gilden der Germanischen Völker, Bd. ii. (1891); Blok, Geschiedenis van het Nederlandsche Volk, translated by Bierstadt and Putnam, i. (1898); The Lex Frisionum, in vol. iii. of Monumenta Germaniæ Historica, sect. Leges ; The Vetus Jus Frisicum and other Frisian codes are given by Von Richthofen ; Eichhorn, Deutsche Staats und Rechtsgeschichte, vols. ii. and iii. ; Motley, Rise of the Dutch Republic ; Menzel, Geschichte der Deutschen ; Dunham, History of the Germanic Empire, i. and ii.

CHAPTER XI.

Emancipation and Revolution in the Netherlands.

During the Middle Ages the Netherlands formed politically, if not geographically, a rather indefinite region. In the tenth century, indeed, the greater part of it appears as a political unit under the name of the Duchy of Lower Lorraine, which stretched from the Scheldt to the Rhine, from the marshy coast of the north to Sedan in the south, and formed one of the ducal provinces of the empire. Westwards of the Scheldt lay the remaining portion, the great county of Flanders, which was mostly a fief of the French crown. While the Flemish county, with the exception of Artois, ceded to France, remained intact for many centuries under the descendants of Baldwin of the Iron Arm, the Lotharingian duchy erelong succumbed to the feudal attrition which destroyed its unity. A number of petty feudal States was the result of this friction—the duchies of Brabant and Limburg, the great bishoprics of Utrecht, Liège, and Cambrai, the counties of Holland, Namur, Luxemburg, Hainault, Guelders, besides a number of smaller lordships which succeeded for a time in maintaining their independence of the greater magnates. The only bond of union was the common subjection to the emperor, but this subjection to one supreme head did not, as a rule, prove more conducive to peace and order in the Netherlands than in the rest of the empire. These Netherland magnates quarrelled and fought with one another, and filched and wasted one another's lands, in spite of the Pax of their imperial overlord, or the Truce of God proclaimed by the Church. Each had his standing enemy and his standing feud—Holland and Hainault with Flanders, Holland with Friesland, Guelders and Holland with Utrecht, Brabant with Guelders and Luxemburg, Luxemburg and Hainault with Liège, and so on, to the general misery of the wretched people and with small enough results to the magnates themselves. Out of this vortex of contention chance ultimately drew Holland, Zealand, and Hainault together under one count, Brabant and Limburg under one duke; but, otherwise, the turmoil of jealousies and strifes continued until the Burgundian in the fifteenth century dragged all, with the exception of Liège, alike into his net.

The Netherlands, throughout these dark, chaotic ages, thus afford a striking object-lesson in mediæval anarchy. Here, as elsewhere, this history is largely the record of fighting, burning, stealing, harrying, murdering in the name of fist right. Nay, each State had its own internal quarrels to aggravate the turmoil of interprovincial broils—the mighty contention of the Hooks and Cabeljauws, or Cods, for instance, who distracted little Holland for many a generation with their bickerings, though they only weary the historian now; the deadly struggles between prince and people in Flanders, which was no teapot storm at all events, and was fraught with very momentous consequences in many ways, as shall appear directly. Friesland, as we have seen, was the only spot in these Netherlands flats which kept the feudal magnate at arm's length and presumed to govern itself with some measure of consideration for the general good.

Despite all this turbulent pugnacity, there was substantial progress in the arts of peace in these little States, particularly in Flanders and Brabant, from the twelfth century onwards. Their quarrels might be petty and sterile, but they are indicative of the force of character which was to secure for this flat land a marvellous *rôle* in modern history. These mediæval Netherlanders were a strong, tough race, which was training for its future destiny in fighting the sea, ever prone to submerge it, as well as fighting its own quarrels—a gritish race of fishermen, sailors, agriculturists, merchants, manufacturers, artists, which was to leave its mark on history. From these lowlands was to spring the republic, which in the seventeenth century, held for a season the naval, commercial, and political supremacy of the world.

Among these mediæval feudal States, Flanders played the chief *rôle*, though Brabant and, by-and-by, Holland also bulk largely in the history of the time. Flanders was partly a county, partly a lordship, partly allodial territory. The county embraced most of the land west of the Scheldt; the lordship included Alost, east of that river, and Waes and the Four Ambachten on its north-western bank. As count, its ruler held of the French crown; as lord, he was a prince of the empire; as an allodial proprietor, he was an independent superior. Its population was a mixture of Gallic and Germanic elements, but though the Germanic element predominated, the county, by far the largest division, was subject to the overlordship of the French kings. The count was in fact one of the twelve peers of France, and the first in rank of his order. He was, however, by no means a dutiful subject, and strove to make himself independent by the help of the English and imperial enemies of France. It was the policy of his overlord, on the other hand, to curb his insubordination and extract as much as possible of Flemish territory as appanages of the French crown. This policy triumphed at Bouvines where Count Ferdinand drew his sword against Philip Augustus, under the banner of the Emperor Otto IV., and definitely lost the province of Artois as the penalty of his defeat (Treaty of Melun, 1225). Philip's successors, especially Philip the Handsome, did not neglect to improve their advantage, and the struggle for supremacy between the houses of Avesnes and Dampierre supplied them with frequent opportunities for interference, both as superiors and as arbiters. To maintain his position against Jean D'Avesnes, who cultivated the support of the emperor, Guy de Dampierre (1280-1305) sought the protection of the French monarch. In the person of Philip IV., the protector threatened to become the master, the great fief of former days a royal province. From this fate it was saved by the democracy of the towns.

In the Netherlands, as in Western Europe generally, the revival of commerce brought the cities into prominence. From the twelfth century onwards they appear as thriving centres, which were possessed of a considerable measure of freedom, and were striving to increase it. In Flanders, in particular, the progress of civic life was extraordinary, and the fame of the Flemish cities erelong filled the whole civilised world. Towards the end of the century there were over forty of these rising towns in Flanders, to twelve for Brabant, seven for Hainault, half a dozen for Liège, four for the bishopric of Utrecht. During the next century the increase of the population and enterprise of Ghent, Bruges, Ypres, Douay, Lille, were phenomenal. Of these, again, Bruges, the centre of the English wool trade, and Ghent, and Ypres, the great centres of its manufacture, were the most magnificent. Bruges was the capital of the Hansa of London, as the association of Flemish towns, which held the monopoly of the trade with England, was called, and which was afterwards incorporated with the German Hansa. Hither came merchants from Italy and other southern lands to buy at the wool markets in exchange for the merchandise of the East : hither, too, the traders of the Hansa Bund from the Baltic and the North Sea to dispose of the products of the north. Before the rise of Antwerp in the sixteenth century, Bruges was the grand mart of Western and Northern Europe, where Italians, Germans, English, French, Scots, met to buy and sell the wares of many lands. Their sumptuous residences made Bruges a city of palaces, and the chroniclers vie with one another in lauding its splendour and opulence. The merchants of seventeen kingdoms had domiciles at Bruges, boasts one of them, besides the strangers from almost unknown lands, who resorted thither. The population of Ghent, the centre of the woollen industry, was even larger than that of Bruges. The chroniclers would, in fact, have us believe that it was the largest city in Europe, and Guicciardini still counted thirty-five thousand houses within the area enclosed by its walls, though at the period at which he wrote its prosperity had materially declined. Ypres, famed for its linen, was second only to Ghent as an industrial centre, and, along with it and Bruges, formed the Flemish triad. Thus in the thirteenth century it could be said, not without some exaggeration perhaps, that the Flemings were the cloth makers of Europe. The fineness of their workmanship gave them an easy predominance over those countries where textile industry was but in its infancy. England, France, Germany were in the thirteenth century a long way behind Flanders as industrial nations, and it was only at a later period that the manufacture of wool in England itself greatly lessened the export to Flanders, and thus injured its industry. They were equally expert in the manufacture of linen from the hemp and flax brought from the north in the ships of the Hanseatic League.

The growth of these prosperous cities owed much to the sagacity of the Flemish counts, notably Count Philip of Alsace (1168-1191), who founded a considerable number of towns on the coast, constructed harbours, exploited the waste lands. This sagacious policy, together with the advantages of natural situation, contributed to their phenomenal development. Count Philip was none the less hostile to the aspiration after municipal independence, but the rights granted by his predecessors were only temporarily curtailed by his vigorous government, and expanded under his successors into complete autonomy. From this period, " the municipalities," to quote M. Blok, a recent historian of the Netherlands, " really form small republics within the State." They were republics only in appearance, however, for their government was a monopoly in the hands of an aristocracy of wealth. The Flemish municipalities resemble in this respect those of the empire. A class of wealthy cloth merchants (*Poorters, Geslachten*) secures municipal self-government. This wealthy caste reserves to itself the exercise of power, and excludes the artisans—the weavers and fullers. These artisans organise themselves in gilds and attempt to break down the usurpation of power in the hands of this wealthy oligarchy, while this oligarchy opposes a staunch resistance to the attempted invasion of its privileges. This complication was not peculiar to Flanders. It was repeated, though at a somewhat later date, in all the important towns of the Netherlands, and the struggle of the gilds with the patrician caste was waged in Brabant, Liège, Hainault, as well as in Flanders. The political complications which it evoked, and the number and importance of the Flemish cities invested it, however, with larger issues in Flanders than elsewhere. It played into the hands of the French king, and it gave Count Guy the opportunity of attempting, with the aid of his self-seeking and meddlesome patron and the discontented artisans, to recover his sovereign rights. It began in the first half of the thirteenth century; it reached a crisis in the reign of King Philip IV. at its close.

The gilds of Bruges, Ghent, and Ypres accused the oligarchy of extortion and corruption, and demanded a yearly account of expenditure as well as a share in municipal government. On the refusal of these demands, the men of Bruges and Ypres attacked and pillaged the houses of their patrician antagonists (1280-81). Count Guy espoused the side of the rioters, cancelled the charters of Bruges, executed some of the chief men of the oligarchy, and coupled the grant of a new charter, which he at last conceded in deference to the representations of his overlord (Philip III. the Hardy), with the right of receiving appeals from the jurisdiction of the municipality, and the obligation to render an annual account of expenditure to the citizens. He compelled the patricians of Ghent and Ypres to submit to similar terms, in spite of appeals to the French king. Count Guy was no democrat in feudal guise, however. He had no sympathy with the democratic aspirations of the gilds, and was merely playing for his own hand. He had made the city aristocracy amenable to his sovereign jurisdiction; he left them in exclusive possession of office, and allowed them to promulgate strict regulations against the assembly of the people in the offending cities. The tactics of Philip the Handsome very soon compelled him, however, to cultivate his democratic friends once more. Philip was resolved to reap the fruit of his predecessors' policy and annex the county to the French crown. Though hostile to the French communes, he was ready enough to seek the aid of the city oligarchies of Flanders in the attainment of his design. To maintain their exclusive privileges, these oligarchies were ready to go even this length in their opposition to the count, and only too faithfully earned the nickname of the Leliaerts (men of the lily, *Fleur-de-Lys*). The gilds, on the other hand, were the staunch opponents (the Clauwaerts, or adherents of the Flemish Lion) of a policy which not only ensured their subordination to the oligarchy, but doomed the independence of Flanders as well. Unfortunately they had in Count Guy but a shifty champion of their cause, which, had he only realised it more clearly and consistently, was also his own. The count acted by fits and starts; cringed to King Philip; asserted himself for a moment against his overbearing demands; cringed again, only to find himself outwitted once more by his crafty antagonist; took renewed courage and allied himself in 1294 with Philip's enemy, Edward I. of England, and agreed to marry his daughter Philippa to the Prince of Wales; allowed himself to be lured to Paris, and was thrown into the Tower of the Louvre and kept a prisoner until he became penitent enough to renounce the English alliance and consign his daughter to Philip's keeping as a pledge of his future good conduct; fell foul of the city dignitaries in co-operation with his crafty patron, who deserted him in the complication that followed; to be finally declared to have forfeited his county on the pretext of having seized the goods of some Scottish merchants to the detriment of the Franco-Scottish alliance. Then came a spurt of defiance in dependence on the gilds and the promised help of Edward I., in spite of threats and interdicts from France. This spurt exhausted itself at Furnes, where, without waiting for his procrastinating ally, the hapless count was forced to give battle to a French army under Robert of Artois, and was deserted, with disastrous consequences, by the Leliaerts. Edward landed only to agree to a truce of two years, and left Count Guy to face, single-handed, a second invasion at the end of this term. He was forced to surrender with two of his sons to Charles of Valois, to whom the cities opened their gates, while the count was thrown once more into the Louvre, despite the conditions of surrender. His discomfiture was the triumph of the oligarchy as well as of Philip, and when the royal victor paid Flanders a visit in 1301, he was everywhere gratified by the fêtes and acclamations prepared by the ruling class.

Very different was the attitude of the people, who had to pay for these sumptuous feasts and gorgeous dresses of their rulers, and only broke their sullen silence, as at Ghent, by cursing the exactions of the oligarchy. In spite of all this parade of luxury and loyalty there was no love lost between the conquerors and the artisans, especially as conquest meant increased exaction by Philip's greedy tax-gatherers, as well as by the local taskmasters. Anon other cries than those of "Vive le Roi" were heard in the streets of Bruges, where Peter Coninck, a weaver by trade—small of stature and one-eyed, but endowed with a fiery eloquence and public spirit—denounced the extortion of the corrupt oligarchy, which fleeced the people in order to pay for the rich dresses, the sumptuous banquets that had graced the royal entry. On the arrest of the audacious Coninck and his associates, the people flew to arms, broke the prison doors, attacked the "burg," and massacred such of the magistrates as did not succeed in saving themselves by flight. The rising was put down, and Coninck and his friends driven in turn into flight. A few months later (May 1302) it broke out anew, and this time Coninck and Jean Breydel, his butcher associate, took a terrible vengeance on their oppressors. Uniting their 5,000 followers outside with the mass of the artisans inside the city, they fell on the French garrison and slaughtered over 3,000 of it. It was a gruesome revival of the Sicilian Vespers on Flemish soil. The dead bodies of 24 knights-bannerets, 1,300 chevaliers, 2,000 men-at-arms lay heaped on the streets as the result of these bloody " Matines de Bruges."

King Philip swore vengeance on this artisan rabble that had dared to reward treachery with treachery, but the crafty conqueror was a trifle supercilious in his estimate of these bold burghers, as the victory of Courtrai was to show. Here in July these Flemish artisans (those of Ghent excepted), arrayed under their gild banners, and led by Coninck and Breydel, with Guy de Namur, Dampierre's son, for commander-in-chief, stood firm behind a canal against the shock of Philip's knights, and hewed in pieces several thousands of them as they tumbled into the ditch on their front in confusion unspeakable. It was a proud day for the stout-hearted workman, who had learned to measure his strength with the might of a haughty chivalry—the precursor of Morgarten and other similar heroic exploits which helped to discredit this haughty, degenerate chivalry for ever. Unfortunately, it was a victory rather than a success, as far as the popular cause was concerned, for Courtrai was followed two years later by Mons-en-Pévèle (August 1304), which reversed the defeat for Philip, though not very decisively, and by the Treaty of Athies, the Iniquitous Treaty (June 1305), concluded by the oligarchy, which bound the Flemings hand and foot to their liege lord of France, exacted a large fine and an annual tribute, directed the demolition of the city fortifications, and gave Philip possession of Lille, Douai, and Bethune. The bitter antagonism of the artisans found vent in frequent revolt, and led to the practical disregard of the more objectionable stipulations; but the despicable pliancy of Count Robert de Bethune, Count Guy's son, and of Count Louis de Nevers or Crécy, his great-grandson, which made them the mere satellites of the French court, gave the upper hand to the double domination of France and the oligarchy.

Against this *régime* Western Flanders revolted in earnest twenty years later. The maladroit Louis presented Sluys to his uncle, John of Namur, who established a market in direct rivalry to Bruges. The men of Bruges protested angrily (selfishly, we might also add); and while Ghent, under the influence of its oligarchy and its jealousy of Bruges, stood aloof, they found combustible materials enough in the insurrectionary mood of the oppressed peasantry to raise a popular conflagration. Under their captains or Hoofdmannen, the peasants rose against their feudal superiors, pillaged their castles, and sacked the churches and monasteries. This miniature Jacquerie gave the Bruges and Ypres artisans their opportunity of settling accounts with the Frenchified Count Louis. Led by Jannson and Zannekin, they took him prisoner at Courtrai, and routed the forces of the Ghent oligarchy, which attempted to intervene in his favour at Deinse (1325). Charles IV. of France dictated the makeshift Treaty of Argues (1326) until he could give Louis his revenge by a new French invasion of Flanders. Not Charles IV. however, but his successor, Philip VI., was to be the instrument of the count's vengeance. As swordbearer, Louis was present at Philip's coronation, at Reims on the 29th April 1328. He remained mute when the herald called his name as Count of Flanders, "I am only Count of Nevers," replied he in explanation, "not Count of Flanders, for I have been driven from my Flemish county by my rebellious subjects of Bruges and Ypres, Poperinghe and Cassel." Thereupon King Philip swore by the holy oil with which he had been anointed that he would not enter his capital till he had avenged him of his enemies. He accordingly summoned his host to assemble at Arras in July, and in August invaded Flanders at the head of a splendid army of the chivalry of

France. He had the remembrance of Courtrai to blot out, as well as the wrongs of Count Louis to avenge, and as the paragon of aristocratic prejudice and *hauteur*, he was at the same time the magnificent champion of aristocracy against democracy. He will teach that Flemish burgher rabble what it means to presume to turn its vulgar pikes against a feudal gentleman. On its part the burgher rabble, under Jannson and Zannekin, was burning with desire to repeat the exploit of Courtrai—this time in the neighbourhood of Cassel. And, in truth, it very nearly succeeded in so doing, would almost certainly have succeeded, had it only had the patience to wait for the reinforcements hurrying thither from Bruges. By a swift and noiseless approach in the dusk of the evening of the 23rd August, the three divisions of the Flemings were upon the three French divisions before a suspicion of their advance could precede them. Philip, who commanded one division, was sitting at supper in his tent. So was the King of Bohemia, John of Luxemburg, the commander of the second division. The Count of Hainault was equally off his guard. Only after desperate fighting did the surprised army, "as by a downright miracle," beat back the shock, and repeat the carnage of Courtrai at their enemy's expense. "Of the 16,000 Flemings, not a soul escaped," says Froissart, with his usual exaggeration of numbers no doubt. Philip stained his victory by burning Cassel and massacring its inhabitants, but otherwise he showed great moderation in declining to improve it for his own benefit. He reinstated the count with much good advice as to the reform of his despotic ways, and a warning that if he required to come a second time he would not be so generous.

Count Louis did not take this advice to heart. He glutted his resentment with the blood of ten thousand victims. He gratified his patron by casting down the walls of Bruges. He diminished the chartered rights of the towns, and deprived the gilds of their organisation. He had Jannson and the burgomaster of Bruges torn in pieces by horses at Paris. Flemish democracy seemed crushed by this bloody retribution beyond hope of rehabilitation. It was not long in proving the vanity of this judgment. The men who could win Courtrai and just miss winning Cassel were not the men to submit indefinitely to the barbarous tactics of a petty count, who spent most of his time at Paris as the satellite of King Philip, especially as a leader of a stronger type was forthcoming, in the person of Jacques or James van Artevelde, to champion their cause. Ghent, where Artevelde was about to appear on the stage of renewed strife, had escaped almost scatheless from the consequences of the late rising, during which its magistracy had espoused the side of the count. But even the Ghent magistracy had cause to complain of the count's encroachments on its rights of taxation and justice, and was compelled, now that the French king was the steady patron of their cringing sovereign, to cultivate the lesser gilds, as against its arch-enemy, the great weavers' craft. While it depressed the latter, it accorded the former some share in the municipal administration.

These local broils were, however, soon snuffed into insignificance by the momentous political events in which Flanders, under the guidance of Jacques van Artevelde, played a *rôle* of first-rate importance. These events sprang from the quarrel between Philip VI. and Edward III. over the succession to the French crown, and the ultimate resort of both rivals to the arbitration of the sword. This fateful quarrel vitally affected the interests of Flanders as well. Unfortunately for its peace, its obligations as a fief of the French crown were diametrically opposed to its interests as an industrial district. As Philip's vassal, it was the duty of Count Louis and his subjects to follow the standard of his liege lord. The count's indebtedness to Philip and his French sympathies naturally tended, in his case, to turn the scale in favour of France. In the case of the cities, both political and material interests lay decidedly in the direction of England. Let the English king stop the export of English wool, and the Flemish cities must inevitably starve. No wool, no work for the weavers. No work for the weavers, none for the fullers, and almost none for the rest of the crafts which mainly depended on their activity. It was not the first time that Flanders had been face to face with such a contingency, and the remembrance of this made merchants and artisans very anxious about the upshot of this great diplomatic duel. Anxiety changed into panic when Edward, in response to Count Louis' insane arrest of the

English merchants in Flanders, as a first blow on behalf of his patron, King Philip, ordered the arrest of all Flemish merchants in England, and absolutely prohibited the export of English wool (October 1336). This was a harder blow to Flanders than any of his predecessors had dealt, for the prohibition being absolute, there was no chance of getting the indispensable article at second hand, through Brabant or Hainault, as in former contingencies of the kind.* In a short time Flanders was a land of beggars, and Louis de Nevers the best hated man in the county. Clearly Edward III. must be mollified in spite of Count Louis' French proclivities, since Philip's offer of the monopoly of French wool was a mere blind, French wool being much less in quantity and much worse in quality than the staple English commodity. Of what avail, too, was the concession to Bruges to rebuild its walls, if the Bruges market had collapsed, as far as the buying and selling of wool was concerned?

A year of this deadlock and the situation became desperate. It was as the saviour of this situation that Jacques van Artevelde, a rich cloth merchant of Ghent and dean of the gild of weavers, sprang into prominence. Artevelde was no scion of feudal nobility, as some of his modern admirers contend, but at most a burgher patrician with popular sympathies, and his ability and eloquence made him the natural leader of the famished artisans of Ghent, who cried out for "freedom and work." Already the English, who had in November 1337 attacked Cadsand and routed its Flemish garrison, were at the gates, threatening to aggravate the misery of famine by the misery of war. Had not Count Louis, moreover, treacherously seized Sohier de Courtrai, a patrician of Ghent, who had received Edward's ambassadors in the summer of this year, and thrown him into the dungeon of Rupelmonde? It was evidently high time for the patriot to speak and act, and in Jacques van Artevelde the hour brought the man endowed both with the eloquence that moves the multitude, and the wisdom and energy needful to direct it. On the 27th December 1337, Artevelde harangued the people of Ghent in

* Though he subsequently relaxed the prohibition so far as to allow a large consignment to Brabant, it was on condition that it should not be sold outside the duchy.

a field of the monastery of Biloke, outside the city, to the effect that the salvation of Flanders lay in its neutrality as between the two combatants, coupled with a benevolent sympathy for the English king. Neutrality would restore the English wool supply, and it need not prevent Edward and his army from finding a passage through Flanders into France, if they came as friends and paid for what they wanted. As for King Philip (Count Louis being apparently left out of the reckoning), he would have enough to do in fighting his antagonist, and would perforce acquiesce in this attitude rather than drive the Flemings into Edward's arms by retaliatory measures.

The man who made this sagacious proposal was evidently not the vulgar demagogue that Jean le Bel, Villani, Froissart, and other biassed chroniclers, native and foreign, represent. As far as we can judge from his actions, he was a statesman and a patriot, somewhat brusque and autocratic perhaps, but animated, in the first place, by a genuine interest in the welfare of Ghent, and, in the second place, by a patriotic desire to unite the Flemish cities under its hegemony in a common policy, in keeping with their common interests. The cities should sacrifice the mutual jealousies that had weakened their strength in the past, should accommodate their internal dissensions in order to render their union effective. Such an alliance might be the basis of a wider union with the other States of the Netherlands, with Brabant, Holland, Hainault, and thus inaugurate the confederation of the Netherlands. This large policy was certainly not the policy of a shallow, self-seeking demagogue, and his fellow-citizens showed their confidence in his sagacity by appointing him captain (*hoofdman*) of the parish of St John and commander-in-chief of the city militia.

The first necessity was to negotiate the restoration of the English wool supply, and the provisional concession of this boon was the best proof of the efficacy of Artevelde's policy. Bruges and Ypres hastened to unite with Ghent, and their union meant the loss of Flanders to the cause of King Philip and the impotence of Count Louis. The execution of Sohier de Courtrai, the fulmination of a papal interdict against the rebels, the attempt against Artevelde's life, the failure of Count Louis and the Leliaert nobility to take Bruges, only played into the hands of the great tribune and his English ally. A change of tactics on the part of both Philip and Louis failed to avert the conclusion of a commercial treaty with Edward (10th June 1338), which, while it asserted the neutrality of Flanders, might erelong prove a handle for a political alliance. Edward did not miscalculate the future, and Artevelde had the satisfaction, Count Louis having fled to Paris, and the war having begun in earnest, and Philip having infringed Flemish neutrality in the interval, of negotiating this alliance eighteen months later (January 1340). If, suggested he, Edward would formally proclaim himself King of France, quarter the French with the English arms, in virtue of this proclamation, guarantee the wool monopoly, and restore the towns filched by the French kings, the Flemings would recognise him as overlord of Flanders, and maintain his cause against the pseudo-French king. To these conditions the English monarch agreed, and the bargain was struck which deposed both Philip and Louis at a stroke of the pen. A few weeks previously another important item of Artevelde's policy had attained its realisation in the conclusion of a close alliance between Flanders, Brabant, and Hainault, which in all essential respects virtually transformed them into a confederate State. That the idea was not a chimera, the example of the Swiss cantons, which the leagues of the German cities promised to emulate, had already demonstrated.

Unfortunately, the establishment of a confederate State, in defiance of feudal oppression, was not destined to strike such deep root in Flemish as it did in Swiss soil. There is no Cassel, no Roosebeke in Swiss annals. The Arteveldes, father and son, had not the satisfaction, like Arnold Winkelried, of winning victories by their deaths. For some years the prospect of the realisation of Artevelde's policy was, however, very promising. In the war, which was interrupted by the Truce of Esplechin in September 1340, the Flemings played an important part on the side of their ally. Though Edward gained no decisive land victory, Philip was forced to recognise their independence of French interference, and Louis to rule in accord with the interests of the three leading cities. The Flemish Triad was in truth now supreme. Each was the head of a district which was subject to its jurisdiction, while their representatives met in a general "parliament" to deliberate and legislate for the whole county. Though this organisation existed before the time of Van Artevelde, its powers had hitherto been wielded by the city oligarchies. Under his auspices, on the other hand, the democracy became predominant both in the municipality and the parliament. The Ghent oligarchy had, as we have seen, countenanced the lesser gilds against the weavers. Artevelde now secured for the great craft of which he was dean, an adequate place in the municipality alongside the patricians and their *protégés*, the lesser craftsmen. Not only so, but the right to elect directly the *échevins* or aldermen was extended to the whole body of the citizens. The patricians thus at last succumbed to the craftsmen, though Artevelde was too moderate a reformer to deny them a share in the municipal government, if, as in Germany, they qualified for office by membership of one of the gilds. And what took place in Ghent, took place in Bruges, Ypres, and other towns. The democracy of the three cities, which each exercised a controlling jurisdiction over its subject district, was supreme in Flanders. Unfortunately its supremacy was not always genuinely democratic, for we hear of attempts to coerce recalcitrant subject towns, not merely for their adherence to Count Louis, who was again plotting its subversion, but to prevent the free development of their industry. Ypres, for example, is found waging a bloody strife with Poperinghe, because Poperinghe refused to stop making cloth at its selfish dictation (1344). Termonde similarly resented the attempts of Ghent to suppress its industry, and along with Poperinghe and other small towns, went over to the side of the count.

Still more unfortunately, the spirit of division within the three leading cities themselves tended to ruin the work of the great reformer, and ultimately cost him his life. Malevolent reports, emanating from the Ghent patricians, who winced under the democratic *régime* of the gilds, began to circulate against his integrity. Was he not intriguing with Edward III. to enslave Flanders to an alien domination? If not, to establish his own tyrannic *régime*? So whispered Jean de Steenbeke and other city magnates of Ghent, and when the time was deemed ripe they accused him of aiming at a dictatorship. The gilds were, however, still staunch in support of their tribune; the men of Bruges, Ypres, Courtrai rallied to their assistance, and Jean de Steenbeke was driven into exile (1344). Count Louis, too, who strove to bring about a rising of Leliaert nobility, was forced to flee over the French border (1343). More serious was the outbreak of strife between the gilds themselves. The weavers, under their dean, Gerhard Denys, and the fullers, under Jean Bake, took to fighting in the market-place of Ghent on Monday, the 2nd May 1345—*den quaden Maandag*, Bad Monday, as it was called—and though the weavers had the best of the struggle, the slaughter of a large number of their antagonists, including Bake himself, left a mortal rancour in the hearts of the fullers and the lesser craftsmen, which was erelong to take a savage revenge on the great patron of their enemies.

For Artevelde the situation was indeed becoming very difficult. In addition to internal dissensions, Count Louis, who could now reckon on a host of malcontents in Ghent itself, was threatening invasion, had in fact taken Alost. It was high time for King Edward to intervene, and in response to Artevelde's urgent appeal, he hurried to Sluys with a powerful fleet, which he had assembled in the beginning of July for operations against Philip in Brittany. Here he held a conference with Artevelde and the representatives of the three cities, who agreed not to acknowledge Count Louis unless he did homage to the King of England, to appoint Sohier de Courtrai, son of him murdered in 1338, as Ruwaert to govern the county, and to despatch an army towards Artois in order to support Edward's expedition against Philip. Thus reassured, Edward set sail and left Artevelde apparently master of the situation once more. Appearance was singularly delusive. The great tribune was indeed acclaimed as their saviour by the people of Bruges and Ypres, but on entering Ghent on the 24th July an ominous change was observable in the attitude of the populace, who greeted him with sullen looks and angry murmurs. The report ran that he had basely bartered the county to Edward III., in order to ensure the continuance of his own tyranny. Had he not proposed to make the Prince of Wales Count of Flanders? Was there not a force of English archers lurking at hand to strike the blow that was to enslave them? Still worse, had he not amassed a great sum out of the count's revenues and sent it to England? Was not, therefore, this would-be friend of the people a corrupt traitor, deserving of death for his treachery? Such were the slanders sown by some of his detractors, during his absence, in the fruitful soil of popular ignorance and passion, and they evidently had not failed to take root in the rancorous hearts of the discomfited fullers and their brethren of the lesser crafts. What grain of truth there is in them is limited to the assertion of the contemporary chroniclers that Artevelde had proposed, and Edward had agreed to, the election of the Prince of Wales as substitute for Count Louis. If so, the proposition was not made with traitorous intent, but as a means of assuring the continued support of the English king, and rescuing Flanders once for all from the misgovernment of its Frenchified ruler. Whether true or false, the story was a handy pretext for calumny, and that calumny had engrained itself deeply in the heart of the multitude was shown by the scowls with which it greeted its former idol. Artevelde read in them the signs of doom, and on reaching his house, barred the doors and windows against attack. Anon, the street was packed with a mob consisting mainly of the workmen belonging to the lesser gilds, among them Denys and others of his implacable personal enemies. "Render account of your doings at Sluys," cried Denys; "where is the great treasure of Flanders?" Artevelde appeared at a window and spoke, "Good people, what will ye? In what way have I raised your anger? Tell me; I shall make all amends in my power." "Where is the treasure of Flanders?" shouted the mob. "Gentlemen," replied Artevelde, "I have never taken a penny out of the treasury of Flanders. Return to your homes, and to-morrow I shall render a satisfactory account of my actions." "Nay, nay," cried his enemies, "we must have an explanation at once. You shall not escape so. We know for certain that you have filched the treasure to England, and you shall die for it." Artevelde clasped his hands imploringly, "Gentlemen," said he, "you know what manner of man I have been, and you have sworn to protect me against all men, and now you would kill me. You have the power to do as ye list, for I know that a single man has no defence against a multitude.

But, for the love of God, consider of it, and forget not the great services I have done you till now. Know ye not how all commerce had been driven from the land? To me ye owe its return. I have governed you and guarded the peace so well that ye have all things in plenty." Thereupon there was a great clamour, all shouting as with one voice, "Leave off your sermonising and come down, for you shall die." Further remonstrance was useless, and Artevelde retired from the window to seek by a back door an asylum in a neighbouring church. The courtyard, he found, was also in possession of a yelling crowd, which at last burst the door and beat him to death.

Van Artevelde's memory long remained under the cloud of calumny which culminated in this foul deed. History has tardily vindicated his character and his work from the aspersions of petty rivals, and posterity has at last paid a tribute to his merits by erecting a monument to the enlightened champion of his country. He stands out, in spite of the long centuries of misrepresentation that have obscured the lineaments of his life, as the sagacious politician and reformer who gave prosperity to Flanders, and, as far as possible, self-government to the people. Unfortunately he could not give sense to a mad mob. As well argue with a madman as seek to convince that raging multitude that their accusations are hallucinations, craftily infused into their minds by malignant detractors. It is an evil moment for the popular leader, in such circumstances, when the truth must perforce be a lie and the lie a truth. Nevertheless, it appears certain that Artevelde's ambition was the ambition of an enlightened lover of his country, so often doomed to atone for his superiority over the petty, envious spirits of his time with the blight of his soaring aspirations. By the alliance with England, he rescued Flanders from the maladministration of its count and from the thraldom to France, which tended to stifle the spirit of freedom and nationality and destroy Flemish industry. The confederation of Flanders, Brabant, and Hainault which he negotiated, the energy and foresight with which he strove to foster it, the prosperity which he restored to a blighted industry, are a convincing testimony to his patriotism and his political wisdom. "It was a great pity for Jacques," laments the discriminating chronicler of Valenciennes, "for he by no means deserved such a fate, having maintained and governed the people of Flanders against all and sundry, right peacefully and sagely, for the space of nine years, as a good guardian against Count Louis, who never did ought of good to the country. It was in truth a wicked enterprise."

The reaction which followed showed only too well how lamentably the insensate mob had mistaken its friends for its foes. The three cities strove indeed to maintain Artevelde's policy by disclaiming connivance in the dastardly murder, and renewing the alliance with Edward. They forced Louis de Male, whom they accepted as count after his father's death at Crécy, to affiance himself to Edward's daughter, Isabella (March 1347). But the ungallant boy gave his bride the slip, and galloped across the border to renew his father's alliance with Philip and return in the summer of 1348 to force the recognition of his rights. In spite of the affront to his daughter, Edward was fain to conclude a treaty with him in December of that year, on the basis of the Anglo-Flemish alliance and the guarantee of the privileges of the recalcitrant cities. The guarantee was impotent to prevent the reaction which, now that Louis had won the recognition of his sovereign rights, set in full flood. The defeat of the weavers, who fought desperately in defence of their rights in the streets of Ghent and Ypres before they were overwhelmed by the Leliaerts, restored the *régime* of the oligarchy. At Bruges, too, the popular party was forced to give way to its opponents and acquiesce in the loss of power by the drastic expedients of exaction, proscription, banishment. For ten years Flanders lay helpless at the feet of its count and its municipal oligarchies, until the outbreak of the bourgeoisie revolution at Paris gave the cities courage to renew the struggle. Once more the Triad, donning the red and blue bonnet of Parisian revolt, confederated in support of their common cause, but there was no Van Artevelde to lend efficacy to their union, and Edward finally left them to their fate in the Treaty of Bretigny, which restored Flanders to its overlord the King of France. In spite of frequent "parliaments" to concert defensive measures and futile appeals to Edward, the confederation was an utter failure. Ypres was bludgeoned by Count Louis into submission, after fifteen hundred weavers had fallen victims to the new reign of terror. Bruges bowed its head to the decree that " if any one occasion tumult in the town, he shall be decapitated before the town hall." Only in Ghent did the weavers succeed in recovering lost ground, and maintaining it in spite of the hostility of the count, which once more led to deadly strife in 1379.

The immediate cause of the outbreak was the refusal of the men of Ghent to grant a tax, in payment of the expense of a tournament which the count wished to hold within its walls. What Ghent refused, the men of Bruges offered on condition of permission to construct a canal to connect their city with the sea. Its concession was a fell blow to the trade of Ghent, and the Ghenters determined to resist. They chose the popular Jean Hyoens as their captain-general, drove away the labourers engaged in constructing the works, crushed a Leliaert force which attempted to surprise the city, burned Louis' new castle of Wondelghem in the environs, and destroyed the bridge connecting his Ghent residence with the city ramparts. These drastic retaliatory measures were the signal for a rising at Termonde, Alost, Damme, Courtrai, Ypres, and even Bruges, where the popular party resented the domination of the oligarchy. Of all the important cities, Oudenarde alone remained faithful to the count, and for the next three years Flanders was the scene of a fierce warfare between the White Hoods, as the revolutionists were called, and the Leliaert supporters of the count. It was interrupted by an occasional lull of negotiation, followed by a still fiercer access of strife, until the victory of Woumen (23rd August 1380) brought all Flanders, with the exception of Ghent, to its knees, and left the dauntless city to continue the struggle single-handed under the leadership of the resourceful Pierre van den Bossche. Count Louis failed in the attempt to besiege it into submission, and was forced to conclude another of these spasmodic truces (November 1380), which he broke in the following spring.

In this emergency the Ghenters, at Van den Bossche's instigation, had recourse to Van Artevelde's son, Philip, whom they appointed captain-general. Philip was no "chip of the old block," had, in fact, hitherto lived in obscurity, and was dragged, in spite of himself, into a position for which he was unfitted. But his name was a power in itself, and sufficed to stiffen the determination of the citizens to endure even the horrors of famine rather than sacrifice their liberty. Their resolution was sorely tried by a blockade which, in spite of an occasional driblet of provisions from Brussels, Louvain, Liège, and of the enforced sale of the corn in the granaries of the rich, threatened to end in starvation. For the sake of the starving people, Artevelde offered at a conference at Tournay to accept any terms, provided the lives of his fellow-citizens were spared. Sure of his prey, the haughty count demanded that the men of Ghent should surrender unconditionally and come out and implore his grace with bare heads and halters round their necks. Rather than submit to this degradation, the starving citizens determined to follow their leader, sword in hand, and give battle to the tyrant under the walls of Bruges. Before their furious onset at Bevershoutsveld, Count Louis' levies were scattered to the winds, and the count himself barely escaped out of the city as the victors burst in on the heels of the fugitive host. This success completely turned the tables once more in favour of the heroic city. Not only did Bruges supply the dearth of Ghent, but the whole of Flanders sprang into revolt, and Count Louis' cause seemed as hopeless at the end of the three years' struggle as it had been at the beginning. The count, as usual, appealed to the King of France, now Charles VI., whose uncle, the Duke of Burgundy, was Louis' son-in-law. The rebellious mood of Paris, Rouen, and other French cities, which were in touch with those of Flanders, and had profited by their example to demand the drastic reform of abuses, lent force to the appeal. To disarm the seditious spirit of the Parisian democracy, Charles and his uncle determined to strike a decisive blow in Flanders. It was in vain that Philip van Artevelde strove to parry the blow by turning for aid to Richard II., as his father had turned to Edward III. The appeal for English intervention, though futile, was an additional reason for Charles VI. to strike swiftly and decisively. And strike he did with terrible effect at Roosebeke, where Artevelde's army was driven with fell slaughter into panic-stricken rout, and its leader slain (27th November 1382). Even this disaster failed to cow the staunch defenders of their liberty, who, under Van den Bossche and Ackermann, held out for fully another year until the death of Louis de Male in January 1384 delivered them from their oppressor. Two years later they submitted to his successor Philip of Burgundy, on condition of a general amnesty, and the heroic struggle of over a century's duration came to an end.

Though the victory ultimately lay with the count, in the person of Philip, it was not an unmodified victory for the oligarchy. The Arteveldes had not succeeded in their larger policy of emancipating Flanders from the supremacy of France and the jurisdiction of the count. They had at most but checked the former by pitting against it the hostility of England, modified the latter by pitting against it the emancipation of the masses. They had failed to establish a federal republic under English auspices, and had thus proved powerless to emulate the example of the Swiss cantons and the Italian cities. They had failed, too, to realise the scheme of a united Netherlands under Flemish hegemony. Nevertheless, their work was by no means an unmitigated failure. They overthrew the supremacy of the city oligarchies; they substituted for it the *régime* of the industrial gilds, and even after Roosebeke, the oligarchy had to be content to share its power with the craftsmen, and to submit to the principle of the legal equality of all citizens. Under Philip of Burgundy and his successors, the policy of a larger union was achieved in the unification of the Netherlands under Burgundian auspices, though at the expense of the liberties of the confederate States. In spite of Philip's policy of centralisation, the three Estates of Flanders, in which the people had their share of influence, emerged from the struggle as a check on the arbitrary exercise of authority. In one respect that struggle worked irreparable mischief to the Flemish cities. It robbed them of their commercial and industrial supremacy. The emigration or banishment of thousands of skilful artisans created a formidable industrial competitor on the other side of the North Sea. The tyranny of the counts, who shackled both commerce and industry by their repressive edicts, proved equally mischievous. The rise of Antwerp, whither the Hansa League transferred its staple, was fatal to the commerce of Bruges. The heroic era of Flanders was also the beginning of its decline.

In the other provinces of the Netherlands there was also a twofold struggle between the cities and their sovereigns, and between the oligarchy and the gilds. In the united duchy of Brabant and Limburg the struggle between the duke and the cities culminated in a great triumph for constitutional liberty. These cities were neither so numerous nor so popular as those of Flanders, though Antwerp, Louvain, Brussels, Mechlin, Bois-le-Duc, Tirlemont, had grown into prosperous industrial centres by the beginning of the fourteenth century. Their dukes were not, however, at this critical period, rulers of a forcible type, and were fain to charter away a large part of their authority, in response to the energetic demands of the burgher oligarchies. This pliant spirit yielded the maximum of concession in the Joyeuse Entrée, to which John III. agreed in return for the recognition, by the seven larger and thirty-six smaller cities of Brabant and Limburg, of the succession of his daughter Johanna and her husband Wenzel of Luxemburg. This memorable document, improving upon the charter of Cortemberg, granted by John II., emphasises the rights of the subject and limits those of the sovereign with a startlingly modern precision. The duke might not engage in war, or conclude a treaty, or alienate a single hairsbreadth of territory, or coin money, without the consent of the people. He might not levy illegal taxes or interfere with commerce and industry by arbitrary edicts. He was bound to obey the laws, and might not pardon those guilty of grave crimes, such as murder or rape. He must maintain the peace and limit the right of private warfare. He must restrict membership of the Council to natives, and his councillors as well as other officials were responsible to the cities for the discharge of their functions. So suspicious were these assertive burghers of these privileges that they insisted on retaining in their own keeping all documents which guaranteed them. The spirit of these stipulations is drastically democratic. The people both share in the sovereignty and control its exercise. Nevertheless these civic framers of the Joyeuse Entrée were by no means actuated by a democratic spirit. The oligarchy dictated these restrictions of the sovereignty in its own interest, not in behalf of the mass of the citizens. In Brabant, as in Flanders, there was bitter antagonism between patricians and gildsmen, but in Brabant the gildsmen did not succeed, with the exception of those of Louvain and Mechlin, in the attempt to overthrow the oligarchy. Not only were the numbers of the craftsmen far less in Brabant than in Flanders, but they were unfortunate in their leaders. Peter Coutereel and Everhard Tserclaes were not the compeers of Jacques van Artevelde or Nicolas Zannekin.

Like Brabant and Flanders, Liège was the theatre of long feud between sovereign and subject as well as between the patricians and the gilds. As in Brabant, the cities had the best of the struggle, and in the series of treaties, such as the Peace of Fexhe in 1315, which interrupted it at intervals, wrested from the bishop equally extensive rights. As in Brabant, too, the keynote of the constitution, thus gradually elaborated, was the limitation of the sovereign power by the Estates, in which the cities played a leading part. In government, as in legislation, they secured the main share of power. In the Council of twenty-two which supervised the administration of the episcopal principality, the cities had fourteen representatives to four for the nobility and four for the clergy. The oligarchy did not, however, succeed in retaining power in its own hands, as in Brabant. The craftsmen of Liège, Huy, Dinant, Gertruydenberg, forced their patrician masters to yield them a place in the municipal council, and this supremacy they retained till the beginning of the fifteenth century, when Bishop John of Bavaria, whose relentless reactionary *régime* earned him the title of the Merciless, recovered, with the aid of the Duke of Burgundy, a large measure of his sovereign authority at the expense of the city democracies.

In Holland and Hainault, which were united under one ruler in 1299, the development of the cities was more tardy than in Flanders, Brabant, or Liège. It was only at the end of the fourteenth century that Mons and Valenciennes, the principal cities of the southern county, became prominent as industrial centres and secured the increase of their municipal privileges. In Amsterdam, Leyden, Dordrecht, and other cities of the north, which emerge as thriving commercial towns about the same time, the patricians seem to have reigned supreme. They secured from successive counts increased political rights, and appear alongside the nobility and clergy in the assemblies to which the counts were compelled to have recourse in all important affairs. They seem to have asserted their influence in the dynastic quarrels of the Cods, with whom they allied themselves, and the Hooks, who were supported by the gilds, whose miserable party dissensions filled the land with broil, bloodshed, and devastation throughout the latter half of the fourteenth century.

Such, in briefest possible outline, was the political development of the chief States of the Netherlands, in addition to Flanders, at the beginning of the fifteenth century. The struggle between the cities and their sovereigns, everywhere marked by sensitive impatience of tyranny, in Flanders more particularly, had resulted in the acquisition of political rights, greater or less, according to locality. In all the States the cities secured a place in their Estates, or provincial parliament. In all of them municipal self-government was a permanent victory. In some of them the gilds succeeded in wresting from the oligarchy a dominant place in the municipal council. Liberty had thus made substantial progress in the fourteenth century in spite of mistakes, failures, sacrifices, even crimes. The murder of Van Artevelde was an insane attack on liberty by its misguided champions, and threatened to forfeit all that she had gained in Flanders. The mutual jealousies and internal dissensions of the cities dragged the wheels of progress; but substantial progress there had been, and along with it the promise of larger advance to come. Unfortunately, the promise was only remotely fulfilled. The accession of Philip the Hardy, of Burgundy, as Count of Flanders, on the death of his father-in-law, Louis de Male, transferred the sovereignty, as we have seen, to the hands of a strong man, who asserted his authority at the expense of the rights of the municipalities. Philip took a lesson from his kinsmen, the Kings of France, especially Philip the Handsome, who had strengthened the power of the crown at the expense of all other power in the State. With him began, in Flanders, the policy of centralisation, which under his grandson Philip, very dubiously surnamed the Good, was extended to the other provinces. This Philip, who succeeded his father, John the Fearless, as Count of Flanders and Artois in 1419, became, by fair means or foul, lord paramount of the whole of the Netherlands with the exception of Liège, Utrecht, and Guelders. He bought the county of Namur; he inherited the duchy of Luxemburg; he usurped the duchy of Brabant-Limburg; he despoiled his cousin, Jacqueline, Countess of Holland and Hainault, with their dependent provinces of Zealand, West Friesland, and Utrecht, of her wide domains. This last stroke was the triumph of a mixture of craft, cruelty, and perfidy, which have made Jacqueline the heroine of one of the strangest and most tragic stories of modern history—the prototype in misfortune and in the chivalrous championship of her memory, of Mary, Queen of Scots. The Good Philip was certainly unscrupulous and clever at all events, and before the middle of the fifteenth century his unscrupulous cleverness was rewarded by the possession of a realm which extended from the Alps to the North Sea, and outvied, in wealth and splendour, that of any other European potentate. He was practically independent of either his French or his German superior. For which achievement he has been mightily lauded by writers like Philip de Commines, who wrote, " not for the amusement of brutes and people of low degree, but for princes and other persons of quality," and were richly rewarded for their pains. It was he who founded the famous Order of the Golden Fleece, the distinction which it was the ideal of every aspiring warrior to win, and which is significant of the splendour and power of the great duke, whose friendship was an honour to emperor as well as king. He, too, it was who coolly disowned the obligation of the oaths by which, as Ruwaert, he had sworn to maintain the rights and privileges of the provinces wrested from the unfortunate Jacqueline. This was no chivalrous act, at all events, but it expressed the arbitrary and high-handed methods of the smooth-tongued usurper. We are approaching the age of Machiavelli, though the spirit of Machiavelli is by no means a newcomer in history in the fifteenth century.

Philip was, however, not allowed to bear high-handed sway without resistance, especially in Flanders, where the transference of his alliance from England to France and his futile attempt to take Calais, in 1436—involving as they did the disastrous disturbance of its commerce and industry—excited a violent outbreak of rebellion. Ghent and Bruges flew to arms and defied him to his face. Ghent straightway enacted vengeance by hanging or banishing those of the citizens whom it deemed responsible for this disaster. Bruges went the length of laying hands on the duchess and her son, whilst attempting to escape, retaining them under constraint, and even menacing the duke himself, who came to the rescue. Philip managed to slip away, and ultimately blockaded the starving city into submission. Ten years later Ghent was again in revolt against a salt tax, which Philip arbitrarily imposed, and struggled for four years to assert the right of the Estates to consent to taxation, before it was crushed by the strong hand of its master and punished with the loss of many of its privileges. Philip was duke, virtual king by the grace of God, equally with the emperor and the monarch of France, and his jurists, who were trained in Roman law at Louvain and Dôle, and at the French universities, elaborated for him and his successor the theory of that absolute rule which they strove to put in practice. He had his Great Council to assist him in legislation and administration, his Chambers of Accounts to which he entrusted the financial administration, his stadtholders through whom he ruled the provinces; and thus, as in France, the central power made its heavy hand felt, by means of an official hierarchy, on the liberties of the provinces. Happily in the States-General, which he called into existence, in addition to the smaller provincial assemblies, the provinces had a safeguard against despotic rule in the important matter of taxation, for with them, as with the provincial Estates, in regard to local taxation, lay the right to grant or refuse subsidies for general purposes. No such grant could be made until the city deputies had consulted their constituents, and these were quick enough to seize the occasion to demand the redress of grievances. The ducal *régime* was thus subject to a certain measure of popular control in spite of juristic theories of the divine right of this new-fangled Burgundian sovereignty.

Philip's centralising policy was continued by his famous son, Charles the Bold. The son, however, did not possess the craft and political genius of his father, and shot like a meteor along his dazzling course to swift and tragic doom at

Nancy. Nevertheless, his ten years of rulership (1467-77) did sufficient mischief to the Burgundian realm. He sucked the wealth of the cities like a leech. He kept a standing army, and the standing army meant the repression of rights, especially the right to grant or refuse taxes, in spite of riot and revolt. He massacred the citizens of Liège for their repeated and persistent resistance to his aggressive policy, and burnt the city to the ground. He transferred the supreme court of Holland from the Hague to Mechlin, where he established the supreme tribunal for the whole of the provinces, and thus denied to the Hollanders the right, which his father had respected, of being tried within their own county. The policy of centralisation was indeed not without its advantages in welding these petty States into some sort of unity, such as Artevelde had striven for—a unity represented by the States-General as well as by the Supreme Council of Mechlin. But the Netherlanders had only too good reason to complain that the reckless and oppressive *régime* of a Charles was a heavy price to pay for the realisation of Artevelde's nationalist policy, under the auspices of a firebrand prince of despotic instincts. The meteoric reign of Charles sufficed, therefore, to produce an incontrollable reaction in favour of their old rights and liberties, and the tragedy of Nancy gave birth to a constitution which, while it preserved the federal bond under the ducal dynasty, guaranteed and amplified these rights and liberties in each State. At Ghent assembled a convention of the representatives of the States of Flanders, Brabant, Hainault, Holland to demand such guarantees from Charles' hapless daughter, Mary of Burgundy (February 1477). They were conceded and enshrined in the "Groote Privilegie," the Great Privilege. The "Groote Privilegie" is the Magna Charta of the Netherlands. It secured to the States-General sovereign control over the general government of the provinces. It abolished the obnoxious central Court of Justice at Mechlin. It established or rather reorganised the Grand Council of Administration, consisting of twenty-four members, besides the chancellor and the ducal princes, and bound not to infringe the privileges and rights of the provinces and cities. It abolished all the ordinances which conflicted with these privileges and rights. It conferred on the States-General powers which reduced those of the sovereign to a minimum. The States-General and even the provincial States might meet on their own authority. The sovereign could not marry, or declare war, or raise taxes without their consent. She could appoint none but natives to offices; she should allow only the national language to be used in all public documents, and if she infringed any of these stipulations she forfeited the allegiance of the subject.

Not content with these sweeping general concessions, Holland, Namur, Flanders, Brabant wrested from their impotent mistress an equally large share of sovereign control over provincial legislation and administration. The Great Privilege of Holland contains so explicit a recognition of popular rights that it deserves special quotation.

"The duchess shall not marry without consent of the Estates of her provinces. All offices in her gift shall be conferred on natives only. No man shall fill two offices. No office shall be farmed. The 'Great Council and Supreme Court of Holland' is re-established. Causes shall be brought before it on appeal from the ordinary courts. It shall have no original jurisdiction of matters within the cognisance of the provincial and municipal tribunals. The Estates and cities are guaranteed in their right not to be summoned to justice beyond the limits of their territory. The cities, in common with all the provinces of the Netherlands, may hold diets as often and at such places as they choose. No new taxes shall be imposed but by consent of the provincial Estates. Neither the duchess nor her descendants shall begin either an offensive or defensive war without consent of the Estates. In case a war be illegally undertaken, the Estates are not bound to contribute to its maintenance. In all public and legal documents the Netherland language shall be employed. The commands of the duchess shall be invalid, if conflicting with the privileges of a city. The seat of the Supreme Council is transferred from Mechlin to the Hague. No money shall be coined, nor its value raised or lowered, but by consent of the Estates. Cities are not to be compelled to contribute to requests which they have not voted. The sovereign shall come in person before the Estates to make his request for supplies."

Thus all that the Netherlanders had contended for in their

long conflicts with their petty rulers was decreed in the inviolable charters of a free people. Unfortunately, they proved incapable of preserving them, though the men of Ghent evinced their old spirit of resistance to the encroachment of their liberties by beheading ten of the Lady Mary's ministers, accused of treachery to the constitution, under her very eyes, and in spite of her tearful supplications for mercy. The jealousies and dissensions of the States provided too many points of attack to Mary's husband, Maximilian, who, after her death, became regent and guardian of her son, the Archduke Philip. Maximilian was indeed taken prisoner by the men of Bruges in his attempt to force Flanders to recognise his rule as regent, and compelled to sign a compromise which left it to govern itself, while he governed the rest of the provinces during the minority of Philip. The compromise would not work, however, and an imperial army, under the Duke of Saxony, ultimately made Maximilian master of Flanders, and enabled him to wreak vengeance on his enemies (Treaty of Cadzand, 1492). The price of his victory was the practical abrogation of the constitution, which Archduke Philip formally refused to ratify, on attaining his majority in 1494, except with reservations that virtually nullified it, and its result was the relapse of the Netherlands under an autocratic *régime*, whose accumulated abuses prepared the great revolution of the future.

SOURCES.— Jean le Bel, Chroniques, edited by Polain (1863); Froissart, Chroniques (1325-1400), editions of Lettenhove (1866-67), and Luce (1869); Chronicon Comitum Flandrensium, and Chronicon Ægidii li Muisis, edited by Smet in the Corpus Chronicorum Flandriæ (1837); Rymer, Fœdera, vol. ii., Record Edition; Rotuli Parliamentorum, vol. ii.; Continuator of Guillaume de Nangis, edited by Gerard; Commines, Mémoires, in Petitot's Collection; Chastellain, Chroniques des Ducs de Bourgoyne, edited by Lettenhove; MacKinnon, History of Edward the Third (1900), in which the references to Flemish affairs in the English Chronicles of the fourteenth century are incorporated, and the part played by the English monarch delineated; Blok, Geschiedenis van het Nederlandsche Volk (1892-39), English trans. by Bierstadt and Putnam; Warnkönig, Flandrische Staats und Rechtsgeschichte, translated into French and completed by Gheldorf (1835-64); Lettenhove, Jaques d'Artevelde; Lentz, Jacques van Artevelde; Lettenhove, Histoire de Flandre (1847-50); Pirenne, Histoire de Belgique; Pirenne, Les Pays Bas, in t. iii. of Histoire Générale; Vanderkindere, Le Siècle des Artevelde (1874); Ashley, James and Philip van Artevelde (1883); Motley, Rise of the Dutch Republic; Rogers, Holland (1889); Ward, The Netherlands, in Cambridge Modern History, vol. i. (1902).

CHAPTER XII.

COMMUNEROS AND CORTES IN MEDIÆVAL SPAIN.

THERE is not much authentically known of the nascent kingdom of Spain in the Asturian mountains. Legends of battles that were never fought, of heroes that never existed, in the form in which they are portrayed at any rate, distend the pages of the later Spanish chroniclers, but the early records are few and scanty. There is a long list of kings from the heroic Pelayo in the eighth century onwards, and these kings gradually extended their sway, from their mountain-girt territory, southwards into the land conquered by the Moors. These early kings were elected in accordance with the old Visigothic custom, and the election, though confined to the members of the royal family, often fell upon the oldest and ablest relative of the deceased king. There was no rigid noble caste among those mountain fastnesses, for the fugitive Goths, who escaped from the slaughter on the banks of the Guadalete, were levelled by misfortune to equality with the hardy Cantabrian mountaineers, among whom they sought refuge. The little Asturian State had swelled by the reign of Alfonso III., at the end of the ninth century, into the kingdom of Leon, with its dependent countship of Castille. It was torn during the tenth century by civil war, and exposed to the terrible inroads of Almanzor. There was dissension, too, with the Castillian counts, who ultimately established themselves as independent kings, and this dissension continued throughout the next two centuries, in spite of temporary unions under one sovereign, until both kingdoms finally combined under Fernando III. in 1230. Aragon had meanwhile been growing into a third considerable State by the gradual expulsion of the Moors from the north-east of the Peninsula, and the absorption of Catalonia in the middle of the twelfth century. During the same period, the valour of Count Alfonso in the decisive battle of Ourique against the Moors, raised Portugal from a dependent countship of Castile into an independent kingdom, of which the count became the elective monarch. Wedged into the Western Pyrenees was the little kingdom of Navarre, which could boast of a king with the title of Great—Sancho El Mayor—in the eleventh century, but whose earlier history is both petty and obscure. The final union of Leon and Castille under Fernando III., and the consolidation of Aragon under Jayme I. resulted in the further shrinkage of the Moorish dominion to the south of the Peninsula. Ferdinand improved on the great victory which his predecessor, Alfonso VIII., won over the Moors at Las Navas de Tolosa, by the capture of Cordova and Seville, and this exploit was emulated by Jayme, who captured Valencia and subdued the Balearic Isles. By this attrition of Moorish territory in the south-west and the south-east, the Moorish dominion in Spain was reduced, by the middle of the thirteenth century, to the kingdom of Granada among the mountains of the far south. Supremacy in Spain had finally oscillated, after five hundred years of struggle, from the Moor to the Christian.

In Spain, as in other European lands in these mediæval centuries, the crash of battle grates on the ear. The chronicles of these blood-stained centuries contain many a tale of fighting, ravage, slaughter, and unfortunately the battles of the chronicles, in which hundreds of thousands are massacred for the glory of God, whether that God be the Mohammedan Allah or the Christian Trinity, are by no means all legendary. Some of these terrible slaughters, such as that of Covadonga, of Clavijo, of Calatanazor, have been discarded by sober modern historians as fables or exaggerations, but sufficient remain to curdle the blood of the peaceable, civilised reader. The explanation of this torrent of bloodshed lies partly in the fact that for eight hundred years Spain, as the battlefield between Moor and Christian, was exposed to the agony of one long crusade. But the fighting was by no means the sole fruit of the antagonism of Moor and Christian. Nay, Moors and Christians were sometimes allied in battle against other Moors and Christians, and often enough did the Christian potentates of Leon, Castille, Aragon, Navarre, Portugal, draw the sword against one another. The real Cid, when divested of the legendary accretion which embodied in him the Christian champion against the infidel, is found fighting for or against Moor and Christian alike, as it suited his interest. He is the embodiment of the bellicose spirit of the age rather than of the Christian patriot, and this bellicose spirit which the antagonism to the Moors helped to perpetuate, but did not exclusively engender or keep alive, is the soul of mediæval Spanish history.

The mediæval Spanish kings, with few exceptions, are not particularly distinguished by their virtues. Few potentates were, in those rough, wild times. Their main business, when not warring against the Moors, was the business of fighting with their Christian neighbours, and as their neighbours were often their relatives, the scandal of father making war upon son, or son upon father, or brother upon brother, is by no means exceptional in the annals of their reigns. The surname of "the Battler," given to Alfonso I. of Aragon, might almost be conferred indiscriminately on all these pugnacious individuals. "Thus died my father," characteristically says Jayme, son of King Pedro of Aragon, who was slain by Simon de Montfort at Muret, "for such has ever been the fate of my race, to conquer or die in battle." They were certainly more distinguished by their pugnativeness than by their proficiency in the art of government for the benefit of the people. Periodic civil war added to the miseries of international strife. Faction throve in Spain with all the facility of Jonah's gourd.

Strange as it may seem, it was in this war-ridden mediæval Spain that free institutions took early root, and throve as they throve in no other European country at so early a period. War was the grim foster-mother of Spanish liberty, and in spite of its barbarism, it was not incompatible with political development. It produced the Spanish *fueros*, and the *fueros* in turn produced the Cortes or Spanish parliament. Equally strange is it that in a country where the arts, including even agriculture, were long despised as menial occupations, the towns played so important a *rôle*. For centuries the Moors were the artisans of Spain, and Moorish civilisation was an abomination to the true believer. The Spanish town in the earlier Middle Ages was not, however, a hive of industry, but a garrison for defence or aggression against the infidel. Its early importance was derived from its military character. Industry only came after the repulse of the Moor to the mountains of the south afforded a respite from the incessant conflict of several centuries. The kings of Leon, Castille, Aragon, encouraged these settlements or colonies (*poblaciones*) by the grant of exclusive privileges. Municipal self-government did not spring, in Spain, from the economic revival that led to the emancipation of the towns in Italy, France, Germany, the Low Countries, England, and Scotland. Its origin lay primarily in the necessity of defending the frontier and reclaiming the large tracts of pillaged territory that separated the advancing Christians from the retreating Moors. The chartered municipality thus appears in Spain at an earlier date than in any other country, Italy perhaps excepted. Leon obtained its *fuero*, or charter, as early as 1020, and it was probably not the first creation of its kind; Najera in 1035; Iaca (Aragon) in 1064; Sepulveda in 1076; and from the middle of the eleventh century onwards the number of free municipalities, holding of a royal, ecclesiastical, seigneurial, or elective (*Behetria*) superior, increased by leaps and bounds. They were empowered to elect their own magistrates (*alcaldes*) and council (*concejo*), and to maintain their own militia. Their jurisdiction extended over a wide tract of adjacent territory, and was wholly independent of that of the neighbouring nobles, who might become members of the urban community only by renouncing their rank. Neither king nor noble might interfere in the affairs of such a chartered community (*communidad* or *communero*), though the king was represented by an official who collected the tribute for the royal treasury. An appeal was indeed permitted to the royal court of justice, but if the king promulgated an order contrary to the charter, the community was entitled to resist, and a neighbouring grandee who violated its territory might be slain with impunity. The anxiety of the king to encourage their development appears further in the effort to increase their population. Debtors and even criminals—whether Jews, Moors, or Christians—who settled within their walls were, for instance, guaranteed immunity from pursuit, in the charter granted by Alfonso VIII. of Castille to Cuenza.

Equally remarkable is the early attainment of the free towns of Castille and Aragon to political rights. Whilst in France, England, and Scotland, the assembly of the three Estates was not fully organised before the end of the thirteenth century, the free towns of Aragon were represented in the Cortes as early as 1133, those of Castille by 1169. Not only so, but their representatives speedily became the real power in these national assemblies. The voice of the commons was supreme in the Cortes of both Castille and Aragon long before it became predominant in the English Parliament. It would, however, be shortsighted to mistake the Cortes for a modern parliament, though that of Aragon, in particular, undoubtedly wielded very large powers. Its meetings were dependent on the royal summons, and were very irregular. Each city had only one vote, though it might have several representatives, and these representatives were not, from the reign of Alfonso XI. onwards, elected by the whole body of the citizens, but by the town councils, which, as in England and Scotland, became amenable to the corrupt manipulation of the government. The number of cities represented was, too, in Castille at least, gradually diminished until towards the end of the fifteenth century only about a score retained the coveted privilege. Their political power was undoubtedly substantial, but it was intermittent, and to predicate popular representation of the Cortes of the fourteenth and fifteenth centuries at all events would be to misuse language.

The political influence of the Castillian cities was greatly enhanced by their union, as in Germany, Italy, Flanders, and Scotland, in defence of their mutual interests. The oft-recurring anarchy of the age brought these leagues or Hermandades, which included in 1315 as many as a hundred cities, into vogue, and like the Swabian league, they formed for the time being a sort of State within the State, which met in general assembly, or Cortes extraordinary, passed its own laws, fulminated its own penalties, and maintained its own military force. In the most flourishing period of their history the Castillian Hermandades overshadowed even the Cortes in their influence on affairs. They were as much political associations as police organisations, and the tone of some of their articles of association betokens the assumption of very large rights. If the king, for instance, should attempt to assess an illegal tax, his agents should, according to one of these articles, be put to death. If a noble robbed a member of his goods, and refused to restore them, his house should be razed to the ground. Oftener that not, however, the king and the Hermandad were allied against the nobility, their common enemy, and in the fifteenth century the Santa Hermandad formed an apt institution, in the hands of Ferdinand and Isabella, for the building up of the fabric of the absolute power of the crown.

As Castille and Aragon were independent States before their union in the latter half of the fifteenth century, and differed considerably in their political institutions, their constitutional history demands separate treatment. In both cases this history centres in the Cortes. The origin of that of Castille is to be looked for in the early mediæval council of the magnates—ecclesiastical and secular—whose consent seems to have been necessary to all important measures. This council, again, may be affiliated to the old Visigothic national council that met to legislate at Toledo in the days of a Leovgild, a Reccared, a Chindaswinth. These kings, as well as their mediæval successors, seem to have wielded an authority absolute in theory, but limited in practice by the council of the great men of the nation, with whom the people are sometimes found associated in the character of assenting spectators at least. The old Visigothic code of the Leges Visigothorum, the Fuero Juzgo of the thirteenth-century Castillian translation, ascribes large powers to the kings, but we must discriminate between the attributes conferred on the monarch by the clerical scribe, familiar with the phraseology of the imperial dignity, and the real power of an individual who was often enough hurled from his throne by some conspiring faction. While the king might in theory be supreme in Church and State, the source of justice, the maker of the laws, the arbiter of peace and war, the head of the army, his power was in reality small, and every important exercise of it was circumscribed by the magnates, lay and ecclesiastical. The Visigothic code has its law of treason, and savage enough it was, but we may see in its very savagery as much the relaxation as the rigour of authority in a turbulent age.

Even the royal office was not deemed strictly hereditary before the eleventh century, and the old usage of election survived long after in the formal recognition of the title of the heir-apparent by the Cortes. The Moorish conquest, moreover, diminished the power, such as it was, of the Visigothic monarch, and a king of Asturias, and even of the expanding States of Leon or Castille was for long rather a shadowy personage, whose nobles were his equals rather than his subordinates. The fact that they claimed and did not hesitate to exercise the right to renounce their allegiance and defy the monarch on the slightest provocation, amply shows how brittle was the bond between king and subject. A king whom any magnate might lawfully defy if he did aught to his disadvantage, and from whose jurisdiction he might withdraw to some neighbouring State, was about as "absolute" as a master whose employees strike work and transfer their services to another, if their terms are not conceded. To speak of these kings, with Mariana and Dr Dunham, as "absolute," even on the strength of some high-sounding expressions in the statute-book, which the jurists, whom they patronised, borrowed from Roman law, is to make a Diocletian, a Charlemagne, a Philip II., a Louis XIV., look very small indeed. On the contrary, the monarch in mediæval Castille was often little more than a figurehead, whose weakness contrasts with the strength of the greater nobles or *ricos hombres*. From their ranks were drawn the great officers of the crown—the admiral, constable, governors of provinces (*adelantados*), members of privy council. They furnished the grand masters of the great military orders. They exercised the rights of private war. They were exempted from taxation, and many of them were enormously wealthy. Clemencin has estimated that the total revenue of the chief grandees of Castille amounted to one-third of the whole kingdom. Don Juan of Biscay, for example, whose enormous possessions were confiscated by Alfonso XI. in 1327, was lord of more than eighty towns, villages, and castles. Alvara de Luna, the all-powerful minister of John II., could place in the field 20,000 vassals. Of the Constable Davalos, who flourished in the reign of Henry III., it is said, surely with exaggeration, that he could ride all the way from Seville to Compostella through his own estates. It was one of the most highly prized prerogatives of such magnates to keep their heads covered in the presence of the king, and they did not hesitate to confederate in armed opposition to the crown whenever the opportunity of aggrandisement presented itself. Though the feudal system seems to have secured but a partial footing in Castille, the Castillian grandees were as factious as the petty feudal sovereigns of France, as ready to draw the sword in intestine strife as to march against the Moors. The *hidalgos* and *caballeros*, who made up the lesser ranks of the nobility, furnished them with an ample following of trained warriors in addition to their numerous retainers. Against their factious turbulence the king found a mean remedy in treachery and assassination, and the device brings out in grim relief the weakness of the central authority.

If these factious magnates are often found setting the laws at nought, they also appear, in the early records of both Leon and Castille, as partners with the king and the higher clergy in the work of making them. The early Cortes were composed of all men of influence in the State, both lay and cleric—bishops, abbots, and *optimates* or *magnati*. They elected the king, and their consent was necessary to all important legislative acts—laws, charters, grants to churches, &c. Originally the sole members of the legislature, these lay and cleric magnates seem, after the rise of the towns to self-government and political influence, to have played but a subordinate part in the national assembly. The Third Estate became by far the more important factor, and in some of the Cortes of the fourteenth and fifteenth centuries, both prelates and nobles are conspicuous by their absence. It seems, indeed, that while on exceptional occasions members of all the Estates were present in greater or lesser number, the Third Estate was as often as not invited by royal summons to legislate on the matters submitted to it, irrespective of the views of the other two. Among these matters, the most important was taxation, and as both nobles and clergy were exempt from this burden, their presence was not essential on occasions when the main object of the assembly was to grant a subsidy. Hence the distinction between "general" and "particular" Cortes.

It was in the control of taxation that the power of the Castillian Cortes, as of the English Parliament, mainly lay. In Castille, as in England, the principle was clearly enunciated, that no tax beyond the tribute that the towns were by charter bound to pay, might be assessed without the unanimous assent of Parliament. The Third Estate is found during the fourteenth and fifteenth centuries insisting over and over again on this cardinal doctrine in its remonstrances against its infringement, and more than one king explicitly recognised its validity. Alfonso XI., for instance, undertook in 1328 "not to exact from the people any tax, whether particular or general, not hitherto established by law, unless granted by all the deputies in Cortes assembled." Sixty-five years later the Cortes is found conditioning its grant to Henry III. by the stipulation that "he should swear before one of the archbishops not to take, or demand, any money, service, or loan, or anything else of the cities or towns, or of any individual belonging to them, on any pretence of necessity, until the three Estates of the kingdom should first be duly summoned and assembled in Cortes, according to ancient usage. And if any such letters requiring money have been written, they shall be obeyed (for the sake of politeness, that is), and *not complied with*." The Cortes of 1420 were equally explicit in maintaining against the exactions of John II., "the good custom founded in reason and justice, that the cities and towns of your kingdoms shall not be compelled to pay taxes, or requisitions, or any other new tribute unless your lordship ordain it by the advice and grant of the cities and towns, and of their procurators in their name." They withstood the arbitrary tactics of Henry IV. in the same unyielding spirit, and even Ferdinand and Isabella, and Charles I. did not venture to ignore a right thus jealously asserted, however autocratically they might rule in other respects. They were careful, too, on occasion to limit these grants to certain purposes, and to demand an account of expenditure and the redress of grievances before renewing them. They are sometimes found extending their remonstrances to the personal expenses of royalty, as when they naïvely admonished the prodigal Alfonso X. and his queen to eat at the rate of 150 maravedis a day "and no more," and at the same time prescribed a more moderate diet for their attendants.

In addition to the control of taxation, the Castillian Cortes claimed to exercise the right to participate in legislation, and to a certain extent to control the executive. That from an early period they enacted laws along with the king, appears clearly enough from the statement of the fact in authentic records. Alfonso V., to go no further back, confirmed the old Visigothic code in the Cortes of Leon in 1003, and the additions and emendations made by subsequent monarchs were enacted sometimes by the consent (*acuerdo*), sometimes with the advice (*consejo*) of the national assembly. The Fuero Juzgo, the amplified Castillian version of the Visigothic laws, made under the auspices of Ferdinand III., and the more elaborate Siete Partidas, largely based on the Justinian code, and composed in the reign of Alfonso X., received the sanction of the Cortes. It was not, however, till 1348 that the Cortes at Alcala sanctioned the Siete Partidas. The king, indeed, legislated by ordinances (*pragmaticas*), as in England, and a monarch of an autocratic temperament might in this way assert his individuality without regard to the national will, as represented by the Estates, but as a rule the co-operation of king and Parliament was essential to the validity of all important legislative measures. The commons made their power felt, too, in the execution of the laws by the admission, towards the end of the fourteenth century, of several members of the Third Estate to the royal council. As the council exercised very large administrative functions, the Third Estate thus wielded in Castille, in the fourteenth and part of the fifteenth centuries, an influence on government comparable to that of the English Commons, and superior to that of the French Tiers État, during the same period. The Cortes even claimed the right to intervene directly in administration, and the exercise of their right was not confined to the minorities that frequently exposed the State to the misery of faction and misgovernment. The practice came, in fact, to be recognised as a law which rested on ancient precedent. "Since in the arduous affairs of our kingdom," to quote a law of Alfonso XI., of date 1328, "the counsel of our natural subjects is necessary, especially of the deputies from our cities and towns, we therefore ordain and command that on such great occasions the Cortes shall be assembled, and counsel shall be taken of the three Estates of our kingdoms, as the kings, our forefathers, have been wont to do." Nor were the Estates slow to appeal to the law against the misrule of worthless sovereigns like John II. and Henry IV., whose united reigns extended from 1407 to 1474. "When kings have anything of great importance to undertake," protested the Cortes of Ocana in 1469 to Henry IV., "they ought not, according to the laws of the kingdom, to do so without the advice and cognisance of the principal cities and towns of your kingdom."

In spite of such "laws," however, constitutional government did not work well in Castille. Practice did not square with theory, and the Castillian Cortes proved an ultimate failure as an essay in parliamentary rule. The king is indeed found occasionally professing complete amenability to the will of his subjects, and from some of these professions we might imagine that he was the model of a constitutional ruler. "The duty of subjects towards their king," to quote a law of Alfonso X., "enjoins them not to permit him knowingly to endanger his salvation, nor to incur dishonour or inconvenience in his person or family, nor to cause mischief to his kingdom. And this may be fulfilled in two ways: one by good advice, showing him the reasons wherefore he ought not to act thus; the other by deeds, seeking means to prevent his going on to his own ruin, and putting a stop to those who give him ill counsel. Forasmuch as his errors are of more consequence than those of other men, it is the bounden duty of subjects to prevent his committing them." The nobles at least were not slack in carrying out the royal wishes in this respect, and their proneness to do so gave the monarch a handy pretext which he was equally quick in improving to his own advantage. In a kingdom in which rebellion was an admitted right and an oft recurring incident, violence on the part of the king as well as the nobles was common enough. It led him, too, to cultivate the Third Estate at the expense of the aristocracy, and thus aggravate the dissension of the orders which their mutual jealousies fostered. This dislocation of Castillian society was thus unfavourable to the experiment in constitutional government. Nobility and Third Estate were frequently at feud, and when the magnates were not united in coalition against the king or the towns, they as often as not fell to fighting among themselves. This jealousy and contention frustrated that harmony of classes and interests which is indispensable to the successful working of constitutional government. Such a state of things might, indeed, prove the foster-mother of free institutions. The Castillian grandee was certainly not the patron of popular liberty, and antagonism to the grandee might be a necessary condition of popular emancipation. The Third Estate of Castille was not, however, the champion of popular emancipation in the large sense, and the contention between it and the nobility did not lead to any large political result of this kind. It merely enabled the king to play off the one order against the other, and if the Third Estate, under royal patronage, bade fair for a time to become the dominant force in both legislation and administration, it lacked the strength, though not the will, to resist the growing despotism of the series of strong sovereigns that began with Ferdinand and Isabella. Not only did its representatives in the Cortes dwindle to about a score of cities, which jealously excluded the others from the privilege of representation ; it never had been really representative of the mass of the nation, which in Castille, as in other lands, languished in oppression and serfage, and while a revolt of the serfs (*solariegos*) had mitigated, it did not eradicate this evil. It ultimately degenerated into the mere reflex of the municipal oligarchies, to which the parliamentary franchise was confined. Add the fact that these oligarchies were often corrupt, often amenable through the royal *corregidores* to the royal will, and the impotence of the Cortes under the energetic *régime* of a Ferdinand, a Charles, a Philip, was inevitable. The Castillian constitution, however admirable its structure in some respects, thus rested on too shaky a foundation to withstand the shock of despotism. The intrepid defence of constitutional liberty of which the Cortes, with all its faults, showed itself at times capable, certainly deserved a better fate. Castille just missed the honour of leading the van of modern political emancipation which was reserved for England. Along with Aragon, it may claim at least that of showing the way even to England.

Aragon indeed was more precocious and more strenuous than Castille in the assertion of political rights. It was a feudal State, and its political magnates possessed great feudal privileges. They were the equals, almost the rivals of the king, and their independent spirit is re-echoed in their famous oath of allegiance at the advent of the sovereign. "We who are as good as you, choose you for our king and lord, provided that you observe our laws and privileges; and if not, then not." The formula may be the invention of Antonio Perez, the unfortunate minister of Philip II., who has recorded it, but it certainly accords with the traditional restiveness of these proud, insubordinate Aragonese *ricos hombres*. They were not numerous, but their privileges were in the inverse ratio of their numbers. They professed descent from the shadowy twelve peers of the ancient principality of Soprarbe, to which the chroniclers have given a constitution as old as the middle of the ninth century. The existence of these twelve magnates, who, in conjunction with a Justiza, made and unmade sovereigns, and kept a strict watch on their administration, is very problematic. The tradition seems premature by a couple of centuries, though the Spanish antiquaries are by no means unanimous on the subject. Certain it is that with the growth of the kingdom by the conquest of Moorish territory, the power of the king did not increase at the expense of the great territorial nobility. The division of the conquered lands among them as fiefs held of the crown, in return for feudal service, augmented both their high spirit and their restiveness of control. Besides their feudal jurisdiction over their dependants, they absorbed all the great offices of State, and were exempt from taxation, imprisonment, and capital punishment. Their feudal privileges and their constitutional rights made them as formidable a class to royalty as the great magnates of the French crown. They were not so wealthy as those of Castille, for Aragon was small and barren in comparison, especially before the acquisition of Catalonia; but their limited numbers made their union more solid, and consequently more formidable to the royal authority. Though they possessed and exercised freely enough the right of private warfare against each other, they presented a united front in defence of their interests, as the Aragonese kings found to their cost. "It was as difficult," said King Ferdinand, "to divide the great nobility of Aragon as to unite that of Castille." Nor was their political power lamed to the same extent as in Castille by friction with the towns, with which they are found co-operating, on critical occasions, in the assertion or defence of the common rights of all freemen. Nobles and commons had their jealousies and feuds in Aragon, as elsewhere, but they were patriotic and shrewd enough to pull together when their rights were at stake. "There was such a conformity of sentiment among all parties," says Zurita, in reference to the General Privilege, "that the privileges of the nobility were no better secured than those of the commons. For the Aragonese deemed that the existence of the commonwealth depended not so much on its strength, as on its liberties." The rights which the co-operation of nobles and commons wrung from Pedro III. at Saragossa, in 1283, compare favourably with those which the English barons wrested from King John at Runnymeade sixty-eight years earlier, and amply entitle the General Privilege to be regarded as the Magna Charta of Aragon. The victory is all the more remarkable inasmuch as it was won over a monarch who was in no sense the Spanish equivalent of King John. Peter III., as his surname of The Great implies, was unquestionably a strong ruler. Yet the man who had conquered Sicily, defeated the forces of Philip the Hardy by sea and land, and defied Pope Martin IV., was no match for the combination of nobles and commons who swore mutual assistance in resistance to absolutism, and threatened to dethrone him if he persisted in refusing compliance with their demands. Like Magna Charta, the General Privilege placed the barrier of the law between the subject and the arbitrary will of the king. It guaranteed the ancient privileges of both nobles and towns, bound the king not to declare peace or war, or levy taxes, or make laws without the consent of the Cortes, protected the property of the subject from arbitrary seizure and his liberty from illegal encroachment, subjected the jurisdiction of the Justiza, or Grand Justiciar, to the control of a committee of the Cortes, abolished secret trial and torture, except in the case of accusations of issuing false coin, excluded Jews and foreigners from judicial offices, and stipulated that the Cortes should be convened annually at Saragossa.

The nobles did not forget their own interests in their profession of zeal for the public welfare, and the stipulations that they should not be bound to serve the king in war beyond the kingdom, and should have the liberty to renounce their allegiance, if so disposed, and take service abroad, while the king was required to protect their families in their absence, were not creditable to their patriotism. Nor do we discover any anxiety on the part of either nobles or commons to secure a share in these rights for the servile mass, whose lot in Aragon was certainly capable enough of amelioration. "The nobles of Aragon and other lords of a locality, who are not of the Church, may," according to the Observances of Aragon, "treat their serfs, well or ill, according to their pleasure, and seize their goods without possible appeal, and the king may not on any pretext interfere in their domains." The General Privilege, like Magna Charta, guaranteed rights to certain classes; it did nothing for the people in the wider sense. Senor Castelar must have forgotten the serfs when he came to the conclusion that "the aristocracy of Aragon fought at all times, not for power, but for *popular liberty!*" Class egotism notwithstanding, it was in the main a noble essay on behalf of liberty as far as it went, though it does not merit all the enthusiastic, but indiscriminating encomiums which the historians, whether Spanish or foreign, have lavished on it. As an assertion of the right of the subject against the assumptions of absolute power, it is admirable. "Absolute power never was the constitution of Aragon, nor of Valencia, nor of Ribagorca, nor shall there be in time to come any innovation made, but only the law, custom, and privilege which have been anciently used in the aforesaid kingdom." Pity only that this "law, custom, and privilege" did not assure justice and liberty to servile peasant as well as to noble and burgher.

Not content with these guarantees, the Aragonese four years later extorted from Alfonso III., Pedro's successor, the Privilege of Union which sanctioned the right of resistance to arbitrary government. The right of the subject has seldom been asserted in so blunt and thoroughgoing a fashion, even in modern times. These fierce barons and commons of Aragon were not content to invoke the law and secure its vindication by remonstrance or other constitutional means. They drew the sword at once, and bluntly challenged the king to fight. By infringing the rights and privileges of any member of the union, making use of force, that is, to his detriment, without due sentence of justiciary, he ceased to be their king and became their enemy, against whom they might lawfully rise in revolt. The union acted, in fact, on such occasions as a rival sovereign power, with its own seal, on which was displayed a group of suppliants at the foot of the throne, against a significant background of tents and spears, its own standard, army, and council. This readiness to draw the sword in the cause of liberty might easily produce evils at least as great as the arbitrary abuse of monarchic power. However admirable the doctrine of the right of resistance to illegal acts, its systematic practice in this extreme form could only lead to anarchy. There are other ways of securing justice without indulging, at the slightest provocation, in civil war, though as a last resort against illegal government, force may be needful and efficacious. To precipitate the nation into revolution on the slightest pretence of individual wrong was to play into the hands of factious magnates who, in spite of their professions, were not always actuated by the public good. A dispute about the succession which Pedro IV. wished to secure for his daughter, to the exclusion of his brother Don Jayme, developed into one of these internecine struggles which ended in the suppression of the union. Barons and commons swore defiance to the monarch in defence of the Salic law and on behalf of Don Jayme, and during a heated altercation in the Cortes at Saragossa, an armed mob broke into the hall of the monastery of the Preaching Friars, where the sitting was held, and threatened to kill the unpopular Pedro. From this fate he was saved by the intervention of the members, but he choose to risk the arbitration of the sword rather than submit to their demands. His victory over the confederates at Epila in 1348 was a victory for the cause of order, and though Pedro tore in shreds the Privilege of Union with his dagger at a subsequent Assembly of the Cortes at Saragossa, he used his advantage with moderation. Epila was a victory, not for absolute, but for constitutional government. Pedro confirmed the ancient liberties, and in the Cortes and the Justiza, Aragon had a surer guarantee of both liberty and justice than in a factious combination which was a menace to both.

The Cortes of Aragon possessed more actual power in both legislation and administration than that of Castille. It was a compact body which represented all the orders of the State, if not the whole people, and the cohesion of its four Estates (*braços* or arms)—magnates or *ricos hombres*, lesser nobility (*infanzones* and *caballeros*), clergy, and commons—lent its voice a weight which no king before Ferdinand, the Catholic, might ignore with impunity. "My people are free," replied Alfonso IV. to his queen, who exhorted him to follow the forcible example of his brother, the King of Castille, "and are not so submissive as the Castillians. They respect me as their king, and I hold them for good vassals and comrades." The commons both attained political influence at an earlier period, and retained it longer than in Castille, and a town which had once exercised the privilege of representation could continue to avail itself of its right. The Aragonese Cortes was, too, entitled by law to meet every two years, and though the law was by no means scrupulously observed by the kings, it was represented during the intervals between the sessions by a committee of eight members—two from each order—whose duty it was to control the administration. Its deliberations resembled in one particular at least those of a modern parliament, for it usually embraced two parties—the one, which we may denominate conservative, maintaining the rights of the monarch; the other, which we may call liberal, those of the nation. Nor was its meeting a mere constitutional ceremony, as in France or Germany, where the Estates assembled to talk and resolve, without any real power to enforce their will. Every member had the right to veto any measure, and even to bring the business of the session to a standstill by recording his protest. Such an excess of authority was more flattering to the self-esteem of the deputies than conducive to the transaction of business, and seems to have been but rarely exercised. It shows, at any rate, that individual as well as corporate opinion was something to be reckoned with in the national assembly of Aragon. Barring its partial character as a feudal assembly, the representative of certain classes, not of the whole people, it came as near to a modern parliament as a mediæval political assembly could do. It exercised all the powers which that of Castille claimed to exercise, and it did so in a more effective fashion. It legislated, called the executive to account, regulated the succession to the crown, controlled taxation, and supervised the royal household. It possessed in addition the jurisdiction of a supreme court of justice. To its bar, every one, even the most obscure inhabitant of the most obscure village of the kingdom, came who had a suit against any royal official, and if he was too poor to pay an advocate to plead for him, the State was bound to provide one at its own charges. To its action as a court of justice, as well as a legislative body, the laws of Aragon were indebted for many an enactment which went to swell the code of Huesca, the body of laws enacted with its sanction in the reign of Jayme I.

Equally important as a safeguard of justice and a check on the abuse of power by the crown, was the office of Justiza or justiciary of Aragon, whose function it was, according to an old law, " to protect our laws and liberties from arbitrary violation." This redoubtable official, who acquired the full measure of his authority after the suppression of the Privilege of Union, was the supreme judge and guardian of the laws, in co-operation with the Cortes, the referee to whose scrutiny the royal ordinances were subject, and the adviser of the monarch, to whom he administered, seated and with covered head, the coronation oath. Though appointed by the king, he, latterly at least—*i.e.*, from the middle of the fifteenth century—held his office for life, and could only be deprived, in case of maladministration, by the united decision of the king and the Cortes. Great as were his powers, which he did not on occasion hesitate to assert against the royal will, they were not absolute. His decisions were liable to the review of a court whose members were chosen by the king from the Cortes. Subject to this salutary limitation, his jurisdiction was none the less an effective check on the administration of the royal judges and other officials, and even on the action of the king himself, in virtue of the rights of jurisfirma and manifestation, with which he was invested. By the former he was empowered to evoke a suit from an inferior court to his own tribunal, and to protect the accused person from molestation by the royal judges, pending proceedings before himself, and on the defendant giving security to appear for judgment. By the latter he could demand and enforce the release of any one arrested by order of the inferior judges, and transfer him to the public prison, set apart for this purpose, to await trial at his bar. The exercise of these powers thus assured the subject, before the organisation of the Inquisition by Ferdinand the Catholic, against an unfair trial and arbitrary imprisonment, from which no mere parchment Magna Charta was sufficient to protect him. "The grand originality of this magistracy lay in the guarantee which it afforded of the rights of each against the tyranny of all, the liberties of the nation against the encroachment of the government, the property of the subject against the greed of the fisc, the liberty of the individual against the abuses of the various jurisdictions, ecclesiastical and secular." Another benefit of the office, equally important, was the substitution of the arbitration of the justiciary for that of the sword in intestine disputes. The incorruptibility and independence of many of these magistrates invested them with an influence before which party spirit bowed, for even the magnates learned to respect in them an impartiality which did not fear to brave the king as well as check their own turbulent spirit.

Both Valencia and Catalonia had their Cortes, and although they sometimes met along with that of Aragon in the same place, at the same time, for the same purpose, all three sat and deliberated separately, and were usually held in different towns. While their political institutions thus resembled those of Aragon, they were pervaded by a more democratic spirit. Catalonia was, indeed, politically in advance of Aragon, where the aristocratic element was strong, as Aragon was in advance of Castille, where the aristocratic element, though strong, was not so cohesive. In spite of its republican freedom, however, Catalonia was not in advance of its neighbours in the matter of serfage, which was not abolished till 1486 by Ferdinand the Catholic. Barcelona was a virtual republic under the supremacy of the Aragonese kings rather than a subject city. Its thriving commerce and industry raised it to a position of wealth and splendour second only to those of the most famous cities of Italy, and the energy of its commercial and industrial life was reflected in the democratic spirit of its municipal institutions. It was governed by a senate of a hundred, which exercised the legislative function, and by a small council of *regidores* or magistrates, who formed the executive. The members of both the larger and the lesser council were not a mere oligarchy of wealth and rank. They were elected from the merchants and craft gilds alike, though men of noble birth might qualify themselves for office by renouncing their rank. They were invested, as a corporate body, with certain sovereign rights, such as the conclusion of commercial treaties with foreign States, the maintenance of the defence of the city in time of war, the issuing of letters of mark against the enemies of their commerce. The sovereign dignity of their magistrates was expressed by the title of *magnificos*, by the privilege of remaining seated with heads uncovered in the royal presence, and by the special honour accorded to their deputies to court, who were treated with the same ceremony as foreign ambassadors. "The inhabitants of Barcelona," to quote the testimony of the Venetian ambassador to Spain at the beginning of the sixteenth century, "have so many privileges that the king scarcely retains any authority over them." The Aragonese kings were in truth fain to propitiate their democratic spirit, and those who, like Ferdinand I. at the beginning of the fifteenth century, ventured to ignore it, were speedily taught to repent of their rashness.

SOURCES.—Marina, Ensayo Historico Critico sobre la Antigua Legislacion de los Reynos de Lyon y Castilla (1808), and, Teoria de las Cortes (1820), and article in the *Edinburgh Review*, No. 43 ; Mariana, Histoire Générale d'Espagne, translated by P. Charenton, (1725); Zurita, Annales de Aragon (1562-69); Blancas, Aragonensium Rerum Commentarii (1588); Ayala, Cronica de los Reyes de Castilla (1779-80); Froissart, Chroniques (Lettenhove and Luce's editions); Sempere, Histoire des Cortes d'Espagne (1815), and article in *Edinburgh Review*, No. 61 ; Castelar, Estudios Historicos (1875); Ulrich Ralph Burke, History of Spain, edited by

Sources of Chapter XII.

Martin A. S. Hume (1900); Hallam, Europe during the Middle Ages, vol. ii.; Prescott, History of the Reign of Ferdinand and Isabella (1879); Dunham, History of Spain and Portugal (Cabinet Cyclopedia); Robertson, History of Charles V. (1857); Dozy, Recherches sur l'Histoire et la Literature d'Espagne (1860); Watts, Spain (1893); Butler Clarke, The Cid Campeador (1897); Poole, The Moors in Spain (1887); Mariejol, Les Royaumes Iberiques du XIe à la fin du XIIIe Siècle, in Histoire Générale, t. ii. (1893); Desdevises Du Dézert, Les Royaumes Iberiques de la Mort d'Alfonse X. à l'Union de la Castille et de l'Aragon, Hist. Gén., t. iii. (1894); Lafuente, Historia General de España (1887-89); Haebler, Über die Älteren Hermandades in Kastilien, in Historische Zeitschrift, xvii. (1885).

CHAPTER XIII.

CONSTITUTIONAL AND SOCIAL PROGRESS IN MEDIÆVAL ENGLAND.

THE orthodox view of the Anglo-Saxon settlement assumes the extermination, within a large area of Roman Briton, of the native population by the invaders from over the North Sea. It holds that these invaders, similarly, made a clean sweep of Roman institutions, and substituted for them those of their homeland in Jutland and Saxony. This view has been contradicted in both particulars. The Anglo-Saxons, assert its opponents, enslaved many of the Roman Britons instead of killing the population wholesale. And they paid tribute, more or less, like the invaders of the Continental empire, to the jurisprudence at least of Rome. "We have trustworthy evidence," says Sir Travers Twiss in the introduction to volume ii. of his edition of Bracton, "in a letter addressed by St Aldhelm to the Venerable Bede, in the seventh century, that the 'marrow' of the Roman laws was still being drawn out of them by earnest students; and from a poem of Alcuin in the eighth century, we gather that the study of Roman jurisprudence was at that time still maintained in the school of York."

These invaders, it is further assumed, settled down as free village communities, which only very gradually sank into serfage under a lord of the manor, who in turn became a feudal magnate. This doctrine, too, has encountered able antagonists in Mr Coote, and more particularly in Mr Seebohm. Instead of the free village community, Mr Seebohm shows us the Roman *villa*, with its slaves and *coloni*, becoming the English manor, with its cluster of serfs, under its Anglo-Saxon lord. These serfs were the natives, who simply changed masters—and Mr Seebohm has found indubitable traces of the survival of men of British blood in Northumbria, Wessex, Mercia—or the servile dependants whom the invaders brought with them, and established on their conquered estates. Mr Seebohm sees even in Germany itself, not the free village community, but the manorial settlement of lord and serf. In carving the conquered territory into "hams" and "tuns," as their estates came to be called, and settling down as lords of a servile population, the invaders were merely applying the custom of their homeland. This bold theory cannot, perhaps, be regarded as conclusively proved. It has, for instance, found a formidable opponent in Professor Vinogradoff. But the evidence, accumulated by its learned author in its support, should make us receive with reserve the glowing pictures which writers like Mr Green and Mr Freeman have drawn of these communities of Anglo-Saxon freemen, who cleared the country with the sword, and established at its point the institutions of a free race. It is more probable, on the other hand, that they acted, as their Frankish kinsmen acted in Gaul—assimilated, to some extent at least, the institutions of the Roman Britons, which, according to Mr Seebohm, were very like their own in the matter of landownership and servile cultivation.

A most disagreeable conclusion for those who have expended so much fond rhetoric on the free institutions of "our Saxon forefathers," and have coolly consigned the mass of the inhabitants of Roman Britain to wholesale massacre, or to the refuge of the Welsh and Scottish mountains. In view of these enthusiastic periods, Mr Seebohm's sober conclusion is, unintentionally of course, not without a certain humour in Celtic eyes. "However many exceptional instances there may have been of settlements in tribal households, or even free village communities, it seems to be almost certain that these 'hams' or 'tuns' were, generally speaking, and for the most part, from the first, practically *manors* with communities in *serfdom* upon them." And the worst of it is that our unconscionable author does not shrink from the assertion that these serfs were not necessarily of British blood. They were, it would seem, partly at least, of the same blood as the invaders, who are piously supposed by the patriotic English historians to have stepped on the shores of Britain as bands of freemen, and to have planted their native freedom in British soil. Even if this be but a theory (with some evidence behind it, however), we may perhaps, on the strength of it, look for a little less indiscriminating enthusiasm and a little more modesty on the part of said historians, who so complacently claim for "our Anglo-Saxon forefathers" a monopoly of freedom and political genius, and ignore the other elements of the population of "England" in the making of "English" history. Evidently a good deal more went to "the making of England" than what the Anglo-Saxon invaders brought with them in the keels that carried them across the North Sea.

The invaders were, then, probably not all freemen, and the freemen seem to have been much fewer in number than the modern historians assume. They were the lords of a serfish element in the population, Saxon or British, or both, and consequently the free village community in the early Anglo-Saxon kingdoms appears to have been the exception rather than the rule. That the invading bands contained various social grades seems certain from Tacitus' general description of the Germans, the accounts of the Saxons given by later writers, and the testimony of the early laws of Ethelberht of Kent. Tacitus and Nithard, for instance, speak of nobles, freemen, and serfs—the eorls, ceorls, laets of the Kentish laws—and the slave was of course at the bottom of the social scale.

Unlike the Franks, however, the Saxon invaders had no kings. Each tribe was ruled in peace by its chief or ealdorman, and only in time of war did they select by lot one of their chiefs as Heretoga, Herzog, Dux, to lead the united host against the common enemy. Hengist and Horsa, Cerdic and Cynric, were not kings, but Heretoga or ealdormen, leaders of war bands. The kingship sprang into existence in Teutonic Briton as the result of conquest. The war leader, as the founder of a petty State, was rewarded with the title of king. The primitive Anglo-Saxon king was, however, a very humble dignitary compared with the Merovingian monarch of the same period. Though superstition attached a certain sanctity to his person as the assumed descendant of the gods, his power was by no means, in theory or in practice, absolute. He was elected by the people, and if the choice was as a rule limited to the royal stock, he was none the less the representative, not the lord of the nation. And, as among the Franks on the other side of the Channel, he might be deposed if he proved unworthy of his office, and was frequently dispossessed by violence in this early anarchic period of Anglo-Saxon history. Of the fifteen kings of Northumbria in the eighth century, for example, thirteen are recorded to have lost their office by resignation, murder, or expulsion. Examples of the same fate are not lacking in the history of the kings of Wessex. Two of these Northumbrian and Wessex kings were certainly formally deposed by the Witan, or Great Council of the nation, and they are not solitary examples of this supreme exercise of the sovereignty of the people in British history since the Anglo-Saxon conquest. "Six times at least," says Mr Freeman, "in the space of nine hundred years, from Sigebert of Wessex to James the Second, has the Great Council of the nation thus put forth the last and greatest of its powers."

These early kings shared the legislative and executive powers with the Great Council or assembly of the chief men of the kingdom, which, according to Mr Freeman, theoretically at least, represented the nation. Bishop Stubbs, on the other hand, sees in the Witan a select, non-representative body, composed of the ealdormen, the prelates, and *comites* or companions of the king, who did not represent, though they acted on behalf of the nation, and whose numbers increased as the union of the kingdoms proceeded. The Witan seems to have been selected, not elected. Whether representative or not, this select assembly was originally, and for long, invested with very ample powers, and was a far more potent factor in government than the assembly of the Merovingian or Carolingian kings. The laws were decreed by its "counsel and consent," and, except perhaps under a very strong king, this phrase is evidently no conventional formula, as it often is among the Franks. It legislates for the Church as well as for the nation. Its consent is necessary to the alienation by the king of the folk or public land. It is the supreme court in civil and criminal causes. It imposes taxes on extraordinary occasions—in cases, that is, in which the revenue of the royal and public lands was insufficient to meet the emergency, say, of a Danish invasion. It declares war or peace. It disposes of the army and fleet. It fills all high offices in Church and State. It elects the king as well as the bishops and the ealdormen, and deposes him when necessity arises. Theoretically and actually, the royal dignity was doubtless great. The king is the representative of the people; he is consecrated to his office with the rites of religion; if a heathen, he enjoys the prestige of an assumed offspring from Woden; if a Christian, he is regarded as the anointed of the Lord. In reality he possesses, originally, very little power. His action is controlled by the Great Council in the most comprehensive fashion. If the people is bound to the king by an oath of allegiance, the king is bound to the people by an oath to rule justly. Nay, the oath of allegiance is indirectly, if not specifically, conditional. The king must fulfil his part of the bargain, to put it plainly; otherwise fealty lapses. The Anglo-Saxon king, as thus controlled by the nation, was evidently a much less august individual than those imitations of the Roman *imperator* who ruled in Frankish Gaul. While it would be absurd to see in this Anglo-Saxon polity a fully fledged democracy of freemen, with its sovereign popular assembly, as some of the English historians have done, it undoubtedly represents a very limited monarchy. It is rather a practical aristocracy under a monarchic form, for the Witan, which represents the higher classes, both secular and ecclesiastical, is really supreme in legislation, policy, and administration.

This aristocracy is, however, compatible with a system of local government which deprives it in turn of the powers of an oppressive oligarchy, and leaves room for the operation of the popular will in what concerns it most nearly—local administration. The freeman at least, whether lord of a manor or the occupier of a small holding, has his share in the local administration through a series of courts, corresponding to the political subdivisions of the country, in which he makes his voice heard personally or by representative. These subdivisions consist of the township, the hundred, the shire, each of which has its distinctive court and administrative officials. The township, if composed of freemen, has its *gemot*, or what we should call its "parish council," which elected its *tungerefa*, town reeve, or headman, and its four representatives to the larger courts, and made its own bye-laws; if dependent on a lord of the manor, it was probably administered by its superior or his steward. According to Pollock and Maitland we "have no ground whatever for concluding that the township-moot (court) had any properly judicial functions." Above the township came the larger political division of the hundred, with its *gerefa*, or hundred reeve, as headman, and its monthly court or hundred-moot, at which the landlords of the district and the representatives of the townships met to dispense justice in civil and criminal causes. Larger than the hundred was the shire, which was under the jurisdiction of the ealdorman, elected by the Witan, and the shire reeve or sheriff, nominated by the king. The ealdorman was the commander of its militia, the sheriff the administrator of the law, who presided over the shiremoot or folkmoot, as the court of this larger area was called. This court, which was held twice a year, was attended by representatives of the hundreds and townships, and seems to have been invested with legislative as well as administrative powers.

This political constitution did not remain stationary throughout the five centuries of Anglo-Saxon history. It underwent modification in some material points. More especially did the power of the king increase, and this increase of power reacted on the political and social organisation of the nation. The change from a number of petty States to one kingdom under a monarch, whose sway extended from the Forth to the Channel, made the king a far more powerful individual, territorially, than a petty prince of Kent, Mercia, or Northumbria. The predominance of one king over the rest was expressed from an early period by the title of Bretwalda. When in course of time there came to be but one ruler over the whole Anglo-Saxon territory, the increase of his territorial power found expression in the high-sounding title of *imperator, basileus*, of all Britain, which, nominally at least, placed him on a level with the imperial potentates of east and west.

Not only did his territorial power increase, his relation to the nation likewise underwent a change. He was not merely the head of the tribe or petty State; he became its lord and was protected by a rigorous treason law. To plot against the king was to incur forfeiture of life and goods. The clergy, too, elevated his dignity by the emphasis which they laid on obedience as a religious duty. Ethelred, for instance, is "Christ's vicegerent who preserves and holds sway over Christendom and kingdom as long as God grants it." It would be premature, of course, to read into such language the theory of divine right, but it undoubtedly tended this way. The king continues to legislate by the counsel and consent of the Witan, but the Witan tends to become a royal rather than a national council. His official functions are amplified. He becomes more and more the source of justice, the guardian of the peace; and the breach of the peace, the transgression of the law, is an offence against the king. He is the supreme judge in all causes, and his officers consequently encroach on the powers of the local courts. He is, moreover, the grand landowner. The folkland—land held without written title—becomes the king's land, and is practically undistinguishable from the royal domain.

The *gesith* of earlier times, the *comes, miles*, companion who fights for him in battle, resides at his court, and is rewarded with a grant of folkland, by-and-by develops into the *thegn*, the noble landowner, the vassal. The nobility of blood and tradition gives place to an official and territorial nobility, the eorl to the thegn. This nobility has, too, various grades, and ultimately the earl, whose title is borrowed, not from the old *eorl*, but from the Danish *jarl*, appears as the highest in rank. This nobility is not, however, a feudal caste, as on the Continent, for even the ceorl and the merchant may prosper to thegn right. The tendency is, nevertheless, in the direction of feudalism. The king is the universal lord; the great landowners, who hold estates of him and owe him military service, have jurisdiction over the lesser landowners, and by the time of Edward the Confessor a large number of small freemen have, by commendation, placed themselves in dependence on a lord. And while the relation of inferior to superior is still a personal one, it tends to become a relation based on land tenure, and has thus something in it of the feudal tie. In the rise of a class of magnates, too—especially after the four earls of Canute, who turn the kingdom into a seethe of anarchy under his successors—we have a parallel to the aggressive feudal spirit which had triumphed over the central power in France, and threatened to transform England into a feudal state on the French model. From this fate it was saved by the strong hand of the Norman William.

For though William was the lord of a feudal duchy and brought the feudal system to England in his train of feudal barons, he was not minded to engraft that system in its integrity on his English kingdom. He was not prepared to invest his barons with the great territorial jurisdictions which would have made them petty sovereigns and rendered the establishment of an effective central authority impossible. He suppressed the great earldoms. He was determined to be king in fact as well as in name—no mere figurehead on the throne, like his contemporary fellow-potentates of the house of Capet. He sought and obtained the consent of the Witan to the sovereignty which he had wrested from Harold; he would not hold what he had won, in dependence on the swords of his feudal followers. He would hold it as absolute lord, and distribute it on certain conditions. It was the realisation of this policy, so sternly carried out in the face of rebellion, so systematically applied to all estates, whether forfeited for rebellion or not, that resulted in the establishment of the feudal tenure of land in England. All landowners, great and small, became feudal vassals, either directly of the king, or indirectly, through some superior who was the king's vassal, and the trend of Anglo-Saxon institutions towards feudalism made the change a consummation, rather than a revolution. This change would not, of itself, have sufficed to buttress the royal government; it might rather have led to its debility. In France, as we have seen, feudalism reduced the central government to impotence. In England, on the other hand, the power of the feudal hierarchy was strictly subordinate to that of the king. It was more a social than a political organisation. The sovereign jurisdiction which made the French magnate a virtual king within his own dominions, was, with the partial exception of the palatinates of Chester, Shropshire, and Durham, on the Welsh and Scottish marches, reserved by William to the crown. The feudal baron preserved certain rights as against his vassals, but the jurisdiction of the manorial court was not allowed to trench on the royal prerogative. He might be a great landowner, but the policy of scattering the grants of land to one individual over a wide area made it difficult for him to concentrate his forces against his sovereign. The king was master of the nation, not merely, as in France, the virtual equal of a number of petty sovereigns. He exacted an oath of allegiance from the whole nation, from mediate and immediate vassals alike. In France, on the other hand, the vassal who held directly of a lord was bound to obey his summons, irrespective of the royal will, and if this lord fought against the king, he, and not the vassal who followed his standard, was guilty of rebellion. In England, in the same contingency, the vassal was, in virtue of his oath of allegiance, equally guilty with his lord. He, equally with his lord, was bound to answer the royal summons to arms, for the king was entitled to call out the entire military force of the nation—the old English *fyrd*—as well as impose taxes and issue summonses to his own court of justice, irrespective of the jurisdiction of the local superior. He retained the old institutions of the nation—the hundred-moot, the shiremoot, the Witenagemot, which was henceforth known as the Great Council—as media of administration and legislation. He innovated indeed in matters of ecclesiastical custom. To please the pope, he deprived the English bishops of their sees and put Normans in their places. He separated the ecclesiastical from the secular courts, and thus enhanced the ecclesiastical power. But he resisted the papal claim to supremacy, and asserted his own over the bishops.

Thus, as against the feudal hierarchy, William was actual, not merely titular sovereign; as against the nation, his sovereignty was limited by the old constitution on which the feudal system was engrafted. This limitation was, however, only such as the conqueror chose, from politic reasons, to impose on himself. In reality he held his crown in virtue of his sword. He maintained it by his stern, merciless, vigorous personality, and enforced submission to his will on both magnates and people. His will was thus the mainspring of government, and his will was practically absolute. It remained to be seen whether, under his successors, the constitutional forms which he allowed to subsist had sufficient vitality to resist the impolitic and oppressive exercise of this sovereign will; whether, that is, England should remain an absolute, or develop into a constitutional monarchy.

In the more immediate of these successors, William Rufus and Henry I., the absolutist tendency of the crown is equally distinguishable, in spite of the constitutional forms of election and coronation oath. William II. was an execrable autocrat, who broke the laws of God and man with cynical shamelessness, and richly merited the shaft of the assassin. Henry I. was a rigorous ruler, who proved the efficacy of the policy of centralisation by the firm administration of his Curia Regis and his justiciary, Roger of Salisbury. He held down the turbulent Norman barons who resented the bit in their mouths, and strove to throw off the royal yoke; but he befriended the people, the mass against the class, in his own interest at least, and sternly upheld law and order. "He was a good man," says the chronicler, "and great was the awe of him; no man durst ill-treat another in his time; he made peace for men and deer." By contrast with the reign of his successor, Stephen, the thirty-five years of his strong government were regretted as a national benefaction in the midst of the ensuing twenty-five years of war and anarchy.

This miserable period of civil strife between the partisans of Stephen and Mathilda was the opportunity of the great barons. They fought for their own interest, and espoused or deserted the cause of the rivals as it served that interest. Each mighty donjon became a feudal fortress, its owner a petty feudal potentate who waged war, coined money, and exercised a harsh jurisdiction over his dependants, in defiance alike of Stephen's kingship and Mathilda's queenship. The worst excesses of the feudal anarchy of the Continent were perpetrated by the swarm of titled cutthroats who exemplified the *régime* of fist right at the expense of both crown and people. The paralysis of law and government was complete, and their restoration was the apparently hopeless task which Mathilda's son, the young Henry II., first of the Angevin or Plantagenet kings, set himself to accomplish.

This strong-willed, energetic young man was a born organiser, and in his strong hands the administration of Henry I. was not only renewed, but reformed. The experiment of twenty-five years of anarchy made the nation only too glad to welcome the strong man in the place of the weak, and co-operate in the work of reform. The great barons again found the bit in their mouths. Their castles were mostly razed to the ground; they lost the rights they had usurped; they were forced to submit to the law of the land. They were not only taught the lesson of subordination, they were made to co-operate in the work of government, along with the prelates and the lesser landowners, in the Great Council, which Henry frequently summoned, and by which he legislated the greater measures of his reign. This training in a national assembly in national affairs was not without important consequences in the near future, when a worthless, despotic king occupied his father's place and drove the nation into revolt against his tyranny. At the same time Henry lessened their power for mischief, while training them to use their powers for good. He deprived many of them of the influential office of sheriff, and substituted officials whose administration he controlled by his itinerant justices of the Curia Regis. By the device of scutage—the commutation of military service for a sum of money—he obtained the means of maintaining a mercenary army to defend his French provinces, and thus diminished his dependence on the vassals of the crown in his foreign expeditions. For the defence of the kingdom he relied on the old national militia, the fyrd, which he organised and armed with modern weapons (Assize of Arms). He associated the nation more closely in the administration of justice by the establishment, in germ at least, of trial by jury, elected from each hundred and township, in civil and criminal causes in the county courts (the Grand Assize and the Assize of Clarendon). The Assize of Clarendon established in each county a jury composed of twelve lawful men from each hundred, and four from each township, to present and accuse criminals. The Grand Assize ordained that in civil causes four sworn knights of the shire should elect twelve sworn recognitors to inquire into and give a verdict on the case. The system was applied to taxation by Archbishop Hubert Walter in the reign of Richard, and thus the nation was taught to deal in a representative capacity with public questions.

Henry's policy was thus to rule as a national king, with

the co-operation of the nation, and the rally of the nation to his side in the rising of the great barons in support of his rebellious son, shows that his policy was both shrewd and effective. As in the reign of Henry I., it is still king and nation against the barons, and the alliance is to the advantage of the nation as well as the king.

The nation did not follow him in his ecclesiastical policy, which tended to reduce the clergy, like the barons, to submission to the law, and though entirely defensible in itself, was rendered odious by the harsh treatment and the murder of Archbishop Becket. That a criminal in holy orders should be allowed to escape the penalty of death for murder, simply because he could plead privilege of clergy, was, in Henry's eyes, a mere subterfuge to evade the law, and he rightly insisted, in the Constitutions of Clarendon, that he should be handed over by the ecclesiastical to the civil court for sentence. The people, on the other hand, saw in the clergy the protectors of the poor, and in the murdered archbishop its champion and martyr, and the popular feeling forced the monarch to resile in the face of the baronial rebellion of 1173-74. The Church as a national institution was a political force which could not yet be defied with impunity, and Henry was wise enough to recognise the fact to his own humiliation. Fortunately for English political progress, the lesson was thrown away on his son, whose tyrannous rule estranged the nation from the king, and allied barons and people in defence of their rights against the crown. The union of races, of Englishman and Norman, which was in progress by this time, helped to strengthen the union of classes.

Like his predecessors, John owed his throne to the election of the magnates, and if one may trust Matthew Paris, he was expressly reminded of the fact by Archbishop Hubert. "We all," declared the archbishop to the assembled people, "by reason of his merits, no less than of his royal blood, have unanimously chosen him for our king." The archbishop and his fellow-electors were singularly short-sighted. John had yet to prove his merits, and his vices had been in sufficient evidence during his brother Richard's short reign. He broke through every restraint of law and morality, was, in fact, like Rufus, a ruffian pure and simple. He showed, indeed, on occasions, some of the vigour of the ruffian, though he is usually represented as a coward and a trifler. Happily, he was incapable of sustained action. He defied and then cringed to Pope Innocent III. He threw down the gauntlet to his overlord, King Philip II. of France, and allowed himself by his inaction to be mulcted of his French domains. He roused by his tyranny the combined antagonism of barons, Church, and nation, who presented their ultimatum in the Great Charter. He had only the pope and his mercenaries to fall back on, and he shrank from the struggle with a united nation and signed the charter. When he recovered sufficient energy to break his word and take vengeance on the barons, it was only to be confronted with a still stronger combination, with Louis of France at its head, and to end a reign of ignominy in the midst of failure and execration.

The Great Charter, based on that by which Henry I. had forsworn the tyranny of William Rufus, reveals the abuse of power which it seeks to remedy in a series of sixty-three articles. Of these abuses, the most crying are the excessive exactions in the form of reliefs, the oppression of minors and widows under ward, the arbitrary taxes, and the illegal encroachment on the liberty of the subject. Against these evils every freeman secures the most explicit guarantees. "If any count, or baron, or other tenant-in-chief of the crown shall die and his heir shall be of full age, he shall only pay the relief specified by ancient custom." "The guardian of the estate of an heir, who is a minor, shall not take of such estate any but reasonable exit, customs, services, and this without destruction or damage of man or things." "No widow shall be compelled to marry again as long as she prefers to live without a husband, provided she gives security that she will not marry without our consent, if she holds of us, or without consent of the lord of whom she holds." "No scutage or aid shall be imposed unless by the Common Council of the kingdom, except in the case of an aid for the ransom of our body, the knighting of our eldest son, and the marriage of our eldest daughter, and in each case the aid shall not exceed what is reasonable. . . . And for the holding of the Common Council we shall cause to be summoned by letters under our seal the archbishops, bishops, abbots, counts, and greater barons, and in general, through our sheriffs and bailiffs, all those who hold of us in chief, to meet on a certain day and at a certain place; and in letters we shall make known the cause of the summons, and these summonses having been made, the business shall proceed on the assigned day according to the counsel of those who shall be present, although those summoned may not all appear." " No one may exact a feudal aid from his own free tenants except in the three cases above mentioned of ransom, the knighthood of an eldest son, and the marriage of an eldest daughter." " Recognitions shall not be taken unless within the county of the accused and in the following manner—we, or in our absence from the kingdom, our capital justiciar, shall send two justiciars through each county four times in the year, who, with four knights, elected by each county, shall hold on a certain day the assizes of the county." " No free man may be taken, or imprisoned, or disseized, or outlawed, or exiled, or in any other way destroyed, injured, nor will we go against him or send against him, except by the lawful judgment of his peers, or by the law of the land. We will sell to no one, nor will we deny or delay to any one, right or justice." Finally, the king is made to distrust himself, and to concede to the barons the right to elect twenty-five of their number, whose duty it shall be to guard the rights thus conceded, and in case of contravention by the king, to compel him by force to observe them. The king is thus himself made amenable to the law, and resistance to illegal government is not merely no rebellion, but a constitutional obligation. " In brief," as Pollock and Maitland point out, " it means this, that the king is and shall be below the law." Lex thus became Rex, and under this Rex all subjects, whether vassals of the crown, or vassals of those holding immediately of the crown, whether baron or simple freeman, were guaranteed in their liberty and property against injustice and exaction.

As the guarantee of the rights of all freemen, the charter is thus a great landmark in the history of the vindication of liberty from the abuse of arbitrary power. Let us, all the same, not fall into the strain of exaggeration in which the historians usually speak of it. It is a great advance only in reference to the age which produced it. It secures rights to the freeman, indeed—inestimable rights; but the rights are for the freeman only. With the exception of a single insignificant phrase, there is no mention of the unfree, and it does little or nothing to break down the tyranny of the feudal system from which it emanates. It consecrates liberty to those who enjoy it; it does not give it to those who enjoy it not. It homologates a vast and intricate system of privilege and inequality, under which might is often right, and equal justice for all men means, really, equal justice for the few. It remained to be seen, too, whether equal justice for all, even in this limited sense, would stand the test of kingly rule in the future. The frequent demand for the renewal of the charter in future reigns, shows that it was more frequently observed in the breach than in the rule. It is a pious belief that would assume that because Magna Charta was incorporated in the statute-book, misgovernment and oppression were henceforth impossible in English history. The facts are certainly often enough incompatible with this fond belief.

The beginning of the reign of Henry III. witnessed a reaction against the baronial movement of that of John, and the reaction is apparent in the omission in the renewed charter of the two important articles which made the king dependent, in the matter of taxation, on the Great Council, and conferred on the barons the right to resist the infringement of its provisions. The fear of the consequences of the baronial supremacy, which might in England, as in Aragon, have plunged the country into periodic anarchy, was stronger in moderate men than the fear of royal misgovernment, especially as John's successor was but a boy of nine years, and the government was in the prudent hands, first of William the Marshal, Earl of Pembroke, and then of Hubert de Burgh. The case was changed, however, when the fickle, false, and foolish Henry declared himself of age in 1227, and gave power and place to a host of foreign fortune-seekers and favourites, like Peter des Roches, Bishop of Winchester. The insolent *régime* of these greedy minions once more estranged the nation from the king and restored to the barons the influence they had wielded in the preceding reign. Moreover, the royal subservience to the exactions and pretensions of the pope alienated the clergy and transferred them to the ranks of the opposition. This opposition at length found in Simon de Montfort, Earl of Leicester, a leader born to rally it in effective antagonism to a hateful *régime* of favouritism, tergiversation, and oppression. This rally came in 1258, after all classes had been maddened by royal and papal exactions to support the will-o'-the-wisp policy of winning the Sicilian crown for Prince Edmund. The Great Council, or Parliament, as it was now beginning to be called, at Oxford, to which not only the great barons, but the lesser tenants-in-chief crowded in arms, compelled the king to accept a programme of reforms, drawn up by the council of twenty-four barons, chosen for the purpose, and known as the Provisions of Oxford. Their purport is to remedy the evil of irresponsible power by subjecting the administration to the control of a council of fifteen, to be elected by four of the barons. To this end, the council was entrusted with large powers, for to it the royal officials—chief justice, treasurer, chancellor—were virtually made responsible. " They shall have power to counsel the king in good faith concerning the government of the realm, and all things which appertain to the king or the kingdom ; and to amend and redress all things which they shall see require to be redressed and amended. And over the chief justice and over all other people." To keep the nation in touch with the Council, three Parliaments were to be held each year, but their members were limited to " twelve honest men," chosen by the barons to represent the realm, and empowered to deliberate with the Council, in their name, on all affairs of public importance. It was a dubious expedient thus to supersede the Parliament in the name of the Parliament, and it looks very like the establishment of a baronial oligarchy which might easily become dangerous to the general interest. It proved unworkable in the near sequel, owing to the distrust of the subtenants of the baronial supremacy and the dissensions in the ranks of the barons themselves, of which Henry took advantage to declare himself absolved by the pope from his oath to observe the Provisions. The result was the rising of the barons in 1263, and, after the futile attempt at arbitration by St Louis (Mise of Amiens) which was favourable to the king, the battle of Lewes, where Earl Simon not only defeated Henry, but took him and his son Edward prisoners.

Master of the situation, the victor strove to give a wider and firmer basis to the reforms enacted at Oxford. He retained the council of administration, while limiting its membership to nine, but he discarded the representative baronial committee of twelve, which had superseded the Parliament, and in December 1265 summoned an assembly which, besides barons and prelates, included two knights from each shire and two representatives of each town. It is in the presence of the latter class that the importance of Simon's policy lies, for in the civic representatives a new political factor of great potential significance emerges. The towns were the staunch opponents of arbitrary government, and in recognising their right to a voice in the national council, the reformer was at least showing the way to constitutional government as the future was to conceive it.

That way lay not in narrowing representation to baronial committees, but in widening it to the vital elements of the nation. The vitality of the towns in the thirteenth century was proving itself in England, as elsewhere, by the spirit of enterprise which was increasing their prosperity and their capacity for self-government, as their charters bear witness, and it is the merit of Simon de Montfort that he emancipated himself from the shackles of class privilege and prejudice so far as to recognise the political value of civic enterprise and capacity. To regard him as the creator of popular representation is to misuse language, as long as the mass of the people remained in a state of serfdom. Popular representation was still, and continued to be for centuries to come, a misnomer, though found often enough in the pages of the historians; but the presence of these burgher representatives was a step towards it. Simon's Parliament might be a partisan assembly; it might not be, in the larger sense a "popular" one, but it came as near as the circumstances would admit to being a national one, and the work of the reformer must be judged by the actually expedient, not by the theoretically possible. Progress is not the less progress, though it may be limited by the actual, and fall far short of the ideal; it is not the less progress, even if it seem to prove a failure. The victory of Lewes was followed by the defeat of Evesham, but the cause was not lost for which its leader perished.

Bracton and the Supremacy of Law.

The enemy of Simon de Montfort, the conqueror of Evesham, became, in spite of himself, the champion of the cause for which the vanquished earl died. Edward I. discovered that he must perforce submit to the co-operation of the national Parliament which Earl Simon had called into existence. He was king by hereditary right; the feudal principle had strengthened the tendency to hereditary succession; the days of election were past in the meantime; but as the result of a long struggle with misgovernment, the law was supreme and Parliament had become a factor in the making of the law. "The king," says Bracton, the great English jurist of the period, "ought not to be subject to any man, but to God and the law, for the law makes him king. Let the king, therefore, give to the law what the law gives to him, dominion and power, for there is no king whose will and not law bears rule." Moreover, the law is not merely the prince's will, for the words of the pandects that "whatever the prince pleases has the force of law," mean not the mere will of the prince, "but that which is established by the advice of his councillors, the king giving his authority, and deliberation and discussion having been had upon it." "Whilst he does justice," he adds, "he is the vicar of the Eternal King; but he is the minister of the devil when he turns aside to injustice. For he is called king (*rex*) from ruling (*regendo*) well, and not from reigning (*regnando*), because he is a king whilst he rules well, and a tyrant (*tyrannus*) when he oppresses with violent dominion the people entrusted to him. Let him, therefore, temper his power by law, which is the bridle of power, that he live according to laws, because a human law has sanctioned that laws bind the lawgiver himself, and elsewhere, in the same, it is a saying worthy the majesty of one who reigns that the prince should avow himself to be bound by the laws." Law, he repeats, makes him king, and submission to it is greater than mere empire. It is only on this ground that he rates the dignity of king so highly. He calls him the vicar of God. He ought to surpass all his subjects in power. He ought not to have a peer, much less a superior. No one may presume to dispute concerning his acts, much less contravene them. But just because he is God's vicar, he can do nothing but what is right and just.

Though the interpretation of the old Rex Legia is forced,

and Bracton provides no legal means of calling a lawless king to account, it is very significant as an expression of the prevailing contention that the power of the King of England is not arbitrary. The struggles of several reigns, in spite of reactions and failures, had translated this contention into fact. He might ordain in his council without summoning Parliament to approve the ordinance; he could not enact the fiat of his own will pure and simple. He must at least obtain the opinion and apparently the assent of the council.

Significant, too, in the history of English political liberty is this apparition of the jurist, who emphasises the fact of law even to the king whom he serves as justiciary. Bracton is the first of the long line of great English lawyers who elaborated the theory of the supremacy of the law, and impressed it on their contemporaries. The theory might not be philosophic, but it was a good working axiom, and it was destined to play a *rôle* of enormous significance in English constitutional history. Bracton is the most shining light, in the thirteenth century, of that school of legal learning which Archbishop Theobald founded and Vacarius organised at Oxford, and John of Salisbury rendered illustrious in the preceding one. The Oxford school in its turn was the fruit of the revival of the study of Roman jurisprudence in Italy and Western Europe, which, as Pollock and Maitland have shown, powerfully affected the development of English law in the twelfth and thirteenth centuries. But while the study of Roman law abroad tended more and more to buttress the throne of the would-be absolute potentate in France and Germany, the jurist in England became the staunch champion of the limitation of the royal power by the law, of the rights of Parliament against the crown. The names of Fortescue and Coke, among many others, are sufficient to remind us of the fact.

The fact of this limitation is patent enough in the reign of Edward I. Edward was a great ruler and legislator, but he both ruled and legislated in co-operation with the nation, if with the aid of his lawyers. If he did not summon a representative Parliament on the model of that of Simon de Montfort till 1295; if the Parliament previous to this date was only a partial assembly of the higher orders, he consulted the various classes, affected by his financial measures, in local assemblies. Happily, the combination of political broils which involved him in strife with France, Scotland, and Wales, rendered an appeal for money to the nation indispensable, and it was under the stress of these difficulties that he summoned the memorable Parliament of 1295, in which, in addition to barons, prelates, and representative knights of the shire, representatives of the towns and the lower clergy* met (whether in one or three chambers is not apparent) to discuss and grant a subsidy. This assembly is usually known as the Model Parliament, and, in form at least, the name is not unmerited. If it cannot be said to have represented the people, it certainly represented the Estates of the realm—lords, clergy, commons—and such representation meant much in view of the fact that the three Estates exercised the power of the purse. The power of the purse is, in some respects, the main thing in government. Without the purse, government is indeed impossible in any great political complication like that which necessitated the appeal to the Estates, and prerogative is an empty pretension. The king can do nothing against Scotland and France unless Parliament pay, and Parliament being in a patriotic mood, did pay on this occasion. But it was not minded to submit to any additional imposition, not freely conceded by the Estates, such as the increase of the export duties on wool and the fresh imposts on the clergy. Edward succeeded in browbeating the clergy into submission, in spite of the resistance of Archbishop Winchelsy. He failed to intimidate Roger Bigod, Earl of Norfolk, and Humphrey Bohun, Earl of Hereford, the marshal and the constable, who would neither take part in a proposed expedition to Gascony, nor be a party to any further grant in support of the war. "By God, sir earl," said the king to one of them, " you shall either go or hang." "By God," was the retort, "I will neither go nor hang." He alienated the merchants by the seizure of their wool, and thus by his arbitrary exactions and threats, roused in turn the defiance of the clergy, the barons, and the commons, at a time when he could not afford to risk their defiance. In this attempt to resort to the arbitrary tactics of

* The lower clergy subsequently preferred, though summoned, not to sit in Parliament, and to make their grant in Convocation.

his predecessors, he was thoroughly beaten. Edward was a far more formidable antagonist than John, but the combination of the Estates proved as effective in vindicating their rights against the strong ruler as the combination of barons, clergy, and nation in wresting Magna Charta from the weak one. This vindication the proud king could not bring himself to concede in person. He went to Flanders, leaving the Prince of Wales as regent to confirm the charter (the *Confirmatio Cartarum*), as renewed by Henry III., and augmented by several special articles bearing on the questions in dispute between king and Parliament. Not only the taxes for special purposes, but all revenue, with certain specified exceptions, should henceforth be levied with the express assent of Parliament. "Moreover, we have granted for us and our heirs to the archbishops, bishops, abbots, priors, and other folk of Holy Church, as also to earls, barons, and to all the commonalty of the land, that for no business from henceforth will we take such manner of aids, tasks, nor prises (arbitrary seizures), but by the common assent of the realm, and for the common profit thereof, saving the ancient aids and prises due and accustomed. And for so much as the more part of the commonalty of the realm find themselves so grieved with the maltote of wools, to wit, a toll of forty shillings for every sack of wool, we, at their requests, have clearly released it, and have granted for us and our heirs that we shall not take such thing, nor any other, without their common assent and goodwill, saving to us and our heirs the customs of wools, skins, and leather granted before by the commonalty aforesaid."

From these words it is evident that the assent of the commons, equally with the barons, was henceforth necessary to taxation, and in this respect the confirmation of the charter is a great advance upon the original of John. It remained for Edward II. to go a step further in 1322, after the defeat of Lancaster's attempt to substitute for the misgovernment of the king and his favourites a baronial oligarchy, on the model of the Provisions of Oxford, and render the assent of the commons indispensable to every legislative act. Henceforth, "the matters which are to be established for the estate of our lord the king, and of his heirs, and of the estate of the realm and of the people, shall be treated, accorded, and established in Parliament by our lord the king, and by the consent of the prelates, earls, and barons, and the *commonalty* of the realm, according as hath heretofore been accustomed."

Who, now, was this commonalty; who were the commons? Within Parliament they were, of course, the non-baronial element, the members for the counties, and the members for the towns. Without Parliament, the commons were those whom these county and town members represented, the freeholders and burghers who elected them. But were the commons in this political sense—the freeholders and burghers who enjoyed the right of representation—identical with the people? The historians, who write so complacently of popular representation during these mediæval centuries, do not seem to have asked themselves this very pertinent question. They burst into enthusiasm over the establishment of the parliamentary constitution of Simon de Montfort, as if Parliament and people were synonymous terms. The fact is that Parliament represented certain classes, certain Estates; it by no means represented the people. Constitutional government at this stage meant government by certain aristocratic and clerical dignitaries in the House of Lords, and certain representatives of the landowners and merchants in the House of Commons; but it reveals a singular innocence to speak or write as if the lords and commons at this time, or for long after, embodied by representation the people of England. "The people of England" did not exist in a political sense, even under its early Anglo-Saxon constitution, because a large part of it was in a state of serfdom and enjoyed no political rights. It did not exist in a political sense in the thirteenth century, in spite of the three Estates of lords, commons, and clergy in Parliament assembled. It did not come into existence until a series of reform bills had deprived these Estates or classes of a monopoly of political right and transferred it to the nation at large. I have, therefore, been intentionally sparing of the terms "people" or "popular" in reference to the constitutional history of Anglo-Saxon, Norman, and Plantagenet times, and have preferred the word "nation" to express the co-operation, in political action, of the classes which produced the Charter and the Model Parliament. Even the word nation can only be used with reserve. The Charter and the Model Parliament are doubtless landmarks in the history of English constitutional liberty, but they are certainly not landmarks in the history of popular liberty. There is nothing popular, democratic in them in the large sense. The Charter respects the rights of the *liber homo*, the freeman. There is no mention of the villein, the unfree man, in the clause that guarantees the freeman from arbitrary imprisonment. The Model Parliament represents the barons, freeholders, burghers; it does not represent the unfree man of the peasantry, in spite of Mr Freeman's contention that "the union of the representatives of the smaller landowners in a single chamber with those of the cities and boroughs . . . made the House of Commons a real representation of the whole nation." Dr Stubbs is more judicious. He does not overlook the fact that the three Estates of the realm were not co-ordinate with the people in the large sense. He reserves the "large residue that lay outside the political body, . . . the townsmen who were not included in the local organisations, and the classes of peasants who neither appeared nor were represented in the county courts." Yet even Dr Stubbs slips into the mistake of speaking of the Commons "as the representative of the mass and body of the nation." With all respect to the enthusiastic panegyrist and the learned historian of the English constitution in mediæval times, nothing is further from the simple truth. The simple truth is that the people was, politically and socially, in a state of bondage and nullity, was not really or formally represented by the landowners and merchants who sat in conclave as "the commonalty of the realm" at Westminster. The number of peasant freeholders, in comparison with the mass of serfs, was limited. "There can be no doubt," concludes Vinogradoff in his book on "Villainage in England," "that in many, if not in most places, the feudal organisation of society afforded little scope for a considerable class of freeholding peasants or yeomen."

The English Parliament was, at the beginning of the fourteenth century, a mighty bulwark of constitutional liberty against an arbitrary king; it was not the champion, the representative of the people, of popular interests, as the trend of the century was convincingly to show. It acted in the name and on behalf of the realm, but the realm and the people were by no means identical terms. It was the embodiment of aristocratic and middle-class privilege and right. It was only in a prospective and potential sense that it could be said to embody the rights or aspirations of the people.

What, now, was the condition of the mass that the Commons did not represent? A glance at the tenure of land will show us the state of things in its real light. Whatever the form of tenure in early Anglo-Saxon times—whether the land was largely held and cultivated in common by free village communities, or held by the mass, on servile conditions, of a limited class of landowners—it appears certain that from the eleventh century onwards "the whole country outside the larger towns," to use the words of Mr Ashley, "was divided into manors." These estates belonged to individuals called lords of the manor, and the lord of the manor was invested with certain rights not only over the soil, but over its cultivators. Part of the manor formed his demesne, which he cultivated for his own use; part might be held by freeholders; the rest was held by tenants in villenage, and was cultivated on the co-operative principle. Among these servile tenants there were, at the time of the Domesday survey, several classes— villeins proper, or the larger holders; the bordars and cottars, or smaller holders, who were most numerous in the midland and southern counties. In the eastern counties there was an additional class of socmen, and some of these socmen seem to have been even freemen. In Kent, indeed, the peasantry seem to have been treated by the law as freeholders. In the west and south-west, in Wales and Cornwall, the *servi* or slaves were most numerous. Whatever the grade, they were all alike bound to render their lord certain services and pay him certain dues. The villein proper had to give two or three, the cottars one or two days' labour a week throughout the year, with additional days during the seasons of sowing and harvest, and to render so many payments in money or kind. The unfree socmen, though ranking higher than the villeins, and not obliged to render week work, were liable to assist their lord at seedtime and harvest. Here is an extract from the "Liber Niger" of Peterborough Abbey, of date between 1125 and 1128, which reproduces for us in contemporary terms the features of the mediæval manor and its servile cultivators. "In Kateringes, which is assessed at 10 hides (1,200 acres), forty villani hold 40 yardlands or virgates (usually 30 acres each), and there were eight cotsites (cottars) each holding 5 acres. The holders of these yardlands plough for their lord in spring 4 acres for each yardland. And besides this, they find plough teams three times in winter, three times in spring, and once in summer. And they have twenty-two plough teams wherewith they work. And all of them work (for their lord) three days a week. And besides this, they render per annum from each virgate 2s. 1½d. of custom. And they all render 50 hens and 640 eggs. One tenant of 13 acres renders 16d., and has two acres of meadow. The mill with the miller renders 20s. The eight cottars work one day a week, and twice a year make malt. Each of these gives a penny for a goat, and if he has a she-goat, a half-penny. There is a shepherd and a swineherd who hold 8 acres. And in the demesne land of the manor are 4 plough teams with 32 oxen," &c.

All these classes were bound to the soil. Their tenure was not protected by law as against the lord. They could not sell their holdings or leave the manor without their lord's consent. If they fled, they could be seized and brought back. Their children inherited their servitude. They might only in rare cases defend themselves in court against their lord, though they might sue for justice against all others. They were practically at the mercy of the man of whom they held their holdings. They were bound, in some counties, to monopolist exactions for their lord's benefit. They could, for instance, only grind their corn at his mill, at so much per bushel or sack. They had to pay a fine to him on the marriage of their daughters (*merchetum*). They could not sell an ox or a horse without his license, and the lord might seize both their chattels and their land. Even the freeman who held lands in villenage was subject to the services and dues inherent in his holding, though he was free from the arbitrary treatment of person and property to which the villein was subject, and might leave the manor if he pleased.

What has just been said applies to serfs living on the manor of a lord. The condition of those living on the crown lands was relatively higher. "The peasants belonging to the manors, which were vested in the crown at the time of the Conquest, follow," according to Vinogradoff, who cites Bracton, " a law of their own. Barring certain exceptions . . . they enjoy a certainty of condition protected by law. They are personally free, and although holding in villainage, nobody has a right to deprive them of their lands, or to alter the condition of the tenure by increasing or changing their services. Bracton calls their condition one of privileged villainage, because their services are base, but certain, and because they are protected . . . by peculiar writs which enforce the custom of the manor."

During the three centuries following the Conquest, the condition of the servile class undoubtedly improved. In England, as on the Continent, a gradual rise is apparent in the condition of the villeins from the thirteenth century onwards, though even in the thirteenth century they were still subject, according to Bracton, to very arbitrary treatment. " The wave," to quote Vinogradoff, " begins to rise high in favour of liberty even in the thirteenth century." Here, too, custom tended to harden into legal right, and self-interest and sometimes the spirit of humanity ameliorated the servile state. A hundred years after the Conquest, the *servi*, the slaves of the west and south-west, had nearly disappeared, had risen, that is, to the status of villein holders, though on more onerous conditions. The number of free tenants materially increased ; in other words, a considerable proportion of the large holders in villenage had succeeded in commuting the obligation to render so much labour to their lord for a fixed rent in money or kind, and in lessening their disabilities. They became free tenants, *libere tenentes*. They were no longer compelled to pay a fine for the consent of their lord to the marriage of their daughters. They could sell their oxen without his permission. They could, according to Bracton, defend themselves, in some actions, against the lord in a court of justice. In the thirteenth century some of them are found obtaining charters conferring the possession of their holdings " for ever," or " on themselves and their heirs." Commutation of services for a money payment did not, however, in a large number of cases—the molmen for instance—raise the villein to the position of a free tenant. In such cases, his tenure was still a servile tenure ; he was still bound to the soil. His freedom of action was still limited in a variety of matters by his dependence on his lord's consent, and this consent was dependent on the payment of a fine. He became, at most, a customary, not a free tenant. He might rid himself of the more onerous services due to his lord by paying instead of working; he was still liable to exceptional services in the busy seasons, or bound to find labourers to perform them for him. His status before the law was still that of the villein, as the peasant rising in the fourteenth century was to show, even if, unlike the ordinary villein, who was unable to commute, he had freed himself from the more servile duties of his tenure. According to Bracton, the law knew only two classes of men—the free and the unfree—and in the eye of the law the man who had not attained to freeman status was still a serf, though his social condition might have improved. "As to the general aspect of villainage in the *legal* theory of English feudalism," remarks Vinogradoff, "there can be no doubt. The 'Dialogus de Scaccario' gives it in a few words: the lords are owners not only of the chattels, but of the bodies of their *ascripticii*, they may transfer them wherever they please, and 'sell or otherwise alienate them if they like.' Glanville, Bracton, Fleta, and Britton follow in substance the same doctrine, although they use different terms." In spite of legal theory, however, the serf had in practice some right even against his lord, and might sue him, for instance, if he seized his wainage. Despite theory, too, improvement by commutation was becoming a pretty general practice, and this improvement was rendered easier by the rise of a class of labourers, as distinct from tenants, who held little or no land, and offered their services for hire. The lord was all the more willing to accept money instead of service, if he could command with it the labour necessary for the cultivation of his demesne.

It is a general assumption that the Church contributed largely to the improvement of the status of the villein. It was, perhaps, ready to do so at the expense of the secular proprietors. It was none the less extremely jealous, in England as on the Continent, of any diminution of its corporate rights, and it was not disposed to champion social progress at its own expense. "There is plenty of evidence," according to

Pollock and Maitland, "that of all landlords the religious houses were the most severe—not the most oppressive, but the most tenacious of their rights; they were bent on the maintenance of pure villein tenure and personal villeinage. The immortal but soulless corporation, with her wealth of accurate records, would yield no inch, would enfranchise no serf, would enfranchise no tenement. In practice the secular lord was more humane, because he was more human, because he was careless, because he wanted ready money, because he would die. . . . It is against them (the professed in religion) that the peasants make their loudest complaints." In the fourteenth century, in fact, as we shall see, the peasant was ready to revolutionise an over-wealthy Church root and branch.

The servile condition of the masses might thus give scope to a certain measure of progress. It was, doubtless, during periods unaffected by political or natural disturbances, fairly prosperous. There was not in England, as on the Continent, the oft-recurring misery and depression which made the lot of the common man a chronic purgatory. There were, indeed, times of terrible suffering—of civil strife, of iron-handed despotism, of baronial anarchy, of dearth, of pestilence,—but the limitation of the feudal jurisdiction by the central power saved the English peasant (with the exception of the lawless period of Stephen's reign) from the worst excesses of feudal anarchy, from the frequent feuds and devastating expeditions of factious and hostile magnates. In a political sense, however, the villein counted for nothing in England, as on the Continent. The possession of a parliamentary constitution, which meant so much for the English landowner and merchant, conferred no benefit on the English villein, as long as it did not take into account his political existence, and as long as his lord was invested with rights which were incompatible with citizenship and rendered political emancipation so difficult.

His rights as a member of the State were of the smallest, in comparison with the freeman. He might in rare cases plead against his lord, but it was obviously perilous for him to do so. His lord had means enough at his disposal of making him miserable if he pleased. Against third parties he had, indeed, the rights of a freeman. He might sue, though he could not act as the judge of, a freeman who was not his lord. He might make "presentments" in civil and criminal causes. He might even sit as a juror in civil causes. He was, too, so far a citizen in the eye of the State that he was taxable, and was liable to bear arms in the defence of the country. But these were burdens rather than rights, and on the whole his condition was not compatible with either the aspirations, or the privileges of liberty.

In a large number of the towns, as well as in the counties, the franchise, whether parliamentary or municipal, was the privilege of a class, not the common right of the mass. At the period of the Conquest the towns, *burgi*, the Anglo-Saxon *burhs*, numbered eighty, and were for the most part no larger than walled villages. Only London, Winchester, Bristol, Norwich, Lincoln, and York were of importance as centres of trade and population, and with the exception of the capital, these probably did not contain more than a few thousand inhabitants each. These towns had their reeve or *præpositus*, their court leet or assembly, their bailiffs. According to Dr Stubbs, their organisation resembled that of the hundred, rather than the township, was, that is, a stage in advance of the manorial village. They were subject to the jurisdiction of a lord, or even lords, who, in the case of those situated in the royal demesne, was the king. With a few exceptions, such as London, Lincoln, and other considerable centres, their inhabitants were mostly cultivators of the soil, for there was little trade beyond what the weekly or half-weekly market created. As on the Continent, the growth of commerce, which came, in England, in the wake of the Conquest, increased both their prosperity and their population, and the fact is evident from the institution of merchant gilds from the end of the eleventh century onwards, on the model, apparently, of the voluntary associations, of a religious or secular character, of earlier times. The rise of the gilds is contemporary with the grant of charters to these thriving urban communities. Henry I. inaugurated the policy of conceding them a certain measure of self-government, and the policy was both continued and amplified by his successors, Henry II., Richard, John, and Henry III., as well as imitated by the secular and ecclesiastical superiors in the case of the towns subject to their jurisdiction. The aspiration after municipal emancipation thus produced in England, as on the Continent, a communal movement, though this movement did not in all its features follow the model of that in France and Germany. It was not a revolutionary struggle between burghers and feudal superiors. The English towns, with the exception perhaps of London, gained independence of feudal jurisdiction, not by revolution, but by negotiation. They bought their privileges, and their progress towards self-government was more gradual and much less marked by dramatic incident. It began with the conversion of the dues, payable by the inhabitants individually to the sheriff, in the case of those on the royal demesne, or to the steward of the lord, into a fixed annual rent for the whole (*firma burgi*). The stages are denoted by the charters of successive reigns. That of London granted by Henry I. already concedes to the citizens the right to elect their own sheriff and justiciar, and immunity from any other jurisdiction, from certain general impositions, and from liability to tolls and customs throughout the whole of England. These privileges did not, however, involve municipal self-government. London was at this period a shire, not a municipality, and it is not till the reign of Richard I. that the municipality or *communa*, as the chroniclers term it, emerges under its mayor and aldermen as the result of a "conjuration" of the citizens against the Grand Justiciar, William Longchamp (1191). The reign of Henry I. also furnishes us with an example of a charter granted by an ecclesiastical superior to a town subject to his jurisdiction. The privileges conceded by the Archbishop of York to Beverley are, however, far more modest than those granted by King Henry to the capital, and include only the right to have its own gild hall (*Hanshus*), to make its own bye-laws, to pay a fixed annual rent of eighteen marks, and to enjoy immunity from tolls throughout the shire.

Though the other towns lagged behind London in the attainment of political rights, the charters granted by successive kings display a gradual increase in the concession of privileges, a gradual approximation towards complete self-government. Henry II., for example, concedes to the citizens of Oxford all the liberties of the citizens of London; to Lincoln, besides the liberties, customs, and laws which it had enjoyed under his predecessors, Edward the Confessor, William I., and Henry I., the emancipation of the villein who shall have resided within the city for a year and a day; to others, exemption from the jurisdiction of the sheriff,—a general and much-coveted privilege. Richard goes a step further, and grants to the citizens of Lincoln the right to elect their reeve or *præpositus*. In those granted by John to Northampton and Lincoln "the common council" already appears as the embodiment of the rights of the city, while Dunwich is raised by him to the rank of a free burgh and its burghers invested with all the rights previously belonging to its superior.

It was in this progressive fashion that municipal government in England slowly took shape. Emancipation was a business transaction, not the work of a revolution. The town gradually rose to autonomy as one king improved upon the concessions of his predecessor. But the process was by no means uniform, and the municipal constitutions evolved out of these varied concessions by successive kings were in some respects as dissimilar as in the case of the French communes. In some towns the municipal franchise belonged to all householders; in others, it was restricted to those who paid scot and lot, *i.e.*, the ratepayers; in others, to those who paid burgage or rent due by the town to the lord—the burghers proper; in others, to the members of the merchant gild. A few were self-governing communities in the real sense of the term; laws drawn up by the elected officials were submitted to the general assembly of the burghers for approval or disapproval. Dr Gross holds that this town democracy was, in the earlier stage of municipal history, the rule, not the exception. If so, the town democracy seems in the case of the majority to have been evanescent indeed. The greater number soon came to be governed by oligarchies, more or less limited, according to the number of those in whom power was invested. In many of the charters the privileges of the merchant gild are carefully safeguarded, and it would seem that in the larger towns at least, as in the great cities of the empire, the municipal administration was in the hands of this organised wealthy merchant class. The gild in England, as in Germany and the Netherlands, was a monopolist society which not only possessed large and exclusive commercial privileges, but absorbed the municipal administration in all towns in which it was strong enough to do so.

As in Germany and the Netherlands, too, there was friction between the merchant gild and the craft gilds which acquired importance with the growth of English industry in the twelfth and thirteenth centuries, though the struggle was neither so general nor so eventful as on the Continent. A recent writer, Dr Gross, goes indeed so far as to pronounce the struggle "a myth." The assertion seems too sweeping, for while the larger crafts obtained gild rights in consideration of an annual payment to the king, their attempts to secure a voice in the affairs of the community, in resistance to an oligarchy of wealth, were stoutly opposed by the merchants. In the reign of Richard those of London found a champion in the person of the alderman William Longbeard, who declaimed against the oppression of the poor, and was dragged out of sanctuary and executed by Hubert Walter for his pains. In the reign of John the aldermen and reeves of Lincoln are similarly found denying the claim of the fullers and dyers to be free citizens; and according to the London "Book of Customs" the weavers and fullers of Winchester, Oxford, Beverley, and Marlborough were incapable of accusing or giving evidence against a freeman, and did not, therefore, enjoy the rights of full citizenship.*

These rights they did not succeed in securing till the end of the thirteenth century, and even then a considerable portion of the inhabitants—the smaller artisans and the labourers—still remained outside the pale of free citizenship. "From one cause or another," remarks Mrs Green in "Town Life in the Fifteenth Century," "groups of men were formed in the midst of every town who were shut out from the civic life of the community" (the authoress assumes that the earlier *communa* was democratic in the real sense), "and whose natural bond of union was hostility to the privileged class which denied them the dignity of free citizens and refused them fair competition in trading enterprise. The burghers yearly added to their number half a dozen or perhaps even a score of members, wealthy enough to buy the privilege, while the increase in the unenfranchised class, which had begun very early in the town life, proceeded by leaps and bounds, till presently the old balance of forces in the little State was overthrown,

* Dr Cunningham finds an explanation of this in the fact that these artisans were originally foreigners—Flemings or Normans.

the ancient constitution of a free community of equal householders was altogether annulled and forgotten, and a comparatively small class of privileged citizens ruled with a strong hand over subject traders and labourers to whom they granted neither the forms nor the substance of liberty."

The period of expansion was in truth followed by a period of contraction in many towns, during which election to the common council passed more and more into abeyance, and the administration became the monopoly of an oligarchy composed of the wealthier merchants and members of the greater crafts. The attempt to break down this monopoly of power, on the part of the mass of the inhabitants in the fifteenth century, was frustrated by the exclusive spirit of the oligarchy and the royal policy of granting to it charters of incorporation, with the right of selecting the members of this corporation and its representatives in Parliament. Under such a system, the parliamentary representation of the inhabitants of the towns was no more a real representation of the people than that of the inhabitants of the counties by the knights of the shire. It could at most claim to represent the distinctive factor of civic, as opposed to rural life. The larger towns, at least, had become essentially mercantile and industrial in the fourteenth century. Traders and craftsmen embodied the soul of the city, and their representation, however imperfect, brought the Commons into touch with a more democratic force than in the purely agricultural constituencies, though it did not result in what really deserves the name of popular legislation.

SOURCES (in the order of treatment).—Stubbs, Select Charters and Constitutional Documents (1884), and Constitutional History of England (1874-78); Freeman, History of the Norman Conquest (1867), and, Growth of the English Constitution (1872). Older works like Palgrave's History of the English Commonwealth (1832) and Kemble's Saxons in England (1849) still deserve attention, though antiquated in part. Green, History of the English People (1877); Seebohm, The English Village Community (1883), and Tribal Custom in Anglo-Saxon Law (1902); Coote, Romans in Britain (1878); Pike, The English and their Origin (1866);

Sources of Chapter XIII.

Elton, Origins of English History (1890); Lee, Leading Documents of English History (1900); Bracton, De Legibus et Consuetudinibus Angliæ, edited by Sir Travers Twiss, vols. i. and ii. (1878, Chronicles and Memorials); Taylor, The Origin and Growth of the English Constitution (1900); Ashley, English Economic History and Theory (1888); Pearson, History of England during the Early and Middle Ages (1867); Round, Feudal England—Historical Studies in the Eleventh and Twelfth Centuries (1895); Pollock and Maitland, History of English Law (1895); Maitland, Domesday Book and Beyond (1897), and, Township and Borough (1898); Vinogradoff, Villainage in England (1892); Cunningham, Growth of English Industry and Commerce during the Early and Middle Ages (1890); Madox, Firma Burgi (1726); Gross, Gilda Mercatoria, Ein Beitrag zur Geschichte der Englischen Städteverfassung (1883), and, The Gild Merchant (1891); Toulmin Smith, English Gilds, with preliminary Essay on the History and Development of Gilds, by Brentano (1870); Mallet Lambert, Two Thousand Years of Gild Life (1891); Hibbert, The Influence and Development of English Gilds (1891); Adams, London and the Commune, English Historical Review (October 1904); Mrs Green, Town Life in the Fifteenth Century (1894); Fairlie, Municipal Administration (1901); Merewether and Stephens, The History of the Borough and Municipal Corporations of the United Kingdom (1835); Merewether, A Sketch of the History of Boroughs (1822).

CHAPTER XIV.

Political and Social Revolution in England in the Fourteenth Century.

Theoretically the Commons may be said to have represented the people. They acted in the name of the people. Practically, as we have seen, they represented certain Estates, certain classes, and at this stage of English parliamentary history, and for long, popular representation is largely a misnomer. And, as we shall see immediately, the House of Commons, while quick to vindicate the rights and embody the aspirations of certain Estates, certain classes, was not friendly to the social and political emancipation of the masses. It was zealous to maintain the chartered rights which these classes had won from the Norman and Plantagenet kings. It was lukewarm or antagonistic to the demands of the people for the improvement of their social and political lot. It was nevertheless a power in the land, and during the fourteenth century it tended to become more and more *the* power in the land. It derived strength from its representative capacity. It was theoretically the nation, and it actually embodied the vitality of the most important classes of the nation—the lesser landowners, the yeomen, the merchants, the craftsmen. Its representative strength made it increasingly self-assertive in legislation and government. Of the three kings whose reigns fill out the century, it deposed two and kept in check the arbitrary tendencies of the third. And its power as a representative legislative body, though not yet exercised for democratic ends, was at least capable of being so used when the time should come. In spite of itself the House of Commons proved the foster-mother of the democracy of the future. Its principle, if not its practice, is democratic. It speaks and acts in the name of the people, "the commonalty," if it does not really represent it.

The contemptible character of Edward II., the worthlessness of his favourites, the disgraceful disasters of the war with Scotland, would have maddened any nation, which retained some measure of self-respect and public spirit, into rebellion. The people, which had been ruled by an Edward I., could hardly submit to be ruled by an Edward II. for any length of time without vigorous protest. The stroke of fortune which gave him, for a short season, the upper hand over the Earl of Lancaster and his defiant fellow-barons is memorable, as I have already noted, for the recognition of the right of the Commons to a voice in legislation as well as taxation. In order to oust the recalcitrant barons, Edward was forced to cultivate the Commons, and the recognition and amplification of their rights, as against the usurpation of the baronial oligarchy of Ordainers, was a most laudable piece of statesmanship. A baronial oligarchy on the model of the Provisions of Oxford might have controlled the king, and the miserable misgovernment of Edward certainly called for redress by way of control. But it would have closed the way to power for the Commons, and it is very dubious whether the supremacy of these factious magnates, who indeed did good service in ridding the country of a parasite of the stamp of Piers Gaveston, would have been for the general interest and have ensured good government. The attempt on a previous occasion was not reassuring, and happily the spurt of energy on the part of the king, under the inspiration of the Despensers, was successful in making an end of the Ordainers and their ordinances. Edward was, indeed, too poor a creature to profit by success, especially in the face of the discontent which his *régime* had spread broadcast over the land, and which his momentary triumph could not keep under. Under the guidance of the younger Despenser, he steered straight for the breakers, and his shipwreck was tragic enough. In January 1327, he was hustled off the throne by a revolution, of which his queen, Isabella, and her paramour, Mortimer, were the leaders, and in September done to death, at their instigation, and with horrible barbarity, in Berkeley Castle. His enemies deposed him by the will of Parliament, and even proposed to find a sanction for their drastic proceedings in " the voice of the people." Vox Populi, Vox Dei, was, in truth, the theme from which Archbishop Reynolds preached to the assembled legislators, and the acclamations of the London populace gave some colour of justification to the sermon. There could be no doubt at any rate as to the cogency of the grounds of this proceeding. Edward was declared to have forfeited the crown by reason of his misgovernment, and it was consequently transferred to his son. The articles which gave the reasons of his deposition stated no more than the truth. He was incompetent to govern, had refused good counsel, had neglected the duties of his office, had lost Scotland, Gascony, Ireland, had broken his coronation oath, and finally ruined the realm, and should make way for a better man in the person of his son. To these propositions the sorry monarch was compelled to assent in his prison at Kenilworth and to witness the breaking of his staff by the high steward, in token of the renunciation of his authority. The voice of the people, the *vox populi*, might only be the voice of a number of successful revolutionists who usurped the sovereignty of the people for their own ends. It is certain, all the same, that Edward was widely unpopular and merited his fate, though the part of the queen and many of her supporters was neither an honourable nor a disinterested one. It was not the first, it was not to be the last illustration of this exercise of the sovereignty of the people in English annals. Before the century was out another king was to go the way of Edward II. at the bidding of Parliament. Nor was it a novelty in the history of Western Europe in mediæval times. A few years before the deposition of Edward, Emperor Adolf of Nassau had been voted by the electors of the Holy Roman Empire unfit to rule. Emperor Wenzel, too, was within another hundred years to be adjudged the same fate. Further back, the Frankish magnates had made equally short shrift with Charles the Fat, and the fate of the last of the Merovingians might have provided the hapless Edward with the warning that the throne is not the immaculate refuge of weak or wicked potentates.

The son in whose favour he was deposed had inherited the masculine qualities of his shameless mother. He was no craven trifler like his father, but a vigorous, strong-willed, ambitious, self-assertive prince with marked instincts of the "chivalry" order, and it seemed as if the day of the autocrat had returned. His weak side was his keenness to engage in far-reaching schemes of an ill-regulated ambition, without counting either the cost or the possibility of their attainment, and his mad plunge into a war with both Scotland and France, though explicable enough in a young man of fervent temperament and martial proclivities, forced him to cultivate the goodwill of the Commons and made him more dependent on their co-operation than would otherwise have been the case. He certainly did his best by his wild and expensive martial policy to change co-operation into antagonism, and to rouse an unpopularity towards the end of his reign almost as great as that which swept his sire from the throne. Before that long reign of fifty years came to an end, Parliament threatened, from reasons of patriotism as well as partisanship, to take the helm of affairs out of his hands, or at least to entrust it to steersmen of its own choosing and controlling. He began his reign with the sympathy of the nation centred upon him; he died amidst its detestation. It was the oft-recurring and increasingly onerous demands for subsidies that soured the national temper and gradually estranged the nation from the showy, bellicose, and withal selfish monarch, in spite of the victories with which he seemed to merit and justify its generosity. These flaming victories in Scotland and France, which won so many plaudits at first, palled by their very frequency, especially as the struggle with France lengthened out from decade to decade without apparent substantial results, and ultimately ended in total failure and disgrace. France had to pay its kings a terrible bill in defeat and suffering, and, as we have seen, rebelled. England had to pay an equally heavy bill for barren victories, and was more than once on the point of rebellion. Pestilence and dearth, social antagonisms and widespread popular misery added fuel to the political distemper, and the records of Parliament, as well as the pages of the chroniclers, show that the grievances complained of were not merely the captious criticisms of a nation that had taken to grumbling. Each grant was accompanied and conditioned by a petition for the redress of grievances, and the petition, though often left unfulfilled in spite of royal promises, became more pressing as time went on. Among these grievances the Articles of 1340 mention more particularly the maladministration of the sheriffs and the delays of justice, the oppression practised by the royal purveyors, and arbitrary taxation in the shape of unauthorised tallages. Only the redress of these abuses opened the purse-strings of the Commons in the shape of a liberal grant of wool from which the parliamentary revenue of the king at this period was derived. Edward bore the bridle with ill-concealed impatience at times, and was not above wheedling a subsidy out of the refractory Parliament by promises which he never intended to keep, and which he ignored when it suited him. Nor was he slow to give rein to his arbitrary instincts when the angry fit was upon him, as in his harsh treatment of Archbishop Stratford and other ministers who had incurred his dislike, or the ill-will of his courtiers. In general, however, he was forced by the war to make a virtue of necessity, and to connive at the increasing spirit of self-assertion in the Commons. One demand which appears as early as 1341, when Parliament finally crystallised into the two Houses of Lords and Commons, is very significant. It is the demand that the king's ministers shall only be appointed by advice of the peers and the Council, shall be sworn in Parliament to act in accordance with the laws, and shall account to Parliament at stated periods for their conduct in office. It went further than the claim of the baronial oligarchy under Henry III., since it gave the control of the executive to the Commons as well as the Lords, and it anticipated the great seventeenth-century contention of the responsibility of ministers to Parliament. Edward gave way, and the demand passed into a statute, but though he was mean enough to break his word, on the plea that he had only consented by force of circumstances, and annul it shortly after, Parliament took every opportunity of returning to the charge.

The day of triumph seemed to have arrived at last when the Good Parliament met in April 1376 amid the crowning disasters of the close of the reign. The pent-up anger of several years exploded on the Duke of Lancaster and the court party, of which he was the leader, and which was justly deemed responsible for the misery and humiliation of Edward's ignominious dotage. The miscreants in official places should forthwith be brought to justice, and to justice the more heinously guilty of them, particularly Lord Latimer, the king's chamberlain and privy councillor, and Richard Lyons, one of his financial officials, were accordingly brought by impeachment and imprisonment. The dotard king was compelled to give up even his mistress, the shameless Alice Perrers, who was banished from the court by sentence of the Lords. Lancaster, who had ridiculed the incipient threats of these stern commoners, was quickly undeceived. "What!" cried he, in response to the warnings of some of his followers, "humour these upstart hedge knights who think themselves kings and princes of the land? I trow they are ignorant of my power. To-morrow I shall make them tame enough." "Your magnificence forgets," quoth one of those present, "that these knights are supported not by the people only, but by the most powerful of the land, among whom is Prince Edward, your brother. The citizens of London, too, are on their side, and will defend them from injury."

Thus supported, the Lords and Commons resorted to the device, long mooted, but hitherto evaded, of controlling a corrupt and oppressive administration. Amid the many items of a bulky reform programme this demand appears prominent, and the determination with which it was pressed forced the king to embody it in a number of ordinances. Henceforth he should add ten or twelve lords to the Council, who should be consulted in all great affairs of State, and without whose assistance no important business should be determined. In matters of less importance he was to act by the advice of six or four of these additional councillors, who were to be in perpetual residence at court, though they were not to interfere with the official duties of the chancellor, treasurer, and other officers of State. On no account should they receive bribes, or perpetrate any exaction, on pain of paying double the sum so acquired. All ordinances issued by the king with their advice should be faithfully and expeditiously executed by the royal ministers, who were likewise forbidden, under the same penalties, to accept gifts in the performance of their functions. All which Edward decreed in a number of ordinances, and appointed a special committee of advice, including the Archbishop of Canterbury, the Bishops of London and Winchester, the Earls of Arundel, Stafford, and March, and Lords Percy, Brian, and Beauchamp. In return the Commons renewed the wool subsidy of 1373.

The amount of practical reform achieved by this Parliament during its unprecedently long session of ten weeks (it sat till the 6th July) amply entitles it to the distinction of "The Good Parliament." It had cleaned out the Augean stable of ministerial corruption and moral miasma, which made the court and the government a disgrace to the throne and a scandal to the country. It had read a severe lesson to unscrupulous officials, and established as a precedent the right of the nation to demand from its rulers an account of their stewardship. It had shown, long before the days of the Long Parliament and the Reform Parliament, that when English public opinion has made up its mind for reform, an anti-reform government cannot stand, more especially if that government is corrupt. This was a great victory, and unlike the victory of 1341, it represented an important stage in the progress of Parliament to power over the executive. John of Gaunt attempted, indeed, to play the part that his now dotard father had played so unscrupulously in 1341. No sooner had the members dispersed after debating into shape a hundred and forty petitions for the redress of grievances, to which Edward, as usual, professed redress, than Lancaster set the ordinances at nought by dismissing the additional members of Council, denied its title to the name of a Parliament, and reinstated the impeached officials, and even his *protegée*, the discarded mistress. He took the precaution of silencing its leaders by imprisoning the speaker, Sir Peter de la Mare, and banishing Wykeham, Bishop of Winchester, and then packed a new Parliament, which met in February 1377, to grant a poll tax of fourpence a head, and reverse all the Acts of its predecessor. This drastic action was, however, but a temporary check of the parliamentary advance to supremacy.

"The Good Parliament" was the prelude to the "Merciless Parliament." The minority of Richard II. only aggravated the abuses of the last years of his grandfather's reign. The continued ill-success of the French war, the increasing hardship of oppressive taxation, the extravagance and dissipation of the young king and his courtiers, the accumulation of abuse which they did little or nothing to rectify, produced in ten years the whirlwind of angry opposition which raged with unmitigated violence during the sessions of 1386 and 1388. Under the leadership of the king's uncle, the Duke of Gloucester, Parliament began the business of reform, in the former session, by demanding the dismissal of the chancellor, the Earl of Suffolk, and the treasurer, the Bishop of Durham, and answered the dogged refusal of the king by the threat of deposition. The spectre of the fate of Edward II. shook the young king into compliance, but the concession did not save the chancellor from impeachment at the demand of the Commons. Impeached he accordingly was, found guilty of various misdemeanours, deprived of all his possessions, and imprisoned, pending the payment of a fine of £20,000. Still worse fared it with other delinquents during the "Merciless" session of 1388, in spite of Richard's reactionary measures in defence of his prerogative in the interval. The Lords not only impeached the more obnoxious of the king's advisers, including Suffolk, whom he had released, in defiance of their former sentence; they condemned them to be hanged, and two of them, Tressilian, the chief-justice, and Brember, an ex-mayor of London, were actually hanged. Suffolk and Vere, Duke of Dublin, only escaped the same punishment by flight. Neville, Archbishop of York, another fugitive, was deprived of his temporalities, and removed from his see by the pope, Urban VI. Against the lesser delinquents the Commons were equally implacable, and as the result of their demand, four additional victims, of knightly rank, were sent to execution. Such stern vindication of the principle of the responsibility of ministers to Parliament is only paralleled by the seventeenth-century republicans, and in the relentless assertion of this principle the Merciless Parliament was as thoroughgoing as the Long Parliament. Prerogative should not be allowed to protect ministers deemed guilty of culpable misgovernment, and if the judges should try to intervene and disqualify the bill in which the charges of misgovernment and treasonable practices were drawn up, Parliament as the supreme judge should decide the matter for itself, and act accordingly. "The King of England," says Froissart, "must obey his people, and do wha they wish." Froissart should have written Parliament, and then his assertion would have been no exaggeration, even in the fourteenth century. Langley had also noted the fact, though the king in "Piers the Plowman" boasts that he is supreme :—

> "I am king with the crown the commons to rule,
> And Holy Church and clergy from cursed men to defend;
> . . . . . . I am head of the law;
> For ye are but members, and I above all."

Parliament might virtually be the faction of Gloucester, and Gloucester might be a scheming, ambitious politician, but in claiming and exercising such powers, it made all the same a large stride in the direction of subordinating king and Council to a parliamentary supremacy. The importance of its Acts is not to be measured by the ambitious character of its leader, or the factious spirit of his associates. These Lords and Commons were making constitutional history in their own rough, harsh fashion, and if the men were not above reproach, their action in smiting a government of corruption and favouritism was defensible enough. If government by royal prerogative meant simply misgovernment, to substitute Parliament for prerogative is a proceeding that appeals to the common-sense of every person not blinded by the conventional prestige of a throne. Happily in English history, tradition, usually the inveterate enemy of common-sense in politics as in religion, has never proved wholly faithless to liberty, in spite of the decrees of would-be absolute kings and their sycophant abettors, in cabinet or pulpit, to silence or discredit the voice of freedom that echoes from a hoary past. Magna Charta could never pass into the realm of archæology. The fate of John and Edward II., to go no further back, could never be ignored in English history as the fate of a Carloman, a Charles the Fat, might be by their distant successors on the throne of France. Tradition had its precedents in England, and these precedents have been invoked from generation to generation by the men who have done battle with despotism and misgovernment. Reform may be delayed, reaction may set in, but reform is never permanently shelved, reaction never permanently triumphant.

In Richard's case, the reaction came to a swift and melancholy end. With one of those spurts of energy, which he could show on occasion, he threw off the tutelage of Gloucester a year after the session of the Merciless Parliament. It seemed for a few years as if he had profited by the lesson in constitutional rule which that Parliament had so sharply administered. He did not turn upon his enemies and smite them down, as they had smitten his friends. He showed himself surprisingly moderate and accommodating, and while he insisted on the recognition by Parliament of his prerogatives, he submitted the administration of his ministers to its approval. There was a lull in the strife of party during which king and Parliament seemed to work harmoniously for the reformation and rehabilitation of the State.

This lull was fallacious, was in fact the prelude to the thunderstorm of royal vengeance. The constitutional monarch suddenly developed into the absolute king. If he had not gone mad, as has been supposed, the part he acted was mad enough. The French marriage doubtless drew him into a current of association and aspiration which made him impatient of constitutional control. His relations with Gloucester became strained, and the old distrust of his scheming uncle returned and deepened into hatred. Ambition and hatred seem to have got the upper hand of his impulsive nature, and he set himself to play a *rôle* for which neither nature nor circumstance had fitted him. He affected imperial dignity ; he compelled the Commons to apologise for complaining of the extravagance of his court ; he seized Gloucester and Arundel as suspects of treason, and had them impeached and sentenced to death, and the legislation prejudicial to the royal power repealed by a packed Parliament, convened in September 1397. To crown its craven subservience, it granted him during a second session, held at Shrewsbury in January 1398, the wool subsidy for life, and deputed its authority to a legislative committee of eighteen, composed of the king's friends. By thus both abdicating its control of the purse, and surrendering its legislative power to the crown, it committed parliamentary suicide, and placed the nation in the hands of an irresponsible master. It was the climax of parliamentary cowardice and self-abnegation, for which we can only find a parallel in English annals in the reign of Henry VIII. Evidently there were traitors to the cause of English constitutional liberty among those highly titled legislators who had been its foremost champions ten years before. They certainly were not martyrs to principle, and their opportunist attitude reminds us that as yet it was but a handful of weathercock politicians, not the people as such, that shaped the parliamentary history of England in this fourteenth century. When the people, as distinct from its magnates, takes up the task of vindicating the constitution, there will be heroism and martyrdom in the struggle. As for Richard, if he was unconstitutional, he was at least thorough. He made no secret of his determination to be absolute master of the realm, and no scruple in declaring that, as king, he was at liberty to break his word and do as he pleased. Parliament could not complain that it had been overreached into compliance, and its self-effacement is only the more disgraceful in consequence.

Happily it was too extreme to be lasting, especially as its master was, after all, but a man of straw, and the magnates whom he had temporarily overawed, were men of turbulent, pugnative nature, who took to quarrelling with him and with one another at the first provocation. A personal dispute about the inheritance of John of Gaunt, of which Richard took possession to the detriment of his son, the Duke of Hereford, grew into a storm which swept him from the throne. In language as abject as that of Edward II., whom, in his final collapse of nerve and dignity, he closely resembled, Richard declared his unworthiness to rule, and Parliament, after the recital of the long list of his offences against the constitution, summarily deposed him and substituted Hereford as Henry IV. in his stead. Henry claimed the crown by right of descent "from the good lord, King Henry Third," but it was only after Parliament had considered his claim, and "with one accord agreed that the said duke should reign over them," that he was seated on the throne. Moreover, Henry explicitly undertook to eschew the arbitrary ways of his predecessor, to govern, not according to "his proper will," but "by the common advice, counsel, and consent" of Parliament. His substitution was one more crushing blow to the practice as well as the theory of absolute right. For a precedent and a proof that the English kingship is based only on the will of Parliament, the fourteenth century thus furnishes as convincing evidence as the seventeenth. In the struggle with Richard the issue between absolute and limited monarchy stands forth in the clearest outline, though it was not yet finally decided in favour of Parliament, as subsequent struggles were to show. His deposition is the crushing answer to the express assumption of a foolish monarch that he was above the law and independent of Parliament. If only Parliament had been the people's representative in fact as well as in theory, that answer would have been altogether indefeasible.

Parliament had asserted its mastery over an arbitrary king. It had also by this time become the source of law to the nation. In England, law became national or "common" under the Norman and Angevin kings. The king, after the Conquest, is the virtual owner of the land, the universal superior, and his justices dispense the law throughout the kingdom. They gradually formulate this law which is binding on the whole nation. Thus the system of common law came into existence, whilst in France and other Continental countries each district was, more or less, a law unto itself. The unity of this system was completed when the legislative function was largely concentrated in Parliament in the reign of Edward I., and this legislative function lent it a far greater power, a more splendid *rôle* than that of a German Reichstag, or a French States-General. In Germany, in France, there was the diversity of local custom which even an absolute potentate could not ignore by the fiat of his will. In England Parliament was supreme and all-embracing in its legislative activity. Up to the Reformation, indeed, its activity did not embrace the Church, which had its own law—the law common to the Roman Catholic Church. After the Reformation even this exception disappeared. "Despite certain faint theoretical doubts," says Mr Jenks, "the law which issued from the Parliament at Westminster was supreme over all customs and privileges; it covered the whole area of human conduct in England, at least after the Reformation."

That Parliament was not the representative of the people, except by an abuse of language, is conclusively evident throughout the reign of this deposed king, as well as in that of his predecessor. Parliament was in truth often but a faction, or at most the tool or ally of a faction. No greater mistake than to assume that English constitutional history is the reflex of a conscious national progression towards the definite goal of political liberty. Each reign from the period of Magna Charta onwards contributed something to the great result, but this contribution was often a step in the dark, and conditioned by the history of the age. English constitutional history is an evolution, but it is an evolution that is shaped by history rather than by law. It unfolds certain political principles, but the men that champion them do not necessarily see the full bearing of them, and often enough espouse them from personal, even factious motives. Simon de Montfort was a great constitutional reformer, but it would be absurd to credit even Simon de Montfort with more than an indistinct sense of the significance of his political action. He sought a remedy applicable to his time, and he was led to do so, not so much by intention as by the situation in which he found himself. That is to say, he was a practical politician, not a philosopher, and the English constitution is the work not of philosophers, but of practical men acting from higher or lower motives, as the case may be. Still more absurd would it be to mistake a Duke of Gloucester or a Duke of Hereford for theoretic reformers. Their motives are of a personal and political, not of a transcendental nature. Nay, Parliament itself, as I have remarked before, is the representative of a class, not of the nation in the real sense, and defends its own interests, strives to realise its own aspirations in the name of the nation. In so doing, it enunciates and defends principles favourable to political liberty and progress. From the constitutional point of view its legislation during these years of struggle with the crown might lay claim to enlightenment. It made a dead set against the abuse of power by the king and his ministers, but it did so only in order that power might become the monopoly of the class which it chiefly represented —the landowners, the territorial magnates more particularly. This class was quick enough to cry out against oppression and misgovernment when its own interests were touched; it had no sympathy with the demand of the masses for social and political amelioration. It did its utmost to bar the way to their elevation, and is found all through the century legislating for the benefit of class against mass. It is in the mass that we may look for the theoretic impulse to action, which circumstances indeed provoked, but whose scope circumstances did not limit. In the struggle of mass against class, which was contemporaneous with the struggle of class against crown, even larger issues were raised than those which divided king and Parliament. The question was not whether Parliament was to be supreme over the king, but whether the people was to be supreme over both king and Parliament. A much bigger question, certainly, but one for which the fourteenth century had no other solution than that of the repression of the people.

The terrible visitation known as the Black Death proved a blessing in disguise to the English peasant. Its ravages were indeed tragic enough. From its appearance in the towns of the south coast in August 1348 till well into the following summer it breathed death and panic over the land. In London alone 100,000 persons are said to have perished, in Norwich 57,000. At Yarmouth, Leicester, York, and other centres the mortality was proportionately appalling. From the towns it spread to the villages and hamlets, which in many cases were completely depopulated. The ruined, deserted houses, the grass-grown streets told for years to come the mournful tale of its remorseless ravages. Universal horror struck the nation, and drove the people in terror-stricken flight into the woods and wastes. In January and March 1349 the meeting of Parliament had to be postponed for fear of the contagion. The administration of justice ceased, divine service was suspended in many of the churches. Despair drove men mad, and their madness took the form of religious mania. Panic tore asunder the ties of family affection, blunted the feelings of humanity. Not only the physician and the priest shunned the pestilential dens of the dying; parents forsook their children, children their parents in their terror of the deadly infection.

The moral effects were sad enough, the material effects were not less crushing. They were likewise far-reaching. In thinning the ranks of the peasants, the pestilence sapped the social and economic system of the time. A murrain swept away the herds. In one pasture, for instance, as many as 5,000 carcases of dead cattle poisoned the air with a deadly stench. The result was a scarcity of food and a dearth of labour. The land fell out of cultivation for want of hands to till it. Corn and meat rose in price. Famine threatened to complete the ravage of pestilence. What was an unmitigated calamity to the landowner was, however, opportunity to the villein and the labourer. If prices rose in consequence of dearth, why should not the wages of the labourer rise in proportion? If the number of available hands for working the lord's demesne had decreased to a third or more of what it had been, why should not the landlord double or treble the labourer's daily earnings? Very cogent reasoning from the labourer's point of view, but most outrageous from that of the lord of the manor, especially as the villeins whose services had been commuted for money were not available to take the place of the hands who laboured for hire. There were only two expedients for coping with the situation in the landlord's opinion. One was to compel the labourer by legislation to work at the former wage: the other to compel the villeins to render the services which by commutation had fallen into disuse. In the refusal to work, except at double or treble the old wage, the landlord saw only the excuse of laziness, or the airs of overweening arrogance. Let the king, therefore, ordain as a remedy the obligation of every able-bodied person, free or unfree, under sixty years of age, without a vocation or a competence, to work at the former rate of wages. This the king did by proclamation in 1349, and added a clause that victuals should be retailed at the former prices. The rate of wages and the price of provisions should thus be equalised by royal authority. In such a contingency, however, it is the law of self-interest, not the law of royal councils, that regulates the course of things, and the proclamation was a failure. Parliament considered itself wiser than nature, and two years later sought to give efficiency to the proclamation by transforming it into a statute—the celebrated Statute of Labourers (1351), which not only fixed the rate of wages of labourers and artisans at the old rate, but prohibited them from moving from one county to another, contravention of both regulations being punished by fine and imprisonment.

The statute proves the failure of the proclamation. When threatened by the landlord, the labourers took to flight or simply defied him, and as they formed unions in defence of their interests, the landlord had the worst of it in spite of the law and its penalties. To save his crops from rotting he was forced to pay 6d. or 8d. a day for reaping, in place of the legal rate of 2d. or 3d. If he refused and set the law in motion, his neighbour was only too glad, under pressure of necessity, to accept the services of the fugitives on their own terms. Equally futile was the attempt to force the free villein to give service instead of a money rent, service being more desirable than rent. Still worse, many of the villeins whose services had not been commuted became endued with the refractory spirit of the time and demanded the same privilege. If the landlord demurred, they, like the labourers, took to flight and swelled the vagabondage of the age. Or, following the same example, they formed local unions to enforce concession. In many cases the landlord was forced to yield, and commutation became increasingly common. He was forced, too, to abandon the custom of cultivating the larger part of his demesne, and to turn it into pasturage. The change was not, at first at least, a profitable one, and his discontent found repeated expression in Parliament, and occasioned renewed legislation against both labourer and villein. The sheriffs were empowered to declare runaway labourers outlaws, who might be killed wherever they were caught. Many of these fugitives had in fact degenerated into thieves and cutthroats, and were a serious menace to social order. "Many of them," complained the Commons in the Good Parliament, " become staff-strikers, and also live wicked lives, and rob the poor in simple villages, in bodies of two or three together. And the greater part of the said servants increase their robberies and felonies from day to day." The villeins, too, had become increasingly defiant and threatening during the thirty years following the great plague. They were not satisfied with the commutation of their services. They banded themselves together to free themselves utterly from every mark of bondage and assert their claim to the rights of free men. According to the testimony of a statute passed in 1377, " they affirm themselves to be quite and utterly discharged of all manner of serfage due, as well of their body as of their tenures, and will not suffer any distress or other justice to be made on them; but do menace the ministers of their lords of life and member, and still worse, gather themselves together in great routs and agree by such confederacy that every one shall aid other to resist their lords with strong hand, and much more harm do they in sundry manner to the great damage of their said lords, and evil example to others to begin such riots."

This is, of course, the one-sided testimony of an aggrieved class. Its keynote is the assumption that any attack on class privilege or legal right is a wrong and a crime, and doubtless the landlord had some cause for grumbling at the counter-assumption that class rights and privileges, even if sanctioned by law and custom, are not, therefore, inassailable. The villein might be an anarchist from the landlord's point of view, a presumptuous varlet who had taken it into his mulish head to kick against the rights of his master and do things that shocked the legal mind. He is clearly, from the standpoint of law and custom, in the wrong. But is it so certain that law and custom are in the right? The landlord has law on his side because he made the law, but the fact that he made the law could not prevent those at whose expense it was made from questioning its validity. This is the problem which the villein has been resolving these twenty years back, and which some of his preachers have been suggesting and helping him to answer. There is John Ball, for instance, who has been haranguing these rustics all over the country, proclaiming the gospel of the brotherhood of man, which even the Middle Ages have not lost sight of, though the Church has long ceased practically to inculcate such heretic opinions. Some of John Wiclif's poor priests, too, have translated into plain rustic English the communistic theories of their master as to the rights of property, though their master in practice leaves property in possession even of the wicked, and eschews a social revolution. The itinerant friars were equally outspoken in their demand "that all things under heaven ought to be in common." Many of the villeins had thus arrived at some notion of the difference between right and law as thus enunciated, and it is certain that, while fairly prosperous, they had come to hate the servile status to which the law doomed them, and were determined to be free.

The age was peculiarly favourable to such aspirations.

The Black Death had produced an economic crisis which gave the villeins the consciousness of their power, the sense of their own interests. It had given an impulse to the demand for commutation, and the amelioration of their servile condition had begotten the desire for full emancipation. Authority was relaxed in Church and State. Not only was Parliament impugning the government and taking the reins out of the hands of a dotard king and his worthless ministers; in the mediæval Church itself, that great engine of subordination to authority, that mighty instrument of religious and intellectual thraldom, men were heard denying the claims of pope and prelate alike to the obedience of Christians. In such an age the wayfaring preacher, who denounced injustice in high places and proclaimed the rights of man, became a prophet, with more power over the masses than king, Parliament, and Church combined. Such a prophet was John Ball, "the mad priest of Kent," as Froissart contemptuously calls him, whose vehement denunciation of the social wrongs of the age had increased in violence with the persecution that had dogged his steps these twenty years past. He anticipated Wicklif in his onslaughts on the wealth and luxury of the higher clergy, and he seems to have adopted his doctrinal heresies towards the end of his career. It was, however, rather as a practical preacher against social abuses that he acquired popularity and power with the rustic congregations that gathered round him in the fields or on the village green. He thundered, in the intervals of freedom from prison life, against class privilege and oppression with a fervour of democratic and socialistic argument that seems an echo of Wace, and might have been caught from the "Social Contract" of Jean Jacques Rousseau in later days. "Good people, things will never go well in England so long as goods be not in common, and so long as there be villeins and gentlemen. By what right are they, whom we call lords, greater folk than we? On what grounds have they deserved it? Why do they hold us in serfage? If we all come of the same father and mother, of Adam and Eve, how can they say or prove that they are better than we, if it be not that they make us gain for them by our toil what they spend in their pride? They are clothed in velvet, and warm in their furs and their ermines, while we are covered with rags. They have wine and spices and fine bread, we oatcake and straw and water to drink. They have leisure and fine houses; we have pain and labour, the rain and wind in the fields. And yet it is of us and of our toil that these men support their pomp. We are called slaves, and if we do not perform our services we are beaten."

The villeins' indictment of the landlords, like the landlords' indictment of the villeins, is an extreme outburst of class irritation. It is only fair to remember that they had their good times in years of plenty, and that the wages of labourers had risen in spite of repressive legislation. According to Langland, or, more correctly, in deference to Professors Skeat and Pearson, Langley, the labourers had been spoiled by prosperity. They had become fastidious in their diet and increasingly bumptious.

> "Labourers that have no land to live on but their hands,
> Deigned not to dine a day on worts a night old,
> Penny ale will not do, nor a piece of bacon,
> But if it be fresh flesh or fish fried or baked,
> And that hot and more hot for the chill of their maw.
> And unless he be hired at a high rate he will chide.
> .   .   .   .
> And then curseth he the king and all his Council after
> Such laws to enforce labourers to grieve."

So much must be subtracted from this overwrought picture of the misery of the people.

At the same time the note of indignant protest against the oppression of the poor by the rich is very marked in Langley. "He pictures," to quote Skeat, "the homely poor in their ill-fed, hard-working condition, battling against hunger, famine, injustice, oppression, and all the stern realities and hardships that tried them as gold is tried in the fire. Chaucer's satire often raises a good-humoured laugh; but Langley's is that of a man who is constrained to speak out all the bitter truth, and it is as earnest as is the cry of an injured man who appeals to Heaven for vengeance." Moreover, though Langley was no revolutionist, his fearless denunciation of social abuse tended to excite the revolutionary spirit, while his glorification of honest labour, as in the case of the German popular scribes of the next century, helped to nurture in the peasant the sense of his worth.

The significance of John Ball's invectives lies not in their literal accuracy (supposing Froissart, who only writes from hearsay, to be giving a true version of his sermons, and not, as is probable in so ardent a votary of chivalry, exaggerating the irrational element in them). It lies in the spirit of revolt against convention which they excite. His insistence on the natural equality of men is the point that tells, the gospel that makes him omnipotent in every manor village, where villeins and labourers were brooding and talking over their grievances. His communistic ravings were probably not taken seriously, for they do not seem to have been formulated in the demands for the redress of grievances, and only incited at most to pillage during the coming insurrection. His appeal to Adam and Eve was far more effective, for it confirmed in the villein the rising hatred of his social status and his determination to enforce his complete emancipation from serfage. It was this doctrine that made the revolution of 1381, as it made the revolution of 1789. Granted that all men are equal by nature (and the villein was in no mood, even if he had been able, to scrutinise the doctrine critically), it is clear to the villein that no man, even with all the force of law and custom at his back, has a right to keep him in bondage. Whether all men are actually in all respects equal by nature or not, the conclusion of the villein is substantially correct. No man *has* a natural right to enslave his fellow, even in the Middle Ages, against his will, and if the villein refuses to submit to his servile condition any longer, he has justice and reason, if not the law of the land, on his side.

But the desire to extirpate serfdom, root and branch, was not the only, though it seems to have been the chief, motive of the insurrectionary movement propagated by John Ball. Among the men of Kent, where villenage was practically unknown, the spirit of revolt was as strong as among the men of Essex or Norfolk, Somerset or Cornwall, Lancashire or York. It had a political as well as a social character, aspired to the reform of the State as well as of society. At such a crisis the ideal co-operates with the real to give verve and strength to the popular upheaval. What boots it to vindicate the rights of the individual, as long as an oppressive class possesses the right to make unjust laws and an oppressive government fleeces the people? The people, therefore, must set its hand to the rectification of abuses, must undo the obnoxious class legislation to its detriment, must take vengeance on these evil designing ministers who exact these nefarious poll-taxes, and cannot, nevertheless, save the country from defeat and misery, must deprive these false "commons" of the power to do the true commons further mischief by their selfish Acts of Parliament. John of Gaunt, especially, must be prevented from carrying out his traitorous design on the throne, and King Richard shall both be delivered from the thraldom of evil councillors and safeguarded in his rights as the leader of the people. In the view of these simple rustics, the king has only to be told of their grievances to become their champion and do their bidding. "With King Richard and the true commons," is the rallying cry of the revolution. The day of the true democracy has dawned at last, and the day of retribution for the usurpers of the rights of the people in Parliament and Cabinet. In this fierce, levelling spirit reasoned the men of Kent, and doubtless the poll-tax, in addition to the burdens of serfage, likewise gave the movement a political as well as a social colouring in the other counties.

It was thus not a mere aimless outburst of blind passion that focussed all the tributary rills of popular aspiration into the surging torrent of revolution, though the villeins indulged in excesses that were brutal enough. The rising was carefully planned, skilfully organised. It had its central committee in London which hatched the "Great Society" or association of the villeins not merely of the home counties, but throughout the length and breadth of the land. Its summonses had been carried far and near, "greeting well John Nameless and John the Miller and John Carter, and bidding them stand together in God's name, and Piers Plowman go to his work and chastise well Hob the robber, and take with them John Trueman and all his fellows ... and know friend from foe." Jack the Miller further "asketh help to turn his mill aright. He hath grounden small, small. The King's Son of Heaven, He shall pay for all. Let thy mill go aright with the four sails, and the post stand in steadfastness. With right and with might, with skill and with will, let might help right, and skill go before will and right before might—then goeth our mill aright.

And if might go before right, then is our mill misadight." Again "Jack Trueman doth you to understand that falseness and guile have reigned too long." And again, "John Ball greeteth you well all, and doth you to understand that he hath rungen your bell."

Thus organised and summoned to the rally, the villeins burst into revolt with startling suddenness and universality, to the consternation of king, prelates, ministers, and landlords alike. The collectors of the arrears of the poll-tax of 1380, the third within three years, were driven from a couple of Essex villages, and the whole county was up in arms in a trice. The chief-justice of the King's Bench himself, who went down to the revolted district in the beginning of June to attempt to enforce the law, was taken prisoner and his jurymen decapitated. Kent immediately followed the example of Essex, and before a week was over the rustic hosts of both Essex and Kent, swelled by contingents from the neighbouring counties, were swinging along the main roads in their wild march on London. Rather ludicrous those motley bands of young men and old must have seemed from the standpoint of the trained soldier, if their resolute fervour had not bespoken some fell purpose. "They gathered together," says Walsingham, contemptuously, "for the conquest of the kingdom—some with simple clubs, some with rusty swords, some with battle-axes, some with bows blackened by smoke and age, with only one arrow, and even this one had often but a single feather." Not a very formidable army certainly, except in its numbers, which swelled as it went into tens of thousands. Nevertheless at the sight of these rusty swords and musty bows the lords and squires of England trembled, fled into the woods, and the king and his ministers quaked and shut themselves up in the Tower. The surprise was complete. The insurgents were organised; their enemies were not. They had not reckoned with the "Great Society," and they were for the moment paralysed by fear. It looked for a few fearful June days as if the thousands that had gathered on Blackheath from the south, and the thousands that had gathered on the other side of the Thames from the north would succeed by the terror they inspired in transferring England straightway into a democracy. John Ball, the "mad" preacher whom the bishops and the landlords had hunted from manor to manor, and diocese to diocese for over twenty years, was master of the situation, and now John Ball, freed from his prison at Middlesex, was breathing vengeance without stint. On Blackheath he held forth once more from the appropriate text of Adam and Eve:—

"When Adam delved and Eve span,
Who was then the gentleman?"

He thundered anew his doctrine of the natural equality of all men. "If it had pleased God to create slaves," cried he, "would He not in the beginning of the world have decreed who was to be a serf, and who not? No such thing. And as serfdom is offensive to both God and nature, the time has at last come when you shall be freed from a long bondage. Wherefore, take courage and extirpate the weeds that have grown up in the field of the State—lords, judges, lawyers, juries, yea and all and sundry who have done or shall do injury to the commonweal—kill them all without mercy in order that equal liberty, equal nobility, equal dignity, equal power may reign in the land." Such is the murderous philippic which the hostile chronicler puts into the mouth of the fanatic priest, and judging by the terrible deeds of the immediate sequel the exhortation is probable enough. Forward, then, to the bloody work, King Richard having refused to parley with the popular leaders at Rotherhithe, opposite the Tower, or surrender Archbishop Sudbury the chancellor, or Hales the treasurer, and sundry other delinquents for punishment. Forward the southern host accordingly tramped under John Ball and Wat Tyler, on Thursday morning the 13th June, towards London Bridge, after having burned Lambeth Palace and the Marshalsea prison. The drawbridge was lowered by friendly hands; the men of Essex came pouring in through the Aldgate on the north, and the city lay at their mercy. For three days more they continued to crowd in from south, and north, and west, from far and near, and they were not unwelcome visitors to the mass of the populace which had its own grievances to redress, its own hatreds to satiate. The mob made first for John of Gaunt's palace, the Savoy, and sacked and burned it to the ground. The treasurer's mansion at Highbury, the hospital of the Order of St John, of which he was Master, the Inns of Court, the haunts of the hated race of lawyers, shared the same fate. The insurgents at first refrained from pillage, but the ruffians from the Fleet and the Marshalsea, and all the scoundreldom of a large city in revolt would not be denied the opportunity of plunder and murder, and robbed at will in spite of orders to the contrary. Vengeance was, too, unsparingly taken on every one who had the misfortune to be identified with the oppressors of the people, on lawyers and jurymen more particularly, who were haled to a scaffold in Cheapside and beheaded.

There was higher prey in store for the executioner's axe in the Tower, where the king, the archbishop, the treasurer, and the courtiers cowered helpless and terror-stricken, and near which, on St Catherine's Hill, the insurgents finally took up a position. The shouts of vengeance which rent the air, the blazing mansions in the city, which reddened the sky, seemed the foreboders of doom. What course to pursue? Sally out and extirpate the villein host, urged the bolder spirits. Negotiate, promise, concede everything, and thus gain time, suggested the Earl of Salisbury. This course the king ultimately adopted, and next day, in conference at Mile End, agreed to the abolition of serfage, root and branch, over the whole land, and presented to the men of each county a royal banner as the emblem of his protection. To the villeins of every manor and village a charter of emancipation should be accorded, as fast as the thirty clerks, to whom the task was entrusted, could get the precious parchments ready. With this victory the bulk of the insurgents professed contentment. The wilder spirits were by no means satisfied, however; they must have the heads of Sudbury and Hales, and Richard was forced to give way and sacrifice his ministers. The archbishop and the treasurer were torn from the chapel of the Tower by the invading mob, and dragged to their doom on Tower Hill. Sudbury bore himself with dignity and courage, but his expostulations fell on deaf ears, and could not stay the executioner's maladroit blows that tortured him to death. It was the chancellor, the reputed author of the poll-tax, the persecutor of the people's friend, John Ball, whose life was forfeited to the people's vengeance. It mattered not, therefore, that, personally, Sudbury was by no means an invidious person, that he was lukewarm in the persecution of heretics, and kind and gentle in disposition. He was the head of a Church, synonymous with the neglect of the poor, with corruption and grovelling worldliness; the representative, to boot, of a hated government, which spent the poor man's earnings in heartless profusion, and must die, high priest though he be, and his head, along with that of Hales, be stuck on London Bridge as a testimony that the people may not be oppressed with impunity. Besides Hales, other delinquents in high places—John Leg, the farmer of the poll-tax, and John Lynn, who had escaped the penalties of the Good Parliament—shared the archbishop's fate. Nor was political resentment the only motive of bloodshed. Many others, notably the Flemish weavers, fell victims to the rancour of the London mob. The city was turned into a pandemonium of murder and pillage, and, as usual in such an upheaval, the fanatics by their excesses ended in undoing the cause of liberty, and bringing upon themselves a terrible retribution. Every schoolboy knows the oft-told tale of the episode at Smithfield, where Richard met the insurgents in conference once more, where Wat Tyler was struck down by the Mayor of London during an altercation in the king's presence, and where the boy king disarmed the rising ire of his followers by his fortitude and presence of mind. "I am your king, your leader," cried he, riding straight in the face of the bent bows of the threatening mass. "Follow me, everything you demand is granted." The ruse succeeded. The insurgents confidently followed the king, whom they had always desired for their leader, to a field at Clerkenwell, while the mayor raised the city militia. Before they were aware of the trick, they were surrounded and disarmed, and the revolution was at an end as far as the capital was concerned. There was no massacre, as the fiercer spirits demanded. The duped peasants were allowed to disperse to their homes, but summary vengeance was taken by the mayor on those who had loitered in the city, as well as on the cutthroats of the London mob.

The failure of the revolution in the capital entailed its bloody repression in the counties, where the villeins had meanwhile been busy burning the manor rolls and murdering obnoxious landlords, clerical as well as laic. It had been already checked in Norfolk by Henry Spencer, the bellicose Bishop of Norwich, who hunted the roving bands, and paralysed further developments by hanging their leaders. The fugitive landlords came out of their hiding-places and swelled the forces which, under the king and his lieutenants, swept the counties, slaying all who resisted, and gathering prisoners for the bloody assize of Chief-Justice Tressilian. Tressilian had his profession and his predecessor, Sir John Cavendish, who had been caught and decapitated in Suffolk, to avenge, and his fury knew no pity. Terror reigned supreme, until the juries, disgusted with the gruesome business, refused to convict, and Parliament in November passed an act of amnesty. Between the sword, the gallows, and the executioner's axe, the number of victims, which was swelled by a few desperate rallies of the hunted peasants, amounted to about 7,000, among whom was John Ball himself. This savage retribution, which swept away so many of these deluded rustics, swept away the charters of emancipation. "Serfs you are, and serfs you shall remain," burst out Richard to a peasant deputation at Walsham. Revoked the charters accordingly were by letters patent, which bore that "all should render the burdens, customs, services which they owe to us and to other lords, as they were accustomed before the said rebellion, without contradiction, murmur, resistance, or objection." The king might indeed plead that he could not do by his own fiat what touched the interests of a powerful class so closely, without asking its consent, and when he did submit the question to an ensuing Parliament, it unanimously voted against emancipation.

The rising had failed as an organised attempt at reform, though local outbreaks continued for long to show that the restive spirit of the peasants had not been quelled. As a bold bid for liberty it deserved a better fate. The social demands of the rustics, as interpreted by the charters of emancipation, were moderate enough. All they asked was the total abolition of serfage, and the fixation of a rent of 4d. an acre for the land they tilled. To say that they had forfeited these concessions by their violence is to forget that they had received great provocation to violence, and that without drastic measures they would never have received the slightest consideration from an oppressive government, or a prejudiced Parliament. The blame for the violence lies, in the first place, on the shoulders of those who had persistently refused redress for over thirty years, and had thus conjured the storm. The peasants had ample justification for believing that both government and Parliament were the mere tools of class against mass, and would only give way to force. They had good reason, too, for demanding retribution on the royal officials, whose rule was both oppressive to the people and disgraceful to the nation. To condemn the movement on account of its excesses is easy enough, but where there are glaring abuses to redress, there will perforce be excesses, when remedy can only be had by force. To allow things to come to such a pass was simply to tempt doom. On the other hand, to indulge in pillage and murder in the prosecution of desiderated reforms was equally fatal policy. Even if Richard had failed at Smithfield, it is questionable whether the democracy of John Ball and Wat Tyler would have succeeded in sober actuality. The peasants needed education as well as freedom. Without education democracy of the type of John Ball must have tended to anarchy, and anarchy usually ends by strengthening the system it seeks to overthrow.

The rising was not wholly futile, however. In spite of the misguided energy which brought about its immediate suppression, at such terrible cost in bloodshed, it did something to inaugurate a better state of things. While Parliament became still more jealous of its class supremacy, and petitioned the king in 1391 against the education of the children of villeins, it was forced to modify the Statute of Labourers to the extent of substituting a sliding scale for a fixed wage. The emancipation movement continued in spite of its opposition, for the villeins did not eschew their local unions, or even risings for the purpose of extorting the concession of their demands for freedom. The remembrance of 1381 had its salutary lessons for both government and Parliament. The peasants had won influence as a class, though they failed to gain a recognised political standing, and their social status shows a gradual improvement until, under the Tudors, the remains of serfage finally disappeared, and every Englishman was free before the law.

Contemporary with the movement for emancipation from serfage was the movement for emancipation from ecclesiastical thraldom championed by Wicklif, and carried on after his death by the Lollards. The religious had, however, very little connection with the social movement. The Lollards were not political or social reformers. They were not as a rule in sympathy with the war of class against class. Wicklif, like Luther, was first and foremost a clerical controversialist who strove to reform the Church in doctrine and practice, and allied himself with the dominant class of the day in order to attain his end. The *protégé* of John of Gaunt was not the man to stir up a social or political revolution. Like Luther he denounced the resistance of the peasants to oppression, and meekly preached submission. Like Luther, too, he thus belied the principle of resistance in regard to things mundane, which he was staunch enough to exemplify in regard to things spiritual. The spirit of insubordination to the dominant social order was the spirit of the devil, not of Christ. "The fiend moveth some men to say that Christian men should not be servants or thralls to heathen lords, sith they ben false to God and less worthy than Christian men; neither to Christian lords, for they ben brethren in kind, and Jesus Christ bought Christian men on the cross, and made them free. But against this heresy Paul writeth in God's law. But yet some men that ben out of charity slander poor priests with this error, that servants or tenants may lawfully withhold rent or services from their lords, when lords ben openly wicked in their living."

The writer had himself propounded this doctrine, and even advocated a thoroughgoing Christian communism in his book "De Dominio Civili." His doctrine of lordship, or *dominium*, tended, in fact, if practically applied, to result in universal confiscation. All men, according to Wicklif, "hold" directly of God. All are alike dependent on him. In this respect they are all equal; there is no difference between lord and servant, priest or layman. The notion is feudal, but it is a feudalism pervaded by a democratic idea. It is enunciated in the "De Dominio Divino"; it is elaborated in the "De Civili

Dominio." In this elaboration Wicklif applied the principle of feudalism to ethics. In the moral sense man stands to God in the relation of vassal to superior. God is the universal overlord; all men are His dependants, and as the vassal of a lord loses his right to his fief by rebellion, the sinner by transgression forfeits his moral right to possess anything. On the other hand, the righteous man is lord of all things; as God's vassal, his fief is the whole sensible world. Consequently all goods in a really Christian State must be held in common. John Ball did not utter anything more revolutionary than this. But then John Ball was a fiery demagogue, Wicklif a mere theorist and a theologian. Ball's is the social, Wicklif's the theological conception of man, and the theologian evidently spoke very differently from the socialist to his rustic hearers at Fillingham and Lutterworth. Wicklif's conception is at most an ideal which the future may realise. Nay, it deals with the spiritual not the temporal side of man, and a state of material felicity is not necessary to man's spiritual good. Such felicity is rather to be looked for in the blessedness of the life to come. A very different doctrine from the earthly communism of the popular preacher, though not very comforting to those who resent the injustice and hardship of their lot, and demand its improvement as a natural right. Wicklif, in fact, expressly blunts its revolutionary edge by maintaining that God is the author of human society, however imperfect it may be, and that it is not permissible by the divine law to apply such a theory by force.

Nor is Wicklif's teaching on the subject of government, to which he devotes some chapters of the "De Civili Dominio," by any means revolutionary. There is indeed a democratic note in some of his arguments, but here again it is the theorist, not the publicist, that speaks. The only two legitimate forms of government are, he holds, the monarchic and the aristocratic. A State should be governed by a king or by a number of judges, an aristocracy, as in Israel. He gives the arguments for and against both forms, and his own preference is for aristocracy. The king derives his power from God, and his subjects are therefore bound to obey him. He is supreme in all causes, ecclesiastical as well as civil, and may deprive any ecclesiastic or ecclesiastical corporation of Church property used unworthily. "The king is invested with the supreme donative power of his realm, and if, for example, it is expedient that the clergy be deprived, even against their will, of their temporalities, the duty pertains in an especial sense to the king." But he is bound, in virtue of his divine right, to rule his subjects justly and to preserve his people in peace, though he states explicitly in another work, the "De Officio Regis," that he is not himself limited by the laws. Moreover, the rule of an aristocracy of judges is more in accord with a state of innocence and the law of God. Worst of all is the government of priests, as the Old Testament shows. Granting, however, that a people is subject to monarchic government, it is bound to render obedience even to a tyrant. The reasons adduced are, of course, theological. Christ obeyed, and so should we. Such suffering is divinely ordained for our good. There is only one exception, but it is sufficiently comprehensive—if the refusal of obedience were likely to end his misgovernment, we should be justified in refusing. In other words, we should take advantage of whatever promising chance of relief from his tyranny should come within our reach. He is, in truth, not a consistent supporter of absolute monarchy. For while in the "De Officio Regis" he inculcates passive obedience to a degree that seems to leave no room for resistance, he nevertheless in the same work insists on the right of rebellion, and even of tyrannicide in certain contingencies. When it would be sin against God to obey the king, he must be resisted, but all offences against men are to be borne with patience.

In regard to the question whether hereditary succession or election be the best, he gives the arguments *pro* and *contra*, and opines that both have their advantages. He treats the subject of slavery in the same fashion. Whilst he reminds us, on the one hand, that slavery is an Old Testament institution, he emphasises the fact that it is contrary to the law of nature, and to our own instincts, and we should therefore not seek to enslave our fellow-creatures. Even slavery, however, may be defended on theological grounds. Christ took upon Himself the form of a slave, and even a slave may be a freeman in the moral sense, and boast his lineage from Adam with the proudest baron. All Christians are equally noble, and true nobility depends on nature, character. Certainly democratic enough as far as it goes, but democracy of this kind would as certainly not very readily lead to the emancipation of the masses from inequality and injustice in the practical prosaic world outside the theologian-idealist's study.

From all which it appears that the "De Civili Dominio" is a mere academic treatise which could never have produced the revolutionary movement of 1381. Its doctrines were probably unknown outside the walls of Wicklif's lecture-room at Oxford, except to the heresy hunters on the outlook for matter of accusation against the heterodox divine. In any case their author, though he spoke out against the oppression of the poor by selfish and heartless masters, would be no party to the forcible redress of grievances. Some of his poor priests may have helped to swell the rising tide of popular anger; but if so, they must have taken their cue from the spirit of the age, not from the teaching of their master. Wicklifism, Lollardism was a purely religious movement begotten of the reaction, not from social, but from ecclesiastic abuses. It was a war of creed, not of classes. Wicklif challenged the absolute supremacy of the pope, and ultimately disowned the papal headship of the Church. He attacked the power of the hierarchy, subjected it to the secular authority, and demanded the confiscation of ecclesiastical property which that hierarchy had forfeited by its worldliness and luxury. He denounced the ignorance, rapacity, and turbulence of the friars. He denied the dogma of transubstantiation, appealed to the Bible against tradition as the grand authority in matters of faith, and translated it into English for the instruction of the people. He demanded the preaching of the Gospel in place of the mummeries with which the Church services were overlaid, and thus strove to lead men from the traditional Church back to Christ. He taught men to see the Church not merely in its ministers, but in its members, and implied, if he did not expressly teach, the Lutheran dogma of the priesthood of believers. He laid stress on spiritual in contrast to formal religion, on the direct relation of the soul to God instead of to the Church, and inveighed against the abuses of indulgences and the worship of images and relics.

The significance of the Wicklifite reformation thus lies in

the fact that it aroused and kept alive the spirit of revolt against a corrupt and tyrannic ecclesiastical domination, in spite of statutes for the burning of heretics (*de hæretico comburendo*) which the Church obtained from Henry IV., and the faggots which they set ablazing around these martyrs of the early English reformation. The ultimate effects of this revolt were far-reaching indeed. It led directly or indirectly to great social and political changes. But these changes were still beneath the horizon of the age of Wicklif and his followers. The Bohemian revolution, as we have seen, which was inspired by Wicklif, was only a local attempt to realise his ideal of reformation, though it produced one of the most dramatic struggles of modern history, and perpetuated its influence in the quasi-social, quasi-religious movements in Germany in the fifteenth century. Wicklif and his followers did not see the full bearing of their principle of the right to worship God otherwise than accorded with mediæval creed and practice, and with the exception of Lord Cobham's spasmodic rising against Henry V., they did not seek to push their principle of liberty further, and apply it to abuses that were not religious.

The fourteenth century, which thus closed its stormy career in social and religious strife, is in some respects one of the most noteworthy in English annals. It was one of the most bellicose on record, for the struggle with France went on, with fitful interruptions, for the better part of sixty years. Its pre-eminence in this respect is unique, for though Europe has had its Thirty Years' War in more modern times, it had never before, and has never since witnessed a Hundred Years' War. For two generations Englishmen and Frenchmen had fought over the wretched question who was the rightful king of France, as they were to do for two generations longer. Judging from results, and having regard to the misery entailed on both nations, its pre-eminence in this sort of Quixotic enterprise is certainly not an enviable one. Happily, it has other claims to distinction. From the social, the religious, the constitutional point of view, it was undoubtedly a century of progress. In spite of the failure of the attempt to force social reform, the lower classes had risen considerably in the social scale. Serfage was doomed and was slowly dying out, though the system of enclosing and appropriating the common lands as pasturage for the lords' use, to which the landowners had recourse, unfortunately started a new agrarian grievance, and gave rise to new strife and violence in the course of the following century. In spite, too, of the fierce persecution of the Lollards, the demand for doctrinal reform, involving the emancipation of the conscience from the tyranny of the mediæval Church, marks the beginning of a new age of intellectual and religious life, of enormous potential significance. In the constitutional history of the century, too, progress is unmistakable, and if here also there are checks to record, there are also notable victories. In the assertion of its claims, Parliament, as we have seen, became increasingly insistent with the century. It forced the royal will to bend to its demands, and though there were evasions and high-handed reactions in favour of prerogative on the part both of Edward III. and Richard II., the victory finally lay with the Parliament and not with the king. Constitutionally the fourteenth century deserves to rank with the seventeenth, not merely in the assertion, but in the vindication of parliamentary rights. If it did not behead a king for attempting to trample on these rights, it deposed two. Henry IV. of Lancaster held his crown by parliamentary title, if he professed to claim it by hereditary right, and both he and his two successors of the House of Lancaster were forced to comport themselves accordingly in the great essentials of parliamentary government, viz., control of taxation and expenditure, responsibility of ministers, right of legislation, and the guardianship of the laws. More especially did the House of Commons become more and more the directive force in both legislation and administration. If the thirteenth century created, the fourteenth century made the House of Commons. True, the Commons were largely the representatives of a class and the tool of this class against the mass; often, too, the creature of baronial faction. The tendency of representation was unfortunately, in the fifteenth century, to contract both in town and county. The gilds became, as we have seen, narrow and exclusive, the municipality a royal corporation, and as the common councils were elected by these privileged burgesses, and in turn elected the borough representatives to Parliament, the borough representatives really represented only a few privileged individuals. "With the definite recognition conferred by the charters of incorporation," says Dr Stubbs, "comes in a tendency towards restriction. The corporate governing body becomes as it were hardened and crystallised, and exhibits a constantly increasing disposition to engross in its own hands the power which had been understood to belong to the body of the burghers. The town property comes to be regarded as the property of the corporation; the corporation becomes a close oligarchy; the elective rights of the freemen are reduced to a minimum, and in many cases the magistracy becomes almost the hereditary right of a few families. The same tendency exists in the trading companies also. The highest point of grievance is reached when by royal charter the corporation is empowered to return the members of Parliament. And this power, notwithstanding the legal doctrine that such a monopoly, although conferred by royal charter, could not prejudice the already essential rights of the burgesses at large, was in many cases exercised by the municipal corporations until it was abolished by the Reform Act of 1832." Similarly the statute of Henry VI. which in 1430 restricted the county franchise to freeholders holding land of the value of forty shillings a year, excluded leaseholders and copyholders, who are contemptuously classed "as of no value, whereof many of them pretended to have a voice equivalent with the more worthy knights and esquires dwelling within the same counties." Nevertheless, the Commons had been surely winning their way to power, and the growth of their power, if we may be allowed to anticipate, meant ultimate gain for democracy. "The constitutional result of the three reigns that fill the fourteenth century," says Dr Stubbs, "is the growth of the House of Commons into its full share of political power, the recognition of its full right as the representative of the mass and body of the nation (?), and the vindication of its claim to exercise the powers which in the preceding century had been possessed by the baronage only." Representative "of the mass of the nation" it was not, except in name, but in spite of class legislation, we to-day, who have seen the realisation of its claim to be a truly national assembly, may rejoice in the growth of its power against an arbitrary king, if not as against the people. And this power it maintained far into the fifteenth century, throughout the reign of the Lancastrian kings and the anarchy of the Wars of the Roses, to experience a temporary check under the nipping frost of the Tudor despotism. What the barons, who fought themselves to death in the long civil anarchy, lost, was gain to the Commons, for the time being at least, as well as to the king. "Both sides," to continue Dr Stubbs, "look to the Commons for help, and while they employ the Commons for their own ends, gradually place the decision of all great questions irrevocably in their hands."

SOURCES.—Chronicles of the Reigns of Edward I. and Edward II., edited by William Stubbs; Murimuth, Continuatio Chronicarum, edited by E. M. Thompson; Walsingham, Historia Anglicana, edited by H. T. Riley; Scalachronica, edited for the Maitland Club by Jos. Stevenson; Hemingburgh, Chronicle; Chronicon de Lanercost (Maitland Club); Robert of Avesbury, De Gestis Edwardi Tertii, edited by E. M. Thompson; Chronicon Angliæ, edited by the same; Knighton, Chronicon, edited by J. R. Lumby; Higden's Polychronicon, edited by the same; Chronicon of Baker de Swinebroke, edited by Giles; Froissart, Chroniques, editions of Lettenhove and Luce; Rymer, Fœdera, Record edition; Rotuli Parliamentorum; Statutes of the Realm; Barnes, History of King Edward the Third; Birchington, Vitæ Arch. Cant., in Anglia Sacra; Eulogium; Wyclif, Tractatus De Civili Dominio, edited for the Wyclif Society by R. L. Poole (1885 *et seq.*); The De Dominio Divino, edited for *idem* by Poole (1890); The De Ecclesia, edited for *idem* by Prof. Loserth (1886); The De Officio Regis, edited for *idem* by Pollard and Sayle (1887); Hook, Lives of the Archbishops of Canterbury; MacKinnon, The History of Edward the Third (1900); Stubbs, Constitutional History of England; G. M. Trevelyan, England in the Age of Wyckliffe; Trevelyan and Powell, The Peasants' Rising and the Lollards; Reville et Petit-Dutaillis, Soulèvement des Travailleurs en Angleterre en 1381 (1898); Poole, Illustrations of the History of Mediæval Thought (1884); Skeat, Piers the Plowman (1879); Jusserand,

Sources of Chapter XIV.

Piers Plowman, English translation (1894); Denton, England in the Fifteenth Century (1888); Green, History of the English People; Rogers, A History of Agriculture and Prices in England, i. and ii. (1866); Cunningham, Growth of English Industry and Commerce (1890); Jenks, Law and Politics in the Middle Ages (1898); Sergeant, John Wyclif (1893).

CHAPTER XV.

The English Parliament from Henry IV. to Henry VIII.

In the fourteenth century the keynote of English constitutional history is the development of the power of Parliament at the expense of that of the crown. It was a century of constitutional life and progress. The fifteenth century was a century of constitutional life, hardly of constitutional progress. It did not make any marked advance upon its predecessor. The Lords had obtained the control of the State, and the Commons did not seek to go beyond the constitutional claims already vindicated. "If the only object of constitutional history," says Dr Stubbs, "were the investigation of the origin and powers of Parliament, the study of the subject might be suspended at the deprivation of Richard II., to be resumed under the Tudors. During a great portion of the intervening period, the history of England contains little else than the details of foreign wars and domestic struggles, in which parliamentary institutions play no prominent part. The parliamentary constitution lives through the period, but its machinery and its functions do not much expand; the weapons, which are used by the politicians of the sixteenth and seventeenth centuries, are taken, with little improvement or adaptation, from the armoury of the fourteenth. The intervening age has rather conserved than multiplied them, or extended their usefulness."

Throughout the fifteenth century Parliament, if not progressive, was nevertheless very active. It was frequently summoned by Henry IV., who as a rule submitted to its direction, and governed as a parliamentary king. "Never before," to quote Dr Stubbs once more, "and never again for more than two hundred years, were the Commons so strong as they were under Henry IV." It was equally active under

Henry V., whose history, as Dr Stubbs points out, exhibits to us a king acting throughout his reign in the closest harmony with his Parliament, both in his internal and foreign policy. Whether as the suppressor of heresy, or as the aggressive champion of the English claim to the French crown, Henry was the hero of the nation, the executor of the will of its Parliament. During the minority of Henry VI., as well as during his active reign, no important step could safely be taken without its mandate, and when Henry, under the guidance of Suffolk, attempted to go against the strong, though unwise national feeling it represented in opposition to the disastrous peace negotiated with France, he jeopardised not merely his popularity, but his crown. "By its steady maintenance of ministers, whom the nation detested and abhorred," says Mr Plummer, "by its disregard to the wishes of the nation constitutionally expressed, by its attempt to tamper with the independence and liberties of Parliament, the House of Lancaster (under Henry VI.) destroyed its own best title to the throne, and its fate, however melancholy, cannot be called undeserved." Even in the terrible dynastic strife that unsheathed the sword to settle the rival claims of Lancaster and York, Parliament was the arbiter to which both sides appealed, for their own selfish purposes, no doubt, in the intervals of battle. If the sword actually settled the contest for the time being, the one way or the other, it was the Parliament that gave the national sanction to the accession of Edward IV. of York and the deposition of Henry of Lancaster in 1461. Nine years later, on the successful invasion of Warwick in Henry's behalf, it was Parliament that reversed the Act of 1461, and restored the deposed monarch to his throne. Edward won back his crown by the sword a few months afterwards, and practically held it in virtue of his sword, but even under his drastic sceptre, Parliament continued to meet and legislate, though at much longer intervals. His brother Richard III., like his predecessors, turned to it for the acknowledgment of the dignity he had usurped, and when Richard was in turn displaced by Henry of Richmond on the field of Bosworth, it was only in virtue of a parliamentary declaration that his claim obtained validity. By its frequent changes of front, Parliament might be merely the mouthpiece of the dominant faction, but the fact that faction sought its sanction at every important step of these dynastic revolutions demonstrates the formal deference at least which it was compelled to show to its authority.

And its activity throughout the Lancastrian period clearly exemplifies the great constitutional principles inherited from the fourteenth century. The House of Commons appears, together with the Lords, as the representative assembly of the nation, though representation was limited by a narrowed franchise. It vindicates freedom of debate, and resents the interference of the king in its deliberations. It applies this right of free debate to all important questions bearing on the national welfare—to foreign policy as well as internal administration. It insists that its petitions shall be turned into statutes without alteration or amendment, and that redress of grievances shall precede supply. It grants taxes "with the assent of the Lords, spiritual and temporal." It claims the right to appropriate supply to specific purposes, and to scrutinise and criticise the royal expenditure. It practises the right to call obnoxious ministers to account either by impeachment or bills of attainder, though it does not by any means always do so in a wise or just spirit.

Its aspirations were, however, premature. Parliamentary government did not work well under the Lancastrians. It weakened the executive; it bred anarchy. It was not equal to the task of curbing dynastic ambitions, or forcing its will on contentious magnates, and the result was a reaction which substituted the virtual autocracy of the Tudors for the parliamentary *régime* of the Lancastrians.

If Parliament made no appreciable constitutional advance in the fifteenth century, it was during the period of faction and dynastic strife known as the Wars of the Roses that the theory of constitutional government was elaborated by Sir John Fortescue, who was born about the beginning of the fourteenth century, and became Chief-Justice of the King's Bench in 1442. He was an ardent Lancastrian, and fought and suffered for his political creed. He spent several years of exile in Scotland and France, and witnessed on the fatal field of Tewkesbury the final discomfiture of the Lancastrian cause. He won his pardon and the restoration of his estates by accepting the indisputable arbitration of the sword, and agreeing to write in support of the victor's title. His pliability cannot fairly be called defection. He had strenuously championed Henry's cause with pen and sword till it was irretrievably lost. His party was annihilated, and though it would have been more heroic to refuse to eschew his party allegiance, even to save his head, his martyrdom could not have helped in the least to recreate that party. And in professing allegiance to Edward IV. he did not renounce his political creed. The constitutional doctrine of the " De Laudibus," which he wrote between 1468 and 1470, for the instruction of Prince Edward, Henry VI.'s son, is not essentially different from the constitutional doctrine of "The Governance of England," which he wrote after the final triumph of Edward IV. He remained the champion of constitutional government, though he sought to suggest remedies for the misgovernment of Henry VI.

According to Fortescue, who takes his nomenclature from Aquinas and the Schoolmen, the English monarchy is not exclusively a regal or absolute dominion, nor is it exclusively a political or popular dominion. It is both regal and political; in other words, it is a mixed or limited monarchy. In an exclusively regal dominion the will of the monarch is absolute, as in the case of the Oriental kingdoms, and later of the Roman empire. In a State at once regal and political, the will of the people forms the body politic, of which the king is the head, not the master. It is the law that binds the members of this body together, and the king cannot change the law or deprive the people of their property without their consent. His power is strictly limited by the laws. "For he was appointed to guard the laws and protect the subjects in their lives and goods, and this power he has received from the people for this purpose, and may not arrogate to himself any other power over them." No people ever formed itself into a kingdom by its own freewill and compact for any other end than the security of its laws and property. It would never have submitted itself for this purpose to an arbitrary will which endangered these, and consequently arbitrary power could never originally be derived from the freewill of the people. Like Bracton, long before, Fortescue ignores the notion of the divine right of kings in a monarchy such as that of England. Such a notion is excluded by the constitution, though it had already been mooted in the Bishop of Carlisle's speech on the deposition of Richard II., and was to find ardent champions in little more than a century after he wrote.

Nor is the maxim of the imperial jurists that "whatever pleases the prince has the force of law" admissible under the English constitution. The laws of England are not enacted by the will of the prince, but by the assent of the whole kingdom as represented in Parliament, consisting of over three hundred elected persons. Whilst, however, these three hundred persons theoretically represented the kingdom, they could not, on a forty shilling franchise, be said to represent the people. We must allow our theorist some latitude of assumption in these predemocratic times.

From this it follows that the king cannot, as in France, change the laws, or enact new ones, or inflict punishments, or impose taxes at his own will and pleasure. He does not even give judgment in person in the courts of justice, though the decisions of the judges are called the king's judgments. The king is entrusted by prerogative with a certain discretion in the matter of pardon, but he cannot by prerogative contravene the laws. He may not even modify laws that are found to be imperfect, without the common assent. Under the English constitution king and Parliament co-operate in legislation, and the government is thus "regal" and "politic." "The sovereign power is limited by political laws." And such restraint is not derogatory to the royal dignity, though English kings have sometimes been impatient of it, and have sought to exercise absolute power. It is in the interest of the king as well as the people. Compare the state of England with that of France. How prosperous the former, how miserable the latter! In England a man is convicted by the evidence of witnesses before a jury; in France the law makes ample use of the inhuman practice of torture to extort confessions of guilt—a practice which our author denounces in the name both of humanity and justice. The contrast in other respects is to the advantage of England, and the secret of this advantage lies in the superior legal and financial administration of the State constitutionally governed. It secures the general welfare, and the general welfare is the true test of good and stable government. The records of Parliament, the testimony of, say, the "Paston Letters," might not bear out Fortescue's contentions as to the general prosperity of the people and the superior administration of justice in England in contrast to other nations. We should have to make extensive reservations in confronting theory with practice, especially in the case of the local courts of justice, which were often at the mercy of the local magnate and his host of armed retainers. The Cade rising a few years before Fortescue wrote, shows that the theory of the general welfare was certainly capable of improved exemplification in England, as elsewhere. The enunciation of the principle nevertheless does credit to our author's enlightenment and public spirit.

The great civil war between the adherents of Lancaster and York tended to dislocate the constitutional government which Fortescue appraises so highly, and a few years after he wrote the "De Laudibus," he attempted to show Edward IV. in his "Governance of England," otherwise called "The Difference between an Absolute and a Limited Monarchy," how to remedy the rampant evils of the time. The change of dynasty made no appreciable difference in his constitutional creed. He was still the warm friend of liberty and the people. The fruit of tyranny is the oppression of the people, as in France, whose king has made himself absolute and taxes his subjects at will. In his eyes a Charles VII. or a Louis XI. is a tyrant, and such tyranny is contrary to both the law of nature and the law of God. Nay, it defeats itself, for it keeps the people poor and miserable, and thus impairs the tyrant's power. "A king's office standeth in two things, one to defend his realm against its outward enemies by the sword, the other to defend his people against inward wrongdoers by justice." The king is the minister of the people, as the pope is the servant of the servants of God. Though his office be the highest temporal office on earth, it is none the less a ministry. He thus sets himself in the "Governance," as in the "De Laudibus" in direct antagonism to the rising tide of absolutism on the Continent. If good and stable government is the chief desideratum in England after the Wars of the Roses, it should still be government broad built on the people's will, as expressed by Parliament at least. More especially should it prove its efficacy in the welfare of the commons. The democratic note of the "Governance" is very pronounced. Fortescue shows a keen sense of the value of the commons to the State, and a warm interest in their welfare. If you impoverish the commons, he reiterates, you expose the kingdom to invasion from without, and rebellion within. You will make of this prosperous realm a second Bohemia, "where the commons for poverty rose upon the nobles and made all their goods to be common." You will, moreover, dry up the fountain of the revenue, and thus paralyse the government. The general prosperity is the best guarantee of both order and justice, the highest honour of which a king can boast. "The greatest surety truly, and also the most honour that may come to a king is that his realm be rich in every estate; for nothing may make his people to arise but lack of goods or lack of justice. But yet, certainly, when they lack goods they will arise, saying they lack justice. Nevertheless, if they be not poor they will never arise unless their prince so leave justice that he give himself altogether to tyranny."

To secure good government for the future our author elaborates a scheme of reform, which shall make the royal administration more effective than it has lately been. He has not lost faith in parliamentary government, but he sees the necessity of placing the helm of the ship of State in stronger hands than those of a Henry VI. "While remaining true to the great constitutional principles which he had previously enunciated," says Mr Plummer, the erudite editor of "The Governance," "he urges the king to avoid the main weaknesses of Lancastrian rule, its unsound finance, its subserviency to aristocratic influence, its lack of 'governance' and justice." The need of these reforms was only too clamant. The power of the lords had risen to a pitch which was incompatible with the general weal. The king was poor; the great nobles were rich. They were in reality petty sovereigns within their vast domains, and their local influence was far stronger than that of the king. They waged private war in pursuit of their ambition or their resentment. They controlled the local administration, they browbeat or bribed juries to give decisions in favour of themselves and their creatures. The fruit of their predominance was rampant lawlessness, scandalous maladministration. The judges were powerless or too corrupt to withstand the local tyrant who had a band of liveried retainers to execute his will. The "Paston Letters," which give such a sinister picture of the abuses incident to this aristocratic predominance, could only have been written in an age of unblushing corruption, unbridled lawlessness. There was ample need of the strong ruler to teach these arrogant, quarrelsome, selfish barons a lesson in subordination to authority. The Star Chamber was an urgent as well as an efficacious reform. The Tudor monarchy was the inevitable outcome of the Wars of the Roses, and the trend of the next hundred years was in reality away from the constitutional principles which Fortescue championed, and with which he sought to combine reform.

Although the fifteenth century witnessed no marked constitutional advance on the fourteenth, it was none the less a century of great changes—social, political, religious, intellectual. In England, as in other lands, it was the century of the dawning Renascence, of the depression of the power of the feudal magnates, and the consolidation of that of the crown, of the beginnings of a new nobility, of the growing prominence of a prosperous middle class, of the depreciation of the power of the Church. Even the evangelical reformation has its root, in England, in the century that witnessed the persecution of the Lollards. It had hardly closed when the new movement which was to quicken the embers of English Lollardism, broke out in France, Germany, Switzerland. These changes made for progress. In England, as in the rising Continental nations, they denote the trend from the mediæval to the modern world. Even the revival of the power of the crown, which seems retrogressive, was a move forward from the anarchy of the Wars of the Roses. The Tudor despotism was in its initial stage the necessary vindication of order, the guarantee of immunity from a repetition of the bloodshed and misery of the reigns of Henry VI., Edward IV., and Richard III. England gained by the repression of feudal anarchy even at the cost of the temporary suppression of liberty. The turbulent, self-seeking magnates who confounded liberty with license had ridden for a fall, and they deserved to fall. If the crown under Henry VII. became strong, it also showed itself effective in the administration of justice, the uprooting of conspiracy, the maintenance of prosperity. The welfare of the nation was for the time being bound up with the strong government of the Tudor Henrys and the Tudor Elizabeth. They were born rulers, or, at least, rulers born for their times. They were strong-willed, yet they understood how to make their will seem identical with that of the nation. They made use of strong men as ministers, but they could discard the strong minister in order to humour the nation or cover a necessary change of tactics. They knew, too, the value of money in government, and taught England's enemies to respect that power of the long purse which has played such a mighty *rôle* in modern English history. Henry VII. and Elizabeth hoarded carefully for purposes of State as well as from motives of avarice, and if Henry VIII. was extravagant, he knew where to find plunder on occasion, as the clergy and the monks experienced to their cost. By their adroitness and their ability they piloted England through the century of stress and storm which followed half a century of civil war and revolution, and from this point of view their despotism was necessary and salutary. In times of transition from anarchy to liberty an interval of strong government is indispensable. A country which has passed through a long period of civil strife, must find its equilibrium before reaction can safely make a new start in political progress. The absolute king was for a time a necessity in the history of the great modern nations. Happily, in the case of England, the personal *régime* was much shorter than in France, Spain, or Germany.

The elements of political liberty were stronger and came earlier to maturity in England than across the Channel. The mediæval constitution had prepared the way for the modern constitution, and when the crisis came in the seventeenth century, under the series of maladroit and unpopular Stuart kings, the political genius of the English people found the remedy for misgovernment ready to its hands.

The long interval of personal rule under the Tudors thus did not paralyse the English parliamentary machine, as the much longer interval of personal rule under the Bourbons did in France. The Tudors continued to govern through Parliament, though they were strong enough to bend Parliament to their will. They professed, while they violated constitutional principles, and took advantage—a mean advantage at times—of the cardinal principle of the responsibility of ministers by making them the scapegoat for unpopular measures. They did not eschew Parliament, as the French kings eschewed the States-General. And thus when the fulness of time came, the English Commons of the seventeenth century were able to take up the work of the English Commons of the fourteenth. All they had to do was to impart new force to the machine and adjust it to the circumstances of the time. The *rôle* of Parliament even under the Tudors, when the Commons form the more influential element, though by no means always a very honourable one, is, therefore, of great prospective importance.

Nor need its servility surprise us at a time when a new nobility, which owed its rise to the crown, was paying for royal favours and distinguishing itself from the proud feudal aristocracy of the fifteenth century, by its abject abasement. It grew rich on the royal generosity in the matter of confiscated ecclesiastical property, and could consequently not afford to be high-spirited or independent. "For the first time almost in our history," says Mr Brewer, "even subordinate offices in the king's household, in his chamber or his kitchen, were the passports to wealth and distinction. Secretaries, chamberlains, lords of the bedchamber, grooms of the closet and the stole supplanted the ancient, proud aristocracy." The Tudors employed new men and cultivated the upper middle class, by whose submission they could play the master. Their ministers in Church and State—men like Wolsey, Cranmer, Cromwell—belonged to this class, which was devoted body and soul to their government. Moreover, the king could manipulate Parliament practically *ad libitum* through the influence which he wielded over the middle-class representatives in the Commons—the borough members. The towns returned two-thirds of the House of Commons, and as they were ruled by their municipal oligarchies, all that was necessary to secure a subservient majority was to manipulate the town oligarchy. The task was certainly not a difficult one, and the efficacy of this kind of manœuvring was proved by the result.

The subservience of this upstart nobility and this rising middle class in Parliament was, indeed, to judge from the action of Parliament, shockingly conspicuous under the eighth Henry. Parliament did almost mechanically the most contradictory things. It showed itself Catholic or Protestant according to the humour of the king. It declared the illegitimacy of the Princess Mary, Henry's daughter by Catherine of Aragon, and, notwithstanding, subsequently declared her capable of the succession. It settled the crown on the children of Queen Anne to the exclusion of Mary in 1534, and two years later annulled her marriage, and therewith its own act, in deference to the behest of the sensual and jealous monarch. It sanctioned the outrageous treason laws of Henry, and revoked them at the accession of Edward VI. It established Protestantism under Edward, disestablished it under Mary, and finally established it again at the accession of Elizabeth. It legislated, in fact, to order, and it did things at the dictation of Henry VIII. which gravely endangered liberty, and proclaimed its own slavery. "To Henry, as to others of his race," says Mr Brewer, "Parliament was nothing better than a court to register the king's decrees, and assume a responsibility for acts, the unpopularity of which he did not care to take upon himself." It indeed vigorously opposed Wolsey's exorbitant demands for a subsidy in 1523, and granted less than half the sum demanded; but it relieved the king by explicit acts on two occasions—in 1529 and again in 1544—from the obligation to repay money borrowed by him; in other words confiscated the claims of the State creditors. It submitted—in 1525 and again in 1545—to benevolences and other arbitrary exactions of the royal commissioners, who threatened and bullied the lieges into compliance with their demands. It passed treason laws, which exposed men to death who could not suborn their religion and their conscience to the king's passions or policy. It condemned men by bill of attainder without hearing them in their defence. It declared that the royal proclamations should have the force of law, and empowered the king to bequeath the kingdom by will to whomsoever he pleased. The age of the strong man seemed dead to the struggles that had produced a Magna Charta, a Model, a Good, or a Merciless Parliament. It rallied round Henry VII., though his administration, if efficient, could not be called popular. It idolised Henry VIII. in the earlier years of his reign at least, though in his reign, as in that of his father, there were risings for redress of grievances to chronicle. "Love for the king is universal," wrote a Venetian observer of Henry VIII., "with all who see him, for his highness doth not seem a person of this world, but descended from heaven." England had become an autocracy as thoroughly as if Parliament had been an unknown institution. Henry VII. had prepared the way by his pursuit of a peace policy, which induced prosperity, his practical turn for the business of government, which was not too scrupulous in the attainment of ends. Henry VIII. was more unscrupulous and masterful than his father. He might have boasted fully a century before Louis XIV. that he was the State. He enforced his will both on Church and State as potentially as if he had been king and Parliament in one. Parliament thus went a long way in abrogating its own rights, and placing the liberties and rights of the nation at the feet of an autocratic potentate and his masterful ministers. It certainly could not have continued indefinitely to risk the experiment of humouring a despotic monarch like Henry VIII. without jeopardising its own existence. A succession of kings of the stamp of the eighth Henry, and of Parliaments like those which lent themselves as his servile tools, would have reduced England to the level of France, would have enabled the monarch to dispense with Parliament altogether.

Happily the Tudor monarchs did not go the length of ignoring Parliament, as their Valois contemporaries ignored the States-General. It continued to play an active, though too often a sorry part in legislation, to preserve parliamentary traditions, to maintain at least the form of parliamentary institutions, against the day when the reaction from autocracy should renew the consciousness of its rights and inspire it with the belligerent spirit to vindicate them. Moreover, Parliament, in its subservence to the Tudor autocracy, did not always represent the spirit of the nation. It certainly did not represent the poor man on whom taxation pressed hard, who had social grievances to redress, and who resented the drastic ecclesiastical policy of his rulers. In 1497 the men of Cornwall rose under Thomas Flammock and Michael Joseph to resent the oppressive taxation of Henry VII. In 1536 the men of the northern counties sprang to arms to resist the ecclesiastical policy of Henry VIII., and enforce the redress of social grievances. Under Somerset's *régime* the rising was repeated, from religious or social motives, in the eastern counties and in Cornwall. There were, too, even under the strong hand of Henry VIII., forces at work in the nation which tended to the ultimate undoing of autocratic government—forces which sprang from the revival of learning and the reformation of religion—and, in fostering these great movements, the Tudor sovereigns were unconsciously laying the axe to the root of the system of personal government. The new culture meant the spread of education, the quickening of the individual mind, the growth of inquiry and criticism, and these things in the long run made for political as well as intellectual progress. In the reign of Henry VIII. himself we have a remarkable example in Sir Thomas More of the political aspirations of the English humanist. In a country in which political liberty could already boast of so many champions in the arena of practical politics in bygone centuries, it was only natural that the intellectual awakening should make its influence felt on English political thought. From Fortescue onwards, through Sir Thomas More, Sir Thomas Smith, and Hooker, there is a continuity of testimony against arbitrary government in the English publicists of the higher type, and the tradition of antagonism to unconstitutional government which lives in their works contributed to nurture the spirit of political liberty throughout the Tudor period.

SOURCES. — Fortescue, De Laudibus Legum Angliæ, Latin text and translation by Amos (1825), and, The Governance of England, otherwise called The Difference between an Absolute and a Limited Monarchy, edited by Plummer (1885); Statutes of the Realm; Stubbs, Constitutional History, iii. (1878); Gairdner, The Paston Letters (1874-75);

Sources of Chapter XV.

Calendar of State Papers, Henry VIII., edited by Brewer (1862-70); Brewer, Reign of Henry VIII., edited by Gairdner (1884); Gairdner, York and Lancaster, in Epochs of Modern History, and Life of Henry VII., in Statesman Series (1889); Pollard, Henry VIII. (1903); Hallam, Constitutional History of England from the Accession of Henry VII.

CHAPTER XVI.

Constitutional and Social Progress in Mediæval Scotland.

In Roman times Britain north of the Forth was inhabited by a number of tribes, two of which gave their names to the confederacies formed to attack or resist the Roman invaders. In the days of Columba this twofold division, though under different names, still appears in the Northern and Southern Picts, who are found in possession of this northern region, with the exception of Dalriada (Argyleshire), which was colonised by Scottish settlers from Ireland. According to Dio the government of the tribe in the third century was "democratic," not monarchic. Each tribe apparently governed itself under its chief, and like the Teutonic peoples on the other side of the North Sea, they only elected a common leader—the later Toshach, corresponding to the Heretoga of the Germans—in time of war. There was no hereditary sovereign of the whole land, as in later times, for Galgacus seems to have been merely the war leader of the occasion. When the temporary war leader succeeded in rendering his office permanent, when the Toshach of some critical emergency became the king, as he seems to have become before Columba's day, the lesser confederacies of Northern and Southern Picts were combined into an elective monarchy. While this monarchy tended, further, to become hereditary within the royal family, the succession was not necessarily limited to the nearest heir, who, as among the Welsh Celts, might be passed over on grounds of expediency, and who, among the Picts—succession being through the mother—was not the eldest son, but the brother, or the sister's son of the deceased king.

The dim period of Scottish history, preceding the amalgamation of the Picts with the Scots of Dalriada, boasts a long list of these nebulous kings. Some of them are historic in the sense that they are known to have ruled in the flesh. Others are purely legendary, and very probably fabulous, the offspring of the fancy of patriotic chroniclers, eager to invest Scottish history with a national antiquity that would dumfounder the Saxon, Danish, or Norman intruder. The best authenticated of the series are but shadowy rulers at most; their authority was not greater than what their swords could gain for them over the subordinate chiefs who paid them tribute, entertained them on their journeys, and followed them to the fray. Further their jurisdiction probably did not extend. The politics of the day seem to have been confined mainly to war—war within, and war without—war with some rebellious Mormaer, or provincial governor, war with Strathclyde Britons, or Dalriadic Scots, with Bernician Angles, or Norse invaders. Bede and Adamnan cast but an occasional side-light on the doings of these shadowy potentates, before the accession of Kenneth MacAlpin united Pict and Scot under one dynasty. What grains of political history may be gleaned from the chaff of legend do not concern us further. The important point for us to note is that out of these misty ages a central monarchy north of the Forth had displaced the third century "democracy" of Dio.

The establishment of the Scoto-Pictish monarchy north of the Forth, in the ninth century, was by no means contemporary with the formation of a homogeneous nation in what came to be afterwards known as Scotland. It is difficult to speak of a Scottish people till after Bannockburn, and even after Bannockburn there was for long a deep rift between Highlander and Lowlander. The Anglo-Saxon stamped his nationality on England soon after the Conquest. With the exception of Wales, Cumberland, and Cornwall, the inhabitants may be described as the English people even before the petty Anglo-Saxon kingdoms became merged into one State. The invaders were all of the same race and language, were one in institutions and character, and held the natives, whom they did not succeed in exterminating, in subjection. Very different was it in that northern part of Britain, afterwards known as Scotland. Here the Teutonic invader did not, in anything like the same degree, displace the native Celt. For long he only occupied the south-eastern corner of the land, between the Tweed and the Forth. West of him in Strathclyde were Brythonic Celts; south-west, the Picts of Galloway; north-west, the Scots, or Goidelic Celts; north, Picts again; while far away in Caithness and the Hebrides were Norsemen. These Picts may be taken as Celts, with an admixture of an earlier non-Celtic people, who added to the racial variety of the population. Until these varied racial elements became so far fused as to own, through conquest or otherwise, allegiance to one central authority, the Scottish kingdom in the larger sense did not exist, and even then "the Scottish people" was still in the womb of the future. It was not till the reign of Malcolm II. (1005-1034), the last of the direct line of Kenneth MacAlpin, the stout warrior who, by the victory of Carham, won Saxon Lothian for the northern kingdom, and virtually incorporated Strathclyde, that the Scoto-Pictish crown appears as the emblem of substantial authority. This Malcolm evidently had a stronger grip than any of his predecessors on the land which he ruled through his dependent Mormaers or provincial governors, and his dependent thanes or barons, who held their estates of him, and both of whom he held under the curb for thirty years. He kept his court in royal state at Scone, and on its moothill gathered not merely, as of yore, the virtually independent chiefs of Scoto-Pictland, but the dependants of the monarch to deliberate on affairs of State. Mr Robertson, at all events, whose opinion must still carry weight with every student of this period of Scottish history, sees in Malcolm II. the germ of the feudal king, the author of changes in the direction of feudalism, "which undoubtedly seem to point to his reign as the era of a certain advance towards the consolidation of the royal authority."

It is usual to regard the Anglic settlers of Lothian as freemen who enslaved the conquered Celtic population. As we have seen, in reference to the Saxon settlers farther south, the evidence yielded by the more recent study of Anglo-Saxon land tenure seems to contradict this theory. In the region between the Forth and the Tweed, the Anglian settlers were apparently not all freemen who settled down in free village communities. Here, as in the south, the village community was more probably, in many cases, a community of serfs living

on the manor of a lord, such as the Cartulary of Kelso
Abbey reveals to us in the thirteenth century, and bound to
render him services, according to the size of the individual
holding. Among such serfs Anglo-Saxon names occur, and
the suggested explanation that these names were probably
adopted by men of Celtic descent is very far-fetched. Nor
does it obviate the difficulty to assume that in course of time
many of the Anglo-Saxon freemen lapsed into villeins. Mr
Seebohm, on the contrary, adduces evidence to show that the
opposite process was the rule. The original villeins gradually
—very gradually, it would appear—rose to the rank of the
freemen. The facts he brings forward in support of his theory
should at least make us more diffident in assuming that the
Teutonic invader north of the Tweed was necessarily a freeman and the conquered Celt necessarily a serf. The fact is
that the social organisation of Teuton and Celt was more or
less identical. Among the Celts, as among the Teutons, in
primitive times, the land belonged to the people, not to the
individual. Among both Celts and Teutons, however, the
tendency was towards individual possession, the creation of a
class of landowners, and by the period of the Anglo-Saxon
invasion, common ownership would seem to have largely given
place, among the invaders, to the manorial system of tenure.
The freemen settled down as landowners, and their estates
or manors were cultivated by their dependants, in part for the
use of their lord, in part for their own use. These servile
dependants held a certain number of acres in return for service
on the lord's demesne, or portion reserved for his own use, and
for dues in money and kind. They were bound to the soil,
and were, as we have seen, subject to other restrictions of
their liberty. There were, moreover, slaves as well as villeins
in these so-called free communities of Mr Freeman's and Mr
Green's fancy, and in certain regions, where the conquered
population was numerous, slavery rather than villenage was
the rule. Such is the theory in support of which Mr Seebohm
adduces plausible arguments from a study backwards of the
tenure of land in mediæval and early England.

Let us cross the Forth from Saxonland (the Saxonia or
Lothian of the chroniclers) into Celtland. What do we find?
Applying, with Mr Skene, who traces the connection, the

condition of things prevailing in Goidelic or Gaelic Ireland to Goidelic or Gaelic Scotland, we find essentially the same agrarian and social features in Dalriada, and by inference in Pictland. The land belonged, indeed, theoretically to the tribe, but practically a large portion of it was held by a class of landowners, or " Flaith," who had in the course of time succeeded in rendering the portions of the tribal land, which they cultivated or grazed, their hereditary property. The landless tribesmen, such as " the broken men " of other tribes, or the conquered population of an earlier time, became, on the other hand, the tenants of these " Flaith," or Celtic lords of the manor, and rendered rent in kind or money for their holdings. The same process would seem to have been exemplified in Gaul, where in the age of Cæsar, there was a large class of serfs (*servi*) dependent on a limited class of *equites*, who had succeeded in gaining possession of the soil and in absorbing political rights. In Celtland, as in Saxonland, then, we find the same social distinction between lord and serf based on the tenure of land, while the distinction is capable of minor gradations according to the wealth of the landowner on the one hand, and the greater or lesser servile burdens of the tenant on the other. We may call the one a tribal, the other a manorial system. Practically the system was the same. In Wales, for instance, where Mr Seebohm does not admit the manorial system or the village community—whether free or servile—there is the same distinction between the free tribesmen, who own the land, and the other inhabitants (*aillts* and *taeogs*) who held land on more or less servile terms. And what holds of Wales holds of that part of Celtic North Britain known as Strathclyde, whose population was composed of Brythonic or Welsh Celts.

The identity of the social organisation of Celt and Saxon appears in another important particular. The Anglo-Saxon had his *wergeld*, his personal value in case of murder; the Celt had his " honour price " (*enéchlann*), which, as in the case of the former, varied according to rank.

Politically, too, the Teuton deviated far less from the Celt than is usually assumed by German, English, and most Scottish historians. The resemblance between the political institutions of Gauls and Germans is in truth certified by as ancient an authority as Strabo. According to Strabo, "Gauls and Germans resemble each other both physically and politically. They live the same kind of life, and have the same institutions." The fact has been insisted on by a modern French writer, whose erudition entitles his opinion to deferential consideration. "There is not a single trait of the social and political state of the ancient Germans," says M. de Coulanges, "which we do not discover among the Gauls. The institutions and domestic life of the Germans, their habits and their beliefs, their virtues and their vices, were those of all the nations of Europe." And the resemblance which strikes the ancient and the modern writer in the political institutions of Gaul and Germany holds in reference to those of Celt and Saxon in North Britain. The Anglo-Saxons at the time of the invasion, unlike most other people of Teutonic race, had no kings. They followed the tribal leaders whom they had elected as generals of their war bands. Similarly, the Celtic tribes of the days of Galgacus confederated under a war leader to resist the Roman advance; they owned no allegiance to an hereditary king. In a couple of generations the Anglo-Saxon king appears at the head of the petty States formed by the invaders, and the mutual wars of these kings make up much of Anglo-Saxon history until one of them — whether Northumbrian, Mercian, or West Saxon — predominates for the time being over the others, and the whole people coalesces under this supreme monarch. The same phenomenon appears in North Britain, where the North and South Picts are ultimately found united under one king and fighting for predominance with the kings of Dalriada, Strathclyde, or Northumbria, until the whole land, north of the Tweed and the Solway, is unified under the later kings of the Scoto-Pictish dynasty. Further, these kings both north and south of the Tweed are theoretically, and often practically, elective, within the limit of the royal stock at least, though for long the Pictish peculiarity of succession through the mother prevailed in Celtland. In regard to the evolution of the kingship, then, the Anglo-Saxon and the northern Celt move on parallel lines. Nor does there seem to be any radical difference in regard to the royal jurisdiction. The Anglo-Saxon king was far from being an absolute potentate, and the authority of the Scoto-Pictish king was, as we have seen, limited enough. An Eadwine or an Alfred governed in co-operation with the Witenagemot, or assembly of the magnates of the realm; a Constantine or a Malcolm even so at the moothill of Scone, whither the chief men of Alba or Scotia came at the royal summons to deliberate in council. The Anglo-Saxon king had his ealdormen and his shire reeves, to whom he entrusted the military, fiscal, and judicial administration of the shires. The Scoto-Pictish king had his Mormaers or governors of the seven provinces (the later earls), his Maers and Toisechs (the later thanes), who administered the smaller subdivisions of the kingdom. The Scottish version of Glanville's treatise on the Laws of England, known as the "Regiam Majestatem," translates in fact the *prepositus* of the hundred by the words "vicecomitatus, vel le Toshederach," and thus equates the Toisech or Toshach with the head of an English county. We may, if we follow Sir Henry Maine in his study of the Brehon Laws, even descry in Celtic institutions north of the Forth, as in Ireland, the parallel of the Teutonic mark or village community, while the hundred and the shire moots of the Anglo-Saxon landowners may be paralleled by the district and provincial assemblies of the Celt, held perhaps within those circles of standing stones which remain as the memorials of forgotten institutions.

Where, then, is the radical difference between the political organisation of Saxons and Celts which most English and Scottish historians have been wont to assume? Nowhere, except perhaps in matters of detail. The two developed on parallel lines, and the only difference lies in the fact that the Anglo-Saxon line was more advanced in some respects than the Celtic. The State was more consolidated under the Anglo-Saxon than under the Celtic king, for the tribe continued to assert its individuality among the Celts longer than among the Saxons. Anarchy is accordingly assumed to be an inherent mark of Celtic political institutions; order and consolidation of those of the Anglo-Saxons. But even in this particular our complacent historians, prone to assumption, do not always look facts in the face, in their biassed generalisations. Was there, then, no anarchy under the Anglo-Saxon monarchs, and must we look to Ireland, Wales, and Scotland only for political disorder, a weak central authority? On the contrary, there seems often enough little difference, even in this respect, between the state of things prevailing in Saxonland and the state of things prevailing in Pictland. The chronicles of both are full of broil, war, and murder, and there were probably as many kings murdered or deposed, as many civil wars, as much maladministration in the former as in the latter. In both there is discernible the same tendency towards feudalism, towards the domination of the class at the expense of the mass, the tendency that bespeaks the growing potency of the greed and the sword of the strong man against the weak. Where then, I ask again, is, in matters essential, the difference, emphasised by the historians, between the order of things Celtic and Saxon? What ground for ascribing, as the historians, as a matter of course, do, the merit of the political development of the Scottish people to the Anglo-Saxon fraction of it? The political development of the Scottish people would in all probability have been much the same, though it would perhaps have come later, had neither Saxon nor Norman invader penetrated north of the Tweed. Much is made of the influence of Queen Margaret, the English wife of Malcolm Canmore, who was himself of mixed Saxon and Celtic blood, but Margaret's influence was purely social and religious. It affected the Church rather than the State, society rather than politics. The essentials of political development were all there already, and in the long run we should have had a Scottish parliament, and Scottish towns under a municipal *régime*, in the Celtic sense of the term Scottish, without the non-Celtic infusion to which it is customary to ascribe all manner of benefits in the political making of the Scottish people. But the horrible anarchy of Pictland, exclaim the historians! And what of the horrible anarchy of Saxonland? But if not of Pictland, then of Ireland? Perhaps we had better not ask, in present circumstances, what Ireland might have become but for Anglo-Norman invasions.

At the same time, every impartial historian, even if he recoils from the cool superiority of conventional assumption in this matter, will admit that the Anglo-Norman infusion into the Celtic population of North Britain was an advantage in itself. It hastened the political development of Scotland. It brought it into touch with a more advanced civilisation. It lent to the Celtic element a staying power in which the more volatile and imaginative Celt is wanting. The blend was good, but it is to the blend and not to the alien infusion only that we owe modern Scotland. In view of this fact, a little less of the "guid conceit" of themselves, characteristic of the Anglo-Saxon and other Teutonic peoples, and their historians, is a desideratum at present. Sir Henry Maine evidently felt this when he wrote: "Many, perhaps most, of the differences in kind alleged to exist between Aryan sub-races are really differences merely in degree of development. It is to be hoped that contemporary thought will before long make an effort to emancipate itself from those habits of levity in adopting theories of race which it seems to have contracted. Many of these theories appear to have little merit, except the facility which they give for building on them inferences tremendously out of proportion to the mental labour which they cost the builder."

Scotland, like England, developed into a feudal kingdom, and though the feudal tendency is perceptible among the Scottish Celts, the feudal system in its maturity came to Scotland, as to England, from Normandy. In Scotland, too, as in England, it tended towards the consolidation of the State, except in the Highlands, where its growth was retarded by analogous local customs, which would not easily bend to the written law and the central authority of the king. Elsewhere the king gradually became, by a legal fiction, theoretically at least, the supreme landowner, of whom all other landowners held by charter, directly or indirectly. We are not to suppose, however, that David I. or his immediate successors dispossessed the old proprietors of Celtic race, though a large portion of land must have been granted, at somebody's expense, probably not always at the king's, to the Norman and Anglo-Norman adventurers who sought refuge and fortune in Scotland. They appear to have confirmed their proprietary rights by charter, and thus transformed the old social hierarchy into a feudal one.

The introduction of the feudal land tenure accentuated in Scotland, as elsewhere, the difference between the freeholder, the holder by charter, and the non-freeholder, who might be a free tenant, but was usually a serf of various degree of bondage (*nativus*, Scottish neyf, *cottarii*, cotters, *husbandi*, husbandmen). It did not, indeed, create the distinction between freeman and serf, for the distinction existed, as we have seen, from early times in both Celt and Saxonland. But it systematised the rank of the upper classes, and in stereotyping by charter these social distinctions, deepened the gulf between free and non-free. On one side of the gulf stood, according to a statute of Alexander II., "all knights, sons of knights, or holders of any portion of a knight's fee, and all who held their lands by free service or by *fie-de-hauberc*, hereditarily and by charter," who were alone accounted of free and gentle birth. On the other, "the churl born tenant of land, the man of ignoble birth, and all who had neither free tenement nor free parentage." Feudalism, then, in Scotland, as in England and on the Continent, gave a recognised status and rights to the upper classes; it did nothing for the lower except to confirm their inferiority and their bondage. The bondsman owed his emancipation, not so much to the philanthropic sentiments of Church or society, as to the economic factors which in Scotland, as elsewhere, substituted a money rent for service, and to the exigencies of the War of Independence, which afforded him the opportunity of earning his freedom on the field of battle. The emancipation was probably not complete before the fifteenth century in the Lowlands, and presumably later in the Highlands, though, according to Mr Cosmo Innes, "the last claim of 'neyfship' or serfdom proved in a Scotch court was in 1364." Happily there was one door of escape for him, even in the twelfth century, which feudalism could not shut. He could run away to a neighbouring town and acquire freedom by a full year's residence and the purchase of a burgage tenement. The feudal king was the foster-father of the Scottish burgh, and the Scottish burgh was, comparatively speaking at least, an oasis of freedom in the desert of feudal privilege. It doubtless contained an unfree element, like the country around it, and like all towns in mediæval times, but it was a centre of activity, and its chartered privileges were the recognition of the rights of work, of the industry of merchant and craftsman.

VOL I.   Z

The chartered community, the municipality, was in Scotland, as elsewhere, the focus of progress, though here, too, progress was shackled by the thralls of burgher privilege and monopoly.

These burgh communities did not owe their existence to David I., or his immediate predecessors and successors. The origin of town life in Scotland goes back into Celtic times. "The oldest burgh charters are," according to Mr Cosmo Innes, "only of the reign of William the Lion (1165-1214), but like the early English charters they point plainly to a previous burghal organisation." The ecclesiastical charters of David I. (1124-1153), for instance, already contain references to "the burghs of Dunfermline, Haddington, Perth, Stirling, Edinburgh, Elgin." The Scottish town community did not spring into existence with the charter, though Mr Robertson invests it with merely an Anglo-Norman origin. William the Lion was not the creator, but the patron of the Scottish burgh, which, as in England and elsewhere, had grown up around the king's castle, or the bishop's seat, or the "keep" of some great landowner, or the monastic foundations of Columba and other Christian missionaries, perhaps even of Ninian and Kentigern, and had attained a certain measure of self-government. Nor was there in Scotland a struggle for emancipation with the feudal superior, as in France and Germany. Not only was the king favourable to their development; he found zealous imitators in the bishops and in some of the great landowners, who gave chartered rights to the burghs that had sprung up around some cathedral church or baronial "keep" (burghs of Regality and Barony). Another characteristic of the mediæval Scottish burghs, which they shared, however, with the free imperial cities of Germany, was their union in groups for commercial and political purposes. Such a union was the Hansa of the northern burghs to which David I. and William the Lion accorded special privileges. More famous was the union of the four burghs of the south—usually Edinburgh, Stirling, Roxburgh, and Berwick—with their own court, which was invested with large powers and met under the presidency of the king's chamberlain. In this union we may see the germ of the Convention of Royal Burghs, and its customary laws, which were confirmed by David I. in the first half of the twelfth century, form, in the opinion of Mr Innes, the oldest extant municipal code, though a recent writer, Sir A. C. Laurie, it is only right to say, does not consider them "to be genuine productions" of David's reign. Their adoption by the other Scottish burghs adds to their value as a mirror of Scottish municipal organisation at a period when, in other countries, we are left to grope our way to generalisation from individual charters. While the Scottish charters tell us nothing very definite on this point, the burgh laws inform us that the burgh was governed by magistrates (*præpositi*— aldirman and bailyeis in the Scottish translation), "who shall be elected by the common council of the good men of the town, shall swear fealty to the king and the burgesses, shall conserve its customs, and shall do justice according to the constitution, council, and judgment of the said good men." The municipal organisation is still more definitely outlined in the "Laws of the Gild," enacted a century later (1249) for the town of Berwick, and serving as the model for all other Scottish gilds. "We ordain by common consent that the community of Berwick shall be governed by twenty-four good men, of the better, more discreet, and trustworthy of that burgh, thereto chosen, together with the mayor and four bailies. Item, we ordain that the mayor and bailies shall be chosen at the sight and by the consideration of the whole community. And if any controversy be on the election of the mayor and bailies, then their election shall be made by the oath of twenty-four good men of the said burgh, elected to choose one person to rule the said community."

The system of civic government thus outlined is that of a community administering its own affairs through its elected officials—the alderman and bailies of the Scottish translation— and the laws which they were elected to administer embrace the whole range of a rude civic life. The possession of a rood of land, for which he pays a rent of fivepence to the king or other superior, constitutes a burgher, and each burgher was bound to be present at the fortnightly moot or court. The merchant plays, of course, an important *rôle* in the town organisation, and the buying, selling, making of articles are subject to minute regulations. The merchant gild appears as a privileged corporation to which no dyer, butcher, or tanner who worked with his own hands is admitted, and which possessed a monopoly of trade within the burgh and the trading district attached to it. The common craftsman was evidently as yet in a semi-servile condition, for if "any keemster (wool comber) leaves the burgh to dwell with upland men, while having sufficient work to occupy him within such burgh, he ought to be taken and imprisoned." It was not till the fourteenth and fifteenth centuries that the Scottish craftsman, like his English and Continental brethren, succeeded in fighting his way to a share in municipal rights. While in Scotland, as elsewhere, the gild was originally a trading association, and the right of electing the town council was evidently exercised by every burgher who possessed a rood of land, the gild members gradually absorbed the civic administration and developed all the pretentious pride and tyranny of local privilege and monopoly. Its petty magnates displayed a prodigious dignity on £10 a year, and one of the old gild laws, enacted in 1249, informs us that it was essential to their dignity to possess a "decent" horse under penalty of a fine. "We ordain that any burgess having in goods ten pounds shall have in his stable a seemly horse (*equum decentem*) worth at least forty shillings. And if he be deprived of his horse by any chance, death, sale, gift, or in any other manner, he shall within forty days provide another. If not, he shall be fined eight shillings to the gild." It was, as we have seen, derogatory to his dignity to work with his own hands, and it was against this petty spirit of purse pride and pretension that the craftsmen arrayed themselves in their craft gilds and fought for the recognition of the rights of labour against the usurpation of capital. The struggle ended in a compromise, which shows that the Scottish craftsmen had to be content with a much smaller share of municipal power than that which some of their brethren in the German and Netherland towns extorted from the municipal oligarchy. Each craft gild was empowered by Act of Parliament in 1469 to elect a member, who in turn had a voice in the election of the town council along with the outgoing councillors. "The choosing of the new officers (shall) be in this wise, that is to say, that the old council of the town shall choose the new council in such number as accords to the town—alderman, bailies, dean of gild, and other officers—

and that each craft shall choose a person of the same craft that shall have voice in the said election of the officers." With this modest recognition of its claims, the democracy had to be content for many a long day.

It would, however, be shortsighted to limit the influence of the people to its formal representation in town council or even Parliament. There are times when the popular will expresses itself in some great wave of popular conviction which tells, consciously or unconsciously, on the destiny of the country. Such an influence one may clearly discern in some of the great crises of Scottish history, though the masses might have no direct or adequate representation to voice their convictions. The history of a nation is shaped sometimes as much by its spirit as by its institutions. In the War of Independence, in the struggle of the Reformation, for instance, it is public spirit rather than constitutional action that tells, and in this sense we may subscribe to the panegyric of the Scottish burghs prefaced by the editor to their "Ancient Laws and Customs." " In the homely burghs of Scotland we may find the first spring of that public spirit—the voice of the people—which in the worst of times, when the crown and the law were powerless, and the feudal aristocracy altogether selfish in its views, supported the patriotic leaders, Wallace and Bruce, in their desperate struggle, and sent down that tide of native feeling which animated Burns and Scott."

The Scottish Parliament was not, strictly speaking, the substitute of the older Celtic assembly on the moothill of Scone. It developed directly out of the "court" of the feudal king—the court to which the immediate vassals of the crown were summoned. Feudalism gave a more definite organisation to the social hierarchy, but it merely deepened tendencies that existed already, and the legislative court of the feudal king only differs in form from the assembly of the older Celtic monarch. In both, legislation is the result of deliberation with the chief landowners, whether secular or clerical, the only difference being that the landowner in the thirteenth century is a vassal in the full feudal sense, a large freeholder by charter of the crown. In this sense, we may regard the later Parliament as essentially, though not formally, the old assembly under changed conditions of land tenure. The feudal king, though exercising a more concentrated authority, was hardly more powerful than his Celtic predecessor. In all important acts his authority was limited by the court of magnates, and in theory, at least, we find him at times legislating by the authority of the whole community of the realm. We might, in fact, if we did not know better, mistake a court or council of William the Lion for an ancient democratic assembly. These councils profess, at any rate, more than once to be national, even democratic. Such and such a statute in the reign of, say, William the Lion, is enacted by the advice and with the consent of the magnates *and the whole community of the realm*. When, however, we turn to the record of those present for an explanation of this democratic assembly, we find the meeting to consist of, say, one bishop, two earls, one prior, the Justiciar of Lothian, the High Steward, and one other baron—eight in all, including the king. " The whole community of the realm" is, therefore, evidently a mere formula, which points to the custom of an earlier time—a custom which may be predicated of Celtic as well as Teutonic practice. The testimony of an English chronicler, John of Hexham, may not be conclusive on such a point, but it may be adduced as written evidence that the tradition of the election of the king by the popular assembly still lived in Celtland, from which it filtered to the chronicler of Hexham. " The whole people of the land," says he, in reference to the accession of Malcolm IV. in succession to David I., "constituted Malcolm King of Scotland, *in accordance with the custom of that nation*." " The whole people" (*omnis populus terræ*), who met on the moothill of Scone, or elsewhere, in the twelfth century, is, of course, as empty a phrase as "the whole community" (*tota communitas*) of the clerk of the " national " assembly in William the Lion's time. As in the case of the Merovingian and the Carolingian assemblies, its only significance lies in the reference to a hoary tradition. Mr Cosmo Innes, one of the least culpable of Scottish historians in the matter of sins of omission against the Celtic race, saw the incongruity of the phrase with the reality. He did not see its significance as bearing on Celtic as well as Saxon custom. Like most of the Lowland Scottish historians who write on these matters, he calmly assumes that the tradition refers to the Teutonic practice of election by the people. "Some memory perhaps remained of the old Saxon, and, indeed, general Teutonic principle, which looked to the assembly of the whole nation as the source of all law and power." Why not Celtic, as well as Teutonic? Even John of Hexham, who explicitly refers to a Scottish (*apud Scotiam*), not a Saxon custom, might have afforded him a hint of the desirability of looking further afield for precedent than to the eternal Teutonic "source of all law and power." He might not, as he confesses, have known Gaelic. He did know mediæval Latin, and even from mediæval Latin he might have discovered that ancient democracy was not the sole possession of "old Saxon or general Teutonic principle."

Democratic phraseology, notwithstanding, it is not until the end of the thirteenth century that Parliament in Scotland, as in England, may be regarded as actively representing, if not the whole community, at least the three Estates of the realm. During the previous century, its evolution from the Curia Regis, the king's court, appears in progress. The court which William the Lion held at Perth in 1166 was, for instance, composed of "his bishops and good men" (*probi homines*). Twenty-two years later there was present, in addition to bishops, earls, and barons, "an infinite multitude of his men." These assemblies recur in the reigns of the second and third Alexanders, and in the stormy period of John Baliol, William Wallace, and Robert Bruce, the name of Parliament is applied to them in contemporary records. In some of these early parliamentary assemblies representatives of the burghs seem to have appeared along with the nobles, clergy, and other freeholders who held directly of the crown. There can be no doubt at any rate as to their presence in the Parliament held by Robert Bruce at Cambuskenneth on the 15th July 1326, in which "the earls, barons, burgesses, and all other freeholders" stand out as a definitely constituted body with recognised rights. Among these is the right to grant or refuse a subsidy. The king asks, the Parliament grants, a tenth-penny of all rents, but it adduces grievances, stipulates conditions. The intolerable exactions arising from a long war, and assessed without its sanction, must cease. The king shall levy no other "collectæ," and shall lessen the legal dues accruing to the crown (*prisæ et cariagia*). The grant is made for life but it shall be null if the king allows any remissions. With the right to control taxation is combined the right to legislate, as the bulky volumes of the Acts of the Parliament of Scotland show.

The original principles of the Scottish constitution are thus identical with the English. The nation is represented by the Three Estates of clergy, barons, burgesses, and other freeholders (though the clergy were evidently not present at Cambuskenneth), and these Estates control taxation, stipulate the reform of abuses, make the laws. As in England, too, the Estates sought to extend their rights during the troubled period of the fourteenth century. The continuation of the war with England, the capture of David II., the antagonism to his contemptible person, and his unpatriotic union policy roused the assertive spirit in the Scottish Parliament. It flatly refused to agree to the union proposal of Edward III., which David had the hardihood to offer for its acceptance at Scone in March 1364. To this unpatriotic plan it curtly and decisively replied that "they would in no wise concede, or assent to, the wishes of the King of England and his council in this matter. They would have no Englishman to rule over them in preference to the lawful heir." It persisted in this firm attitude for years, in spite of Edward's importunities and threats and David's weakly abetment òf them, and risked even the renewal of war in its staunch resistance to the will of both kings. "Intolerable and impossible," was its final retort at Scone in 1368. We find it, too, during the same period encroaching on the prerogative of the crown in matters of coinage and currency, directing the administration of justice, calling the royal officials to account, though they held their offices by hereditary right, forbidding the alienation of the crown lands or the conferring of privileges prejudicial to the crown revenue, requiring the king to renew his coronation oath to eschew such alienations, controlling the royal expenditure, and debarring any justiciar, sheriff, or other royal official from executing any royal warrant "against the statutes and common form of law."

All this gave promise of the development of parliamentary power in Scotland, equal to that of the English Parliament. The promise was not fulfilled, unfortunately. With the exception of the revolutionary period of the reign of Charles I., and to some extent the age of the Reformation, the Scottish Parliament did not attain the power, nor did it play the *rôle* of the English Parliament in the government of the country, and its history is, therefore, by no means so dramatic, so fruitful in constitutional progress, as that of the more famous assembly at Westminster. For this result it had itself, not the forcible character of its kings, to blame. The War of Independence was indeed succeeded by a period of intense patriotic and parliamentary effort, during which Scotland continued to maintain its integrity against the southern usurper, in spite of repeated defeat and the incapacity of Bruce's more immediate successors. Anarchy and civil war blasted, however, the germs of this incipient political development for many a long year. Moreover, the members of the Scottish Parliament fell into the bad habit of shirking their duties. The expense and inconvenience of a journey to the capital disposed the smaller freeholders, who did not yet enjoy the benefit of the English device of attending by representative, to acquiesce, in 1367, and again in 1369, and on sundry later occasions, in the devolution of the judicial and legislative business on two committees. From these committees were gradually evolved the Court of Session or College of Justice—the supreme law court of Scotland—and the Lords of the Articles, whose function it was to draw up the bills to be voted by Parliament. Legislation was thus virtually handed over to a small section of members, and if the government, as frequently happened, succeeded in influencing the election of the Lords of the Articles, the Parliament became a mere voting machine of such measures as the government for the time being thought fit to entrust to it. Though James I. attempted in 1428 to redress the grievances of the smaller freeholders by introducing a system of representation, it was not till the latter half of the sixteenth century that it was successfully put in operation.

"The Parliament," says Mr Cosmo Innes, our Scottish constitutional historian, "in theory sat all together—the Three Estates in one chamber. But whatever the theory, it is certain that from the time of David II. till the Great Rebellion in England" (it would have been more correct to add, the

National Covenant), "had roused some parliamentary feeling in Scotland, our Parliament really cannot be said to have sat at all. It assembled only to adjourn, and met again finally only to receive and adopt the reports of its committees. During all these centuries—from the fourteenth to the beginning of the seventeenth century—I am not aware that an article—as we should now say, a bill—was brought in and discussed, opposed, supported, voted upon in Parliament—I mean in open and plain Parliament."

Power, when the throne was weak, as it so often was during the reign of the second and third Roberts and the first three Jameses, was monopolised by the leaders of aristocratic faction, who entered into regular alliances for personal and political purposes. In these wild times Parliament might enact in the name of the king; it was, as a rule, powerless to enforce or control, and was often the mere plaything of faction. The great lords were formidable both in the number of their retainers, and the powers with which their heritable jurisdictions invested them, and they were not slow to make use of both for political ends. The Scottish feudal magnate was, in virtue of these jurisdictions, a far more powerful individual than his English equal in title. To murder or carry off the king, and thus dictate the policy to be followed for the time being, was the policy of a Douglas, a Home, an Arran, and as the policy was dominated by the self-seeking spirit of the successful faction, the country had to pay a terrible price on such occasions in confiscation, bloodshed, anarchy, civil war, for this rough and lawless species of party government. It was the sword rather than the debate that made or unmade laws in Scotland. Yet this turbulent factious spirit, if it kept alive a fierce insubordination, prevented the establishment of a royal despotism that might easily have ridden roughshod over so invertebrate an assembly as that of the Three Estates. As we shall see later, royal despotism, when it did come, found stern, stubborn antagonists in the descendants of the men who were so accommodating in regard to their parliamentary rights. Moreover, a people which had fought so stubbornly for its independence could never become a people of slaves to an absolute king.

The misery of the people under this *régime* of savage fist-law was terrible enough, as both official records and chroniclers prove. The complaints and enactments of Parliament reveal the excesses which it was impotent to repress. The local despot and brigand, disguised under the name of baron, acts in defiance of crown and law, quarrelling, fighting, slaughtering, burning, robbing, ejecting his tenants, without restraint, according to his savage instincts. Truly, if this was Anglo-Norman, in contrast to Celtic civilisation, the Celt had no reason to credit himself, as the historians usually assume, with more than his share of "savagery." There were more "savage" deeds enacted in the fifteenth century in Anglo-Norman Scotland, or Anglo-Norman England for that matter, than among all the Highland clans put together. In no country was the anarchic oppression of the feudal magnate more inhuman than in Scotland, and the pictures of it which the Scottish chroniclers have etched are as full of horror as those of the chroniclers of France, Spain, and Germany.

SOURCES.—For the early period—Skene, Celtic Scotland; Robertson (E. W.), Scotland under her Early Kings; Rhys, Celtic Britain (1884); MacKinnon, Culture in Early Scotland (1892); Burton, History of Scotland, vol. i. (edition 1873); Tytler, History of Scotland, vol. i.; Mackintosh, History of Civilisation in Scotland; Cosmo Innes, Scotland in the Middle Ages, Sketches of Early Scottish History (1861), and, Scotch Legal Antiquities (1872); Seebohm, English Village Communities, and, Tribal Custom in Anglo-Saxon Law (1902); Maine, Early History of Institutions (1875); Coulanges, Histoire des Anciennes Institutions Politiques. The Regiam Majestatem, a version of the Tractatus de Legibus ascribed to Glanvill, and written in the reign of Henry II., is given in the Acts of the Par. of Scot., i.—a Scottish translation exists under the title of Auld Lawes and Constitutions of Scotland, collected by Sir J. Skene, 1774. Sir A. C. Lawrie, Early Scottish Charters Prior to 1153 (1905). For the later period—Ancient Laws and Customs of the Burghs of Scotland (1124-1424), edited by Cosmo Innes for the Scottish Burgh Records Society (1868); The Records of these Burghs, edited by various editors for the Society; Calendar of Laing Charters, edited by J. Anderson (1899); Sir James D. Marwick, The Municipal Institutions of Scotland, in the Scottish Historical Review for January and April 1904; The Acts of the Parliaments of Scotland, with Preface by Cosmo Innes; Fordun's Chronicle of the Scottish Nation, edited by W. F. Skene; The Orygynale Chronykil of Scotland, by Andrew of Wyntoun, edited by D. Laing; MacKinnon, The History of Edward III. (1900), in which other original authorities for the history of Scotland in the fourteenth century will be found; Robertson (Alex.), Lectures on the Government, Constitution, and Laws of Scotland; Brown, History of Scotland, i. (1899); Lang, History of Scotland, vol i. (1900).

I am indebted to my friend, Professor MacKinnon, Professor of Celtic Languages and Literature in the University of Edinburgh, for his kindness in reading the manuscript of this chapter.

The references of Greek and Latin writers to early Britain will be found in the Monumenta Historica Britannica.

CHAPTER XVII.

Mediæval Political Thought in Relation to Liberty.

Thus far we have followed the historical development of institutions which made for social emancipation and political progress in the Middle Ages. Our path has lain in the rough track of actuality. We have refrained from venturing into the byeways, shall we say, labyrinths, of theory. We have shunned the gates of the schools, for to us the schools offer no attractive vistas. For our purpose so far, indeed, the schools might as well have had locked doors. The babble of verbosity which echoes from within over the shibboleths of Nominalism and Realism seems to belong to a totally different sphere from that of the world of action in which we have been moving. Nominal or Real, the conflict of the schools has appeared to our passing glance very artificial indeed, in the midst of the world of contention in which men fight for social and political rights against social and political wrongs. The "Realism" of the schools seems but an air-bubble, mere gossamer compared with the realities of actual life. The most passionate realist is but a nominalist when measured by the actualities that are at work under the crust of feudalism, and are slowly changing the world, amid stress and storm, from its mediæval to its modern form.

And yet this is but a passing impression. The babble of the schools is, after all, not wholly babble, even from the point of view of the historian of the origins of modern liberty. The schoolmen were not all given over to mere hairsplitting over abstruse and often childish points of theology and metaphysics. There were some earnest thinkers among them, some who were in close contact with the world of their day, some whose minds were inspired by the political contentions of the time, more especially by the tremendous conflict between the ecclesiastical and the secular power. In so far, then, the war of the doctors has a certain interest for us. When it touches social and political institutions the doctors may indeed be found fighting the same battle, in a different fashion, as the militant reformer who wages a bitter warfare against the social and political abuses of the age.

Our interest is certainly not lessened by the discovery that some of these scholastic theorists enunciated, in their own mediæval fashion, truths which were to be the battlecries of the army of modern political reformers.

It is, nevertheless, well to differentiate. The contrast between mediæval and modern political thought is, in its general aspects, very striking. The theological element in mediæval political speculation is very pronounced, especially in the earlier Middle Ages. At a later period, Aristotle in his Latin form exercises a marked influence, but Aristotle is made to square with the Bible and the Fathers. Philosophy is dominated by theology. Aristotle only strengthens the authority of the Scriptures and the Fathers. There is little independent thinking; there could, indeed, be little in an age in which the Church and its doctors bear decisive sway over the minds of men. We hear of an occasional heretic, but the heretic is an outcast and has few followers.

Mediæval political thought is markedly affected by this theological bent. It is impregnated by the ecclesiastical atmosphere of these ages. We are a long way from the era of a Machiavelli. The theorists, for the most part, looked at things political through ecclesiastical spectacles. Their theories, in fact, grew out of the tremendous conflict between the ecclesiastical and the secular power. Much of the reasoning of their authors is, therefore, wasted on a modern mind. It rests too largely on Scripture, and, what is worse, on a strained interpretation of Scripture. It appeals too much to the Bible, to prophets, apostles, fathers. In its appeal to ancient history, it mistakes assumptions for fact. It is great in Scripture, logic, subtleties, trivialities, assumptions, but its great things are often puerilities in the eye of the modern historian. They fail to convince, while they weary and irritate the modern mind. Much of all this passionate argumentation about pope and emperor is in fact pure verbiage. Not only are we far removed from the actual state of things that gave it an interest to the disputants concerned; we feel ourselves to a large extent strangers to the type of mind, the trend of thought and feeling, which begat it.

While this is so, it is well to remember that questions are touched, if not decided, which possess an intense human interest. Sometimes we light upon a refreshing modern thought, a thought which wells up out of these arid tomes, like an oasis in the desert. The source which inspired these thoughts is not properly mediæval. It is what has been translated from the German as "antique-modern." It is classic, Aristotelian, and its tendency is distinctly modern.

The conflict between the ecclesiastical and the secular power—of which so much of mediæval political thought was, as I have said, the offspring—was inspired by the dominant mediæval idea of unity. To the Middle Ages the unity of nature in general and of mankind in particular was a cardinal doctrine. The universe, so reasoned the schoolmen, is one in God, and of this general whole the world is a subordinate whole. In the subordinate unity, again, the spiritual and the secular constitute two further unities, with distinct, if co-ordinate functions. It is the function of the spiritual power to rule the world in things spiritual, of the secular power in things secular. Pope and emperor are the supreme heads of Christendom, and in their harmonious co-operation are realised the ends of both Church and State—the reign of the kingdom of God. The mediæval idea of government is theocratic— the theocracy of the Jews modified by Roman and Christian institutions.

Such is the theory; but the theory, it is almost needless to say, did not square with fact. As a matter of fact, this unity never existed, for owing to the rift between East and West, the supremacy of one imperial and one ecclesiastical authority was never recognised. The emperor at Byzantium refused to own the supremacy or even the title of the emperor at Aachen or Frankfurt, and the patriarch of Constantinople spurned allegiance to the pope of Rome. It is astonishing with what audacity assumption will sometimes slap fact in the face, and to the modern historical student this mediæval battle about unity is a mere pretence. The insistence on unity is in truth in strange contrast to the actual state of mediæval society. Not only are there two emperors who each advance the empty claim to supremacy over the world. Not only is the pretension of the pope to universal sway in the Church disowned by the East. Not only is a large part of Western Europe independent of the western empire. In the actual state of society anarchy, not unity, is the striking characteristic. The feudal magnate is sovereign in his own domain; the feudal king of France, England, Scotland, Spain, claims an independent dominion in spite of the pretensions of would-be universal sovereigns.

And well was it for the political progress of the world that history refused to square with the theories of the doctors. To posit God as the omnipotent ruler of the universe, and then draw the conclusion of the omnipotence of pope and emperor in things ecclesiastical and secular, was not only to be false to the actual facts of history; it was not to read the trend of history aright. It was the echo of an exploded empire which had proved itself, by its effeteness and its despotism, hostile to true progress. The Roman ideal of a world dominion centred in one man was not an ideal favourable to political liberty, and, what is impossible without political liberty, political progress. The spring of progress lies in the quickening forces of the individual mind acting through free nations, free institutions, free initiative. This being so, the permanent revival of this world machine in the alliance of a universal Church and a universal State, subject to the divine right of pope and emperor, must have turned the world into a nursery, and doomed mankind, politically at least, to an eternal minority. The paternal rule of the nursery must have sacrificed liberty to subjection, progress to stagnation. Let us be thankful that mediæval history, as we have seen, took another road, and that this idea of oneness was a pure assumption, based on dialectical subtleties and mystical fallacies, and proved an ultimate impossibility.

For it would not work in practice. In practice, indeed, the emperor was for a time the more powerful of the two units, and the pope was content or constrained to reckon with the fact. He was not, could not, indeed, from his situation, be aggressively self-assertive at the emperor's expense. But not for long. As head of the Church, as the supreme governor of souls, he is by-and-by found claiming to be the more exalted functionary of the two. Is he not the successor of Peter, the vicar of Christ, the representative of God on earth? And is not the ecclesiastical office superior to the secular as being concerned with the eternal, not the temporal, the spiritual, not the material interests of man? And has not the pope made the emperor, from the days of Charlemagne at any rate? Clearly, therefore, for these and a variety of additional reasons, of which the orthodox schoolmen are cram full, his holiness is above his imperial majesty, and ought not to dishonour God and the Church by waiving his rights in any contingency in which they seem to suffer detriment at the imperial hands. In the question of investitures, for example. On this question Gregory VII. spoke in no uncertain tones. And thus the quarrel was initiated which, as we have seen, thundered on in the murky atmosphere of the Middle Ages for several centuries. In the progress of the quarrel the pretensions of the popes increased in arrogance, and the doctrines of their scholastic champions consequently grew in bulk, until they appear in modern eyes utterly infatuated and even blasphemous. Humility was certainly not a failing of those mediæval ecclesiastical Cæsars, in spite of the cant about "dust and worms," and the "*servus servorum.*" They will be satisfied with nothing less than second place to the Almighty in the whole range of creation, and neither emperor, nor king, nor, we believe, even the angels themselves, may presume to equality with the successors of Peter the Galilean fisherman. His mediæval sanctity is, for instance, declared to be "not a man, but the vicar of God." He is a kind of glorified mediæval ghost, at whose apparition the mediæval world turned pale and trembled—the talisman that mediæval superstition could pit not merely against the mediæval emperor, but against the mediæval devil. Nay, "he is in a certain sense God Himself, because he is His vicar." His sentence is that of God, and there can, therefore, be no appeal from it. He had only to plant his spiritual battery in position, and men who would otherwise face the wild charge of a host of armoured horsemen, would, in the long run at least, quail before the discharge of his supernatural artillery.

This ghostly mediæval pope of the type of a Gregory or an Innocent could not indeed ignore the secular power. It, too, though in papal eyes it originated in an act of sinful pride, is ordained of God. But it is only through the channel of the Church that it receives the divine sanction, and it is, therefore, subordinate to the Church's head. The mediæval popes and the mediæval doctors constantly emphasise the superiority of the secular to the spiritual power. "That the emperor, and likewise all other rulers" (to quote Dr Gierke) "derive their offices but mediately from God, and immediately from the Church's head, who in this matter, as in other matters, acts as God's vice-regent—this became the general theory of the Church. It was in this sense that the allegory of the 'Two Swords' was expounded by the ecclesiastical party. Both swords have been given by God to Peter, and through him to the popes, who are to retain the spiritual sword, while they deliver the temporal to others. This delivery, however, will confer, not free ownership, but the right of an ecclesiastical office-holder. As before the delivery, so afterwards, the pope has *utrumque gladium*. . . . The true ownership of both swords is his, and what he concedes in the temporal sword is merely some right of independent user." The emperor in particular, and all rulers in general, are, therefore, the vassals of the pope, who is the supreme head of the feudal hierarchy, and may summon them to do him homage, and use the temporal sword in the service of the Church. He is the supreme owner of all property, and may dispose of it in the last resort as he pleases. He may further intervene in secular affairs, may even deprive a ruler of his power, may loosen his subjects from their obedience, and confer the crown on another.

The claim, from the historical point of view, was a mere pretence, though the popes succeeded for a time in foisting it on a credulous and ignorant world. To utter or maintain such pretensions on behalf of the Bishop of Rome from the first to the tenth centuries—in the days of the old Roman emperors or their Carolingian successors—would have seemed both impertinent and ridiculous. From the eleventh century onwards the popes and their champions not only maintained it; they did not hesitate to move heaven and earth to realise it. For a time it seemed as if they were to secure a permanent triumph in the struggle with the emperors. Gregory VII. brought Henry IV. to his knees at Canossa. His successors had the best of it in the mighty quarrel with the Hohenstaufen. The antagonism of the Italians to the Germans, of Guelf to Ghibeline, played into their hands. The incoherence of the empire and the vigorous rise of the nations within as well as without its borders, the recognition of the papal headship by Western Christendom, the weakening effects of the feudal system in Germany and Italy on the central power, all told against the imperial idea. The pope remained master as against his imperial antagonists in the twelfth and thirteenth centuries, maintained his position, too, on the revival of the struggle with the Emperor Ludwig in the fourteenth century. But he had succeeded too well. The victor was assailed by new antagonists who ultimately compassed the ruin of the papal system. The principle of nationality which proved too strong for the imperial pretension to the dominion of the world, proved too strong for the papal pretension to supremacy over both king and emperor. Philip the Fair of France would not bend or break before the ecclesiastical artillery of Boniface VIII. He treated his Bulls with contempt and his person with obloquy. " Let your most distinguished Fatuousness be assured that in temporals we are subject to no one.' " My power," cried Boniface wrathfully to Peter Flotte, Philip's envoy, " embraces both the spiritual and the temporal." " Maybe," replied the imperturbable Peter, " but your power is *verbal*, that of the king is *real*." " God," raved the impotent Boniface, " has set us over the princes of the earth and their kingdoms, to root up, destroy, disperse, scatter, build, plant in His name and by His doctrine. Persuade not yourself, therefore, that you have no superior, and that you are not subject to the head of the Church. He who so thinks is a madman ; he that maintains this impious opinion an infidel." Philip's reply, if tradition speaks truly, was still more drastic. He threw the papal Bull into the flames publicly at Paris in February 1302, and for the next seventy years the popes became the dependants of the French kings at Avignon. Still worse, after the Babylonish captivity, the great schism rent the Church in twain for another half-century, and the General Council contested the papal supremacy even in things ecclesiastical, and strove to enforce the rights of the Church against the Roman tyrant. The sovereignty of the Church, contended the more advanced leaders of the Conciliar party, resides in its members, in the whole body of the faithful. A very democratic sentiment certainly, which, as we shall see, sprang from a similar view of the secular sovereignty, the view, namely, that the sovereignty inheres not in the head of the State, whether emperor or king, but in the people, the members of the State. Applied to the Church, the logical conclusion is that a General Council, as a sovereign assembly representing Christendom, is superior to the pope, and may call him, if need be, to account for his actions, pass judgment upon him, and even depose him. To it belongs the right of electing him, and the cardinals in performing this function are but its representatives. To Cusanus, in particular, who went furthest in the assertion of the sovereignty of the Council, all authority in Church as well as in State is based on common consent, and election is the medium of its delegation to all the various members of the hierarchy, from priest to patriarch and pope. The pope, as well as the lesser orders, derives his power from this source. He is the servant, not the master of the Church. It follows, as a matter of course, in the opinion of men like Marsilius and Occam, the champions of Ludwig of Bavaria against John XXII., that even the laity, as members of the Community of the Faithful, should by its representatives take part in the deliberations of the sovereign assembly of the Church, which has indeed no coactive power without their co-operation. "Upon them," in fact, according to Marsilius, "lay the duty of summoning the Council, deciding who were its members, and executing its resolutions by force and punishment." Occam goes so far as to assert that even women may be admitted, if their presence is deemed expedient.

Thus from the extreme of the ecclesiastical autocracy of arrogant mediæval popes, reaction swung to the extreme of democratic self-consciousness within the Church, in the fourteenth and fifteenth centuries. Not that the Conciliar leaders of the stamp of a Gerson and a D'Ailly countenanced such radical reactionary views. Gerson and D'Ailly championed the rights of a hierarchy, not of the faithful *en masse*, of an ecclesiastical aristocracy, not an ecclesiastical democracy, as against the pope. The Council of Constance burned Hus, the protagonist of the revolutionary doctrine that the true Church consists of all Christians, not of hierarchy or pope, and a quarter of a century earlier the English hierarchy had vented a savage vengeance on the ashes of Hus's predecessor Wicklif. The time was not ripe for such revolutionary doctrines. The pope, in fact, triumphed in the end over the Council as he had triumphed over the emperor. But, as in the case of the struggle with the secular power as represented by the King of France, his victory was but the prelude to discomfiture. A century after the burning of Hus came the trumpet blast of the reformers against Antichrist, and the overthrow of the papal authority, both spiritual and temporal, in a large part of Europe. And the triumph of this reaction meant much, as we shall see, for the political emancipation of the peoples, as well as for their rulers.

The champions of the imperial *versus* the papal power were equally insistent on the divine right of the emperor to rule. They claimed for the imperial crown absolute power, power independent of pope or people. The doctrine of the divine right of the secular ruler is already clearly enunciated (though for the purpose of refutation) by Hincmar, Archbishop of Reims, in the first quarter of the ninth century. "Other wise men say that the prince . . . is subject to the laws and judgments of none but God alone . . . and as he ought not to be excommunicated for any delinquency by his own bishops, so he cannot be judged by other bishops, seeing that he ought to be subject to the government of God alone, by whom only he is established on the throne, and all his actions, of whatever kind, in the government are by the divine command." In confirmation thereof the imperial champions quoted St Paul and St Peter, and thus met the pope with his own weapons. Had not Paul declared explicitly that "the powers that be are ordained of God," that "whosoever resisteth the power resisteth the ordinance of God," and that the emperor " is the minister of God to execute wrath upon him that doeth evil "? And was not Peter himself, the pope's assumed patron, equally explicit? "Submit yourselves to every ordinance of man for the Lord's sake, for so is the will of God." The emperor is, therefore, God's temporal vicar, and as such holds his crown immediately, directly of God, not mediately, indirectly through the pope. These texts were most inconvenient. They would not yield a plausible evasion even to the ingenuity of papalist exegetes. The evasion was straight in the teeth of common-sense, and in general it was admitted that the secular (*imperium*) equally with the ecclesiastical power (*sacerdotium*) was derived from God. The more moderate theorists on either side were content to regard them as co-ordinate, though the spiritual, as concerned with religion, might be allowed the higher rank. They might, indeed, to some extent be interdependent, for if the pope might intervene in certain cases in temporal affairs, it might be the duty of the emperor or other secular ruler to interpose in certain crises in things ecclesiastical—to summon, for instance, a General Council to decide some question of universal interest.

On historical grounds, too, how could the successor of the Bishop of Rome compare himself with the successor of the lord of the ancient empire? Even by dint of forged decretals and fables that passed for history, the Roman bishop could not well blink the fact that a Constantine was supreme lord of the civilised world, the patron of the Bishop of Rome. But a Charlemagne, retorted the papalists, was no Constantine, for was he not created emperor in virtue of the *translatio imperii* by Pope Leo? On the contrary, returned the jurists, the continuity of the empire is unbroken (*imperium continuum*), and Charlemagne, in assuming the imperial crown, assumed the power of the ancient emperors. The ceremony of coronation merely emphasised the fact before Christendom, for the *Populus Romanus*, not the Roman pope, is the source of the imperial power. So reasoned the jurists of the school of Bologna, where the study of Roman jurisprudence was revived and patronised by Barbarossa. So reasoned, too, the most famous of the imperial protagonists, the immortal Dante, in the "De Monarchia"—that powerful defence and panegyric of the universal monarchy—in protest against papal pretension and mediæval anarchy. The jurists did not hesitate to apply to the emperor the absolute attributes of the old imperators. To the "Decretum" of Gratian and the dicta of the papalist doctors, they opposed the "Institutes" of Justinian. In so doing they attributed to the emperor a plenitude of power over the State as stupendous as that claimed by the pope over the Church, and still more ridiculous, in contrast to the actual state of things, than that assumed by Boniface in the height of his ecclesiastical arrogance. The emperor is *de jure* lord of all the world, in spite of the fact that nearly all the world repudiates the audacious pretence. He is, of course, above the law, and whatever he wills is law. What is true of a Constantine or a Justinian is true of a Frederick Barbarossa, " Quidquid principi placuit legis habet vigorem." Hence " the tendency," according to Dr Gierke, " to exalt the person of the ruler. In his own proper person he was thought of as the wielder of an authority that came to him from without and from above. He was set over and against that body whereof the leadership had been entrusted to him. He had a sphere of powers which was all his own. He was raised above and beyond the community. The universal whole being taken as type, the relation of monarch to State was compared with that of God to world. Nay, even a quasi-divinity could be ascribed to him as to the Vicegerent of God. The lengths that the pope's supporters could go in this direction are well known; and their opponents lagged not behind when kaiser and king were to be extolled."

Thus it is roundly asserted that the emperor is "lord of the whole world and God on earth." " To him is due devotion as to God present and incorporated." " As God is to be adored on high, so he is to be adored on earth." The most slavish exponents of the modern doctrine of the divine right of kings could not beat this. Even Bossuet is tame compared with a Baldus, and Louis XIV., with all his supernatural pose, is but mortal in contrast to the divine Barbarossa, to " God present and incorporated." And the French jurists did not lag behind their imperial brethren in the assertion of the divine right of a Philip the Fair. The king rules by divine right equally with emperor or pope. The royal as well as the imperial majesty is a reflex of the divine. " Philip," insists the author of the " De Utraque Potestate," " holds and possesses his kingdom from God alone." Witness the miracles which the kings of France have wrought. Priesthood before the advent of Christ, contends John of Paris, was typical, and, therefore, kingship is the older and higher of the two. "The King of France," insists Raoul de Presle, "holds and possesses his kingdom from God alone, without any intermediary in any manner whatever. He holds of no man, nor from the vicar of Jesus Christ." According to Peter Dubois, the French king has a better right to universal dominion than either emperor or pope, on the practical ground that he has the force to maintain it, while they have not. The pope's business is to save souls, and by interfering in politics and thus neglecting his function, he has sent many to hell. The emperor is but a figurehead, and Philip, who has might as well as right on his side, is, therefore, the very man to assume the headship of Christendom.

The jurists' doctrine of the divine right of the French kings was, however, not allowed to pass without question on political as well as ecclesiastical grounds. Against such claims we may set the protests of men like Nicholas Oresme, the preceptor of Charles VI., who emphasised the rights of the community. Even if the community may have allowed itself to be outwitted into subjection to an arbitrary government, it may seek to recover its liberty. "The king," he protests, "though greater than any one subject, is inferior to the whole community."

Even in England the king is, according to Wicklif, not only independent of the pope, but above the law, and therefore rules by divine right. Wicklif was, however, not prepared to accept a tyrant without demur. Such a ruler has in truth no real dominion, which is based on God's grace, and ought to be resisted, though only on religious grounds. A people may rebel because of the injury done to God, not to itself. Resistance on grounds of utility is damnable. "The main drift of the work" ("De Officio Regis"), says Mr Figgis, "is to inculcate the universal authority of the crown and the religious duty of submission to it on the part of all classes." And Richard II. was not loth to claim the full rights of an absolute king, independent of both pope and people. He was as insistent on his prerogative as the most obstinate of the Stuarts. He alone is lawgiver, master; "in him alone is invested," according to the articles of deposition, "the right to change and make the laws." In short, he is omnipotent in spite of Lords and Commons, and there were not wanting voices, besides his own, to proclaim the fact, as we learn from Shakespeare as well as from other sources. That such views had not, however, taken root in England, the Parliament, by Richard's deposition, gave ample proof.

The emphasis laid on the absolute rights of emperor or king against the vast assumptions of the popes was, however, in its day, a contention on behalf of liberty. It was the vindication of the independence of the State from the worst of all despotisms—that of the priest. The priest assumes the right to dictate to man in the name of God, being indeed God on earth, and reduces both God and society to the measure of the priestly conceptions. The priest might formulate as God's will the most grovelling superstition. It must be received in a spirit of unquestioning obedience. He might be a scheming politician, an ignorant obscurantist, a raving fanatic, with the tiara on his head. Nevertheless, he must be allowed the absolute right to enforce his schemes, his obscurantism, his fanaticism at whatever cost to the true wellbeing of mankind. He might turn the world into a pandemonium of contention, but all his antagonists were *ipso facto* wrong and guilty of rebellion against God. To question such assumptions was to deliver humanity from a fatal thraldom, even if the pope's adversaries invested the rights which they vindicated in a rival potentate. Happily some of them did not stop here, for they ended by denying the claims of both would-be dictators and emphasising a sovereignty which was alone indefeasible—that of the people.

On the other hand, it may fairly be admitted that the papalist champions, in exalting the power of the pope, made some strong points in the same direction against the imperial pretensions to divine right. They thus, in their turn, appear as the defenders of political liberty against monarchic despotism. They could talk the language of democracy when it suited them (saving always the supremacy of the pope) and thus helped to quicken the sense of popular rights as against the absolute sovereignty of the individual. When the kaiser was told that he was not the absolute sovereign he mistook himself for, the contention might be salutary in leading men to question claims incompatible with political liberty. A Gregory VII. might be no champion of popular rights as against the civil power, but some of the champions of the system he represented went so far as to enunciate and defend them.

We detect, in fact, a tendency to question the indefeasible right of monarchy, not only on the part of the more moderate and philosophic theorists, like Thomas Aquinas, but on the part of some of those who apotheosised the secular ruler in the person of the emperor. They disputed the claim of monarchy to be the exclusive form of government, and pointed to the expediency of other forms in certain circumstances. The republic, for instance, may be legitimate and serviceable, for the republic represents a unity of power, equally with the monarchy, in virtue of the conception of its governing assembly as a composite man. They laid stress, too, on the office rather than the person of the monarch, on duties rather than rights, on law rather than command. To the plenary power (*plenitudo potestatis*) of pope or emperor they opposed a limited power (*potestas limitata*). The sovereignty of both pope and emperor is, therefore, not omnipotence. The Church, the community have also rights, and obedience is conditioned by these rights. Government was instituted for the sake of the governed, and if the ruler does not observe this cardinal law, he becomes a tyrant. In all this we may perceive what has been called the antique-modern spirit—the influence of Aristotle working through the Middle Ages in a modern direction.

The tyrant may be resisted on political as well as religious grounds. As a matter of course, the command of God must be obeyed before that of man in any case in which the two conflict. The law of necessity holds against both pope and emperor. But even in things secular the subject is not bound to yield obedience to oppressive acts or ordinances, and may resist such even by force of arms. Injustice, as an act of violence, may be met by violence; yea, the tyrant may be put to death. "Princes," says Thomas Aquinas, "are instituted by God, not that they may seek their own advantage, but that they may preserve the common utility." "The kingdom is not on account of the king," says Ptolemæus of Lucca, "but the king on account of the kingdom." Even Dante emphasises the same sentiment. "The citizens do not exist for the consuls, nor the people for the king, but the consuls for the citizens, the king for the people." "Government," according to Occam, "should promote the liberty and exclude the slavery of the subjects." "Princes who do not rule justly," says Nicolaus Minorita, "are to be regarded as tyrants, rather than kings." Hugh of Fleury would indeed suffer and even pray for a tyrant, and bear the punishment for disobedience to commands contrary to the law of God as a martyr. But John of Salisbury boldly denounces death to the tyrant on the ground that "tyranny is an abuse of power granted by God to man," though he rejects the use of unfair means, such as poison. Thomas Aquinas disallows tyrannicide, but advocates active resistance to a tyrannical *régime*, and holds that such resistance is not sedition unless it induces greater evils than the tyranny against which it is directed.

It is not surprising, therefore, that the tentative tendency to limit the power of the monarch, whether pope, emperor, or other ruler, should end in exalting the rights of the people, and finding the origin of sovereignty in the popular will. Hence the theory of a state of nature in which all men were free and equal and held all things in common, and of the origin of the State by contract. The idea of the contract was derived from the Old Testament, the *jus gentium*, which was regarded as comprehending the *jus naturale*, or law of nature, the *Lex Regia*, and the feudal relation between lord and vassal. The agreement by which the people of Israel set a king over themselves was evidently of the nature of a contract. By the *jus gentium*, according to the jurists, "every free people may set a superior over itself." By the *Lex Regia*, "the people," they contended, "transferred to the prince (by general agreement, of course) all its power and empire." But was not this to ascribe a human origin to the secular power? No, returned the adherents of the divine right of monarchy as against the pope. The people is the instrument of the divine will. Thus, all power derives from the voluntary subjection of the people by way of contract, and even in the case of conquest or usurpation, a tacit consent of the people, by which such violent methods were supposed to be legitimated, was postulated. But the power which the people thus confers, it may resume in certain emergencies. For example, when it recognised Charlemagne as emperor on the assumption that the Emperor of the East had forfeited his right to be regarded as the supreme ruler of Christendom. It was by the consent of the people (*consensus populi*), not by the sanction of the pope that the great Charles acquired the imperial crown. "The pope only declared and executed the will of the people." And the emperor is still elected by the people, for in the case of the Holy Roman Empire the electors are merely its delegates. Hereditary monarchy in the States that had grown up outside the empire might indeed be legally valid. But originally all power was derived from the people by way of election, based on the principle of contract, and the elective system accords best with both the law of God and the law of nature.

But did not the people of Rome, by the *Lex Regia*, alienate the sovereignty to the emperor, and thus deprive itself absolutely of its rights? Certainly, answered the champions of absolute monarchy. The popular sovereignty disappeared in the emperor. Certainly not, returned the advocates of popular rights. The transaction was a concession; it did not amount to an alienation. The people is therefore superior to the emperor (*populus major imperatore*), and may resume its power. Even in a monarchy the people is the true sovereign, though the monarch may not be deprived of his office as long as he observes the conditions of the contract. *Populus major principe*, the sovereign people is greater than the prince or ruler, whoever he be. Even the opponents of this view refused to confer unlimited sovereignty on the ruler in virtue of the popular alienation. The people still had its rights, and its consent was necessary to all important acts affecting the interest of the whole. Some even conceded the right to depose him in case of tyranny. Others found the best constitution in a division of power between the monarch and the community, that is, in a mixed constitution.

The popular sovereignty in virtue of the contract is already stated, as against emperor or king, with modern precision by Manegold of Lautenbach as early as the eleventh century. "Since no one can create himself emperor or king, the people elevates a certain one person over itself to the end that he govern and rule it according to the principle of righteous government; but if in any wise he transgress the contract (*pactum*) by virtue of which he is chosen, he absolves the people from the obligation of submission, because he has first broken faith with it." The prince is in fact merely the executor of the people's will, and if he fails in his duty the people may exercise judgment upon him. "King," says Manegold further, "is not a name of nature, but a title of office; nor does the people exalt him so far above it in order to give him the free power of playing the tyrant in its midst, but to defend it from tyranny. So soon as he begins to act the tyrant, is it not plain that he falls from the dignity granted to him, since it is evident that he has first broken that contract by virtue of which he was appointed. If one should engage a man for a fair wage to tend swine (the simile is not a flattering one), and he found means not to tend but to steal them, would one not remove him from his charge?" "If a king imposes unjust taxes, denies justice, fails to defend the country, or otherwise neglects his duty, the people may" (according to the "Somnium Viridarii") "depose him and choose another ruler." Even the pope in exercising this right is only the executor of the people's will.

This doctrine of the sovereignty of the people advances in Marsilius or Marsiglio of Padua to pure republicanism, though Marsilius, like Occam, wrote on behalf of the Emperor Ludwig. According to Marsilius, who anticipates Rousseau in a remarkable fashion, the people, or the majority of it, is the legislator, and the legislator must be sovereign of the State. The legislator exercises his sovereign will through a general assembly, a council, or an individual. But the executive, the *pars principans*, whatever form it may take, is strictly subordinate to the legislator; it is expressly the agent of the people's will, and subject to its absolute control. It has in effect no will of its own, and performs its function best when it is in closest accord with that of the legislator. It may legislate in the ordinary sense, but only as the exponent of the popular will, which is the supreme law, and in which the State consists.

Equally insistent on the doctrine of the sovereignty of the people is Nicolas of Cues or Cusanus, one of the protagonists of the superiority of a General Council to the pope, and author of the "Concordantia Catholica," written for the edification of the Council of Basle. With him, as with all these theorists, power derives from God, but it is expressed in the will of the community. Hence the axiom that the validity of a law depends on the consent of those to whom it applies. Otherwise expressed, government must be based on the common consent, "*concordantia*," of the governed. Its only sanction lies in the people's will. This follows from the law of nature as well as the law of God. By the law of nature all men are free, and can only become subject by their free will. "But if men are naturally all equally powerful and free, there can be no law, no rightly ordained power of one over them unless by the election and common consent of the others. The law, too, owes its force to their common consent." Hence it is their function to make the laws; theirs also to control their administration, and in the case of maladministration to depose the ruler.

Very notable is the stress laid on the law of nature by these mediæval theorists, irrespective of party adhesions. They posited the traditional natural law of antiquity, and this law they held to be irrefragable. The legislator could not infringe it, for it was implanted in man by God. He could at most only improve it by positive law. Positive law, on the other hand, might be modified according to the will of the sovereign, whoever he might be, whether individual or community. To the champions of the absolute monarch the sovereign was thus above the law (*Princeps legibus solutus est*). "The prince is not bound by the laws." Equally so, the champions of popular sovereignty claimed that the sovereign assembly is superior to the law, though they vigorously protested against the assertion that any individual, apart from the consent of the community, is so. Both thus exalted the power of the State in reference to positive law, while differing diametrically in their interpretation of the State. The former virtually regarded the monarch as the State, the latter identified it with the people or community—the general will—and insisted, against the assumptions of their opponents, that not only is the people by divine and natural law supreme, but that its supremacy, its sovereignty is inalienable and indestructible.

Both parties, too, gradually came to ascribe to the State a

natural, not a supernatural origin, to seek its origin in a rational act, which took the form of a contract, to consider it as a commonwealth rather than a theocracy, though they differed as to the meaning and scope of this contract. While the one conferred, by means of this contract, absolute power on the ruler, the other posited the inalienability of the sovereignty, and gave the State a republican form, or made reservations which found expression in the idea of a limited monarchy, a mixed constitution, representative government. The postulation of the contract might not be a scientific explanation. It was not in accordance with history, but it was destined to have vast historical consequences in modern times. The idea of the sovereignty of the people which was based on it passed into a fundamental doctrine for future champions of popular rights, in the arena of practical as well as theoretical politics, to appeal to. On it was based the call for the States-General, as at Tours in 1484, and the defence of its rights as against the absolute monarch. Writers like Marsilius or Cusanus were only putting in theoretical form the contentions which men were already formulating in practical politics. Marsilius is so modern, indeed, that in one important respect he went far beyond his mediæval contemporaries, theoretical and practical. He advocated a thoroughgoing toleration four and a half centuries before John Locke. No man shall be persecuted for his opinions. Christ alone, not the Church, is the judge of heresy, and every man must answer to Him for his beliefs in the world to come. The doctrines of the heretics, if dangerous to civil society, may come within the cognisance of the secular judicature. Generally speaking, opinion lies outside its province.

In this debate of the mediæval political theorists we have clearly the foretaste of the contentions of the moderns. Many of the stock arguments of the later champions of popular rights are contained in the dogmas of the state of nature, the law of nature, the contract, the sovereignty of the people, the inalienability of this sovereignty, the general will, limited monarchy, mixed constitutions, toleration, &c. The modern writers will only repeat and amplify, wittingly or unwittingly, a great deal of what their mediæval predecessors proclaimed. The idea of representation is also strongly emphasised and even worked out by some of these mediæval doctors, by Marsilius, William of Occam, Cusanus. Power being based on common consent and election, it follows that all power is representative. The emperor is not the empire, but only its representative. The pope is not the Church; he, too, is only its representative. Thus the notion of representation in Church and State came to be theoretically worked out as it came to be practically applied in States-General, or other corporations, and General Council. The people, the community, the congregation of the faithful, are conceived, not as a mass of individuals, but as a corporate body. It is in a collective, not in a distributive sense that the people is sovereign. The sum of all individuals does not form the people. It is composed only of fully qualified citizens (even the radical Marsilius excludes boys, slaves, strangers, women), and sovereignty can only be predicated of it in its composite capacity—in the sense of a duly constituted corporation. Such a corporation the States-General or the General Council is held to be, in virtue of their representative character, and even smaller bodies, such as the College of Electors, or the college of cardinals, who ought, strictly speaking, to be elected, are representative assemblies, and execute their functions in behalf of the people and the faithful respectively. Marsilius, Occam, and Cusanus even attempted to formulate schemes of representation which should secure an equitable and real reflex of both numbers and class, according to area. Marsilius, for example, would have "the world of Christian believers so represented in a General Council that each province or community have delegates according to the number and quality of its inhabitants." Occam goes further, and demonstrates how such a scheme could be worked. The inhabitants of the parish or commune might choose representatives to the diocese or larger territorial district, and these in turn might select the delegates to the General Council, which would, in this wise, really represent the whole Church, not merely the hierarchy. Certainly a startling proposition on the part of a churchman in the fourteenth century, but one which serves to show that democratic notions of a distinctively modern type were at least being seriously mooted in the Church as well as in the State.

Let us, however, beware of reading into the word democracy a modern sense. Theoretically, perhaps, democracy in the mediæval sense may stand for the people, and it is refreshing to find a Cusanus proclaiming the people to be "all by nature equally free and powerful." But Cusanus is dealing with an abstraction, and it is questionable whether the most thoroughgoing champion of abstract popular rights would have subscribed to the emancipation of the mass from oppressive traditional class distinction, from the limitations of popular liberty derived from feudalism. In this respect, to judge from the dicta of some of the most distinguished doctors, the Middle Ages had not advanced beyond ancient times. Occam, for instance, argues strenuously against the papal power, that Christians cannot be the slaves of such a power. But he accepts slavery as an institution, and it does not occur to him to strengthen his argument by condemning slavery in the State as well as in the Church. We have occasionally, indeed, heard a solitary compassionate voice crying in the social wilderness of these ages on behalf of the real brotherhood of man, and demanding emancipation as a humane and religious duty. We have seen, too, how under the operation of economic laws, in particular, emancipation from social oppression became common, though it did not involve the political elevation of the masses. The teaching of the Church was likewise to a certain extent favourable to emancipation, when its own composite interests were not affected thereby, though the opposite doctrine found exponents among the higher clergy, and the prelates were among the staunchest adversaries of the communal movement. And among the theorists the tendency to assume slavery as a natural and even a divine institution, in spite of the New Testament, claimed many distinguished votaries. It may be hard for men to shake themselves free from the prejudices of their age, but it is at least surprising to find learned doctors quoting the sayings of Christ and the apostles, and yet belying the spirit of Christianity by accepting as a matter of course an institution so contrary to Christian brotherhood. Theology and philosophy might mislead them, but theologians should at least have known their New Testament, as well as Aristotle and the Fathers. Augustine and Aquinas, in fact, improve on Aristotle to the extent of adding some far-fetched arguments of their own. Aristotle had defended slavery on the ground of the mental inferiority of a large percentage of mankind. Augustine saw in it the wages of sin, and therefore found a place for it in Christian society, in spite of St Paul. Aquinas added the consideration that the fact of slavery tends to make good soldiers. Men will fight for their liberty all the more bravely if they are actuated by the fear of losing it, since the lot of the conquered freeman is slavery. Nay, in this matter, according to St Thomas, the law of nature is not binding, and may be infringed on grounds of utility. If it is expedient for the community to have slaves, slavery is admissible. Always presuming, let us suppose, that St Thomas himself is not among the number. On the other hand, it is to be remembered to his credit that he insists on the care of the poor by the State as a distinct function of the ruler, and in this respect he represents the better side of mediæval Christianity which, with all its prejudice and superstition, could hardly ignore the fact that the mission of Christ, whatever that of the pope and the lordly prelates of a half secularised Church might be, was to the poor and the miserable. The reason given by Aquinas is singular enough, and sounds characteristically mediæval. By remembering the poor the ruler may thereby atone the more surely for his sins. Even to Wicklif slavery is not offensive, because to him, as to Augustine, it is the result of sin, and at all events, it is a matter of indifference, since spiritual, not personal freedom is the great thing. One might be tempted to conclude that in the Middle Ages there were no sinners among the higher orders of society. Men like Augustine and Aquinas do not seem to have asked themselves the question. But what has a mediæval theologian to do with common-sense?

The works of the chief political writers of the Middle Ages referred to above are the following:—Hincmar (Migné, vols. 125-126); John of Salisbury, Polycraticus (*ibid.*, vol. 199, and Schaarschmidt); Aquinas, De Regimine Principum (Opera, vol. 27, 1871-80); John of Paris, De Potestate Regia et Papali in Goldast, Monarchia Sancti Romani Imperii, vol. 2 (1611-1614); Dante, De Monarchia, ed. Giuliani

Sources of Chapter XVII.

(1878), and in Syntagma Tractatuum de Imperiali Jurisdictione, 1609, translation by F. I. Church (1878), affixed to R. W. Church's Essay on Dante; Marsiglio of Padua, Defensor Pacis, in Goldast; William of Occam, Dialogus, in *ibid.*; Wickliffe, De Civili Dominio, ed. by Poole for the Wyclif Society (1885, *et seq.*); Nicolas of Cues or Cusanus, De Concordantia Catholica, in Syntagma. The chief modern writers are Gierke, Political Theories of the Middle Ages, trans. by F. W. Maitland (1900), as valuable for its notes, which contain copious extracts from the whole range of the mediæval political writers, as for its text; Poole, Illustrations of the History of Mediæval Thought (1884); Dunning, A History of Political Theories, Ancient and Mediæval (1902); Figgis, The Theory of the Divine Right of Kings (1896), and, Politics at the Council of Constance, Transactions of the Royal Hist. Soc., New Series, 13 (1899); Janet, Histoire de la Science Politique, t. i. (1887); Blakey, History of Political Literature, vol. i. (1855), which is, however, very superficial; A. J. Carlyle, Mediæval Political Theory in the West (1903).

Printed at THE DARIEN PRESS, *Edinburgh.*

INDEX TO VOL. I.

Abelard, 48
Ackermann, Flemish popular leader, 229
Adalbéron of Laons, 92
Adalbéron of Reims, 14, 15
Adolf of Nassau, Roman King and Emperor, 189, 193, 296
Adrian IV., Pope, 41, 49
Æneas Sylvius, description of German cities in fifteenth century, 180
Agincourt, Battle of, 129
Alaric, 2
Albizzi, The, 55-57, 59, 60, 64
Alcuin, 260
Alemannia, Duchy of, 185
Alexander II., King of Scotland, 353, 359
Alexander III., King of Scotland, 359
Alexander III., Pope, 41, 49
Alexander VI., Pope, 74, 81
Alfonso I., King of Aragon, 241
Alfonso III., King of Aragon, 253
Alfonso IV., King of Aragon, 255
Alfonso III., King of Leon, 239
Alfonso V., King of Leon, 248
Alfonso VIII., King of Leon and Castile, 240, 242
Alfonso X., 247-249
Alfonso XI., 245, 247, 248
Alphonse of Castile, 137
Altorf, 194, 195
Ambühl, Swiss patriot, 197
Amiens, Commune of, 96, 100, 115; Mise of, 275
— Count of, 89
Anastasius, Emperor, 4
Anghiari, Baldaccio da, 63, 64
Anglo-Saxons, The, 5, 260-266
Anjou, Duke of, 125
Anne Boleyn, Queen of England, 340

Anne, Queen of England, 159
Antique-Modern spirit, 378
Aquinas, Thomas, 378, 385, 386
Aragon, Kingdom of, 239 *et seq.*; nobility of, 251; the "General Privilege" of, 252
Argues, Treaty of (1326), 216
Aristotle, Authority of, in the Middle Ages, 366, 367, 386
Arles, Commune of, 96
Armagnac, Count of, and the Armagnacs, 127-129, 131
Arnold de Brescia, 48, 49
Arnulf, Emperor, 135
Arrabbiati, The, Florentine faction, 80, 81
Artevelde, James van, Flemish statesman, 218-226
Artevelde, Philip van, 227-229
Articles of 1340, 298
Artois, Robert of, 214
Arundel, Earl of, 300
Assega Book of the Frisians, 200
Assize of Arms, 270; The Grand, 270; Assize of Clarendon, 270
Ataulf, 2
Athens, Duke of, 55, 56
Athies, Treaty of (1305), 215
Augustine, St, 385
Auxerre, Treaty of, 127
Azzos of Este, 44

Babylonian Captivity of the Church, 371
Baldus, 375
Ball, John, 310-322
Barcelona, 257, 258
Baumgarten, Conrad of, Swiss patriot, 194
Bavaria, Duke of, 136
Beauvais, Commune of, 96, 116
Becket, Archbishop, 271

VOL. I. 2 C

Index.

Bede, The Venerable, 260
Berengar, 16
Bernard, St., 31
Bernicia, Angles of, 345
Berry, Duke of, 125
Beverley, Commune of, 289
Bevershoutsveld, Battle of, 228
Béziers, Commune of, 95, 96, 125
Bezold on German peasants, 176
Bigi, The, Florentine faction, 80
Bigod, Roger, Earl of Norfolk, 279
Blackheath, 316
Böheim, Hans, German popular preacher, 171-173
Bohemia, King John of, 219
— Religious and Social Revolt in, 158-168
Bohun, Humphrey, Earl of Hereford, 279
Boniface VIII., Pope, and Philip IV., 106, 108, 371
"Book of Customs," The London, 291
Bossche, Pierre van den, Flemish popular leader, 227-229
Bourbon, Duke of, 125
Bouvines, Battle of, 210
Brabant, Duchy of, 208 et seq., 230, 231
— John II., Duke of, 230
— John III., Duke of, 230
— Wenzel, Duke of, 230
Bracton, 5, 260, 277, 278, 285, 286
Brehon Laws, The, 350
Brember, Mayor of London, 301
Bretigny, Treaty of (1360), 226
Bretwalda, The, 265
Breydel, Flemish popular leader, 215
Britain, Roman, 260, 261
Brokmerland, Freemen of, 202
Bruce, Robert, 357, 359
Bruges, 125, 211, 213, et seq.; Massacre of French at, 214, 215
Brunechilde, 9
Buch, Captal of, 117
Bundschuh, The, 173, 174
Burgh, Hubert de, 274
Burghs, The Mediæval Scottish, 353-357
Burgundy, Archduke Philip of, 237
— Duchess Mary of, 235-237
— Duke Charles of (The Bold), 131, 234, 235

Burgundy, Duke John of, 127
— Duke Philip of, 125-127, 229, 232
— Duke Philip of (The Good), 232-234

Cabochiens, The, 127-129
Cadzand, Treaty of (1492), 237
Calixtines, The, 163, 166, 167
Calle, King of the Jacques, 117, 118
Cambrai, Commune of, 96
Cambuskenneth, Parliament of, 359
Campagnacci, Florentine faction, 81
Capet, Hugh, 14, 15, 105, 107
Capponi and Charles VIII., 75
Carrara, The, of Padua, 44
Cassel, Battle of, 215
Castile, Kingdom of, 239 et seq.
Castilian Monarchy, The, 244, 245
Castruccio, 55
Catalonia, 257, 258
Catherine of Aragon, 340
Causis, Michael de, 161
Cavendish, Sir John, 319
Celts, Institutions of, 19, 20; identity of institutions with those of Saxons, 346, 352; subdivisions of British, 345, 346
Century XI., The, 38
Cerchi, The, 54
Cerdic and Cynric, 262
Charlemagne, 5, 10, 19, 23, 135, 144
Charles, Duke of Calabria, 55
Charles, Duke of Normandy, Regent of France, 110-119
Charles IV., King of France, 109, 216
Charles V., King of France, 109, 125, 137
Charles VI., King of France, 124-129
Charles VII., King of France, 109, 129, 130
Charles VIII. of France in Italy, 74-76, 81; minority of, 132
Charles Martel, 22
Charles IV. of Bohemia, 49; Emperor, 112, 138, 141, 156
Charles the Bald, 13
Charles the Fat, Emperor, 16
Chaucer, 312
Cid, The, 240, 241
Ciompi, Revolt of, 56

Index. 391

Clarendon, Constitutions of, 271
Clauwaerts, Flemish political party, 213
Clermont, Marshal of Normandy, Murder of, 114
— Commune of, 116
Clotaire II., 4
Clovis, 4, 7
Cods, or Cabeljauws, Dutch faction, 209, 232
Cœur, Jacques, French statesman, 129
Collective Superior, The, 98
Cologne, Conjuration of, 147
Columba, St, 344, 354
Commines, Philip de, 131
Commons, The House of (Reign of Edward I. and II.), 281, 282; (Reigns of Edward II. and III.), 294-303
Communeros of Spain, 241-244
Communes, The French, municipal constitution of, 96, 97
Commutation of services in England, 285, 286
Conciliar Party, Opposition of, to Pope, 371-373, 384
Concordantia Catholica, 381
Conflans, Marshal of Champagne, Murder of, 114
Coninck, Peter, Flemish popular leader, 214, 215
Conjuration, The, its rôle in emancipation movement in France, 88; in Germany, 147; German peasant, 171
Conrad III., Emperor, 49
Conrad, The Poor, Society of, 171
Constance, Council of, Hus at the, 160-162; Treaty of, 42
Constantine, King of Scotland, 350
Contract, Doctrine of the, 383
Corbie, Robert de, 110
Cornwall, 354
Cortenuova, Battle of, 44
Cortes of Aragon, 243, 255, 256; of Castile, 243, 246-250
Council, The Great, of England, 270, 275
Court of Session, 361
Courtrai, Battle of, 215
Courtrai, Sohier de, Ghent patrician, 219, 220
— Sohier, son of former, 223
Coutereel, Peter, Brabant popular leader, 231

Cranmer, 339
Craw, Paul, Hussite, burned at St Andrews, 168
Creçy, Battle of, 110
Cromwell, Thomas, 339
Crusades, The, influence on commerce and industry, 38, 39
Cumberland, 345
Curia Regis, The, 270, 359
Cusanus, 381, 383-385

Dagobert, 7
D'Ailly, 372
Dalriada, 344, 345, 349
Dante, Exile of, 54; political views of, 374, 378
Davalos, Constable, 245
David I., King of Scotland, 352, 354, 355, 358
David II., King of Scotland, 360, 361
Death, The Black, 307, 308, 311
Decretum of Gratian, 374
Defensor Civitatis, 37
Deinse, Battle of, 216
"De Laudibus Angliæ," 333-335
Denys, Gerhard, Flemish popular leader, 223, 224
Despensers, The, 295
"Dialogus de Scaccario," 286
Dio Cassius, 345
Domenico, Fra, 81
Donati, The, 54
Dozen, Hungarian popular leader, 171
Dublin, Duke of, 301
Dunois, Count de, 129
Dunwich, Commune of, 290
Durham, Bishop of, 301

Edmund, son of Henry III., 275
Edward the Confessor, 266, 289
Edward I., King of England, 275, 278-280; and the Flemings, 214
Edward II., King of England, 280, 294-296
Edward III., King of England, 111, 119, 124, 137, 296-300; relations of, with the Flemings, 218-225; with the Scots, 360
Edward IV., King of England, 156, 331, 333, 337
Eginhard, 10

Index

Ehrbarkeit, Revolt against the, 181
Electors, The, of the German Empire, 138
Emancipation movement in Italy, 39 *et seq.*; in France, 88 *et seq.*
Emmius, Frisian chronicler, 198
Emperors, Struggle of, with the Pope, 370-374
England, 125, 134
English towns, Emancipation of, 288-292
Epila, Battle of, 254
Eric, King of Denmark, 156
Erlach, Rudolf von, 197
Esplechin, Truce of (1340), 221
Estate, The Third, of France, 104 *et seq.*
Etablissements of St Louis, 108
Ethelbehrt of Kent, 262
Ethelred, Anglo-Saxon King, 266
Etterlin, Swiss chronicler, 193
Evesham, Battle of, 276

Ferdinand I., King of Aragon, 258
Ferdinand the Catholic, King of Aragon, 257
Ferdinand, King of Naples, 74
Fernando III., King of Leon and Castile, 239, 240, 248
Ferrara, 45
Ficino, Marsilio, 66
Firma Burgi, 289
Flaith, Celtic lords of the manor, 348
Flanders, Count of (Louis de Mâle), 125, 226-229
— County of, 125, 208 *et seq.*
— Ferdinand, 210
— Guy de Dampierre, 210-215
— Louis de Nevers, 216-226
— Philip of Alsace, 212
— Robert, 216
Flemish cities, The, 210-214
Florence, Constitution of, under Cosimo de Medici, 63; Council of Seventy of, 66; early government of, 47; greater and lesser arts of, 54, 56, 57, 59, 62; Popolari of, 55, 61, 62, 81; reform of constitution of, by Savonarola, 76-80; restoration of the Medici at, 82
Flotte, Peter, French minister, 371
Fortescue, Sir John, Lord Chancellor, 332-336, 342

Foulques, Archbishop of Reims, 135
Fournier on enfranchisement of serfs, 93
France, 24
Franchise, Restriction of the English, 326-328
Franconia, Duke of, 136
Frankish kings, 9, 12
Frateschi, The, Savonarola's followers, 81
Fredegonde, 9
Frederick Barbarossa, 41, 42, 136
Frederick II., 43, 44, 136, 147, 170, 186, 187
Frederick III., Emperor, Reformation of, 170
Friends of God, The, 168
Friesland and the Frisians, 198 *et seq.*
Frisians, Charlemagne and the, 199; the "Privilege" of, 199; East and West Frisians, 199, 200; subject to the empire, 200; laws of the, 201; constitution of the, 201, 202; character of the, 203; revolts against the Counts of Holland, the Archbishops of Bremen, and the Counts of Oldenburg, 202-204; spirit of the laws of, 204-206; love of liberty of, 206; Albert of Saxony, Podesta of, 204; subject to Charles V., 204
Fritz, Joss, German peasant leader, 171, 173
Fuero Juzgo, Castilian code, 244, 248
Fueros, Spanish, 241, 242
Furnes, Battle of, 214
Fürst, Swiss patriot, 191, 195

Galgacus, 344
Gaston, Count of Foix, 117
Gaudri, Bishop of Laon, 96
Gaunt, John of, 314, 321
Gaveston, Piers, 295
Geiler, German popular preacher, 175
Genazzano, Fra Mariano da, 71
Genoa, 47
Gerard, King of Denmark, 155
German free imperial cities, 151

Index. 393

German industry in fifteenth century, 178, 179
German municipalities, Origin of, 142-148; constitution of, 148; powers of, 152, 153
German peasants, Condition of, in fifteenth century, 168-177
German towns, Growth of, 141, 142, 146; slow development of, 145; their struggle for emancipation, 147, 148; leagues of, 153-155; prosperity of, in fifteenth century, 178-180
Germany, 24
Gerson, opposes Hus at Constance, 161, 164; advocates supremacy of General Council, 372
Geschlechter, The, 148, 181
Gessler, Governor of Schwyz and Uri, 193, 194, 196
Ghent, 211, 213 *et seq.*
Gilds, Craft, of England, 291, 292; of Germany, 149-151; of Scotland, 355-357
Gilds, Labour, of Florence, 56, 57, 59
Gild, The merchant, in England, 290-292; in Germany, 146, 148; in Scotland, 355, 356
Giremei, The, of Bologna, 45
Glaber, Raoul, 31
Glanville, 286
Gloucester, Duke of, 301-304, 306
Golden Bull, The, 138
Gontram, Frankish king, 7
Gonzaga, The, of Mantua, 44
"Goyernance of England," The, 335, 336
Granada, Kingdom of, 240
"Great Privilege," The, of the Netherlands, 235, 236
"Great Privilege," The, of Holland, 236
Gregory VII., Pope, 369, 371, 376, 377
Gregory IX., Pope, 43, 44
Gregory XI., 56
Guelfs and Ghibelines, 17, 43, 44, 51, 54-57, 371
Guesclin, Du, 124
Guizot, criticism of the feudal system, 30

Habsburg, Count of, 185
— Count Rudolf the Silent, 188
Habsburg, Count Rudolf III. 188
— Duke and King Albert, 189, 191, 193, 196
— Duke Leopold of, 197
— Frederick of, 196
— King Rudolf, 188, 193, 196
Hainault, Count of, 217
— County of, 208, 231, 232
Hales, Treasurer of Richard II., 317, 318
Hansa League, The, 155-157, 211, 212, 229
Harold, King of England, 267
Hemerlin, Swiss chronicler, 193
Hengist and Horsa, 262
Henry I., the Fowler, Emperor, 141
Henry III., Emperor, 136, 272, 288, 289
Henry IV., Emperor, 371
Henry V., Emperor, 186
Henry VII. of Luxemburg, Emperor, 196
Henry III., King of Castile, 247
Henry IV., King of Castile, 247, 249
Henry I., King of England, 269
Henry II., King of England, 269-271, 288
Henry III., King of England, 274-276, 280, 288
Henry IV., King of England, 127, 304, 330
Henry V., King of England and France, 129, 331
Henry VI., King of England and France, 129, 331-333, 336, 337
Henry VII., King of England, 338, 341, 342
Henry VIII., King of England, 338-342
Henry I., King of France, 108
Hereford, Duke of, 304, 306
Heretoga, 262, 344
Hermandad, The, 243, 244
Hincmar, Archbishop of Reims, 373
Hohenstaufen emperors, 39, 136, 137
Holland, County of, 208 *et seq.*, 231, 232
Hooker, 342
Hooks, The, Dutch faction, 209, 232
Huesca, Aragonese code, 256
Hugh of Fleury, 379

Index.

Hundred Years' War, 109 *et seq.*, 325
Hus, John, 158-162, 273
Husinec, Nicolaus de, 173
Hussite congregations in Germany, 168
Hyoens, Jean, Flemish popular leader, 227

Independence, War of, 361
Innocent III., Pope, 43, 272
Innocent IV., Pope, 44
Innocent VIII., Pope, 69
Isabella, Queen of Edward II., 295
Italian cities, Municipal constitution of, 40

Jacqueline, Countess of Holland and Hainault, 233
Jannson, Flemish popular leader, 216, 217
Janov, Bohemian preacher, 158
Janssen on condition of German peasants, 174, 175
Jayme I., King of Aragon, 240, 259
Jeanne D'Arc, 129
Jerome of Prague, 162
John II., King of Castile, 247, 249
John, King of England, 271-274, 280, 288
John, King of France, 110, 112, 113, 121
John XII., Pope, 16
John XXII., Pope, 372
John XXIII., Pope, 161, 166
John of Hexham, 358, 359
John of Paris, 375, 376
John of Salisbury, 278, 379
Joyeuse Entrée of Brabant, 230
"Jus Frisicum, Vetus," The, 201, 204, 205
Justinger, Conrad, Swiss chronicler, 192
Justiza, The, of Aragon, 251, 252, 256, 257

Kentigern, St, 354
Kiersey, Edict of, 13
Kyburg, Count of, 185

Labourers, The Statute of, 308
Laelierts, Flemish political party, 213, 214, 220, 223, 226

Lambertazzi, The, 45
Lancaster, Duke of, 298-300
— Earl of, 295
Landenberg, Beringer of, Governor of Unterwalden, 193, 194
Lando, Michael de, 59
Langley or Langland ("Piers the Plowman"), 302, 212
Laon, Commune of, 92, 96, 100, 101, 125
Latimer, Lord, 299
Laupen, Battle of, 197
Law, Natural and positive, 382
Le Coq, Bishop of Laon, 110, 111, 113, 115
"Leges Upstalboomicæ," 201, 204, 205
Legnano, Battle of, 41
Leo III., Pope, 10, 374
Lex Frisionum, 199, 200, 204
Lex Regia, 277, 380
Lex Romana Burgundiorum, 4
Lex Romana Wisigothorum, 4, 244
Lewes, Battle of, 275
"Liber Niger," 283, 284
Liège, Bishopric of, 231
Ligue du Bien Publique, 131
Limburg, Duchy of, 208, 230
Lincoln, Commune of, 289, 290
Lipany, Battle of, 167, 168
Lisieux, Bishop of, 131
Lollards, The, 324-326
Lombard republics, 44, &c.
Lombards, 5
Lombardy, League of, 40-42
London, Commune of, 289
Longbeard, William, 291
Longchamp, William, 289
Loqui, Martin, Taborite preacher, 165
Lords of the Articles, The, 361
Lorraine, Lower, Duchy of, 208
Lothaire, Emperor, 16
Louis II., 16
Louis VI., King of France, 85, 96, 100, 101, 135
Louis VII., King of France, 85
Louis IX., King of France, 101, 105, 107, 108
Louis X., King of France, 109
Louis XI., King of France, 106, 130, 131, 133
Lucius II., Pope, 48
Ludovico Moro, Duke of Milan, 74
Ludwig of Bavaria, Emperor, 49, 141, 196, 371, 372

Index.

Luna, Alvara de, 245
Luxemburg, County of, 208
Lyons, Council of, 44
Lyons, Richard, 299

MacAlpin, Kenneth, 345, 346
Machiavelli, " History of Florence," 56-61
Magna Charta, 272-274, 281, 282, 302
Maillotins, The, 125
Malcolm II., King of Scotland, 346
Malcolm Canmore, 351
Malcolm IV., King of Scotland, 358
Manegold of Lautenbach, 380, 381
" Manor Rights," Book of, 175
Marcel, Etienne, leader of revolt against John of France, 110-122, 128
Mare, Sir Peter de la, 300
Margaret, Queen of Denmark, 156
Margaret, Queen of Scotland, 351
Mariana, 244
Marseilles, 96
Marsilius of Padua, 372, 381, 383, 384
Martin IV., Pope, 252
Martin V., Pope, 166
Mary, Princess, of England, 340
Marzfeld or Maifeld, 6, 8, 11
Masselin, Jehan, 132
Mathias of Neuenburg, Swiss chronicler, 192
Mathilda, Queen of England, 269
Maximilian, Emperor, 170, 237
Meaux, Siege of, 117
Mechlin, Supreme Council of, 235
Medici, Alamanno and Antonio de, 60
Medici, Cosimo de, 60-68
Medici, Giovanni de, 60
Medici, Giovanni de (Leo X.), 75
Medici, Giuliano de, brother of Lorenzo, 66
Medici, Lorenzo de, 64-72
Medici, Piero de, son of Cosimo, 64, 65
Medici, Piero de, son of Lorenzo, 72-76
Medici, Salvestro de, 56, 59
Medici, Veri de, 59, 60
Melchthal, Swiss patriot, 191, 193, 194
Melun, Treaty of (1225), 210

Mercia, Kingdom of, 261, 265
Merovingian period, 8, 10
Mersen, Edict of, 13
Milan, 41, 45, 48, 64, 74, 81
Milic, Bohemian preacher, 158
Minorita, Nicolas, 379
Mirandola, Pico, 66
Mons-en-Pévèle, Battle of, 215
Montdidier, Battle of, 118
Montfort, Simon de, 241
Montfort, Simon de, Earl of Leicester, 275, 276, 278, 281, 306
Montpellier, 95, 96
Moothill of Scone, 350
More, Sir Thomas, 342
Morgarten, Battle of, 197
Mormaer, 345, 350
Mortimer, 295
Municipia, Ancient, of Italy and Gaul, 37
Muret, Battle of, 241

Naefels, Battle of, 197
Nancy, Battle of, 235
Naples, 44, 64, 74, 81
Narbonne, Commune of, 96
Navarre, King of, 111, 113, 115, 118-120
— Kingdom of, 240
Nemours, Duke of, 131
Neroni, Diotisalvi, 65
Netherlands, Extent of, in Middle Ages, 208, 209
Nevers, Count of, 89
Neville, Archbishop of York, 301
Niklashausen, 171, 172
Ninian, St, 354
Nismes, 95
Nogent, Guibert de, 31, 92, 97, 101
Nominalists, The, 365
Northampton, Commune of, 290
Northumbria, Kingdom of, 261, 263, 265

Occam, 372, 379, 381, 384
Odoacer, 3
Ordainers, The, 295
Ordinance of 1413 (French), 129
Oresme, Nicolas de, 376
Orleans, Duchess of, 117
Orleans, Duke of, 126, 127
Otto IV., Emperor, 210
Otto of Saxony, 16, 136
Ourique, Battle of, 240

Index.

Oxford, Commune of, 289; Provisions of, 275, 291

Palec, Stephen, 161
Palleschi, The, Florentine faction, 80
Papal supremacy, The, 369-372
Paris, 113-115, 118-120, 125, 126; Parliament of, 101, 128
Parliament, The English, authority and power of (fourteenth century), 297, 298, 305, 326-329; (fifteenth century) 330-332; position of, under the Tudors, 338-342
— The Model, 279; the Good, 298-300; the Merciless, 300-301
— The Scottish, 357-362
Paston Letters, The, 335, 337
Peasant proprietor, The, free, 33
Peasants, Risings of, in England, 309-319; in France, 115-118; in Germany, 169 *et seq.*
Pecquigny, Jean de, 110
Pedro III., King of Aragon, 241, 252, 253
Pedro IV., King of Aragon, 254, 255
Pembroke, William the Marshal, Earl of, 274
Perigueux, Commune of, 96
Perrers, Alice, 299
Petit, Jean de, 127
Philip I., King of France, 108
Philip II. (Augustus), King of France, 85, 100, 101, 107, 210, 272
Philip III., King of France, 105, 213
Philip IV., King of France, 105-109, 137, 210, 212, 213, 371, 375, 376
Philip V., King of France, 109
Philip VI., King of France, 109, 216-225
Piagnoni, The, Savonarola's followers, 81
Picts, The, 344-346
Pippin the Short, 10
Pistes, Edict of, 13
Podesta, The, 41, 44, 45, 97
Poitiers, Battle of, 110
Poliziano, Angelo, 66
Portugal, Kingdom of, 240
Pot, Philip, Lord de la Roche, 132

Pragmatic Sanction (Charles VII. of France), 130
Prague, Four Articles of, The, 163
— University of, 159, 164
Presle, Raoul de, 376
"Privilege of Union, The," of Aragon, 253, 254
"Privilege, The General," of Aragon, 251, 252
Procopius, Hussite leader, 166, 167
Puglia, Francesco da, Franciscan monk, 81

Ravenna, Diet of (1232), 147
Realists, The, 365
"Regiam Majestatem," 350
Reichsfreiheit, secured by freemen of Schwyz and Uri, 186-188
Reichstag, (1427) 169, (1522-1523) 181
Reynolds, Archbishop, 296
Ricci, The, 55
Richard of Cornwall, 137
Richard II., Duke of Normandy, 88
Richard I., King of England, 270, 271, 288, 289
Richard II., King of England, 300-304, 314, 334, 376
Richard III., King of England, 331
Richemont, The Constable de, 129
Richthofen, criticism of Frisian democracy, 198, 199
Ricos hombres, 245
Rienzi, 49
Robert, King of Naples, 54
Roches, Peter des, Bishop of Winchester, 274
Roger of Salisbury, 269
Rolewinck, Werner, popular German writer, 169
Roman cities in Germany, 140
Romano, The, of Verona, 44
Romans, The, 19, 20
Rome, Republic of, restored, 48-50
Roosebeke, Battle of, 126, 228
Rosenplüt, popular German writer, 169
Roses, Wars of the, 328, 331, 332, 337
Rouen, 115, 125, 126
Rudolf of Habsburg, 141
Russ, Melchior, Swiss chronicler, 193
Rütli, Oath of the, 194

Index. 397

Salisbury, Earl of, 317
San Gimignano, Savonarola at, 69
"Sarnen, White Book of," 193
Savonarola, first visit and recall to Florence, 68, 69; his sermons, 70, 71, 73, 75, 77, 79; his political activity, 77-80; reaction against, and death, 80, 81; estimate of man and work, 82, 83
Savoy, Count of, 185
Saxony, Duke of, 136
Scala, La, The, of Verona, 44
Schwyz, Early struggles of freemen of, 186, 187
Scotland, 345 *et seq.*
Seebohm, views of Anglo-Saxon village communities, 260, 261
Sempach, Battle of, 197
Sens, Commune of, 96
Servile classes, English, 283-288
Siete Partidas, Castilian code, 248
Sigebert of Wessex, 263
Sigismund, Emperor, 163, 166; reformation of, 170
Silvestro, Fra, 81
Slavery, Doctrine of, 385
Smith, Sir Thomas, 342
Society, The Great, 314, 315
Soderini Antonio, 77
Soderini, Niccolo, 65
Somerset, The Protector, 342
"Somnium Vividarii," 381
Spain, Municipal institutions of towns of, 241, 242
Spencer, Henry, Bishop of Norwich, 319
St Aldhelm, 260
Standing army of Charles VII., 130
States-General of France, Philip IV. and the, 104-109; Philip VI. and the, 109; activity of, in the reign of King John, 110-113; meeting of, at Tours, 131-133, 383
States-General of Languedoïl, (1412) 128, (1439) 129
Stauffach, Swiss patriot, 191, 194
Statute De Hæretico Comburendo, 325
St Aulde, Jean de, 110
St Denis, 118, 120
Steelyard of London, 156
Stephen, King of England, 269
Stephen II., Pope, 10

Stephen Porcaro, 51
Stoss, Battle of, 197
St Pol, Count of, 131
Strabo, 349
Stratford, Archbishop, 298
Strathclyde Britons, 345, 349
Sudbury, Archbishop, 317, 318
Suffolk, Earl of, 301
Suger, Abbot, works quoted, 91, 92, 100, 101
Swabia, Duke of, 136; Duchy of, 185
Swiss Confederation, Constitution of, 197
Swiss, The, 185 *et seq.*; Bund of (1291), 189-191

Tabor, Mount, and the Taborites, 163, 168
Tacitus, 2, 16
Tell, The story of, 191-196
Templars, The, and Philip IV., 106
Teutons, The, 19, 20
Theobald, Archbishop, 278
Theodoric, 3.
Theories of the origin of German municipalities, 142-144
Toko, The Saga of, 195
Toleration, Hus an advocate of, 161, 162
Tolosa, Las Navas de, Battle of, 240
Torriani, The, 45
Toshach, 344, 350
Toulouse, Commune of, 95, 96; Estates of Languedoc meet at, 13, 56, 111
Toussac, Charles, 110
Tressilian, Chief-Justice of England, 301, 319
Troyes, Jean de, 128
Tschudi, Swiss chronicler, 190, 191, 193-195
Tserclaes, Everhard, 231
Tudor monarchy, The, 337-342
Tuscan cities, League of, 43
Tyler, Wat, 316, 318, 320

"Ueberküre, The," Frisian code, 201, 204, 205
Uguccione, Lord of Pisa, 54, 55
Ulman, Hans, German peasant leader, 171, 173
Unity, Mediæval idea of, 367, 368

VOL. I.   2 D

Index.

Unterwalden, Freemen of, 188
Upstalboom, The Assembly at the, 198, 201, 202
Urban VI., Pope, 301
Uri, Early struggles of freemen of, 187, 188
Utraquists, The, 163
Utrecht, Peace of (1474), 156
Uzzano, Niccolo da, 60

Vacarius, English jurist, 278
Valais, self-governing community, 186
Valencia, 257, 258
Valentinian, Roman emperor, 37
Valois, Charles of, 214
Venice, 42, 46, 47, 64, 75, 77, 81
Vespucci, Florentine statesman, 76, 77
Vézelai, 89, 96
Victring, Abbot of, chronicler, 191
Villari, estimate of Lorenzo de Medici, 66-68
Villeins, Condition of the Scottish, 346-348, 353 ; Revolt of the, in England, 309-319
Visconti, Duke Philippo, 61
Visconti, The, 45

Wace, 311
Waldemar, King of Denmark, 155
Waldenses, The, 168
Waldhauser, Conrad, Bohemian preacher, 158
Wales, 345
Wallace, William, 357, 359
Walsham, 319
Walsingham, 315

Walter, Hubert, Archbishop, 270, 271, 291
Wencelaus, King of Bohemia, 159, 160, 162
Wessex, Kingdom of, 261, 263
White Hoods, The, Flemish political party, 227
Wicklif, John, reformer and political writer, 320-325, 373, 376, 377 ; and Hus, 158-161
Wido, 16
William I., King of England, 267-269, 289
William II., King of England, 269, 272
William the Breton, 93
William the Lion, King of Scotland, 354, 358, 359
Wimpfeling, Jacob, German peasant leader, 171, 173, 174
Winchelsy, Archbishop, 279
Winkelried, Arnold von, 197
Witan, The, 263-265, 267
Wolsey, Cardinal, 339, 340
Worms, Diet of (1231), 142
Woumen, Battle of, 227
Wykeham, Bishop of Winchester, 300

Ypres, 211, 213 *et seq.*

Zacharias, Pope, 10
Zaeringer, The, 185 ; Duke Berthold IV., 186
Zannekin, Flemish popular leader, 216, 217
Zbynek, Archbishop of Prague, 159
Zizka, 163, 165-167